TEACHING CONTENT READING AND WRITING

SECOND EDITION

Martha Rapp Ruddell

Sonoma State University

Allyn and Bacon

Boston • London • Toronto • Sydney • Tokyo • Singapore

To all my students, wherever they are
To Mom and Fred and Sis and Sharon
To John and Toni, Sarah, Kenny, Katie, and Kristin,
And to my family of friends whose love sustains me

Senior Editor: Virginia Lanigan
Editorial Assistant: Kris Lamarre
Senior Marketing Manager: Kathy Hunter
Editorial Production Service: MARBERN HOUSE
Manufacturing Buyer: Megan Cochran
Cover Administrator: Linda Knowles

Copyright © 1997, 1993 by Allyn & Bacon
A Viacom Company
Needham Heights, MA 02194

Library of Congress Cataloging-in-Publication Data

Ruddell, Martha Rapp.
    Teaching content reading and writing / Martha Rapp Ruddell. — 2nd
  ed.
        p.   cm.
    Includes bibliographical references and index.
    ISBN 0-205-26563-4
    1. Content area reading—United States.   2. Language arts-
  -Correlation with content subjects—United States.   3. Literacy-
  -United States.   I. Title.
LB1050.455.R84   1997   96-30835
428.4'071'2—dc20   CIP

Printed in the United States of America

10 9 8 7 6 5 4 3 2 1   01 00 99 98 97 96

Photo Credits
Photo credits, text credits and acknowledgments can be found on page 420, which should be considered an extension of the copyright page.

C O N T E N T S

PREFACE

This is a book about literacy; specifically, it is about the role of literacy in subject area learning. Its title, *Teaching Content Reading and Writing*, is intended to convey that meaning, and the book addresses in detail the many ways that literacy—reading and writing—interact with and support learning. As you read, I hope you will choose to be reflective, to consider how my descriptions and explanations of literacy transactions in subject area classrooms reflect your own experience; particularly, I hope you will spend a good amount of time considering how you developed the interest and expertise that you have in your academic discipline and the role literacy played in that development.

In this second edition, I've added an entire chapter about second language acquisition and development and appropriate instructional practice for teaching bilingual students in multilingual classrooms, so that you will have the requisite knowledge and information to address the needs of second language learners in your classroom. I've retained the chapter on Developing Lifelong Readers and Writers (Chapter 12) because of my ardent conviction that we as teachers are responsible for developing students' ability and willingness to be literate beyond the classroom walls. I sincerely hope that you will spend some time in that chapter even though it's the easiest one to forego.

Keep in mind that many of the ideas you meet in this text will be new to you and may take some time to digest; some may even be quite contrary to how you were taught and how you expect to teach. That's okay. It's simply one more reason to be reflective as you read the book, and to look for ways to find intersections, or points of confluence, between your ideas and mine. Three features in the book are designed to guide your reflective thought and assist in transferring ideas from this text to your teaching repertoire and classroom.

"Double Entry Journal" (DEJ) activities occur at the beginning and end of each chapter. At the beginning of the chapter, the DEJ activity is intended to stimulate your memory, thinking and ideas about the main topic of the chapter you're about to read; essentially, the before-reading DEJ is a way of introducing topics, bringing your own prior knowledge and experiences to bear on the upcoming discussion, and giving you an experience-based foundation for the reading. The after-reading DEJ then builds on what you did before reading, and combines that thinking with ideas from the chapter to extend your understanding of the text. The best way to do the DEJ activities is to keep a journal specifically for them and to compare your DEJ thinking with a partner or small group.

The "How To Do" feature occurs at irregular intervals in chapters focusing on instructional approaches (Chapters 3, 4, 5, 6, 9, 10, 11, 12). The purpose of "How To Do" is to give you a step-by-step list of the things you need to plan, prepare and/or consider in order to make a specific instructional strategy work in your subject area and classroom. "How To Do" generally follows explanations and discussions that are necessarily long and involved; my students like the succinct, listed format of How To Do and use it to guide their lesson and unit planning.

Finally, the "Building Tables" that occur at the end of instructional chapters are intended to summarize in yet another way critical information about how to apply and combine the instructional approaches from this text in your teaching. Additionally, the purpose of the "Building Tables" is to allow you to see instructional connections across chapters that you may not see on your own (chapters have a way of creating rigid, and perhaps unnecessary, barriers), aid your planning efficiency, and give suggestions for increasing the power of the instructional strategies themselves. I hope you will find this book challenging, interesting, and useful in your teaching career.

ACKNOWLEDGEMENTS

This second edition of *Teaching Content Reading and Writing* is truly a collaborative work: It has grown from the comments and criticisms of my students over the last six years as well as from responses of friends and colleagues who've used the book in their classes. My students were unblinkingly honest, but always kind, in their evaluations of the text; they certainly never let me get by with inconsistencies or bombast. My friends and colleagues—MaryEllen Vogt, Brenda Shearer, Elizabeth Willis, Norm Unrau, Betty McEady Gillead, Anne Lewis, Susan Neuman, and others—have been extraordinarily generous in telling me what they and their students liked and didn't like, needed and didn't need from the first edition. I must thank MaryEllen Vogt, especially, who began using the first edition of this text in pre-publication form at California State University, Long Beach, and has continued using it over the years; MaryEllen and her students have been an ongoing source of thoughtful comment and critique, to the book's (and my) benefit for this second time around.

It is most felicitous, I think, when students' work becomes part of what a teacher does, and it gives me extraordinary pleasure to acknowledge what students have contributed to my thinking and to this book. Hearty "thank yous" to Janet Rasmussen and Heidi Hayman-Ahders for their study maps in Chapter 5 (carried over from the first edition); to Jenny Burcham for her insightful map in Chapter 2 of the thinking-reading-writing processes; and to Peter Santucci—one of MaryEllen's Long Beach students—for the CSSR visual in Chapter 4 (I've needed something like it for a long time). Thanks also to Lisa Iwatsubo, Peter Bell, Darlene Pullen, Amy Holcombe, Eric Bohn, and Eric Wycoff for letting me use their lesson plans in the Appendix to illustrate how ideas from this text may be applied to classroom practice.

To my reviewers—MaryEllen Vogt, California State University, Long Beach; Catherine Bell, Castleton State College; and Patricia Perkins, Southwestern Oklahoma State University—I offer thanks for judicious, helpful responses that guided my thinking in revising each part of the text. And to the editorial and production staff at Allyn and Bacon—Virginia Lanigan, who waited patiently for manuscript when I was unable to work, and Nihad Farooq, the sweet presence in Needham, MA, who made things happen when I could not, I am eternally grateful. To my gentle, but thorough, copyeditor, Carmen Wheatcroft (once again), and Marjorie Payne (formerly with Allyn and Bacon), production editor, I am indebted for invaluable assistance and support.

And finally, I give heartfelt and loving thanks to my family and friends who have been with me during this year of good times and some very tough times; their constancy and love have been my strength. To my "group"—Perry and Paul and Pat and Rick—I can only say an inadequate "thank you" for always being there and always believing in me. I am truly blessed by your presence in my life.

CHAPTER 1

LITERACY IN MIDDLE AND SECONDARY SCHOOLS

DOUBLE ENTRY JOURNAL

List everything you remember about reading in school

using the following headings: Reading in Elementary

School, Reading in Junior High School, and Reading

in High School. List as many memories for each head-

ing as you can. You may add ideas as you read the

chapter.

Teaching in middle and secondary schools is a job for people with stamina, enthusiasm, knowledge, endurance, discipline, and a seemingly inexhaustible supply of energy. Nowhere else in schools are faculty expected to do so many things: teach five, six, or seven classes a day; sponsor clubs; coach sports; do hall duty; supervise dances; publish newspapers and yearbooks; direct plays; and sell refreshments at school events, to name a few. Life is hectic and, more often than not, regulated by forces outside teachers' control.

I once taught in a consolidated school district in which one high school, one junior high, and six elementary schools served a rural community of about 13,000 people. Nearly all of the junior and senior high students were bused to school, so starting times were staggered to allow a limited number of buses to run multiple routes. The senior high began at 7:40 A.M., the junior high at 8:05 A.M., and the elementary schools at 8:45 A.M. At the beginning of one school year, about half of our junior high students were arriving five minutes late every day because the buses were unable to make their second run within the allotted time. In a school of 600 seventh- and eighth-graders, this created a situation bordering on chaos, and something clearly had to be done. Possible solutions seemed obvious: start the senior high five minutes earlier and change the early bus schedule, or start the junior high and elementary schools five minutes later and adjust those bus schedules. Instead, the administration *set the junior high clocks back five minutes* and left everything else exactly as it was. So now, when the tardy bell rang at 8:05, it was really 8:10, but the students were in their seats, and the problem had been "solved," for everyone except us, of course. During the entire academic year, we lived and taught in a warp between "real time" and "junior high time" in which any discussion of out-of-school activity schedules was generally lost among confusion, laughter, and conjecture about the prevailing logic behind this decision.

School and classroom conditions, especially at the junior high and senior high levels, frequently make teachers' personal teaching goals and ideals exceedingly difficult to achieve. Class loads of 50 to 150 students a day, pressure to "get through the book" or "get students ready," minimum competency tests, insufficient or inappropriate instructional materials, absenteeism, and constant schedule interruptions are standard components of the secondary teacher's working milieu. Recently, changing school schedules (e.g., 100-minute class periods and year-round schools) and instructional approaches (e.g., schools within schools and integrated studies) have increased considerably teachers' responsibilities and time demands for planning and preparation for teaching. Add to that the recurring and widely broadcast media reports about how schools are failing and the persistent tendency for teacher salaries to be well below levels in business and other professions, and you wonder why anyone remains a teacher at all. To their credit, middle school, junior high school, and senior high school teachers generally accept these conditions with a certain amount of grace and continue on.

Students' reading and writing abilities, and other issues surrounding literacy, are among the many important issues facing middle, junior high, and senior high teachers and schools today. Concern and discussion about these issues are not new. In fact, literacy and literacy achievement have been topics of widespread public and professional interest, discussion, and debate over the past 50 years. Where previously much of the focus of literacy issues, at least in the popular press, centered on elementary reading instruction (the relative importance of phonics and sight word learning, for example), much of today's discussion is aimed directly at issues in secondary school.

For clarity and consistency within this text, I refer to junior high and senior high schools and students as "secondary" because of distinctions between elementary and secondary teacher credentialing and school organizational patterns that are common to many states. Middle schools and students are called "middle" to distinguish them from elementary and junior high students and schools, which may or may not have overlapping grade levels. Although this usage of "secondary" and "middle" may not match standard usage in all states or geographical areas, no one set of labels is likely to do so. Nonetheless, at least we now have operational definitions useful for discussion throughout this text.

LITERACY ISSUES IN MIDDLE AND SECONDARY SCHOOLS

Middle and secondary school students' reading and writing abilities are currently the subject of much concern, and the debate over who is responsible for what continues. One reason for such intense and prolonged scrutiny is the critical role of literacy in students' overall academic success. (Until the past decade, discussion focused almost solely on reading; we have just recently begun serious national discussion of the similarly important contribution of writing.) At each of these levels—middle school, junior high school, senior high school—a steadily increasing amount of information is transmitted through the medium of written text; consequently, increasingly refined reading and writing skills at each level are necessary for continued learning in nearly all academic areas. These skills do not develop at the same rate for all students: In a class of thirty sophomores, we can expect, and do find, reading achievement levels ranging from second grade through sixteenth grade (college senior), with concomitantly wide ranges in writing ability. Even in smaller, special classes—remedial reading or advanced placement chemistry, for example—a range of five to seven grade levels is not uncommon. Experienced teachers *know* what the situation is—we have watched daily as students struggled or idled their way through text—but feel relatively powerless to do anything about it. It is impossible to find one textbook that meets all students' needs, and it is equally difficult to rewrite or retell sufficient information so that everyone receives his or her full share of assistance and/or challenge. Wide differences in students' writing abilities create parallel dilemmas in assigning and evaluating writing tasks.

Tracking systems, honor programs, and "basic" classes, no matter how they are conceived and implemented, do not successfully deal with the problems associated with differences among students' reading and writing abilities. Such approaches can only reduce the ability and achievement ranges to supposedly more manageable limits, but even then, substantial within-class achievement differences still occur. More importantly, perhaps, these tracking plans create as many problems as they solve and are themselves the source of serious concern and debate with respect to educational equity and equality, the effect of teacher expectations on student achievement, and the quality of the educational experience in various school tracks (Oakes, 1992; Wheelock, 1992).

Recent research (McMahon & Villanueva, 1993) highlights the benefits of detracking for all students, particularly those in lower tracks. More and more middle and secondary schools are, in fact, moving toward nontracked student assignment into classrooms in which new organizational patterns and new instructional approaches (collaborative learning groups or themed instruction, for example) are expected to reduce teaching problems created by differences in student abilities and achievement levels. These changes appear to be a step forward, particularly in light of the rapidly changing population of today's schools; to be successful, however, these new patterns and approaches must be seen as means for *accommodating and supporting* different abilities and various kinds of student diversity rather than systems for reducing achievement ranges within classrooms.

LEARNING AND LITERACY NEEDS

When we add to the wide student differences that have always been present in U.S. secondary schools (or at least since the advent of mandatory attendance laws), the new diversity brought about by rapidly changing school populations and the recent entrance of large groups of non- or new-English-speaking students into secondary schools (with even larger numbers projected for the future), we begin to realize the extraordinarily complex responsibility teachers have for adjusting instruction to meet the literacy and learning needs of all of their students. The fact is that our schools are populated by students who have come through our own K–12 system with widely disparate literacy achievement and abilities. Many, many students are progressing academically at a rate we consider highly satisfactory, others lag behind, while yet others are academically gifted or talented in special ways.

Immigrant students add to this diversity and are often immersed quite suddenly in a cultural and language environment that is considerably different from their home language and culture and that may or may not honor their home language and culture (Nieto, 1994). These and other bilingual students come to school with widely varying oral fluency in their first language and proficiency in first-language literacy, and so have diverse linguistic abilities to support their progress in achieving English language fluency and literacy. It is not unusual today for immigrant and native-born bilingual/bicultural students to choose to maintain strong ties with their cultural heritage and retain their first languages. For these students, and others, we need programs and classes that provide support for developing English language fluency and literacy in content areas while at the same time maintaining students' primary language and culture.

Adding further to this mix in middle and secondary schools are students of all races and ethnicities who live below the poverty level, some of whom may come from homeless families. All of these students, whether they are mainstream, immigrant, bilingual/bicultural, or representative of other types of diversity, are generally taught by teachers who are much more thoroughly trained in their respective content areas than they are in teaching a diverse population of students how to read and write in those content areas.

RESPONDING TO STUDENTS' LEARNING AND LITERACY NEEDS

Whatever the characteristics of a given school or district student population, it is not enough for middle and secondary teachers to accept the popular belief that "the kids can't read" or to blame elementary teachers for not doing their jobs; nor is it helpful to deny, ignore, or attempt to escape the diversity of student abilities and needs in our classrooms. First of all, the kids *can* read, albeit with very different degrees of success and achievement. With few exceptions (excluding newly arrived immigrants), middle and secondary students *can read something:* Watch them go through *Mad* magazine, comic books, driver's training manuals, *Rolling Stone,* or whatever the current literary fad happens to be. Second, elementary teachers *are* doing their jobs. They are teaching youngsters how to read and learn from elementary texts and to write in response to that reading. To expect them to "preteach" all the literacy skills necessary for success in middle and secondary school is unrealistic, if not unreasonable. Beginning in middle school and continuing through high school, textbooks and writing task demands grow increasingly more difficult and different from those at the elementary level; literacy skills needed for success in reading and writing are similarly more complex and can be learned most efficiently as they are needed.

Today, we see increasing cultural, ethnic, socioeconomic, and economic diversity of students in schools; to deny or attempt to narrow this diversity is unnecessary and, ultimately, impractical. Mike Rose, in his stunning book, *Lives on the Boundary* (1989), reminds us that in 1890 only 6.7 percent of 14- to 17-year-olds attended high school; by 1978, that percentage had grown to 94.1. This statistic alone accounts for much of the diversity in today's schools and represents, in Rose's words, ". . . a system attempting to honor—through wrenching change—the many demands of a pluralistic society" (p. 7). Diversity, then, must be viewed as the *reality*, the true fabric of U.S. middle and secondary schools. The real issue is the fact that middle and secondary school teaching—what goes on every day in every content classroom—must undergo a fundamental change if any of our students' needs are to be met (Goodlad, 1984). Middle and secondary students—all of them—need additional literacy instruction to extend and refine the reading and writing abilities they already have. For this instruction to be most useful, classroom teachers, not reading or writing specialists, must provide it for them. *That classroom teachers may do so without sacrificing attention to content subject matter—and, in fact, that subject matter instruction may be considerably improved by attention to reading and writing—is the major underlying assumption on which this book is based.*

This assumption is not the product of wishful thinking or unrealistic ideals. Rather, it comes from knowledge acquired by researchers and educators over the past sixty to seventy years about secondary students and their literacy needs (Moore, Readence, & Rickelman, 1992), from a new focus on the special literacy needs of middle school students (Atwell, 1987; Duffy, 1990; Montague, Huntsberger, & Hoffman, 1989), from the knowledge we have about how individuals develop fluency and literacy in a second language (Freeman & Freeman, 1994; Kang & Golden, 1995; McQuillan & Rodrigo, 1995), and from the accumulated experience of middle and secondary teachers themselves. A quick history of the advent and growth of attention to middle and secondary reading and writing instruction in public schools in the next section of this chapter gives a sense of how this assumption came to be and how it has been operationalized in the past. The remainder of this book then focuses on middle school and secondary reading and writing instruction *as it applies to content learning* and presents effective ways for content reading and writing instruction to be implemented today and in the future.

The history that follows next focuses exclusively on reading instruction (as opposed to writing) up until the 1970s and 1980s because issues, instruction, research, and professional and public attention to reading have predominated heavily over writing in modern American education (Clifford, 1987). Not until the late 1980s did writing begin to receive the same kind of emphasis and attention.

MIDDLE AND SECONDARY LITERACY INSTRUCTION IN PERSPECTIVE*

Literacy issues in middle and secondary schools are relative newcomers in the history of education in the United States. The reason is, in part, because U.S. reading instruction began in the mid-1600s as burgeoning communities organized to provide education for young children. Reading instruction was the nucleus of that education and was developmental in nature. That is, the major purpose for instruction was to move children from nonreading or prereading stages into beginning reading; from there, individuals advanced more or less independently toward mature reading.

Attention and emphasis on reading instruction beyond early grades, on the other hand, extends back only to about the late 1920s and early 1930s. At that time, educators and educational movements began to acknowledge differences between literary and technical reading and to promote the practice of providing organized reading instruction for middle-grade and secondary students (Moore et al., 1992). Concurrent with this movement were revelations that many adolescents and adults were unable to perform well on newly developed reading tests, along with concerns regarding the literacy demands for soldiers during the First and Second World Wars. The major focus of secondary reading instruction in its earliest years was therefore *remedial*, rather than developmental, in nature. This difference accounts for the content and format of contemporary middle school and secondary reading instruction, and it assists us in understanding how this instruction evolved.

THE 1930s

The 1930s could be characterized as the incubation period for secondary reading instruction. It was a time when professional interest and concern about secondary reading, growing from issues raised in the late 1920s, led to the initiation of research efforts to determine the nature and extent of adolescent and adult reading problems. A major impetus for this research was the combined effect of the discovery, more than a decade earlier, that thousands of soldiers could not read well enough to do their jobs in the army and of the availability of newly refined, standardized tests for identification and analysis of reading problems. Although few, if any, instructional programs were established during the 1930s, the interest and study during this period provided the foundation for much of the subsequent research and program development.

THE 1940s

At the beginning of the 1940s, once again we were involved in a world war, and once again we discovered that many soldiers could not read. This discovery served as a final catalyst for the implementation of remedial reading programs in junior and senior high schools. Although not widespread, such programs were our first attempt to provide systematic reading instruction to even one segment of the secondary school population. By

---

*Much of the information for the first three-and-a-half decades of this discussion is taken from Nila Banton Smith's classic study, *American Reading Instruction* (1965).

the mid to late 1940s, leaders in the field of reading were recommending—not for the first time, but with growing strength—that systematic reading instruction for all students continue into the middle grades and secondary school (Bond, 1941; Gray, 1948) and called for the establishment of developmental reading programs for this purpose.

THE 1950s

During the 1950s, considerable expansion of secondary remedial programs occurred. During this period, reading instruction in general, and reading disability specifically, received intense professional and public scrutiny. With the publication of Rudolph Flesch's *Why Johnny Can't Read* (1955) and with the launching of the Soviet satellite *Sputnik* in 1957, serious questions were raised concerning the quality of American education, with specific attention directed toward reading and reading instruction (science and mathematics were examined similarly). Increased interest in developmental secondary reading programs and content area reading instruction resulted. In 1958, the National Defense Education Act (NDEA) provided massive federal funds for research, teacher education, school programs, and curriculum projects, much of which was allocated for both elementary and secondary reading.

THE 1960s

Secondary remedial reading programs continued to grow during the 1960s. Most programs were funded wholly or in part by the Title I section of the Elementary and Secondary Education Act (ESEA) of 1965 and were subject to strict federal guidelines concerning testing, student selection, and teacher certification. One of the most immediate problems was staffing these programs with certified secondary reading specialists at a time when few, if any, were available. Consequently, many programs, especially in junior high schools, were taught by relocated elementary reading teachers. Newly organized "developmental" reading classes appeared in greater numbers, usually designated as "Basic English" or "Remedial English" classes and were taught by willing and courageous, but untrained, English teachers who went on to become the secondary reading specialists of the 1970s and 1980s. Rarely did these developmental programs reach all of the students in a junior or senior high school. For the most part, they were intended to provide additional instruction for students who did not qualify for Title I programs or those who had mild reading problems. In some schools, accelerated reading classes were established for college-bound seniors, either as separate courses or as units of study in senior English classes. By the mid to late 1960s, content area reading instruction was receiving increasingly widespread recognition and support. Its proponents made a clear distinction between their instructional approaches and traditional developmental reading instruction (Herber, 1970, 1978); however, this distinction was not always fully understood or practiced.

THE 1970s

Wide expansion and growth of remedial reading programs occurred during the 1970s. Emerging programs in learning disabilities, English as a Second Language (ESL), and other special education fields were frequently combined with the reading program to form Learning Resource Centers that served an ever-expanding population. Developmental programs also grew, especially in junior high schools, and were still generally intended for students identified as "reading below grade level." By the end of this decade, every major publisher of elementary reading textbooks had added, or was in the process of adding, seventh- and eighth-grade books to their reading series to meet the demands of newly extended developmental reading programs. Even with this expansion, however, "developmental reading" was almost universally interpreted as something that goes on outside the regular classroom. So, some junior high schools supplemented English classes with an additional hour of developmental reading class, and others replaced English with a reading class for some students.

RIGHT TO READ AND MINIMUM COMPETENCY MOVEMENTS

During this same period in the 1970s, the Right to Read and minimum competency movements were launched. The Right to Read campaign was aimed at achieving universal national literacy by 1980. The slogan "Every Teacher a Teacher of Reading" (Early, 1957) was adopted as its rallying cry, causing no small amount of frustration and anger among junior and senior high school teachers. The general feeling was that secondary teachers were being asked to replace subject area instruction with reading instruction—to teach phonics instead of physics—a task for which they felt no sympathy and had little, if any, preparation. Subject area teachers were not happy about this turn of events and made no effort to disguise their feelings. Because of this negative reaction (and it was substantial) many secondary reading people felt that "Every Teacher a Teacher of Reading" had done more harm than good for secondary reading programs (Herber, 1978).

Certainly, during this time, the reading teacher was often not the most popular person among secondary school faculties. (Remember, many of them were relocated elementary teachers to begin with!) Few of their efforts to convince subject area teachers to incorporate reading instruction into content teaching met with much success. To remedy this, schools and districts began sponsoring in-service meetings, in which college and university professors in secondary reading met with junior and senior high school faculties to convince teachers of their responsibility and to demonstrate ways to incorporate reading instruction into content classes. I have faced many a tight-lipped, arms-crossed faculty under such circumstances, and I'm not alone in that experience. The success of these efforts varied widely (just as it does today).

Concomitant with Right to Read was the growing impetus of the minimum competency movement. As with Right to Read, the goal of the minimum competency movement was universal literacy, with much of the emphasis placed on testing to determine who would pass or graduate from junior high and senior high school, and on a highly publicized "back-to-basics" approach to teaching the so-called basic skills of literacy. By the end of the decade, most schools were doing some type of minimum competency testing, either voluntarily or in compliance with state legislative mandate, and providing compensatory programs for students who did not meet the test standards. These testing programs created many new problems: They required educators to examine such issues as the fine-line distinction between "teaching students how to take the test" and "teaching the test," what to do about students who repeatedly fail the tests (or, how many times can one repeat the eighth grade?), and what to do about the alarming increase in dropout rates (clearly, the students *already knew* what to do when faced with repeated failure). Easy answers to these and other problems were not found, and, in fact, the problems still exist.

Despite disgruntled faculties and new problems, however, the combined impact of Right to Read and the minimum competency movement served to focus attention on the reading needs of secondary students. For all the negative effects, the result was further expansion of secondary school reading programs, increased university and state requirements for secondary teachers to take one or more reading education classes, and growing acceptance of instruction advocated by content area reading proponents.

WRITING INSTRUCTION

Significant innovation in writing instruction occurred on a small scale in the 1970s that would have enormous impact in the following decades. In 1973, the Bay Area Writing Project (affectionately called BAWP) was introduced at the University of California at Berkeley with James Gray at its helm (Gray, personal communication, 1989). This project—with its emphasis on writing as a medium of understanding and learning, the teacher as writer, writing for different purposes, extension of classroom writing opportunities, and teachers teaching teachers—formed the nucleus for sweeping reforms in writing instruction. Initially, the project served English and elementary teachers in northern California classrooms, but it has exerted increasing national and international influence since 1976, when it expanded to become the National Writing Project.

THE 1980s

By the early 1980s, reading programs of one type or another were well established in most secondary schools. While the emphasis was still remedial, developmental programs, accelerated programs, and attention to content reading instruction were growing. Greenlaw and Moore (1982), in a survey of junior and senior high schools, found that over 75 percent of the schools reporting had separate reading courses available to their students. Of these courses, 74 percent were remedial, 44 percent were developmental, and 36 percent were accelerated. (Many schools reported two or more types of courses.) Schools without separate reading courses reported that reading was taught as part of English, social studies, mathematics, and science courses. Although based on a small sample of schools, this survey suggests national trends at that time.

Most, if not all, of the remedial reading programs in schools were funded through Chapter I of the Education Consolidation and Improvement Act of 1981 (ECIA), which superseded Title I of the old Elementary and Secondary Education Act of 1965. "Reading Across the Curriculum" replaced "Every Teacher a Teacher of Reading" as the slogan for secondary reading in-service programs and became the rationale for increasingly widespread requirements for all secondary teachers to have at least one course in reading methods.

In the mid-1980s, the middle school movement gained increasing attention and momentum. Rooted in the 1960s, the ideals of the movement grew from educators' beliefs that junior high schools did not adequately meet the needs of the students they served (Moore & Stefanich, 1990). A primary assumption underlying the middle school movement was that educational structure and instructional practice must allow for the rapid changes associated with "transescence"—the period between the ages of 10 and 14—and concomitantly provide experiences to promote students' transition into adolescence (Eichorn, 1987; Irwin, 1990; Moore & Stefanich, 1990). Embedded in the middle school movement was the goal to provide instruction focused on ". . . higher literacy and thinking strategies . . ." (Moore & Stefanich, 1990, p. 8), and throughout the 1980s, growing numbers of school districts converted junior high schools or formed new middle schools to begin implementing these ideals.

Midway through the 1980s, the nation experienced a major wave of educational reform triggered by the report, *A Nation at Risk: The Imperative for Educational Reform*, sponsored by the National Commission on Excellence in Education (1983). This report was followed in rapid succession by (among others) *High School: A Report on Secondary Education in America* (Boyer, 1983), which was commissioned by the Carnegie Foundation for the Advancement of Teaching; *Horace's Compromise: The Dilemma of the American High School* (Sizer, 1984); *A Place Called School* (Goodlad, 1984); and *Becoming a Nation of Readers: The Report of the Commission on Reading* (Anderson, Heibert, Scott, & Wilkinson, 1985). In each report, literacy was a focal point, and in each, teachers, schools, textbook publishers, teacher education programs, and any other group even remotely responsible for schooling were severely taken to task for the failure of some students to become literate and of other students to move beyond the most basic, minimal literacy levels.

This great storm of criticism led to much discussion, more than a little finger-pointing, and legislative as well as other types of reform. The Hawkins–Stafford School Improvement Amendments Act of 1988 repealed the Education Consolidation and Improvement Act of 1981 and brought with it much more stringent educational accountability, but fewer fiscal regulations, for Chapter I reading programs. A major reform emphasis was movement away from "basics" and toward a "critical thinking" and "critical reading" focus. Prominent also was discussion regarding the importance of connecting reading and writing processes, and, by the end of the decade, "Writing Across the Curriculum" had joined "Reading Across the Curriculum" as a major goal of secondary schools (the most telling picture of pre–reform movement writing practices in secondary schools is Applebee's 1981 study, *Writing in the Secondary School*).

The National Writing Project was, by now, well established. Its influence had spread within schools as well as geographically among them, so that Writing Across the Curriculum projects involved teachers in all subject areas and at all levels of middle, junior, and senior high schools. Thus, writing instruction in middle and secondary schools began to change, bringing into more common practice literacy instruction, planned and taught by classroom teachers, that reflects a view of reading and writing as different sides of the same coin, each of which contributes substantially to learning and cognitive growth.

THE 1990s AND BEYOND

By the end of the 1980s, then, not only had reading instruction expanded in middle and secondary schools, but writing across the curriculum was gaining acceptance at an increasingly rapid rate. This trend continues today, but with an interesting twist. As educators call for and schools restructure toward the end of more integrated, inquiry-based learning in middle and secondary schools (Harste, 1994; Pace, 1995; Stevenson & Carr, 1993) and a more student-centered, caring curriculum (Chaskin & Rauner, 1995; Noddings, 1992), legislators and others outside the educational community are crying, once again, "back to basics" (Lucas, 1995) in an effort to separate literacy instruction from content learning, while the national standards movement grows apace (*Phi Delta Kappan* themed issue, 1995). These critics view efforts to integrate middle and secondary school learning and to embed reading and writing instruction into that integrated whole as yet another indication that schools have been remiss, that we have failed to teach youngsters how to read and write, and, because of this failure, now must establish more and larger secondary programs to "take care of the problem." A growing number of educators, however, think just the opposite; we understand "the problem" to be one in which fundamental changes are needed in how middle and secondary school students are taught (Atwell, 1987, 1990; Rose, 1989; Ruddell, 1996; Sizer, 1992). We believe that expansion of reading and writing instruction into middle schools and junior and senior high schools—with emphasis both in content area literacy instruction and in special reading and writing programs—is a *positive* factor in contemporary education for all of the following reasons:

1. Expanded reading and writing instruction acknowledges that literacy growth is continuous and does not stop at the end of fourth or sixth grade. Neither should instruction. All students can, and should have, the opportunity to experience continued growth as readers and writers, and in order for them to do so, various types of instruction must be available.

2. Expanded reading and writing instruction provides for diversity of student literacy abilities and needs. Middle school and secondary classrooms are filled with students who represent wide variation in literacy achievement and English language fluency. This diversity in no way suggests that there is anything "wrong" with any students or casts aspersions on students' previous classroom learning or life experience; nor does it mean that only the bilingual/bicultural students require assistance with English-language fluency and literacy. Rather, it recognizes and celebrates human differences. Middle school and secondary reading and writing instruction provides for all students: those who are achieving satisfactorily, those who simply need more time to arrive at expected achievement levels, those who are in the process of becoming fluent and literate in a second language, and those whose achievement goes well beyond the norm.

3. Expanded reading and writing instruction allows students to learn new, more difficult reading/writing/study skills *as they are needed* to complete school tasks (Herber, 1978). Many students find that the skills that served them well in elementary school simply are not adequate for success with the more difficult texts, heavier assignment load, and generally less personalized atmosphere of middle and secondary school. Reading and writing instruction in content area classrooms assist students in extending and adapting their skills to meet these new conditions.

4.   Expanded reading and writing instruction place remedial reading and writing programs into a perspective that more accurately reflects reality. When the only literacy instruction in middle and secondary schools was remedial, all discussion of reading, writing, and literacy was negative, and all attention and concern were focused on the relatively small percentage of the school population with literacy problems. Certainly, that population did and does exist; it would be foolish and irresponsible to suggest otherwise. The net effect, however, was that students, teachers, administrators, and parents alike saw reading and writing instruction as appropriate only for students who were experiencing serious difficulty. Little effort was made to acknowledge and provide for the many, many students who were progressing well. Negative attitudes linger, but expanded efforts to address reading and writing in all classes have done much to reduce this disparity.

Contemporary middle and secondary reading and writing instruction thus appears to be moving toward the goals and ideals first voiced by reading educators in the 1920s: continued, systematic literacy instruction for all students throughout their school years. As such instruction increasingly characterizes middle, junior high, and senior high schools, we will be able to turn our attention from literacy *problems* to address more adequately the literacy *processes* of the students we teach.

PLAN OF THIS BOOK

Throughout the remainder of the book, we will explore various aspects of middle and secondary school literacy instruction in subject area classrooms. This text presents a number of issues, instructional strategies, and classroom ideas for guiding students' literacy and language development in your particular subject area. Specifically, this book addresses the following:

Chapter 2 describes thinking, reading, and writing processes and lays the foundation for the rest of the book. It presents a theoretical point of view and philosophical stance that are well recognized in the field of reading education and that guide my thinking. The instructional recommendations I make in the text follow logically from that point of view and philosophical stance.

Chapters 3 and 4 address the two processes of reading commonly considered to be preeminent aspects of most people's definitions and conceptualizations of reading: comprehension and vocabulary. These chapters demonstrate how both processes are central to learning in subject areas and how instruction may account for content (subject knowledge) and processes (comprehension and vocabulary) simultaneously.

Chapters 5 and 6 extend the discussion begun in Chapters 3 and 4 by focusing explicitly on reading and writing across the curriculum. Comprehension and vocabulary development are certainly present in these chapters but are addressed as natural, and therefore assumed, parts of learning subject content.

Chapter 7 explores issues of assessment and evaluation of literacy abilities in content areas. While the emphasis here is on reading and writing, the recommended assessment information and practices can be generalized beyond literacy learning in many cases.

Chapter 8 concerns secondary textbooks, issues of readability and difficulty, and alternative ways to evaluate texts. The central focus here is finding out about both readers and texts in order to pair them appropriately.

Chapter 9 is another chapter focusing on instruction. It presents discussion, ideas, and specific directions for using collaborative and cooperative learning activities in subject area classes. The emphasis remains on literacy learning in subject areas, and suggestions are made for connecting these strategies with those learned in previous chapters.

Chapter 10 extends discussions from earlier chapters about student diversity, multiculturalism, and teaching in pluralistic schools. The definition of diversity in this chapter encompasses ranges of learning abilities and achievement (including giftedness), physical disability, and gender, as well as ethnic, cultural, and language differences. Instructional information, strategies, and activities that are presented effectively account for all of these various kinds of student diversity.

Chapter 11 extends the discussion begun in Chapter 10 by focusing on second language acquisition and development; this chapter presents effective instructional activities for teaching subject matter content to bilingual/bicultural students in multilingual/multicultural classrooms.

Chapter 12 encourages you as teachers to promote your students' (and your own) lifelong reading and writing behaviors. It's a chapter devoted to pleasurable, interesting reading and writing, for reading and writing can and should be captivating as well as informative. The premise of this chapter is that, if we are to be truly successful teachers, we must not only teach students how to read and write in content areas, but promote attitudes and behaviors that lead students to choose to do both independently.

REFERENCES

Anderson, R. C., Heibert, E. H., Scott, J. A., & Wilkinson, I. A. G. (1985). *Becoming a nation of readers: The report of the Commission on Reading.* Washington, DC: National Institute of Education.

Applebee, A. N. (1981). *Writing in the secondary school.* Urbana, IL: National Council of Teachers of English.

Atwell, N. (1987). *In the middle: Writing, reading and learning with adolescents.* Portsmouth, NH: Boynton/Cook.

Atwell, N. (1990). *Coming to know: Writing to learn in the intermediate grades.* Portsmouth, NH: Heinemann.

Bond, G. L., & Bond, E. (1941). *Developmental reading in high school.* New York: Macmillan.

Boyer, E. L. (1983). *High school: A report on secondary education in America.* New York: Harper & Row.

Chaskin, R. J., & Rauner, D. M. (Eds.) (1995). Special feature edition on youth and caring. *Phi Delta Kappan, 76*(9), 665–719.

Clifford, G. J. (1987). *A Sisyphean task: Historical perspectives on the relationship between writing and reading instruction* (Technical Report No. 7). Berkeley, CA: Center for the Study of Writing.

D O U B L E   E N T R Y   J O U R N A L

_____

_____

_____

_____

_____

_____

_____

_____

Write your own literacy history—an account of your experience acquiring and developing literacy and the instruction you received in school. Use your notes from the prereading DEJ and memories triggered during your reading to help you. Compare your experience with the literacy instruction history provided in the chapter. Share your comparison with a partner or group.

Duffy, G. G. (Ed.). (1990). *Reading in the middle school* (2nd ed.). Newark, DE: International Reading Association.

Early, M. J. (1957). What does research reveal about successful reading programs? In M. A. Gunn et al. (Eds.), *What we know about high school reading.* Champaign, IL: National Council of Teachers of English.

Eichorn, D. 1966. *The middle school.* New York: The Center for Applied Research.

Flesch, R. (1955). *Why Johnny can't read.* New York: Harper & Row.

Freeman, D. E., & Freeman, Y. S. (1994). *Between Worlds.* Portsmouth, NH: Heinemann.

Goodlad, J. I. (1984). *A place called school.* New York: McGraw-Hill.

Gray, W. S. (1948.) *Reading in the high school and college,* Forty-Seventh Yearbook, Part II, of the National Society for the Study of Education.

Greenlaw, J., & Moore, D. (1982). *Reading programs in secondary schools.* Paper presented at the National Reading Conference, St. Petersburg, FL.

Harste, J. C. (1994). Literacy as curricular conversations about knowledge, inquiry, and morality. In R. B. Ruddell, M. R. Ruddell, & H. Singer (Eds.), *Theoretical models and processes of reading*

(4th ed.) (pp. 1220–1242). Newark, DE: International Reading Association.

Herber, H. L. (1970). *Teaching reading in content areas.* Englewood Cliffs, NJ: Prentice-Hall.

Herber, H. L. (1978). *Teaching reading in content areas* (2nd ed.). Englewood Cliffs, NJ: Prentice-Hall.

Irwin, J. L. (1990). *Reading and the middle school student: Strategies to enhance literacy.* Newark, DE: International Reading Association.

Kang, H-W, & Golden, A. (1994). Vocabulary learning and instruction in a second or foreign language. *International Journal of Applied Linguistics, 4*(1), 57–77.

Lucas, G. (1995, July 6). Legislators push basics in schools. *San Francisco Chronicle,* pp. A1, A9.

McQuillan, J., & Rodrigo, V. (1995). A reading "din in the head": Evidence of involuntary mental rehearsal in second language readers. *Foreign Language Annals, 28*(2), 1–7.

Montegue, E. J., Huntsberger, J. P., & Hoffman, J. V. (1989). *Fundamentals of elementary and middle school classroom instruction.* Columbus, OH: Merrill.

Moore, D. W., Readence, J. E., & Rickelman, R. J. (1992). An historical exploration of content reading instruction. In E. K. Dishner, T. W.

Bean, J. E. Readence, & D. W. Moore (Eds.), *Reading in the content areas* (3rd ed.), (pp. 5–29). Dubuque, IA: Kendall/Hunt.

Moore, D. W., & Stefanich, G. P. (1990). Middle school reading: A historical perspective. In G. G. Duffy (Ed.), *Reading in the middle school* (2nd ed.), (pp. 3–15). Newark, DE: International Reading Association.

National Commission on Excellence in Education. (1983). *A nation at risk: The imperative for educational reform.* Washington, DC: U.S. Government Printing Office.

Noddings, N. (1992). *The challenge to care in schools.* New York: Teachers College Press.

Oakes, J. (1992). Can tracking research inform practice? *Educational Researcher, 21*(4), 12–21.

Pace, G. (Ed.) (1995). *Whole learning in the middle school: Evolution and transition.* Norwood, MA: Christopher-Gordon.

Phi Delta Kappan (1995, June). Special themed edition on standards. *76*(10), 744–769.

Rose, M. (1989). *Lives on the boundary.* New York: Penguin.

Ruddell, M. R. (1996). Engaging students' interest and willing participation in subject area learning. In D. Lapp, J. Flood, & N. Farnan (Eds.), *Content area reading/learning: Instructional strategies.* (2nd ed.) (pp. 95–110). Boston: Allyn & Bacon.

Sizer, T. R. (1984). *Horace's compromise: The dilemma of the American high school today.* Boston: Houghton Mifflin.

Sizer, T. R. (1992). *Horace's school: Redesigning the American high school.* Boston: Houghton Mifflin.

Smith, N. B. (1965). *American reading instruction.* Newark, DE: International Reading Association.

Stevenson, C., & Carr, J. F. (1993). *Integrated studies in the middle grades: "Dancing through walls."* New York: Teachers College Press.

Wheelock, A. (1992). *Crossing the tracks: How "untracking" can save America's schools.* New York: New Press.

2

LITERACY PROCESSES: THINKING, READING, AND WRITING

DOUBLE ENTRY JOURNAL

Jot down ideas you have about the processes of think-ing, reading and writing. What is your definition of each? How do you think these processes are connected? When you can no longer think of new ideas, organize your jottings and show any connections you can make.

How we think—how the human intellectual apparatus works—is an endlessly fascinating subject and has been an area of enduring interest to educators, psychologists, and other scientists for many, many years. Modern inquiry into human thinking can be dated to about the beginning of the twentieth century, since which time cognition and cognitive processes have been the focus of much study, research, definition, speculation, and redefinition. Along the way, study of the relationship between thinking and learning as well as the intricacies of various learning processes has led to additional interest in specific learning areas.

Reading emerged very early as a major focus of psychological theory and research, and, as the title of Thorndike's seminal study "Reading as Reasoning: A Study of Mistakes in Paragraph Reading" (1917) suggests, a clear linkage was made between cognition and literacy from early on. Today, information, theory, and research support that linkage and further suggest that the relationship between reading and writing is direct and parallel—that is they are (as mentioned in Chapter 1) different sides of the same coin. In this chapter, we will look first at current theory of cognition and cognitive processes; then we will connect those to reading and writing process theory.

THEORY AND PRACTICE

Before we go any further, however, let us talk for just a moment about theory. Much is made among students in education courses (and others as well) about the separation of "theory" and "practice." Long-standing educational lore has it that to be "theoretical" is to be high-flown, impractical, and out of touch with the real world of the classroom. Nothing could be further from the truth. Although it is possible for a theorist to be all of those things, it is certainly not necessary—nor is it even typical—of good theorists.

Theory is nothing more (nor less) than an informed hunch about how things work. Theories are marked by *cohesion* (things within things "fit together"; things "fit" with other things); *organizing principles* (limited numbers of generalizations or rules explain numerous events); *hypothesis-testing capability* (theories and theory parts may be examined and judged); and *flexibility* (theories change as they are tested and reevaluated on the basis of incremental evidence).

The truly theoretical teacher, then, is one who *fits together* what he or she is doing with what the rest of the school is doing, who understands that how you treat students one day has direct consequences for how they behave the next, and who perceives the relationship of various curricula within the school. A theoretical teacher is also one whose behavior is *rule-governed* rather than random; one who acts with foresight and thoughtfulness; one who reacts to classroom events predictably and reasonably; one who constantly seeks *greater understanding* of the classroom and school ecology by analyzing events and testing hypotheses; and one who *changes* classroom events, procedures, and interactions as conditions warrant. In short, to be theoretical is to make the classroom *make sense*—to yourself, to your students, and to anyone walking into the room. So, then, to be "theoretical" in the classroom is not to be high-flown, impractical, or out of touch with reality, all of which may be inconsiderate, thoughtless, foolish, sometimes silly, and maybe even dangerous—but certainly not theoretical. To be theoretical is to be down to earth, *utterly* practical, and fully in touch with reality. Theory is the foundation upon which all good classroom practice is built. Without it, what we do in the classroom—practice—is uninformed, random, inconsiderate, thoughtless, sometimes silly, and maybe even dangerous. Let us now look at important theory for guiding literacy learning.

COGNITIVE THEORY

I once sat in a teachers' lounge and listened to the vocational education teacher talk about how frustrated he was about a student we had in common. He finished by saying, with equal parts exasperation and affection, "That kid's just like a chicken—he wakes up to a new world every day!" I laughed along with the other teachers and rather admired the down-home flavor and humor of the comparison. Over the years, however, I've come to view that statement as a profound comment on human intelligence. What separates us from chickens is "that we *don't* wake up to a new world every day, and it is our ability to accumulate knowledge—to categorize, differentiate, generalize, and make predictions"—that characterizes our intellectual power. *How* we accumulate knowledge, the cognitive processes that human thinking comprises, is a topic that has fascinated so many so long.

COGNITION

Current understanding of cognition is centered in *schema theory*, derived from the work of Sir Frederick Bartlett (1932) and Swiss epistemologist Jean Piaget (Wadsworth, 1971), and, somewhat in contrast to Piagetian theory, the work of Lev Vygotsky (1978, 1986). Recently, other psychologists and educators (Anderson, 1977; Bayer, 1990; Bransford & Johnson, 1972; McCaslin, 1990; Rumelhart, 1981, 1984) have expanded and refined early theory and research. Piaget defined *schemata* (plural for schema) as ". . . cognitive structures by which individuals intellectually adapt to and organize the environment" (Wadsworth, 1971). Schemata receive, sort, classify, and hold information about environmental events and objects; these events and objects comprise our world knowledge and are connected to one another by the logical operations we are capable of performing. Piaget's classification of developmental stages of cognitive growth identifies specific types of operations in each stage from infant sensorimotor functioning to adult abstract reasoning.

Schemata are acquired, extended, and refined as a result of both direct and vicarious experience, and they carry with them *scripts*, or cognitive maps (Shank & Abelson, 1977), that tell us what to expect and how to behave in specific situations (Rumelhart [1981] even refers to schemata as "little plays"). Knowledge accumulated in schemata and scripts helps us see relationships and interrelationships and to function successfully in various contexts.

Consider, for example, the development of your "library" schema. Remember back to the first time you went to a library. The library was probably rather small; it may have been located in or near a local school. Someone probably showed you where books appropriate to your age were and gave you some information about how to act in a library (speak quietly, take your books to the desk to be "checked out," sit on the floor or in a chair or at a table to read until it is time to leave, etc.). Knowledge residing in this new schema subsequently made it possible for you to return to the library by yourself and function adequately (here is where you're you and a chicken is a chicken—no more "new world" for you, librarywise). You thus were able to *classify* information in your library schema to allow you to know what to expect and how to act, just as you did in your "home" schema, your "dog" schema, your "family" schema, and on and on and on.

Along with classification, we are able to *generalize* schema knowledge and scripts from one specific situation to another. We know that all libraries, even those we have never been inside, use classification systems to store books and periodicals; furthermore, we are able to use the high school card catalogue file after using the elementary school one, we can handle the vagaries of the Library of Congress classification system based on what we already know about the Dewey Decimal System, and we can use the online electronic file based on our knowledge both of traditional card catalogue files and how computer file systems work.

Our ability to *differentiate* occurs when we distinguish between specific items or events both within and across schemata. While we understand that all libraries use a classification system for storing books and periodicals, we also know that finding materials in a neighborhood library differs vastly from finding materials in a major research library. Further, classification systems are equally useful (and used) in department stores, fast-food restaurants, and fish markets; they're all different, and we must apply new classification system rules to each in order to use them. Our ability to differentiate across schemata allows us to make those distinctions and function appropriately.

And finally, we use schema knowledge and scripts to *predict* specifics within a schema so that we enter both known and new situations with a set of assumptions and expectations that guide our behavior. On entering the library on your campus, you expect to find the main desk and major book sections exactly where they were when you were last there, and you expect to follow established procedures for using and borrowing materials; when entering a different library, you look for the same elements in similar or corresponding areas and learn the procedural variations necessary for library use.

COGNITIVE PROCESSING

We continually extend and refine schemata through the processes of *assimilation* (adding new information to old schemata) and *accommodation* (creating new schemata or changing old ones with new information) (Wadsworth, 1971). The sum of our schemata and scripts can be thought of as our knowledge of the world. The more experience we have and the more accurately and precisely we classify, generalize, differentiate, and predict, the more likely we are able to function successfully in many different contexts. Confusion, or *non*-sense, occurs when experience has not provided the appropriate schema or when there is a mismatch between the schema we are using and the actual situation.

If we have no experience with libraries, it is unlikely we would know quite how to use one (luckily, we do have an adaptive schema that says, "When in doubt, observe or ask," so we look for the information desk or a friendly face). Mismatched schemata are typical of those odd, off-center conversations everyone has experienced when two people are talking, but not about the same thing. Comments don't "fit," and nothing makes sense until someone says, "Oh, *you're* talking about . . . ; *I'm* talking about . . . ." Critical to the process of unraveling confusion and non-sense is the monitoring aspect of well-established and refined schemata. Such monitoring signals a problem and lets us know when our behavior, the behavior of others around us, or any variety of interactions are not "right." This monitoring function is crucial to our ability to operate successfully within a complex environment.

CONCEPT FORMATION AND LEARNING

Vygotsky (1986) emphasizes the role of language in concept formation and learning. He states:

> . . . it is the functional use of the word, or any other sign, as means of focusing one's attention, selecting distinctive features and analyzing and synthesizing them, that plays a central role in concept formation [p. 106].

According to Vygotsky, we learn as we move cognitively from murky, undifferentiated object "heaps" to fully differentiated concepts through the medium of inner speech. Social interaction with teachers and peers further serves to guide and direct learning. The distance between what we are able to do (or know) independently and what we are able to do (or know) with assistance Vygotsky calls the *Zone of Proximal Development* (ZPD) (1986, p. 187). The ZPD, in turn, serves as the foundation for Vygotsky's argument that with peer interaction or teacher guidance, individuals can do more than they are able to do alone (p. 187) and, further, that what one can do with assistance today can be done alone tomorrow (p. 188).

THE RELATIONSHIP BETWEEN THINKING AND READING

Reading is the act of constructing meaning while transacting with text. Just as we use information stored in schemata to understand and interact with the world around us, so do we use this knowledge to make sense of print. Notice that I have not said anything about the reader "getting" meaning—from the author, the page, or anywhere else. I believe, as do others (Goodman, 1985, Tierney & Pearson, 1986; Rosenblatt, 1978, 1994), that readers literally *make meaning* from the interaction between prior knowledge and previous experience (what they already know), the information available in text, the "stance" (Rosenblatt, 1994), or position they elect to take in relationship to the text, and immediate, remembered, or shared social interaction and communication (Bayer, 1990; McCaslin, 1989; Vygotsky, 1978, 1986). Of this notion of "transaction," Louise Rosenblatt states,

> Every reading act is an event, or a transaction, involving a particular reader and a particular pattern of signs, a text, and occurring at a particular time in a particular context. Instead of two fixed entities acting on one another, the reader and the text are two aspects of a total dynamic situation. The "meaning" does not reside ready-made "in" the text or "in" the reader but happens or comes into being during the transaction between reader and text (1994, p. 1063).

Consider how active this theoretical view of reading is; in other words, how different it is to "make meaning" from text than it is to "get meaning" from text. Consider also how it focuses on the *reader*, rather than on the text or the author, as the central element of the process and how it emphasizes individual constructions of meaning (who and what the reader is determines in large part what meaning he or she makes) while at the same time accounting for socially negotiated meaning construction through the reader's interrelationships and communication with others. This view is *constructivist* in nature, with its emphasis on the individual as *creator*, rather than *receiver*, of meaning. Just as importantly, this view of the reading process has clear instructional implications—that is, from this theoretical vantage point, one sees many opportunities for teachers to teach in ways that will increase students' reading abilities.

This definition is by no means the only definition of the reading process; others abound—many of them very different and many of them just as supported by research and theory as this one. It is, however, the theoretical view of reading that guides and directs my thinking and thus serves as the foundation for this book. To reiterate:

Reading is the act of constructing meaning while transacting with text. The reader makes meaning through the combination of prior knowledge and previous experience, information available in text, the stance he or she takes in relationship to the text, and immediate, remembered or anticipated social interaction and communication.

Let us now look at the reading process.

THE READING PROCESS

PRIOR KNOWLEDGE AND PREVIOUS EXPERIENCE
At least two types of prior knowledge, residing in schemata, are critical to the reading process. The first is *world knowledge*, which is the total amount of information a person has accumulated through day-to-day living experience. The second is *text knowledge*, which is information accumulated from a reader's experiences with print.

World Knowledge   World knowledge includes information within individual schemata, information involving networks of relationships between and across schemata, and information about embedded characteristics of schemata (Rumelhart, 1981). For example, the "library" schema has within it a large number of schemata we could enumerate: "desk," "chair," "classification system," and "book," to name a few. These schemata are related to, and in fact embedded in, various other schemata. Think about a library desk, a school desk, an office desk, a computer desk, a rolltop desk, and so forth, and you begin to get the idea. Each of these world knowledge schemata carries with it the scripts we discussed earlier, as well as procedural knowledge that makes it possible for the reader to organize information, allocate attention, draw inferences, carry out orderly memory searches, edit and summarize information, and remember information (Anderson, 1985).

During reading, world knowledge serves as both the foundation and the building blocks for constructing meaning—that is, the amount, type, and kind of prior knowledge a reader has about a given topic affects the meaning he or she constructs for text on that topic. World knowledge is constantly changing as the result of our ongoing transactions in the world around us and perceptions of incoming information (Weaver, 1994); thus, no two readings of the same text are ever the same. For the most part, the greater the reader's world knowledge, the greater the likelihood that he or she will construct meaning that is similar to what the author intended. This is not always true, however. Rumelhart (1981, p. 22) suggests three explanations to account for lack of concurrence between reader text and author text:

1. *The reader may not have the appropriate schemata.* In this case, amount of world knowledge is the critical feature in that the reader simply has no basis for constructing meaning. Have you ever read a book as an adult that you'd read as a child and found yourself astonished as you encountered ideas that you didn't even know were there? The child could not make meaning of ideas for which he or she had no world knowledge. We've all experienced technical or other highly specialized text—legal documents, tax forms, bicycle assembly instructions—that left us baffled and defeated. That's "lack of appropriate schemata" in action.

2. *The reader may have the appropriate schemata, but the information available in text may not suggest them.* Here, the reader constructs incomplete or inappropriate meaning, but could possibly construct meaning given addition textual (or other) information to direct attention to the intended schemata. Sadoski and his associates (1992) suggest that text "concreteness," i.e., the degree to which text evokes mental images, may account in some part for the reader's ability to access appropriate schemata. When mismatches do occur, the situation is not dissimilar to the odd, off-center conversations discussed earlier or to reading Gary Larson's *Far Side* cartoons.

3. *The reader may construct a consistent interpretation of text, but not the one intended.* In this instance, the reader "understands text" but misunderstands the author. This situation can occur when prior knowledge is inaccurate (Anders & Lloyd, 1989) or when stylistic devices signaling author intent, such as irony or exaggeration, are not perceived.

Text Knowledge   In addition to using world knowledge, readers also employ prior knowledge about text while reading. This highly specialized information, which is actually a subset of world knowledge rather than separate from it, contains all that the individual knows about how text is organized, how one processes text, how the language of text functions, what expectations are reasonable when approaching print, what procedures are useful in interacting with text, and countless other conventions of text and print.

Knowledge about text ranges in sophistication and complexity from the child's emerging awareness of "Once upon a time" as a stylistic marker for the beginning of a story, to the mature reader's ability to distinguish not only between different types of text (narrative, expository) but between classifications within a given type (technical manual, school textbook, trade book, professional journal, popular magazine). It also includes information about such seemingly minor areas as how pronouns work, use of connectives (such as "and," "because," "in addition to"), and how print conventions (boldface headings, italicized words and terms, footnotes) are used to aid reader understanding of text.

Knowledge about text information becomes increasingly sophisticated and complex as we have correspondingly wider experience with written text. This information forms a set of assumptions and expectations about text that operates each time we begin to read and continues throughout the reader-text transaction. Consider, for example, the different assumptions and expectations you have for what the following texts will bring: advanced physics book, the current "steamy" best seller, a knitting pattern, nursery rhymes, graffiti, a grocery store aisle, a bus schedule, and instructions for programming a computer. Notice how your assumptions and expectations include both your knowledge about text and world knowledge. Even though we have discussed them separately, world knowledge and text knowledge are really rather difficult to sort out at times. Combined, they form the reader's base of prior knowledge and previous experience and thus assist the reader in constructing meaning. The reader's ability to construct meaning congruent with the author's intended meaning depends both on the content of his or her prior knowledge and previous experience and on her or his ability to access that prior knowledge base.

INFORMATION AVAILABLE IN TEXT

The reader's ability to construct meaning also depends on his or her ability to use information available in text. Information in text may be new information or already known. Much of what we discussed in the previous section (on text knowledge) comprises information available in text–textual features that carry meaning. Some features are highly explicit (paragraphing and punctuation, for example); others are slightly less so, such as stylistic differences between comparison-contrast, cause-effect, and effect-cause writing. World knowledge features are similarly available in text and are content-laden; in subject area text, world knowledge features include information about government structures, sines and cosines, musical notation, and much, much more.

Text and world knowledge features are available in text, whether or not the reader's prior knowledge base makes their meaning accessible. When the information in text is already known, that information is considered to be redundant. In other words, the things in text that the reader knows before entering that text are redundant, and, because of their redundancy, require less mental energy and cognitive processing time. So, once a reader's text knowledge base includes the information that quotation marks are used to signal conversation or specialized use of language, that information is redundant and therefore readily processed.

World knowledge information in text may be redundant as well. Consider the differences between your "history book" and "suspense novel" schemata. In each schema resides information that such texts focus on relationships between nations, often involve political conflict, and are concerned with some or all of the following: intrigue, economics, international disasters, famous people, war. Nevertheless, your prior knowledge about how history texts and suspense novels work would lead to quite different expectations for both the form and substance of each, even when the subject matter is identical (World War II, for example). The degree to which individuals have experience reading history books and suspense novels is the degree to which the information is redundant for each person. We create "slots" (Anderson, 1985) in our history book and suspense novel schemata for redundant elements that allow us to encounter them in text and process them with very little mental effort; thus, the amount of redundancy present in text determines, to some degree, the amount of mental energy we have to concentrate on new information.

When readers use information both from their own prior knowledge base and from information available in text, they are thus able to enter text with expectations or predictions that assist in constructing the intended meaning. For example, I can predict with some confidence that a history book will proceed chronologically, will likely use a cause-effect or effect-cause format, will highlight important people and events of historical periods, and, if reasonably new, may use examples of historical "realia" and primary sources to illustrate or expand ideas. Just as confidently, I can predict that suspense writer John LeCarré will keep me in murk and fog for at least the first two chapters; Tom Clancy will give so much detail as to seem to be revealing national security secrets; and Helen MacInnes will create exquisite tension. Such predictions assist readers in processing redundant information rapidly—in filling the "slots"—and allow them to concentrate energy on nonredundant features.

New, or nonredundant, information available in text is understood to the degree that the reader is able to create linkages between the new information and his or her prior knowledge base. New information is the information for which we literally have no slots; therefore, when text is highly abstract or obscure, creating cognitive links between the new and the known is difficult (Sadoski & Paivio, 1994). As readers working independently, we frequently give up or seek help constructing meaning for text with large amounts of new information. In school, instruction and/or social interactions often assist readers in creating links that allow understanding of new information.

READER STANCE IN RELATIONSHIP TO TEXT

Louise Rosenblatt, in her transactional theory of reading and writing (1978, 1994), states that in any reading act, the reader adopts, consciously or unconsciously, a stance that guides his or her progress through text. Reader stance involves selective attention, causing certain aspects of text to come to the forefront and others to recede, and literally creates the reading process for each reading event. What the reader attends to and his or her purpose for reading, in turn, determine to some degree the meaning constructed.

Consider for a moment what you know about sixteen-year-olds. Now consider differences in stance that the following reading materials might evoke among that group: a driver training manual, a current popular novel, instructions for operating a VCR, *Julius Caesar*, a movie theater guide, a physical education class handout "Rules of Baseball," a biographical article on a popular movie star, and 15 pages in a biology textbook. You get the picture. The point is that we cannot really talk about the reading process without discussing the reader, and the reader's intent—his or her reason for reading—is an important influence on the meaning he or she makes in the reading event. Rosenblatt believes that we have generally neglected this aspect of the reading process in our attempts to understand it. She states:

> The reading process that produces the meaning, say, of a scientific report differs from the reading process that evokes a literary work of art. Neither

contemporary reading theory nor literary theory has done justice to this important distinction. The tendency in the past generally has been to assume that such a distinction depends entirely on the texts involved. The character of the "work" has been held to inhere entirely in the text. Such classification of texts as literary or nonliterary ignore the contribution of the reader. We cannot look at the text and predict the nature of the resulting work in any particular reading. Before we can assume, for instance, that a poem or novel, rather than a statement of facts will be evoked for the texts, say, of Frost's *Mending Wall* or Dickens's *Great Expectations*, we must postulate a particular kind of relationship between the reader and the text [1989, p. 158].

Right now, we have a relatively imprecise understanding of how reader stance operates in individuals. Human knowledge, attitudes, beliefs, and motives are hidden from others' view, sometimes even from the individuals themselves, and are therefore difficult to study. We do, however, have some fairly reasonable hunches for explaining variations in reader stance. Rosenblatt, herself, suggests the possibility of a continuum of reading purposes, from *efferent reading* (from the Latin *effere*, to carry away), in which one learns or remembers, to *aesthetic reading*, in which one focuses attention on living through events during reading. Reader stance is determined by the view, efferent or aesthetic, the reader has of the text to be read (1989, p. 159).

My own belief (Haggard, 1988, 1989), and that of numerous others (Stauffer, 1980; Anderson, 1985; Tierney & Pearson, 1992) is that reader stance is shaped, at least in part, by the degree to which the reader "invests" in reading by making predictions, attempting to connect new information with prior knowledge and previous experience, and interacting with peers before, during, and after reading (Bayer, 1990). This viewpoint suggests that reader stance is flexible and can be changed during the act of reading and that intent may become stronger and more positive as investment increases (with the possibility of the opposite effect as well).

SOCIAL INTERACTION AND COMMUNICATION

From the seminal work of Lev Vygotsky in the 1920s and 1930s (Vygotsky, 1986), and the current interest in collaborative thinking in classrooms (Bayer, 1990; McCaslin, 1990), we have recently begun to reemphasize the influence of social interactions on readers' constructions of meaning. The Santa Barbara Classroom Discourse Group, a research consortium of teachers, graduate students, and university faculty, asserts, ". . . literacy [is not] a state of being that one arrives at like a state of grace. Rather, it is a dynamic process in which what literate action means is continually being constructed and reconstructed by individuals as they become members of new social groups" (1990, p. 120). This influence extends to readers' meaning constructions. As readers, we negotiate meaning through discussions, exchanges of information, and other social interactions, even if these interactions are only in our own heads; the result is that the meanings we construct are shaped and changed by others' interpretations of text as well as our own.

And so, we come full circle in our discussion of the components in the reading process. We began with the reader—his or her prior knowledge and previous experience—and end with the influence of social interactions on the reader's constructions of meaning. Let us go back one more time to the original statement of the reading process; hopefully, newly gained redundancy will give it greater meaning than it had before:

> *Reading is the act of constructing meaning while transacting with text.* The reader makes meaning through the combination of prior knowledge and previous experience, information available in text, the stance he or she takes in relationship to the text, and immediate, remembered, or anticipated social interaction and communication.

MONITORING THE READING PROCESS

Recall for a moment the monitoring aspect of schema theory presented earlier—the part that tells you when things do or do not make sense. We call this "metacognition," which means transcending or going beyond knowing. Metacognition monitors knowing; it is the ability to reflect on one's own cognitive processes. Metacognition tells us when we know and when we don't know; it tells us what we know, and lets us glimpse what we don't know. Metacognitive behavior asks the all-important question, "What's wrong with this picture?," that alerts us and causes us to short-circuit action in situations that do not make sense.

This same thing happens during reading. In effect, metacognitive behavior tells the reader, "Whoa! Stop. Go back and look at that again. The meaning you're making here is non-sense." Baker and Brown (1984) call this "dealing with failures to understand." Interestingly, it seems that very good readers have the most refined metacognitive sense while reading (just as interestingly, many not-so-good readers with not-so-good metacognition while reading have excellent metacognitive abilities in other contexts). It appears that knowing when you don't know is every bit as important as knowing itself. At any rate, metacognitive functioning is a critical part of the reading process. It, too, contributes to the meaning the reader constructs by monitoring the quality of that meaning.

THE RELATIONSHIPS AMONG THINKING, READING, AND WRITING

As you have read and analyzed this theoretical view of reading as the act of constructing meaning while transacting with text, you may have already begun to see the relationship between reading and writing and the interrelationship of thinking to both. We could simply substitute "writing" for "reading" in our definition of the reading process—writing is the act of constructing meaning while transacting with text—and have a perfectly valid statement of the writing process.

THE WRITING PROCESS

PRIOR KNOWLEDGE AND PREVIOUS EXPERIENCE

It is a cliché in the lore of writing that one writes what one knows—that the most powerful writing comes from the authenticity of experience. Here, as in many cases, the cliché is true. What one knows *is* prior knowledge and previous experience, and it is from this pool of information that we produce written text. Consider the writing you do: all the many and varied tasks in any given day, ranging from jotting down telephone numbers, to writing grocery lists, to taking notes in class, to writing letters or notes to family members. Prior knowledge and previous experience, both world knowledge and knowledge about text, affect all of these activities.

For example, if we compared an entire class's lecture notes for just one class period, I'm sure we would find large differences among individual notetakers; we can explain these differences, at least in part, by individual differences in prior knowledge. Notetakers use prior knowledge to process incoming information, concentrating their energy on the nonredundant parts, and then record that which they believe to be important based upon what they already know. Some notetakers scribble bits and pieces of ideas whereas others re-create almost verbatim what the lecturer says. Some use various print and textual conventions, such as outlining or indenting, while others write unbroken text or produce "maps," or schematic drawings.

These same individual differences carry over to other kinds of writing. Newly published authors are well known for producing work that is perceptibly, or even boldly, autobiographical. Other forms of writing—grocery lists, for example—are just as distinctive. Mine are organized according to the store's organization, and since I shop at two stores, I organize my lists differently depending on which store I'm shopping. I frequently have such entries as "7 oz. chopped olives" and "13 oz. whole canned tomatoes." That's because I like to try new recipes, and from long (and hard) experience, I know that if I write only "chopped olives" and "whole canned tomatoes" for new recipes, it's awfully easy to get to the store and find myself wondering, "Now, was I supposed to have 7 ounces of chopped olives and 13 ounces of canned tomatoes, or was it 13 ounces of chopped olives and 7 ounces of canned tomatoes?" The difference makes a difference.

Prior knowledge and previous experience influence writing even when we write in a relatively new area. Let's go back to the very first "report" we each copied out of the *World Book* or the *Encyclopedia Americana* (the *Britannica* was too much for us in fourth grade). First of all, we copied those reports because each of us knew so little about the topic that we literally had no words to discuss it. (Isn't it interesting that teachers feel compelled to send students off to do research on topics that the kids know nothing at all about? Wouldn't it be more interesting to find out what students would produce if we sent them off to do research on topics they know a lot about?) Anyway, the choices we made in our copying/writing ("I'll use it all; skip this paragraph; change that word," etc.) were grounded in prior knowledge, even though they often produced strikingly similar texts.

Then, as we became more sophisticated researchers and report writers, our wider base of world knowledge and knowledge about text produced increasingly individualistic text, so that now when we study and write on the same topics as others, we produce widely divergent text. Much of this difference can be explained by what we knew before we began writing. Prior knowledge and previous experience inform us and direct our writing just as surely as they influence how we act in a library and how we read the morning paper or a music appreciation text.

INFORMATION EMERGING FROM TEXT

It is significant, I think, that one of the most important attributes of writing is that it is not only a way to demonstrate what we know—in a report, or a poem, or a set of class notes—it is also a *way of knowing*, a way of working through confusion and fuzzy ideas, and a way of moving toward clarification and articulation of knowledge. This attribute of writing is often overlooked and undervalued. It should not be. Especially at those times when we are struggling to understand a new idea, to "fit" that information into our current knowledge base, and to arrive at coherent meaning, writing becomes a way of working through the process and moving toward insight. Thus, information emerges from text; *new ideas come as and from what* we write. All of us have faced the blank page. All of us have worked to put just the right words on paper, even when we didn't really know what it was we wanted to say. And all of us have had the light dawn, experienced insight, felt the "Aha!" Large or small, this insight grew from our writing, from the very process we went through to fill that empty page. This is the information emerging from text.

You may have noticed that I've changed this part of the reading–writing theory statement. With reading, I talked about information available in text; here, I'm referring to information emerging from text. I see them as mirror images of one another, indicative of the real differences that exist between reading and writing. The important connection between the two types of information is the constructed meaning resulting from or created by each.

WRITER STANCE IN RELATIONSHIP TO TEXT

Here, as with prior knowledge and previous experience, we have a component of the writing process that is directly parallel to the reading process. The writer's intent, his or her purpose for writing, profoundly influences the resulting text. This intent is actually a little more obvious in the case of writer stance than it is for reader stance. As you reflected a moment earlier on the writing you do, in all probability each instance you identified had a purpose attached to it: grocery list (because I have to go to the grocery store and don't want to forget items), report for class (because it was assigned), letter to Mother (because I miss her), or note to roommate (because I want him to clean up his side of the room). Whatever they are, whether efferent or aesthetic, these reasons comprise the writer's stance, which, in turn, directs the construction of meaning in text.

SOCIAL INTERACTION AND COMMUNICATION

As with reading, writing is influenced by social interaction with other thinkers and writers. Nearly always, we write with an audience in mind—even if it is only ourselves. Often we have the opportunity to share our writing with others with the purpose of getting their reaction or response. Such interaction creates and shapes the writing process itself, thus regulating mood, tone, style, and content and establishing our writing "voice."

Here, as with reading, we have come full circle. We began with the writer's background knowledge and ended with his or her voice. Let us look at our definition one more time in the context of writing:

Writing is the act of constructing meaning while transacting with text. The writer makes meaning through the combination of prior knowledge and previous experience, information emerging from text, the stance he or she takes in relationship to the text, and immediate, remembered, or anticipated social interaction and communication.

It seems clear that reading and writing are close, parallel processes. Although the specifics of the two are not identical, a growing number of educators agree. Tierney and Pearson (1986) make a strong case as they compare the reading and writing processes by identifying the "composing" aspect of each: planning, drafting, aligning, revising, and monitoring. Rosenblatt (1989, 1994) applies the efferent-aesthetic continuum to writing as well as reading. A recent spate of articles and books focus on the "reading and writing connections."

MONITORING THE WRITING PROCESS

Metacognitive thought accompanies writing just as surely as it does reading; in fact, it is, if anything, more explicit in writing process than in reading. Consider for a moment the revisions you do when creating text, whether the text itself is informal—a letter to a friend, for example—or polished, carefully honed text such as a term paper. Good writers have a sense of when their writing goes awry, and they have strategies for revising. That is metacognitive thought in action. Much of the currently popular "process writing" instruction focuses on collaborative draft writing of text to increase students' awareness of ways to monitor their writing and to engage them in metacognitive thought.

IMPLICATIONS OF THE THEORETICAL POSITION

In this discussion, we have viewed reading and writing as parallel literacy processes that are inextricably linked with cognition. Figure 2.1 is a map constructed by Jenny Burcham, one of my students, showing her understanding of these relationships. I like Jenny's representation and think it effectively captures the view articulated in this chapter. Further, the map suggests the complexity of the relationships between thinking, reading, and writing. Such a view carries with it the clear implication that learning involves all processes equally. If reading and writing truly are both "the act of constructing meaning while transacting with text" and we believe that the point of school is to make sense (to construct meaning), then it stands to reason that students should do a lot of reading and writing in school. So you see, if we are to produce scientists in our schools, students must be able to read and think and write as scientists do; if we are to produce poets in our schools, students must be able to write and read and think as poets do; and if we are to produce historians in our schools, students must be able to think and read and write as historians do.

Earlier, I said that this view of reading and writing processes has clear instructional implications—that is, from this theoretical vantage point, one sees many opportunities for teachers to teach in such a way as to increase students' literacy abilities.

FIGURE 2.1   *Map of Cognitive Processes*

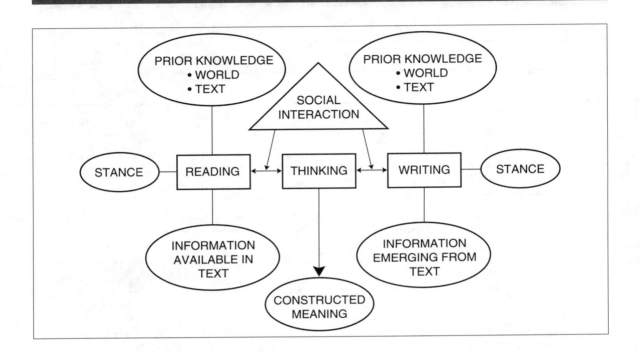

Important here is for you to understand that teaching in such a way as to increase students' literacy abilities *will increase students' learning of content as well.* That is what the rest of this book is about: instructional practices that teach students how to think and read and write within the context of subject area learning. All of the practices are compatible with the theoretical viewpoint we have developed here, and all of them may be used by teachers for developing literacy skills simultaneously with teaching content. In addition, these instructional practices take into account the diversity of secondary school students in today's schools; in fact, they represent at least part of the fundamental change in secondary school teaching we discussed in Chapter 1. As you continue through the text, consider how such instruction may be applied in your subject area.

REFERENCES

Anders, P. L., & Lloyd, C. V. (1989). The significance of prior knowledge in the learning of new content–specific instruction. In D. Lapp, J. Flood, & N. Farnan (Eds.), *Content area reading and learning: Instructional strategies* (pp. 258–269). Englewood Cliffs, NJ: Prentice-Hall.

Anderson, R. C. (1977). The notion of schema and the educational enterprise. In R. C. Anderson,

D O U B L E   E N T R Y   J O U R N A L

_____ _____ _____ _____ _____ _____ _____ _____	*Now rewrite your definition of thinking, reading, and writing using the information you jotted down before reading, as well as information from this chapter, to develop your definitions. Make as many connections between the three processes as you can. How are your definitions like or different from mine? Compare your definition with a partner's. As you continue through the book and your class, occasionally reread and revise your definitions as appropriate.*

R. J. Spiro, & W. E. Montague (Eds.), *Schooling and the acquisition of knowledge* (pp. 415–431). Hillsdale, NJ: Erlbaum.

Anderson, R. C. (1994). Role of the reader's schema in comprehension, learning and memory. In R. B. Ruddell, M. R. Ruddell, & H. Singer (Eds.), *Theoretical models and processes of reading* (4th ed.) (pp. 469–482). Newark, DE: International Reading Association.

Baker, L. & Brown, A. L. (1984). Cognitive monitoring in reading. In J. Flood (Ed.), *Understanding reading comprehension* (pp. 14–21). Newark, DE: International Reading Association.

Bartlett, F. (1932). *Remembering*. Cambridge, England: Cambridge University Press.

Bayer, C. S. (1990). *Collaborative-Apprenticeship learning: Language and thinking across the curriculum, K–12*. Mountain View, CA: Mayfield.

Bransford, J. N., & Johnson, M. K. (1972). Contextual prerequisites for understanding: Some investigations of comprehension and recall. *Journal of Verbal Learning and Verbal Behavior, 11,* 717–726.

Goodman, K. S. (1985). Unity in reading. In H. Singer & R. B. Ruddell (Eds.), *Theoretical models and processes of reading* (3rd ed.) (pp. 813–840). Newark, DE: International Reading Association.

Haggard, M. R. (1988). Developing critical thinking with the directed reading-thinking activity. *The Reading Teacher, 41,* 526–533.

Haggard, M. R. (1989). Instructional strategies for developing student interest in content area subjects. In D. Lapp, J. Flood, & N. Farnan (Eds.), *Content area reading and learning: Instructional strategies* (pp. 70–80). Englewood Cliffs, NJ: Prentice-Hall.

McCaslin, M. M. (1990). Motivated literacy. In J. Zutell & S. McCormick (Eds.), *Literacy theory and research: Analyses from multiple paradigms, 39th Yearbook of the National Reading Conference* (pp. 35–50). Chicago: National Reading Conference.

Rosenblatt, L. M. (1978). *The reader, the text, the poem: The transactional theory of the literary work*. Carbondale, IL: Southern Illinois University Press.

Rosenblatt, L. M. (1989). Writing and reading: The transactional theory. In. J. M. Mason (Ed.), *Reading and writing connections* (pp. 153–176). Boston: Allyn & Bacon.

Rosenblatt, L. M. (1994). The transactional theory of reading and writing. In R. B. Ruddell, M. R. Ruddell, & H. Singer (Eds.), *Theoretical models and processes of reading* (4th ed.) (pp. 1057–1092). Newark, DE: International Reading Association.

Rumelhart, D. E. (1981). Schemata: The building blocks of cognition. In J. T. Guthrie (Ed.), *Comprehension and teaching: Research reviews* (pp. 3–26). Newark, DE: International Reading Association.

Rumelhart, D. E. (1984). Understanding understanding. In J. Flood (Ed.), *Understanding reading comprehension* (pp. 1–20). Newark, DE: International Reading Association.

Sadoski, M., & Paivio, A. (1994). A dual coding view of imagery and verbal processes in reading comprehension. In R. B. Ruddell, M. R. Ruddell, & H. Singer (Eds.), *Theoretical models and processes of reading* (4th ed.) (pp. 582–601). Newark, DE: International Reading Association.

Santa Barbara Discourse Group (1992). Constructing literacy in classrooms: Literate action as social accomplishment. In H. Marshall (Ed.), *Redefining learning: Roots of educational reform* (pp. 119–150). Norwood, NJ: Ablex.

Shank, R. C., Abelson, R. P. (1977). *Scripts, plans, goals, and understanding.* Hillsdale, NJ: Erlbaum.

Stauffer, R. G. (1980). *The Language-Experience approach to teaching* (2nd ed.). New York: Harper & Row.

Thorndike, E. L. (1917). Reading as reasoning: A study of mistakes in paragraph reading. *The Journal of Educational Psychology*, 8, 323–332.

Tierney, R. J., & Pearson, P. D. (1986). Toward a composing model of reading. In E. K Dishner, T. W. Bean, J. E. Readence, & D. W. Moore (Eds.), *Reading in the content areas: Improving classroom instruction* (2nd ed.), (pp. 64–75). Dubuque, IA: Kendall/Hunt.

Tierney, R. J., & Pearson, P. D. (1992). Learning to learn from text: A framework for improving classroom practice. In E. K. Dishner, T. W. Bean, J. E. Readence, & D. W. Moore (Eds.), *Reading in the content areas: Improving classroom instruction* (3rd ed.), (pp. 87–103). Dubuque, IA: Kendall/Hunt.

Vygotsky, L. (1978). *Mind in society: The development of higher psychological processes.* Cambridge, MA: MIT Press.

Vygotsky, L. V. (1986). *Thought and language* (Trans. & Ed., A. Kozulin). Cambridge, MA: MIT Press.

Wadsworth, B. J. (1971). *Piaget's theory of cognitive development.* New York: David McKay.

Weaver, C. (1994). Parallels between new paradigms in science and in reading and literacy theories: An essay review. In R. B. Ruddell, M. R. Ruddell, & H. Singer (Eds.), *Theoretical models and processes of reading* (4th ed.) (pp. 1185–1202). Newark, DE: International Reading Association.

COMPREHENSION INSTRUCTION IN CONTENT AREAS

You've heard the term reading comprehension *many times. List ideas or concepts you associate with reading comprehension and ways you think we learn to comprehend. Now think of your most difficult subject area. How might teachers have made it easier for you to understand this material? How do you suppose teachers teach comprehension?*

PART I: *The Comprehension Process and Comprehension Instruction*

The most common academic goal of reading is comprehension—the construction of meaning that in some way corresponds to the author's intended meaning. (The fact of individual differences in both prior knowledge and stance in relationship to text suggest that this correspondence is never exact nor identical from reader to reader.) In school, however, reading has three additional goals:

1. **Learning.** Students read not only to understand text, but to extend their knowledge in subject areas as well.
2. **Increasing Reading Skills.** At each grade level, students are expected to become better readers and to read increasingly difficult text.
3. **Application.** Throughout the middle and secondary grades, students are expected to apply knowledge constructed from reading text.

Think about this for a moment: It is no small thing we ask students to do. We expect them, from their very earliest reading experiences, to understand the author's intended meaning; at the same time, we expect them to learn more in each and every subject area taught (whether they like it or not), to become progressively sophisticated readers and writers (arriving at some mythical level of "maturity" around the eleventh or twelfth grade), and, finally, to apply newly constructed content knowledge in novel situations. We expect these accomplishments of all students and are often quite vocal in our complaints when we believe that expectations are not being met. Unfortunately, we just as often overlook the fact that what we expect of students—comprehending, learning, developing reading proficiency, and applying knowledge—are interrelated academic abilities. To focus on one ability and exclude the others is to hinder progress in all. The obvious counterpoint is that to develop students' abilities in one area, instruction must address all.

In the past, much of the comprehension "instruction" in secondary schools was little more than teachers telling students to read and understand ("Read Chapter 3 and be prepared to discuss it." "Read pages 54–67 and answer the questions on page 68."). Long a tradition in secondary schooling, this approach today seems more than a little short-sighted, especially when viewed in light of the heavy expectations we hold for student learning and development of literacy skills and abilities. Simply *telling* students to read and understand assumes students will be able to do all that we expect them to do without our help. Further, it equates *telling* someone to do something with *teaching* them how to do it, and such an equation is simply not valid.

If middle school and secondary school students are to meet the expectations held by teachers, parents, the school, and society as a whole, they need *real* instruction—instruction that guides their progress through text, promotes learning, teaches them how to become better readers and writers, and provides adequate support for application of new learning. That is what this chapter is about: first, to examine comprehension as it relates to our agreed-upon view of the reading process (or, if you will, the view presented by this book), and second, to present instructional approaches compatible with that view and the criteria for real instruction that guides students through text, promotes learning, develops reading proficiency, and fosters knowledge application.

THE COMPREHENSION PROCESS

In Chapter 2, we described reading as the act of constructing meaning while transacting with text. The meaning one makes (or what one comprehends) from text during this transaction is a result of the combination of prior knowledge and previous experience, the information available in text, the reader's stance in relationship to the text, and immediate, remembered, or anticipated social interaction and communication. Let's now elaborate on that description of the reading process. Essentially, what happens is this: The reader approaches text with a collection of information and assumptions that make up what she or he already knows about a topic (prior knowledge and previous experience) and a reason (or reasons) for reading (stance). What the reader already knows can range from nothing (in which case, little, if anything, will be comprehended) to total knowledge of a given topic (and there are those who would argue that this reader will comprehend nothing new); most often, however, readers begin knowing something well within these two extremes. Reasons for reading are similarly variable, with an unspecified number of possible affective, cognitive, social, and practical overlays. For example, whether the reader's purpose for reading is intrinsic or extrinsic—internally or externally imposed—is one; others are the degree to which the reader views the material to be useful, interesting, important, and so on.

With this background information and reason(s) for reading, the reader enters text with certain predictions, or expectations, about the text: whether it will be known information or relatively new, easy to read or difficult, interesting or dull, useful or not, and so forth. The reader then progresses by sampling text, making new predictions based on this sample (information available in text), resampling, and confirming or adjusting predictions in light of new information. The amount of redundancy present in text—elements and information already known to the reader—controls to some extent the rate of progress and focus of reader energy and attention.

So, for example, the more one knows about the topic under discussion, the greater the likelihood that reading will be evenly paced, uninterrupted, and relatively rapid; on the other hand, when the reader knows little about the topic, chances are that reading will be slower, somewhat erratic, and interrupted by "thinking" pauses that provide the reader time to process new language and information and/or consider metacognitively how much sense he or she is constructing.

As reading continues, all of the elements of comprehension—prior knowledge and previous experience, information available in text, reader stance, and social interactions—become impossibly intertwined. New information merges with old; reasons for reading change, waxing and waning with value attached to what is in the text; prior knowledge shades or influences the meaning one makes of certain portions of text; previous discussion and/or anticipated social interchange shade interpretations; and on and on. The point is, comprehension is both cyclical and cumulative; it is driven by a predict–read (sample text)–repredict–resample cycle that seems to gather speed and strength and force as it continues successfully forward (the opposite is also true—the cycle very rapidly loses speed and strength and force when progress is hindered). Its complexity is mind-boggling.

Given this complexity and the dynamic aspect of reader-text transactions, it becomes important to get a sense of how successful readers approach and process text if we are to assist students in understanding subject texts. Pearson, Roehler, Dole, and Duffy (1990) summarized a body of comprehension research about what strategies good readers use to construct full, rich meaning from text. From the many studies reviewed has emerged a profile of proficient readers—Pearson and his associates call them "expert" or "thoughtful" readers—that increases our understanding of what happens during successful reader-text transactions. According to Pearson and colleagues, thoughtful readers:

- constantly search for connections between what they know and what they encounter as new information in the text;
- constantly monitor the adequacy of the models of text meaning they build;

- take steps to repair faulty comprehension once they realize that they have failed to understand something;
- learn very early to distinguish important from less important ideas in the text they read;
- are especially adept at synthesizing information within and across texts and reading experiences;
- make inferences during and after reading to achieve a full, integrated understanding of what they read;
- sometimes consciously (almost always unconsciously) ask questions of themselves, the authors they encounter, and the texts they read.

To this profile Paris, Lipson, and Wixon (1994) add the notion of "strategic reading," that is, reading in which the reader not only knows what to do, but knows how to do it and when to do what. They label this knowledge as "Declarative" (knowing what to do), "Procedural" (knowing how to do it), and "Conditional" (knowing when to do what). They emphasize that skilled readers know the purpose of the task at hand and the options for completing it successfully; less skilled readers are often unaware of both (p. 796).

INSTRUCTIONAL APPROACHES FOR GUIDING COMPREHENSION

The clear implication here is that to provide ongoing development of students' comprehension abilities, teachers need to teach in such a way that the characteristics of thoughtful or strategic readers described above are taught and encouraged as students encounter classroom text. The instructional approaches described in this chapter (and, in fact, throughout this text) do just that. This chapter focuses on the immediate goal of comprehension—instruction that guides and assists students in constructing meaning while reading text. In addition, all of the instructional practices in this chapter provide to increase students' ability to learn subject area information, to improve content reading and writing abilities, and to apply new knowledge. I will demonstrate various ways in which they do this. Later chapters focus on increasing students' ability to learn and apply subject area information and improve content reading and writing skills; these chapters similarly demonstrate how to develop comprehension. I will point this out as appropriate.

THE DIRECTED READING-THINKING ACTIVITY (DR-TA)

The Directed Reading–Thinking Activity (DR-TA) was introduced by Russell Stauffer in 1969 as a means for developing reading comprehension and is currently receiving renewed attention and recommendation as an effective means for facilitating students' comprehension (Gillet & Temple, 1994; Tierney & Pearson, 1992; and Tierney, Readence, & Dishner, 1994). Essentially, the DR-TA guides students through text by having the teacher ask students to make and support predictions before reading and then examine their predictions, conclusions, and logic as reading progresses. Frank

Smith (1994) makes a strong argument for DR-TA and DR-TA-like instruction that focuses on students' predictions and subsequent reading of text:

> Now at last prediction and comprehension can be tied together. Prediction means asking questions, and comprehension means being able to get some of the questions answered. Comprehension, basically, is the absence of confusion. As we read, as we listen to someone talking, as we go through life, we are constantly asking questions, then we comprehend. The person who does not comprehend how to repair a bicycle is the one who cannot ask and find answers to such questions as "Which of these nuts and bolts goes where?" at appropriate times. And the person who does not comprehend a book or newspaper article is the one who cannot find relevant questions and answers concerning the next part of the text. There is a *flow* to comprehension, with new questions constantly being generated from the answers that are sought. (p. 19)

The following example is a DR-TA science lesson. Reproduced below is a section of the first page of a chapter of the physics text, *Physics: Its Methods and Meaning* (Taffel, 1992).

DR-TA LESSON EXAMPLE

4   *Vectors, Force, and Motion*

AIMS

1. To note that energy is often associated with matter in motion and that motion is controlled by forces.
2. To learn how to represent forces and motion by vectors.
3. To learn how to obtain the combined effect of two or more vectors acting upon the same point of a body.
4. To understand how a vector can act in directions other than its own.

VECTORS AND SCALARS

4-1   CHANGE, MOTION, AND FORCE

Practically all of the changes we see in the world about us are the result of *motion.* Day and night are caused by the rotation of the earth on its axis. The winds and their effects are caused by the motion of air. The conversion of raw materials into the products we need in everyday living is brought about by various motions. These include transporting the materials to factories, combining them, shaping them into finished products, and transporting the products to market. Change and motion go hand in hand.

Motion is controlled by forces.

When a car stalls, it must be pushed to get it going. When the engine is running, it is the engine which pushes the car forward. In either case, a *force* is being used to change the state of the car from rest to motion. In order to make the car slow down or to stop altogether, the brakes are applied. Again, a force is being applied to change the motion of the car. These examples illustrate that *motion is controlled or changed by means of force.*

4-2   DISPLACEMENT IS A VECTOR

Motion generally involves a change of position of the object being moved. A change of position is called a *displacement*. Suppose a body is moved from a point *A* to a second point *B* 10 meters to the northeast of *A*. How shall we describe this displacement? It is not enough to say that the body has moved 10 meters from *A*. Its final position could then be any point on the circumference of a circle centered on *A* and having a 10-meter radius. To state exactly how the position of the body changed, we must also state in what direction it was moved. Thus, the displacement from *A* to *B* is described as one of 10 meters northeast.

To initiate DR-TA instruction, the teacher asks students to cover everything on the page except the chapter title:

4   Vectors, Force, and Motion

The teacher then asks, "Based upon this title, what do you think the chapter will be about?" Following each student response, the teacher probes for support (if it has not spontaneously been stated): "What makes you say that?" or "Why?" Then the teacher asks students to look at the aims statements below the chapter title:

AIMS

1. To note that energy is often associated with matter in motion and that motion is controlled by forces.
2. To learn how to represent forces and motion by vectors.
3. To learn how to obtain the combined effect of two or more vectors acting upon the same point of a body.
4. To understand how a vector can act in directions other than its own.

At this point, the teacher encourages more predictions, "Now what do you think?" and evaluations of logic and thinking, "Why?" "What makes you say that?"

Students are then asked to read the first three paragraphs of the chapter:

VECTORS AND SCALARS

4-1   CHANGE, MOTION, AND FORCE

Practically all of the changes we see in the world about us are the result of *motion*. Day and night are caused by the rotation of the earth on its axis. The winds and their effects are caused by the motion of air. The conversion of raw materials into the products we need in everyday living is brought about by various motions. These include transporting the materials to factories, combining them, shaping them into finished products, and transporting the products to market. Change and motion go hand in hand.

Motion is controlled by forces.

When a car stalls, it must be pushed to get it going. When the engine is running, it is the engine which pushes the car forward. In either case, a *force* is being used to change the state of the car from rest to motion. In order to make the car slow down or to stop altogether, the brakes are applied. Again, a force is being applied to change the motion of the car. These examples illustrate that *motion is controlled or changed by means of force.*

4-2   DISPLACEMENT IS A VECTOR

Motion generally involves a change of position of the object being moved. A change of position is called a *displacement*. Suppose a body is moved from a point *A* to a second point *B* 10 meters to the northeast of *A*. How shall we describe this displacement? It is not enough to say that the body has moved 10 meters from *A*. Its final position could then be any point on the circumference of a circle centered on *A* and having a 10-meter radius. To state exactly how the position of the body changed, we must also state in what direction it was moved. Thus, the displacement from *A* to *B* is described as one of 10 meters northeast.

Discussion continues with increasingly specific discussion of content: "What other ideas do you think we'll find in this chapter?" "Why?" "What do you think we'll know when we're through?" "Why?" "Anything else?"

Following this, the teacher directs students to read larger sections of text, stop at appropriate points to evaluate previous predictions, draw conclusions, examine and possibly revise logic, and make new predictions.

The DR-TA is relatively simple to do, but it almost needs to be seen to be understood. So, I'm going to demonstrate a DR-TA for an English class lesson using a short story called "The Splendid Outcast" (Markham, 1987). I have chosen to use a sample demonstration of the DR-TA for several reasons: First, because, in my mind, the DR-TA is such an important instructional strategy; it clearly replicates the predict–sample text–repredict–resample process we discussed earlier as a critical component of comprehension; it encourages the behaviors of thoughtful and strategic readers; and it stimulates full, rich understanding of text with its emphasis on prediction and discussion.

Second, I believe the DR-TA is worth knowing a lot about because it is adaptable to many different text styles as well as to other media—two of the best DR-TA lessons I've ever seen were one done in a music appreciation class as students listened to a piece of music for the first time and one in a homemaking class to teach students how to use a dressmaking pattern.

Third, the DR-TA is particularly useful for accommodating the wide cultural, language, and literacy differences students bring to secondary classrooms and for supporting all students in constructing new knowledge. Further, it encourages students to construct meaning collaboratively and stimulates a great deal of student talk and verbal interchange, thus bringing into the classroom the real-life transactions and mutual sharing of knowledge and ability that are characteristic of everyday learning. Most importantly, the wide-ranging, rich classroom discussion of a DR-TA exposes limited English speakers to the very language they are trying to learn. (Of course, language-rich classrooms are just as beneficial for the most accomplished language users as well.)

And finally, the extended lesson here allows me to illustrate the use of four different instructional practices—two in this chapter (DR-TA and group mapping), one in Chapter 4 (Vocabulary Learning in Content Areas), and one in Chapter 6 (Writing Across the Curriculum). After the demonstration, I will discuss the DR-TA further and show other ways it may be applied to various subject area texts.

LESSON PLAN   *DR-TA Lesson*

Setting: Senior English Class   *Topic:* Short Story

Teacher: I'm giving each of you a blank sheet of paper that I will call your "cover sheet." Open your books to page 34 and cover everything except the title and author of the story.

THE SPLENDID OUTCAST
by
Beryl Markham

Teacher: With a title like that, what do you think this story will be about?

Student: About a person who's doing something that's not particularly acceptable, or maybe something outside the ordinary. But something that's exciting.

T: Why do you say that?

S1:   Well, because I know who Beryl Markham is.

T: Who is Beryl Markham?

S1:   If I recall, she's a famous aviator from the turn of the century that was a great flier and lover of the African outdoors . . . a horse trainer. She was also a horse trainer.

T: Yes, she was a horsetrainer. And she's a bit later than turn of the century—more like in this century. Yes, what were you going to say?

S2:   I was thinking it was somebody who was outside of the social clique, but doing quite well on their own.

T: Why?

S2:   Because of the word *splendid.*

T: *Splendid* in the title. Okay. That's an interesting idea. What else? Does anyone know this story? Any other ideas?

S3:   I was thinking of an eccentric who was really having a good time at it.

T: An eccentric who was having a good time of it! That sounds like fun. Any other ideas?

S4:   I think that "splendid" might mean that someone else admired this outcast. This outcast doesn't care whether he's an outcast or not.

T: All right. Move your cover sheet so you can read just the first paragraph.

The stallion was named after a star, and when he fell from his particular heaven, it was easy enough for people to say that he had been named too well. People like to see stars fall, but in the case of Rigel, it was of greater importance to me. To me and to one other—to a little man with shabby cuffs and a wilted cap that rested over eyes made mild by something more than time.

T: (After students read.) Now what do you think?

S1:   It's about the horse.

T: All right, it's about a horse. What else?

S1:   Well, he used to be well known, but something's happened.

T: What do you think it might be?

S1:   Injury?

T: It could be.

S1:   Like a racehorse.

T: Certainly. Any other ideas?

S2:   He had some kind of connection to this little guy. Maybe the guy was a jockey or somebody else that had been connected with him for a while and something that happened to the horse had an impact on this guy.

T: Why do you suggest that he might have been a jockey or might be a jockey?

S2:   Because it said "little man" and I know jockeys are little.

T: All right. Okay. Any other ideas? Read the next four paragraphs.

It was Newmarket, in England, where, since Charles I instituted the first cup race, a kind of court has been held for the royalty of the turf. Men of all classes come to Newmarket for the races and for the December sales. They come from everywhere—some to bet, some to buy or sell, and some merely to offer homage to the resplendent peers of the Stud Book, for the sport of kings may, after all, be the pleasure of every man.

December can be bitterly cold in England, and this December was. There was frozen sleet on buildings and on trees, and I remember that the huge Newmarket track lay on the downs below the village like a noose of diamonds on a tarnished mat. There was a festive spirit everywhere, but it was somehow lost on me. I had come to buy new blood for my stable in Kenya, and since my stable was my living, I came as serious buyers do, with figures in my mind and caution in my heart. Horses are hard to judge at best, and the thought of putting your hoarded pounds behind that judgement makes it harder still.

I sat close on the edge of the auction ring and held my breath from time to time as the bidding soared. I held it because the casual mention of ten thousand guineas in payment for a horse or for anything else seemed to me wildly beyond the realm of probable things. For myself, I had five hundred pounds to spend and, as I waited for Rigel to be shown, I remember that I felt uncommonly maternal about each pound. I waited for Rigel because I had come six thousand miles to buy him, nor was I apprehensive lest anyone should take him from me; he was an outcast.

Rigel had a pedigree that looked backward and beyond the pedigrees of many Englishmen—and Rigel had a brilliant record. By all odds, he should have brought ten thousand guineas at the sale, but I knew he wouldn't, for he had killed a man.

T: (After students read.) Now what do you think?

S1:   The writer is wanting to buy this horse who is an outcast. That's real clear from it. I wish I knew the difference between guineas and pounds. That would be helpful.

T: Yes. I don't really know the difference. I know what pounds are. I don't think guineas are used in the British monetary system anymore, but I don't know. I can't answer it. Anybody know? All right. We'll hang on to that and look it up. What else? What do you think?

S2:   This horse is really special. She's come 6,000 miles to buy him. Breed him, I guess.

T: Okay. What else?

S3:   I get the impression that his price is going to be lower. I'm not sure of the exact cost.

T: The horse?

S3:   Rigel. Because she (or he) is not worried about anybody getting him.

S4:   Either not worried or has enough money that he doesn't have to.

T: Right. (Beryl Markham is a woman, by the way.)

S4:   Right. But I thought in the story it might be a character.

T: I would imagine because she was a horse trainer . . .

S4:   That it's autobiographical.

T: Yes. That she's speaking of herself. Okay. Anything else? The comment that you made about Rigel being cheaper. Why would that be?

S3:   He probably was once a good runner. And he probably had some kind of accident or injury or something happened that made him not a good runner. My guess is that there might be a genetic weakness.

S4:   No one dares to buy him unless they have somebody they think is heaven-sent who is going to take care of this horse.

T: Why?

S1:   Because of the killings, and he's just impossible to take care of. In the back of my mind, though, she's watching this little man who she thought was probably a jockey, so I'm thinking that he figures very closely in the story as somebody in her future with this horse.

T: Okay.

The class continues reading as the story unfolds to reveal that the storyteller and the jockey do, indeed, become rival bidders for Rigel. Both, however, are clearly short on funds. In the meantime, Rigel becomes wildly uncontrollable by the stable hands working at the sale. The jockey enters the ring.

T:	Now what do you think?
S1:	Maybe she'll let him have Rigel because of her admiration for him or because he really won him. He's the only one with courage to approach him.
T:	All right.
S2:	I think she knows the horse is nothing without him—absolutely nothing—that their lives depend on each other.
T:	Anything else?
S3:	I think the auctioneer is going to say, "Sold."
T:	And give Rigel to her?
S3:	No. Give it to the other guy.
T:	To him.
S3:	He's a tight spender.
T:	Oh that's right, that's right. He's got the 480.
S4:	She won't get the 500 out of her mouth, I don't think.
T:	All right.
S5:	I think she'll have the chance if she wants to.
T:	Okay. So, we've got our three suggested alternatives here [suggested earlier]: She's going to get the horse and hire the man; she's going to let him buy the horse; she's simply going to get the horse and he'll be out of it.
S5:	She's going to give the horse to him. She knows it. Even if she could outbid him, the horse would still be his.
T:	All right. Finish the story.

Thus ends the Directed Reading-Thinking Activity (it does not end class discussion of the story, however, but I'll get back to that later). Let's examine the steps in the DR-TA (Stauffer, 1969, 1980); then I will give directions for classroom use and demonstrate other applications.

STEPS IN THE DR-TA

Step 1 Identifying Purposes for Reading

The DR-TA begins with students setting individual and group purposes for reading as they combine prior knowledge with information in text to predict what the text is going to be about. Purpose setting continues throughout the reading each time students repredict, raising new questions ("What connection does the little man have with the horse?" "Will Markham 'let' him buy the horse or will she outbid him?" "What is the bond between the two characters?"), and then sample increasing amounts of text. Students therefore return to text repeatedly with a purpose for reading: to get answers to questions arising from their predictions or to see whether new information will cause these predictions to be revised.

In our lesson-demonstration discussion, notice how broad and speculative early predictions were in contrast to the last ones just before students were directed to finish reading ("About a person who's doing something that's not particularly acceptable, or maybe something outside the ordinary," versus "She's going to give the horse to him. She knows it. Even if she could outbid him, the horse would still be his."). This same progression from general to highly specific predictions is just as typical when reading expository text—our physics text chapter discussion, for example—as it is with narrative.

Notice also how this contrast illustrates what we said earlier about comprehension. In the first prediction, the reader had very little information to go on; the last prediction, however, was focused and informed by prior knowledge, increased amounts of information in the text, the readers' own logic systems, and input from other readers. By this point, the readers had gotten a great deal of information, both from the text and the discussion accompanying reading, and each had clearly made a decision about the final outcome.

This progression of thinking—from broad, speculative early predictions to focused, refined later ones—typifies the DR-TA and a critical aspect of purposeful reading. In fact, general stages of thinking can be identified that are characteristic of DR-TA lessons. The stages below describe the thinking students do as they progress through a DR-TA. Throughout these stages, individual students' contributions to the discussion influence and change other students' constructions of meaning and contribute to individual and group purposes for reading.

1. *Initial Speculation and Conjecture* (title or title and author). In this stage, students have only a title and their prior knowledge from which to speculate (although with some texts, articles, or literature, an author's name may also be available). Students are examining numerous possible contexts, but predictions tend to rely heavily on prior knowledge and various interpretations of title words.

2. *Preliminary Confirmation and Redirection* (first paragraph and/or other preliminary information). Here, first-stage predictions are confirmed or discarded, as text information warrants. This stage is marked by identification of facts and details that do or do not support earlier speculations. Beginning attempts are made to state where the text is going.

3. *Data Collection and Analysis* (more paragraphs, sections, and pages). Lots of discussion in this stage is directed toward fitting together various bits and pieces of the text. Facts, ideas, thematic concerns, and questions are interwoven to make sense of text. Students search for the "big idea."

4. *Focused Speculation and Refined Analysis* (midway or more). At this point, enough text information has been revealed for students to discard ideas that don't work and begin focusing on where the text is going. Predictions become much more focused and definite and much less tentative. Content information is being integrated with prior knowledge.

5. *Final Speculation and Summarizing* (toward the end). Here, tentative conclusions are drawn as speculations incorporate large chunks of content. Conclusions may come from one individual, or be collectively generated, but generally they surface in preparation for the final stage of reading. Here, attention often shifts to higher-order considerations, such as classification and prioritization of ideas, debate over differing viewpoints, or discussion of author or text intent.

6. *Decision Making* (just before final paragraphs or section). By this point, everyone in the room has arrived at conclusions about the content or final outcome of the text. These are often voiced with some conviction. Decisions are not always "right"—that is, they do not always match the actual content or outcome. They are, however, almost always reasonable from the standpoint of what could be.

The teacher's role during discussion is to accept student predictions, making no judgment about how "correct" the predictions are, and to concentrate on follow-up probe questions that assist students in articulating the reasons, logic, and evidence for their predictions. Teachers interject information only when student comments indicate misinformation or misunderstanding (recall the clarification from the teacher about Beryl Markham). Critical to this point is that the teacher's role involves much more listening than it does talking.

Look back at the discussion in the lesson demonstration, and you'll see that the teacher really said very little. The major responsibility for discussion was on the students: They were the ones bringing up new ideas, they were holding the floor most of the time, and they occasionally left the teacher out altogether to discuss the story among themselves. That is precisely as it should be. Good DR-TA teachers quite often find themselves standing in front of a class calling on students, nodding, and saying, "Why?" "What makes you say that?" "Um-hmm," "Really?" and "Any other ideas?" The teacher encourages students to support predictions and opinions through metacognitive thought—that is, to examine aloud how they know something or reveal their line of reasoning. As reading progresses, students re-examine their logic to achieve a "fit" between what is known and what can be predicted. The purpose here is not anything-goes, wild conjecture but, rather, disciplined inquiry in which students use prior knowledge and evidence from text to arrive at new insights and understandings (Haggard, 1988). Because students bring different experiences, cultural backgrounds, and logic systems to the learning task, individual predictions will differ. These differences are to be expected and even celebrated. One of the greatest values of a DR-TA is the sharing of diverse individual experiences and perceptions. Often, these experiences represent a variety of cultural backgrounds and knowledge systems, and when different viewpoints, understandings, and ideas surface, everyone learns something and everyone gains.

It is important that you really listen to what students say during DR-TA discussion—not to see if responses are "right," but rather to hear your students' voices more clearly. As students speculate and support their predictions and conclusions, you can learn a great deal about their prior knowledge base. So, too, you can gain insight into different constructions of meaning that stem from diverse cultural, social, and personal viewpoints. These differences enrich class discussions and add depth and breadth to students' classroom experiences.

The *value* here, then, is the sharing of personal background and reasoning, different as these may be, to increase everyone's fund of knowledge, hone thinking skills, and provide immediate purpose for reading. The net effect is that students engage much more willingly and effectively with content text: Discussion focuses not so much on "right" and "wrong" answers, but rather on the diverse experiences that shape students' meaning construction; purposes for continuing to read grow naturally from questions that arise in the course of that discussion.

Step 2   Adjusting Rate to Purposes and Material

Rate adjustment occurs along two dimensions in a DR-TA: (1) rate and flow of information (teacher-determined) and (2) reading rate (student-determined). The teacher determines the amount of text to be revealed between stop-points and the length of discussion time at each. In the physics lesson, text units varied from one line (the chapter title) to the stated aims of the text and the section title, to the first three paragraphs; the next reasonable unit of text would have been to finish the section; from there, the next entire section could be read. The English lesson was similar: Stop-point intervals went from the title, to one paragraph, to a page-and-a-half, to several pages. This progression, starting with small bits of information and increasing to much larger amounts, is typical of a DR-TA and is generally very workable.

The first stop-point should occur immediately following a title or opening line. Here, students are invited to speculate about all the possible contexts into which the title (or line) might fit. Predictions will vary from literal to highly abstract and from reasonable to silly. (By the way, silly predictions generally go away after one or two DR-TA lessons—the teacher helps them go away by not giving them much attention. Good, hearty, funny predictions happen forever.) As they share predictions in class, students examine a variety of experiences—their own and others'—that not only present a range of possibilities, but also raise the question, "Which of these will it be?"

The second stop-point—one paragraph, and sometimes two—usually provides partial answers to this question. Frequently, much information resides in introductory paragraphs, both in expository and narrative text. Stopping at this point to discuss and make predictions launches students into the cycle of predicting–sampling text–repredicting–resampling that is so important to comprehension. In effect, it gives students practice doing what good readers do (predict–read–repredict, and so on); so, while focusing student attention on comprehension of immediate text, these stop-point predictions help them become better readers as well.

The last stage of the DR-TA—reading much longer amounts of text between stop-points—is important because it increases students' ability to gain meaning from progressively more extended text, and it provides students the satisfaction that comes from uninterrupted reading. Decisions regarding how much text is to be read between stop-points should be based on text difficulty, concept density within the text, and students' familiarity with the topic. Generally, stop-points should occur at logical places—at the ends of sections, following highly abstract passages, at the end of a page, or at points of high suspense—and should not exceed four or five stops per DR-TA lesson in order to allow ample opportunity for discussion, refinement of ideas, and guidance during reading without undue interruption.

Critical to the guidance provided is the amount of discussion time at each stop-point. The amount of time allowed determines how long students will have to think and make predictions about what they are reading. It depends, in part, on the amount of information available and the degree of student participation. Of prime importance is the teacher's sensitivity to student needs and willingness to wait for ideas to occur. There are points when the text does not offer much to be discussed or when students want to get on with the reading. At such times, the best course of action is to let them read. At other times, response is slow because students can't think of the words they need to express an unformed idea. They need time—time to ponder, to consider possibilities, and to synthesize information from a variety of sources. Wait time, when the room is absolutely quiet and no one (not even the teacher) is talking, is necessary for this kind of thinking to take place. It can be uncomfortable for students and teachers who are used to rapid-fire questions and answers; frequently, however, the liveliest discussions and most interesting predictions result from these moments.

The second dimension of rate adjustment occurs spontaneously as students alter their reading rates to meet both their own needs and the needs of the discussion. Some students, being given the direction, "Read to the end of . . ." will first skim quickly through the section to get a general idea of the content (actually, to see if their predictions come true) and then go back and read carefully to fill in details because they know they will be asked to support any conclusions drawn or predictions made. Others will read carefully from the start and go back later to scan the text for ideas that reinforce or support their opinions. The degree and amount of rate adjustment varies considerably from individual to individual.

Important here is that for all students, situational demand requires the application of a reading skill that increases their efficiency and effectiveness as readers. Each time a student scans text to find a word or phrase to support a prediction or conclusion, each time a student races through the reading to see how well he or she predicted and then goes back to get the details, and each time an entire class returns to text to search for overlooked ideas, this skill is reinforced.

Step 3   Observing the Reading

In many classrooms, especially in middle and secondary schools, reading of extended text (text that goes beyond word, sentence, and paragraph boundaries) usually takes place in one of two ways: Either students are assigned such passages for independent seat work or homework, or they take turns reading the entire assignment aloud, paragraph by paragraph, droning up one row and down another, around the room in the dreaded "Round Robin Oral Reading." In the first instance, teachers somehow feel that time spent reading silently in class is wasted, that there are more important things to do, and that students should be able to "get it on their own." In the second, teachers frustrated by students' seeming inability to "get it on their own" resort to Round Robin Oral Reading because it is the only way they know to make sure that everyone is at least exposed to the content of the text.

Unfortunately, neither of these practices is terribly useful. One simply leaves students on their own to sink or swim; the other promotes dependency by removing all responsibility for learning from them. (Just as importantly, perhaps, Round Robin Oral Reading is unfair to everyone: It's deadly dull for good readers and a source of immediate, abject terror for those students whose oral reading skills are not so good. It really does not belong in the classroom.) For instruction to be effective, a certain amount of guided silent reading needs to be done in school; it is not wasted time. Teacher observation during that reading yields much valuable information about students' silent reading abilities and allows the teacher to assist those students who do need help. Whether in small groups or with an entire class, the teacher can quickly learn which students are faster readers and which are slower, which students are actually reading and which are not, which students exhibit signs of serious reading problems (inattention, extreme slowness, stress symptoms, and so on), what strategies students use to get meaning from text or figure out an unknown word, and many other details. Of critical importance here is that unless teachers provide opportunity for students to read silently in class, teachers can have no idea of how students read independently; few, if any, students attempt to complete out-of-class reading assignments by reading text aloud. The most useful, informative way to learn about students' reading abilities is to observe silent reading.

Along with silent reading, purposeful oral reading can take place, either spontaneously—as in our lesson when a student read from text to support an opinion—or focused by teacher direction. Over time, teacher observation of both silent and oral reading yields information about individuals and the group that is useful not only for conducting the lesson at hand, but also in planning subsequent lessons, determining what materials are appropriate and useful with this class, deciding on the amount and kind of guidance needed for future instruction, and making recommendations for students to be screened for special programs. This kind of observation and planning are the essence of reflective teaching.

Step 4 Developing Comprehension

By now, it should be clear that developing comprehension is an integral part of all phases of the DR-TA. It occurs as students combine prior knowledge and new information to make predictions, read to confirm or adjust their predictions, and then draw conclusions and speculate during class discussion. It also occurs during the periodic discussions as students compare their knowledge base with others', review and revise their own logic, and add others' ideas and viewpoints to their thinking. During this process, it is the teacher's responsibility to see that new concepts are developed and reinforced and that students can anchor them within the framework of their prior knowledge base.

Think back to our DR-TA lesson demonstration when the student raised the question of the difference between pounds and guineas. In this instance, the teacher *did not know the answer to the question.* (Surprise!!) The teacher offered what little information she had and then asked if anybody knew anything more. Her final comment, "We'll hang on to that and look it up," was both an acknowledgment of the importance of the concept and a promise to students that she would help them fill in that information when the time was right. This same thing can happen during silent reading; it is not unusual in a DR-TA for a student to interrupt the reading by asking aloud, "What does _____ mean?" The teacher or another student responds and reading continues. Later, during discussion, if the word in question is important to the concept being developed, the teacher extends the immediate definition in an appropriate manner.

Also critical to developing comprehension in the DR-TA are the questioning strategies that teachers use to initiate and extend discussion. It is here, with the questions that teachers use to guide discussion, that the DR-TA differs most remarkably from traditional instruction. The standard DR-TA has essentially two types of questions:

1. Questions that require speculation and prediction:

   "With a title like that, what do you think the chapter (or story or article) will be about?"

   "Now what do you think?"

   "What information do you think we'll find in this chapter?"

   "What do you think will happen next?"

Followed by:

2. Questions that require drawing conclusions and/or providing support:

   "What makes you say that?"

   "Why?"

   "How do you know that?"

I reproduce verbatim teacher questions asked during our physics and English lesson DR-TAs.

Physics

   "Based upon this title, what do you think the chapter will be about?"

   "What makes you say that?"

   "Now what do you think?"

   "Why?"

   "What other ideas do you think we'll find in this chapter?"

   "Why?"

   "What do you think we'll know when we're through?"

   "Anything else?"

English

"With a title like that, what do you think this story will be about?"

"Why do you say that?"

"Who is Beryl Markham?"

"What were you going to say?"

"Why?"

"What else? Does anyone know this story? Any other ideas?"

"Any other ideas?"

"Now what do you think?"

"What else?"

"What do you think it might be?"

"Any other ideas?"

"Why do you suggest that he might have been a jockey, or might be a jockey?"

"Now what do you think?"

"What else? What do you think?"

"What else?"

You get the idea. It is important to note that none of these questions asks students to state literal meaning from text, a fact that probably leads to some teacher skepticism or discomfort with the DR-TA. While DR-TA questions may not specifically ask about literal meaning, this is not to say that literal information is not discussed because, in fact, it is. Students use literal information in the course of making predictions, drawing conclusions, and supporting their responses. It therefore becomes unnecessary to reiterate this information through specific questioning. For example, consider the following response from one student during our DR-TA:

> I think that she and the little man have something in common. They see beyond the trauma the horse has caused. She mentions that the people there like the *idea* of the horses, whereas this man *knew* horses, and probably their motivations for wanting to purchase the horse are different, but they have something deeper than just the way the horse looks. There's some connection; there's a bonding of some kind, a spirituality.

Now compare the quality of that response with anticipated responses to the following literal questions:

"Who are the main characters in the story?"

"Where does the story take place?"

"Why was Rigel an outcast?"

"How did the narrator and the little man differ from the others at the sale?"

The point is that there *is* no comparison between the quality of the student's response to DR-TA questions and the kind of responses the literal questions would encourage. More importantly, it is clear that, in the DR-TA, literal information is used for the exploration of much larger, student-generated questions: "What is the bond between these two seemingly disparate people?" "How does one reconcile her right to the horse and his need for the horse?" "How can the story end in such a way as to reflect reality and at the same time let both characters 'win'?" These qualitative differences are just as apparent in physics and other content-area DR-TA lessons as they are in this one.

The open-ended questions of the DR-TA focus attention on the larger issues, and thus literal meaning remains in rightful perspective. It is only when student response to the open-ended question indicates misunderstanding that literal questions are asked. Literal questions are asked immediately to clarify and remove the misunderstanding; as soon as that is accomplished, teacher questions should return to the types described earlier.

Step 5   Developing Fundamental Skills

When the reading is completed, the teacher directs the class in developing skills that are appropriate to student needs and instructional goals. Activities should *not* require students to write answers to literal questions about what they have just read and discussed. The quality of the discussion and the level of understanding students have achieved have gone well beyond literal comprehension already. Activities *should* extend student response to text in some important way and may include vocabulary study, various activities to organize and combine information, or any of numerous writing activities. We will look at several strategies for developing follow-up activities later in this chapter and in other chapters as well. Of prime importance here is that follow-up activities be thoughtful, meaningful additions to the reading experience.

ALTERNATIVE APPLICATIONS OF THE DR-TA

As the physics-lesson example demonstrates, DR-TAs are useful, not only with narrative, but with expository text as well. Because of obvious differences in narration and exposition, teacher questions for textbook DR-TAs are directed toward consideration of such things as, "What do you think we'll find out in this section?" or "What do you think we'll know when we're through?" Discussion focuses on content as students explore scientific phenomena or mathematics principles or social/political events.

An alternative way to use a DR-TA with textbooks is to prepare DR-TA guidesheets for students to use individually, with partners, or in groups as reading progresses. The following two DR-TA guidesheets are written for the same assignment from a social studies text (Boorstein & Kelley, 1996). This assignment could just as well be done using the DR-TA as we did in our physics-lesson example or our demonstration English lesson.

SAMPLE GUIDESHEET   *From Confederation to Nation*

I.   New State Governments

The following is a list of the subheadings for Section I of our chapter:

Following Old Patterns
Ways of Constitution Making
Written Constitutions
The New State Constitutions
Equality in the States
First Moves Against Slavery

Based on these subheadings, what information do you think you'll find in the "New State Governments" section of our chapter? On the lines for Predictions, list the kinds of information and ideas you think you will find in the reading. After you've finished reading, use the Important Information lines to list important information you find. Put an asterisk (*) beside important information you found that you had predicted you would find. Be prepared to discuss your predictions and choices of important ideas.

Predictions: _____

_____

_____

_____

_____

_____

Important Information: _____

_____

_____

_____

_____

The second type of guidesheet, which follows, is yet another way to engage students in essentially the same process as an in-class DR-TA and the previous guidesheet.

SAMPLE GUIDESHEET   *From Confederation to Nation*

The subheadings for Section I of our chapter, "New State Governments," are given in the following list. For each subheading, use the Predictions lines to write your predictions about the information and ideas you're likely to find in that subsection. Complete all your predictions before reading. Then, as you read, use the Important Ideas lines to jot down important ideas you find in each subsection. Put an asterisk (*) beside any ideas you found that you predicted you would find. Be prepared to discuss your choices of important ideas.

I.   *New State Governments*

Following Old Patterns. **Predictions:** _____

_____

Important Ideas: _____

_____

Ways of Constitution Making. **Predictions:** _____

_____

Important Ideas: _____

_____

Written Constitutions. **Predictions:** _____

_____

Important Ideas: _____

_____

The New State Constitutions. **Predictions:** _____

_____

Important Ideas: _____

_____

Equality in the States. **Predictions:** _____

_____

Important Ideas: _____

_____

First Moves Against Slavery. **Predictions:** _____

_____

Important Ideas: _____

_____

CLOSING THOUGHTS ABOUT THE DR-TA

Students and teachers frequently ask me whether I would use DR-TA's "all the time." The answer is, "No. I wouldn't recommend using anything 'all the time'." But, without getting too overblown about it, I must say that the DR-TA has a way of becoming a habit. It sort of gets in your blood. It does not take long before you find that, regardless of the instructional strategy you're using, you hear yourself asking, "What do you think will be important in this chapter?" and "What made you say that?" and all the language from a DR-TA that causes students to think and to predict and to use prior knowledge. Well, fine. If that happens, it just means you've internalized a process that is useful and effective in the classroom.

If you find some students—those who are shy, or reluctant learners, or limited English speakers—are hesitant to respond to a DR-TA at first, don't fret. Such silence from these students is to be expected; given time, experience, and increased comfort in the classroom, they will begin to participate. Meanwhile, they gain far more by being immersed in animated DR-TA discussion and language exchange than they could possibly gain in a pin-drop quiet class where everyone is working individually or than they're likely to get from question–answer discussions where the teacher does most of the talking. For now, use (and modify and adapt) DR-TA in a way that seems reasonable to you for your subject area, materials, and teaching situation; later, you can make adjustments and decisions about the DR-TA's overall usefulness in your class.

How to do . . . .

A DR-TA

A DR-TA is relatively easy to prepare. The most difficult part of preparation is deciding where to place stop-points, and for novice DR-TA teachers, the tendency is to stop *more* often than necessary, as opposed to less. The only other hard part is learning to ask open-ended, DR-TA-type questions rather than lots of literal questions and becoming used to lesson episodes in which students do most of the talking. Here are the preparation steps:

1. Select the reading assignment (chapter, article, story, and so on).

2. Determine stop-points. Stop first after the title. Then use logical breaks, such as subheadings, chapter parts, and so forth to establish three or four additional stops.

3. Prepare questions to be asked at stop-points; for example, "Based on this title, what do you think the chapter will be about?" "Why?" "Now what do you think?" "Why?" "What do you think we'll learn or find out next?" "Why?"

4. Obtain/prepare cover sheets for students to use to cover text following stop-points (if needed).

THE GROUP MAPPING ACTIVITY (GMA)

The group mapping activity (GMA) was introduced by Jane Davidson (1982) as a means for assisting students in organizing information after reading. Quite simply, maps are schematic and written representations of readers' understanding of text. Maps have become relatively common in classrooms. Many teachers encourage students to use them both to represent meaning constructed from reading as well as to plan and prepare for intended writing. Davidson's approach to mapping begins with these instructions to students (or something like them):

> On your cover sheet, and without looking back at the text, map your perceptions of what we have just read. A map is simply a diagram of what you think the reading (or chapter) was about. There are no right or wrong ways to map. A map may have shapes, lines, figures, words, anything you want it to have. (Adapted from Davidson)

After they have completed their maps, the teacher then invites students to display them. The display shows clearly how different the maps are, and students may, at first, be a bit disconcerted at having to show their maps. The teacher then invites students to share their maps by telling what the symbols and writing on the maps represent and waits for a student to volunteer to share his or her map. (Figure 3.1 shows one way our physics chapter could be mapped.) The wait for a volunteer can seem long, but it

FIGURE 3.1 *Physics Chapter Map Drawn in a Group Mapping Activity*

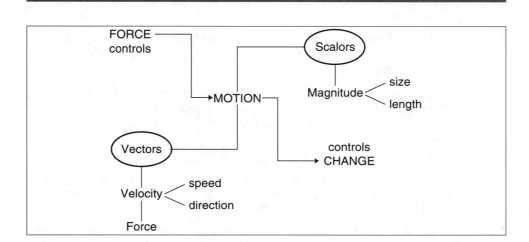

rarely exceeds 20 to 30 seconds. The student explains her or his map and tells why she or he chose to map the reading as she/he did. The teacher asks generative questions to expand the explanation; for example, "What made you decide to put directional arrows between 'force,' 'motion,' and 'change'?" Several maps are shared in this manner, with the teacher leading and guiding the discussion.

Group mapping is an ideal activity to follow a DR-TA lesson. An interesting phenomenon of the DR-TA is that discussion is so rich and full at the stop-points in the reading that there is little need to rehash the text at the end. Thus, the teacher can move directly into an activity such as group mapping that helps students organize and retain information from the text; this is one way teachers assist students in learning and applying subject area information. The discussion that occurs as the maps are displayed and explained allows students to elaborate and expand the knowledge they construct from text. Readers' constructions of meaning continue to be shared during this interchange.

I used group mapping immediately following our DR-TA English lesson with "The Splendid Outcast." Here is one of the map explanations from the GMA for "The Splendid Outcast."

S: I did some highlighting to show that I had two things going at the same time. I had her train of thought—the horse auction, and that she was interested in the horse and that she remembers his dangerous past, but also his breeding. A reference to her own horse business, and that it was getting toward the end of the auction, and then she notices the man (that comes back down here) but prior to that Rigel is brought out in chains—real defiant, real dangerous. And then the bidding takes place in here, and again he comes in (every time I highlight it with pink, he's coming in again).

T: The man?

S: Right. Then the stallion goes berserk, and she passes on the bidding, he gets the horse, and in the end he's revealed as a rebel. So, I just put down train of thought.

T: You show your train of thought there. The man, the jockey, seems to come in there at the beginning, and then come around like this. Did you have a specific reason for highlighting his interaction in there?

S: In the center? Yeah. He seemed to be central to all this peripheral stuff that was going on. It kept coming back to him. Down here, he seemed to be in most of the passages, most of the action. He seemed like a peripheral figure, and yet he seemed central at the same time.

Here is another map explanation. Notice how differently this student organizes and classifies information. Notice also the teacher's role.

S1:   Well, mine's really simple. I saw a parallel between the actual buying ring and sort of like a Venn diagram. If I'd had more room, they'd have been the same size. Rigel, being the center of the story, is the center of the ring. Then the regular buying crowd is all around. Then Beryl and the jockey are each in their own sphere, and they're the only ones who have an interest in Rigel as far as buying him, so they're interacting with him, in a way. Then ending up with Rigel and the jockey, totally overlapped, totally intersected.

T: Oh. This is Rigel and the jockey here? Okay.

S1:   Surrounded by the total interest of Beryl and just slightly overlapped by the regular buying audience.

T: So what you have is this great big circle here that looks real powerful and it becomes this one here. And this small ellipse here has become the big circle here. So, it's a transformation.

S1:   Yeah. But I would have made them more the same size if I'd had more room.

GROUP MAPPING AND MEANING CONSTRUCTION

From these map explanations, it is clear that response to text is a highly individual, personal matter. It is clear, too, that provision for differences in student background and construction of knowledge does not in any way violate or distort the author's intended meaning of a text. These two students, both of whom participated in the same DR-TA lesson, took very different impressions from that reading, illustrating yet again that readers *make* meaning, rather than get meaning, from text. It serves also to highlight one of the two ways that the GMA differs from other mapping strategies (Hampf, 1971).

First, the GMA uses free-form directions to students that *allow* them to respond to text from their own knowledge base and preferred means of representation. Other mapping strategies tell students, step-by-step, how to map. While there is nothing *wrong* with that approach, my experience has been that it tends to lock students in to one "right" way to map; it leaves little room for experimentation and difference. It also tends to focus on literal meaning and thus reduces the possibility that students will move away from the literal into the abstract. The GMA does neither of these. Of particular importance to ESL students, and other students as well, is that free-form maps allow students to use symbols other than words to represent meaning—or to combine symbols, words, and languages—thus broadening and expanding significantly the range and complexity of the ideas they can represent.

The value of allowing students to invent their own means for representing text can be found in the notion of "transmediation"—translation of content from one sign system to another (Suhor, 1984). In this instance, the sign systems we're moving across are written English text and symbolic/pictorial text. Marjorie Siegel (in press), in her work with students reading mathematics text, found that the act of sketching (or mapping) from text produced reflective and generative thinking that increased and deepened students' understanding of the text. She describes Tim and Eric's experience of reading and sketching "Mathematics and the Marketplace":

> As they explained to their classmates, they did not begin the sketching process with much understanding of the text, let alone any way to represent "all that mumble jumble [referring to the article] . . . going around in our head." Instead, they found that experimenting with the new expression plane itself helped them find an entry into the text. In other words, "messing about" with various images gave rise to the star image [the central image of their sketch] and, as they said, this image served as a "key" that allowed them to open the text and begin an exploration of the interrelationship of mathematics and the marketplace. The generative power of the sketching experience thus stands in sharp contrast to Tim and Eric's experience with the "say something" strategy (Harste & Short, with Burke, 1988); words alone, even their own words, did not provide the support they needed to gain meaning from this text. Their own reflections on the experience indicate that literally "picturing" their thinking gave them a way to engage in meaningful learning. (p. 23)

Free-form mapping is not at all unlike the free-form sketching Siegel describes; it is, in fact, so open-ended that it presents the temporary problem of causing student concern about how to invent their maps: The very first time you tell students to "Map your perceptions of what you think the reading was about," they'll get a little anxious. They get anxious because you're not telling them how to do what you want them to do, and they're afraid they'll be "wrong." (They don't believe you when you say there is no right or wrong way to map.) I solve this by displaying "dummy" maps, such as those shown in Figures 3.2 and 3.3, which are maps I've made of texts different from the one students are currently reading. I show them very quickly, saying, "A map can

FIGURE 3.2 *Sample "Dummy" Map for Health Lesson*

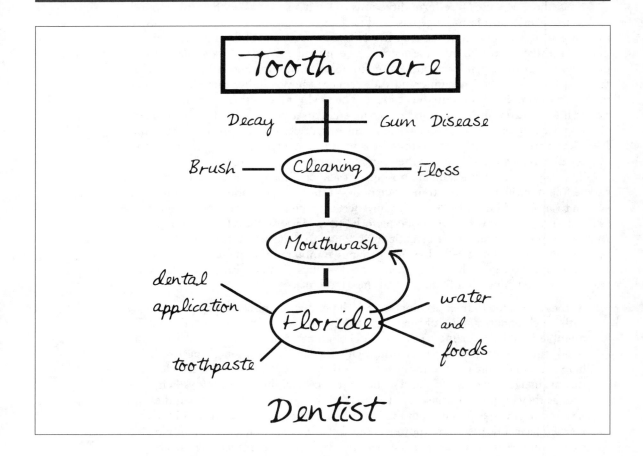

look like this, or like this, or any way you want it to look." That gives students ideas for mapping without providing a pattern they feel compelled to copy. By the time they get to their second mapping experience, students know what you want: They've seen other maps, they have a number of new ideas about how to map, and they've seen that you really do accept their individuality and differences in interpretation and representation.

The second major difference between the GMA and other mapping strategies is sharing the maps in class (that's the 'group' part) and map explanations. Sharing is the most powerful aspect of the GMA and should not be omitted. It is here, after they have mapped, that students can say what they understand about text; explore ideas both in text and beyond; and arrive at conclusions, generalizations, and abstractions. And, as Siegel suggests, the maps serve as a medium for developing insight and generating new ideas; thus, it is not unusual for students to arrive at deeper understand-

FIGURE 3.3 *Sample "Dummy" Map for English Lesson*

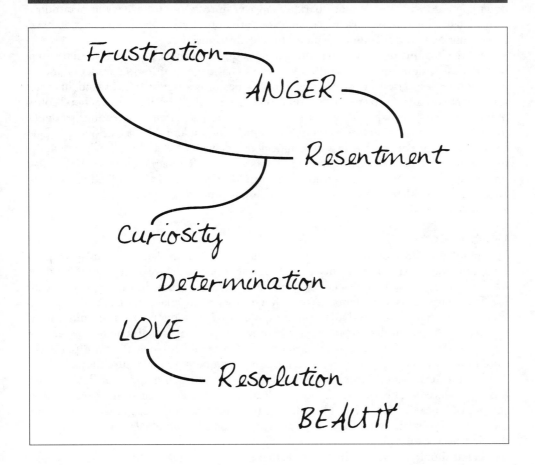

ing in the very act of telling about their maps. This process not only provides for high-level comprehension, but is the cornerstone of learning as well. It gives students practice using new ideas and practice articulating these into oral language. Just as importantly, as students listen to one another explain and explore map meanings, everyone's construction of knowledge is increased and expanded.

Once again, as with the DR-TA, the teacher's role is to facilitate, rather than dominate, the process. The teacher is responsible for asking questions that help students clarify their thinking, articulate new understanding, and arrive at deeper insights. Recall when the teacher asked if the student had a reason for placing the jockey in the center of her map. The student was then able to say what she hadn't said before: "Yeah. He seemed to be central to all this peripheral stuff that was going on. . . . He seemed like a peripheral figure, and yet he seemed central at the same time." That's a very sophisticated conclusion to draw from this story. In some instances, however, students don't come up with a nice, new, sparkling answer in response to teacher or peer questions. That's fine too, because when questions are not fully answered, students do have something new to think about, which often leads to insights.

Critical to this process is that the teacher's question must not place students in a position of being right or wrong; they needn't challenge or question students' interpretation or response to text. Neither should questions attempt to lead students into arriving at conclusions or text interpretations that are all alike. Rather, teachers' comments and questions should be generative, as we've just discussed, leading students into new insights and serving as models for questions students can ask of one another. Important information that may not appear on maps immediately following reading may be added as class discussion and map uses warrant. If a map indicates serious misunderstanding or miscomprehension, this should be handled in an individual conference with the student or through clarifying discussion that allows the student to make an appropriate adjustment.

USING THE GMA

When possible, I prefer full-class sharing of maps and their explanation. Full-class participation is especially important in the first few experiences with mapping. You may not always have time for full-class sharing, however, so other arrangements are possible. Frequently, I have students share with a partner or in small groups. After hearing the teacher's questions, students become quite good at generative questioning; they may need to be reminded to be tolerant of others' representational schemes or text interpretations. When the maps are intended as study aids, which they are perfectly suited for, I ask sharing partners (or small group members) to make sure that all of the "important information" from the reading shows up on each map, regardless of how it is represented. (This request frequently leads to animated discussions about what is and is not "important.") Maps also may be used as "working maps" that change and grow over a unit of study; these may be maintained by individuals, small groups, or the class as a whole.

What should be clear at this point is that group mapping is a flexible strategy that can be adapted in limitless ways to fit classroom needs. As with the DR-TA, the GMA also accommodates for different linguistic, cultural, social, and personal perspectives and provides rich language experiences for all students. Group mapping can be used in conjunction with other activities (not just the DR-TA) and in any subject area. Trust me on this: I have used group mapping from kindergarten to college and beyond, and I have turned any number of student teachers and teachers loose to use it in their classrooms. They all report pretty much the same thing: Their students like it, they like it, and everyone marvels at how much mapping adds to the quality of classroom discussions.

In fact, my own and others' students use mapping for a variety of reasons—to assist in studying for exams or to demonstrate content understanding in course portfolios. In Chapter 2 I showed you my student Jenny Burcham's map submitted as part of her portfolio to demonstrate her learning in the middle school/secondary Literacy

Across the Curriculum course. The map you'll find in Chapter 4 is Peter Sanducci's map submitted as part of his portfolio in a similar class. In content learning, maps serve as useful learning tools. Not only do they help students organize information after reading, they are powerful study tools as well. In later chapters, we will look at yet other ways maps are useful in reading, writing, and learning tasks.

How to do . . . .

A GMA

1. Prepare "dummy" maps.

2. After reading, instruct students to map their perceptions of the reading. Use the following means for clarification and additional guidance:
    a. "A map is a diagram of what you think the reading is about. There is no right or wrong way to map. You may use geometric shapes, words, or pictures on your map."
    b. Show "dummy" maps, saying "A map may look like this . . . like this . . . like this . . . or any way you want it to look."

3. Have students display maps.

4. Allow students to tell about their maps—either to a partner or to the whole class. Focus on how the student chose to map and why rather than on a given standard of "rightness."

5. Encourage, and model, questions that allow students who are sharing their maps to clarify and extend their thinking.

Part II: *Comprehension Levels, Teacher Questions, and Comprehension Instruction*

Earlier in this chapter, we discussed the quality of meaning students construct, both during and after reading, and the teacher's role in guiding students toward insightful, rich comprehension of text. The point was made that what the teacher does, or does not do, has clear implications for all four goals associated with secondary school reading:

1. comprehending
2. learning subject area content
3. increasing reading skills, and
4. applying new knowledge

In this section, we will continue that line of reasoning with some shift of emphasis: Where we earlier characterized the teacher as a thoughtful facilitator of the reading/

learning process—one who designs the instructional progression and then steps back and allows students to lead—in this section we will place the teacher in the more traditional, visible role of thoughtful, explicitly active participant in the instructional episode. Specifically, we will look at how skillful teacher questioning supports comprehension and learning.

LEVELS OF COMPREHENSION

Every reading methods text has a section on "levels of comprehension," and every author uses slightly different labels to identify and discuss these levels. Generally, such taxonomies identify three or four levels of comprehension; a notable exception is the six levels of Bloom's Taxonomy (1956), which a number of people have adopted to discuss reading comprehension. Mainly, however, authors focus on three comprehension levels, with designations varying from "Literal, Interpretive, Applied" (Herber, 1978; Vacca & Vacca, 1996), to "Factual, Interpretive, Applicative, Transactive" (Ruddell & Harris, 1991), to "Text-Explicit, Text-Implicit, Experience-Based" (Readence, Bean, & Baldwin, 1989), to "Literal, Interpretive, Critical and Creative" (Roe, Stoodt, & Burns, 1995).

Differences in these labels mask the fact that everyone is talking about essentially the same thing—only the labeling terminology changes (this is supported by the fact that authors' descriptions of these levels are remarkably similar). I am most comfortable with Herber's (1978) Literal, Interpretive, and Applied labels, and my description shares much with his work. For our discussion, let's use the following definitions of reading comprehension levels:

LITERAL COMPREHENSION

Meaning derived from "reading the lines," in which the reader constructs meaning that accurately reflects the author's intended message. Literal comprehension is text-explicit; that is, answers to literal questions require reader understanding of ideas stated directly in text.

INTERPRETIVE COMPREHENSION

Meaning derived by reading "between the lines," in which the reader perceives author intent or understands relationships between text elements that are not stated directly. Interpretive comprehension is text-implicit; answers to interpretive questions require the reader to draw conclusions in response to unstated cause-effect relationships or comparisons, perception of nuance, and/or symbolic use of language and ideas.

APPLIED COMPREHENSION

Meaning derived by reading "beyond the lines," in which the reader understands unstated relationships between information in text and information in his/her prior knowledge base. Applied comprehension is schema-implicit (or experience-based, if you prefer); answers to questions at this level require integration of new information into the reader's previous fund of knowledge, from which new relationships emerge.

Literal, interpretive, and applied levels of comprehension constitute a hierarchical arrangement of the quality of meaning a reader constructs during and after encounters with text. At the lowest level, the reader understands the author's intended meaning; at the second, the reader draws conclusions and sees implied relationships; and at the highest, the reader perceives new relationships. The goal of comprehension instruction is to teach students how to achieve all three levels.

Our discussion of the DR-TA and group mapping clearly demonstrates their usefulness in developing all levels of comprehension. A more traditional approach than either of these strategies is class discussion led by direct teacher questioning, in a Socratic question–response–question–response sequence. In this type of approach (as with the less traditional approach) teacher questions become critical in determining the quality of student comprehension.

TEACHER QUESTIONS

Teacher questions and teacher-led discussion have been the subject of much study and concern over the past 30 years. In 1967, Frank Guszak published research that reported the kinds of questions teachers ask in reading and subject area instruction. He found that 74% of teacher questions were at the literal level; 8% at the interpretive level; and 19% at the applied level (the applied-level question percentage is somewhat inflated because 15% of those applied questions could be answered by a simple "yes" or "no"— e.g., "Did you like the story?"). Guszak found additionally that 90% of teachers' literal questions were answered correctly, which led him to conclude that students learn very early to give teachers what teachers want: correct answers to literal questions.

Guszak's results have been replicated in studies at various grade levels in many different settings and schools (Durkin, 1978–1979; Mehan, 1979; Heath, 1982; Goodlad, 1984). The pattern of results from such studies continues to say what Guszak's results suggested in 1967: An overwhelming majority of instructional time is devoted to students supplying literal answers to teachers' literal questions. The obvious conclusion must be that we systematically limit the intellectual boundaries of the classroom by focusing on bits and pieces of information rather than using those bits and pieces to explore the larger picture. John Goodlad (1984) describes this as part of the "frontal teaching" practices he found to predominate in junior and senior high schools. Frontal teaching occurs when the teacher stands in front of the class telling, explaining, and asking

> . . . specific questions calling essentially for students to fill in the blanks: "What is the capital city of Canada?" "What are the principal exports of Japan?" Students rarely turn things around by asking the questions. Nor do teachers often give students a chance to romp with an open-ended question such as, "What are your views on the quality of television?" (pp. 108–109).

Life in the classroom becomes a game of "Can you guess what I'm thinking?" in which teachers ask known information questions—questions for which they already have the answers (Mehan, 1979)—and search the room until they get a response that matches the one in their head. Such questioning often produces instructional discussions bordering on the bizarre: I once heard about a discussion in a middle school classroom in which the teacher spent *15 minutes* attempting to elicit the word "clever" from students who had been asked to describe a story character (Gillotte, 1991). This is in direct contrast to real questions that teachers ask to find out how students construct meaning from text (e.g., "What do you think will be important in this chapter? Why?").

I believe that teachers use literal, known-information questions because of their honest (and legitimate) desire to make sure students understand text—that students "get it"—when reading the assignment. Often, these discussions get bogged down in trivia, or time gets wasted in the search for the one correct answer (e.g., *clever*), so that teachers never get around to the higher-level questions they had planned to use; or, teachers simply don't know how to get beyond literal questions. You already know that the DR-TA and group mapping are effective ways to move away from such practices; there are others.

QUESTION-BASED APPROACHES FOR GUIDING COMPREHENSION

THE DIRECTED READING ACTIVITY (DRA)

The Directed Reading Activity (DRA) (Betts, 1946) was designed originally for the purpose of increasing students' comprehension of text by removing barriers to comprehension, encouraging guided silent reading of text, and embedding skill development into lessons focusing on conceptual understanding. Although often associated with the type of reading instruction usually found in the elementary school (what Herber calls "Direct Reading Instruction" [1978]), the five steps of the DRA—(1) preparation for reading, (2) guided silent reading, (3) comprehension development, (4) skill development and application, and (5) extension and follow-up activities—are quite like, if not directly parallel to, the five-step lesson model presented (with varying labels and terminology) in most secondary curriculum methodology texts.

In fact, the DRA has, for some time, appeared in one form or another in secondary textbook teacher guides; it has been and can be successfully adapted for "Indirect Reading Instruction" (Herber, 1978) in which there is clear focus on subject area content, rather than reading skills per se, and reading skills are taught only as they are needed to learn content. The DRA, however, is subject to much variation in how teachers interpret and apply it in the classroom, and therein lies the key to its effectiveness. Let's examine the sequential steps of the DRA more closely. Following that, I will demonstrate a DRA lesson plan.

STEPS IN THE DRA
Step 1   Preparation for Reading   The DRA begins with two types of reader preparation. First is vocabulary presentation, in which selected words from the chapter are

pretaught for the purpose of reducing or removing barriers to comprehension. This is based on two very important assumptions: (1) that the identified words are *critical to comprehension of the passage*, and (2) that the words, as they appear in the passage, *are unfamiliar to the students*. Generally, these words are content-specific; that is, their use and meanings are directly related to the topic under discussion. They do not have to be, however; they simply may be noncontent-specific words in text that meet the two assumptions given above.

Whatever the case, it is important for teachers to select these words carefully, by prereading the text and/or choosing from a list suggested by the textbook author(s), and to tailor their choices specifically for the students being taught. Otherwise, teachers will find themselves standing in front of a class of students teaching words the students already know, only to find later that there were any number of other critical words the students *didn't* know. (Believe me. This will happen even *with* careful selection—I've done it.)

Presentation of the vocabulary words must be done in context so that students will have sufficient information to understand how each word is used in the text and to draw on their prior knowledge base for speculating about possible meanings. The teacher writes the words on the board in sentences or phrases taken directly from text (e.g., "Germany made an *alliance* with Austria and Italy."; "*Points* are ideas."), or asks students to find the words in the passage to be read ("Find the word 'alliance' on page 297, paragraph 2."). Students are invited to contribute ideas they have about each word's meaning based on this context (prior knowledge and previous experience combined with information available in text), and discussion continues until a satisfactory definition is reached. The C–S–S–D progression for analyzing unknown words (Gray, 1946) is useful for this process. (I elaborate on CSSD in Chapter 4.) Here it is in brief:

Context. First, try to construct the meaning of the word from the meaning of the surrounding text.

Structure. Second, look for known word parts (prefixes, roots, suffixes) to help you construct the meaning of the word.

Sound. If that doesn't work, pronounce the word to see if it sounds like any word you know.

Dictionary. When all else fails, look it up.

Because the purpose of vocabulary study during preparation for reading is to help students comprehend text by giving them information about new words and new concepts they will encounter in that text, it is usually short and to the point. It should be, so as not to unnecessarily delay topic discussion and the actual reading. At the most, prereading vocabulary presentation should take no longer than 5–10 minutes. If it does, then reading assignments should be shortened to reduce concept load. It is important, also, to understand that prereading presentation is not the only instruction and practice necessary for long-term vocabulary retention and acquisition. Additional attention to vocabulary can and should follow reading. This is discussed at length in Chapter 4.

The second part of preparation for reading focuses student attention on the subject matter of the text and engages student interest and participation. It begins with the teachers' focusing statements and questions: "Today we are going to begin our unit on woodworking. What do you already know about woods and the handling of them?" or, "How many of you know what an 'empire' is? What empires do you know about in the nineteenth and twentieth centuries, and what was their purpose?"

The discussion following such questions activates students' prior knowledge and previous experience by allowing them to recall both direct and vicarious experience related to a given topic. Further, it creates a pool of shared knowledge that becomes the basis for new learning—in essence, the collective class schema that sensitizes students to the information they will encounter in text. This discussion is valuable for all students and is particularly useful as a means for bringing into play diverse viewpoints, perceptions, and cultural experiences. Just as importantly, it stimulates interest in learning as students perceive points of commonality across various sets of knowledge and experience, points of difference, and unresolved questions.

Step 2   *Guided Silent Reading*   Guided silent reading begins with a statement of purpose for reading given by the teacher; e.g., "Read pages 191–198 to find out how winds affect weather" or, "Read the chapter to find out how environment and culture influence people's needs and wants." This statement of purpose, along with the previous discussion, shapes the reader's stance in relationship to text. The purpose statement should be prepared in advance and should correspond directly to the teacher's instructional objectives.

Discussion leading to statement of purpose for reading may require, however, that the statement change. You may find out that students already *know* how wind affects weather or how environment and culture influence people's wants and needs. If that's the case, seriously reconsider whether the reading should be done at all. If it should, determine what *new* purpose students might have for doing it or develop a new purpose collaboratively with students.

More than likely, you will have a pretty good idea of what your students do and do not know about a subject, so you will not have to deal with major adjustment (although it's not unheard of). But *do* pay attention to discussion before reading, so that you will know what kind and how much adjustment of the purpose-setting statement is necessary. Then adjust as quickly and smoothly as you can and have students begin reading. (This is called "informed decision-making" and/or "reflective teaching." It means that you look at and listen to your students, analyze their response to what happens in the classroom, and change your plans as conditions warrant. It's scary to make such on-the-spot decisions, but learn to do it. If you persist in teaching a lesson that students already know *as though they didn't know it*, you'll destroy your credibility and any interest students have in the topic as well. *Do something—anything*; it may not be perfect, but it'll beat the alternative.)

Frequently, guided silent reading assignments involve an entire chapter, article, essay, or short story that is too lengthy to finish in one class period. You can handle this by initiating silent reading in class, so that you have time to observe students as they read and give assistance to those who need it, and then assigning unfinished reading to be completed as homework.

Discussion of the reading occurs on the next day of class after a short (3- to 5-minute) review period. When the text is particularly long or difficult, however, you may wish to provide more guidance by dividing the reading into sections, stopping at the end of each section for discussion, and then suggesting another purpose for continued reading. This allows you to monitor student progress a bit more carefully and see to it that concepts important to comprehension of subsequent information are developed. I find this "sectional" approach particularly useful with concept-dense texts and books in which text is predominantly numeric and/or graphic (e.g., mathematics books) rather than lexical. Leading students through such a text with purpose-setting statements is useful in teaching them how to read it.

Step 3   Comprehension Development   As with the DR-TA, comprehension development begins the moment we initiate the DRA lesson: in our discussion of the language of text (vocabulary presentation), schema activation and sharing of prior knowledge (focusing questions), and right on into statement of purpose for reading (guiding silent reading). Immediately following the reading (or at the beginning of the next class), the purpose-setting statement is asked as a question to initiate discussion; e.g., "What are some of the effects of wind on weather?" or, "How do people's environment and culture influence their wants and needs?"

It is imperative that you ask the purpose-setting question first and that discussion of it be substantive (involving students' prior knowledge as well as new information from text). If not, students learn that the purpose-setting statement is just something the teacher says, that it has no value and no implications for what is to follow, and that they can ignore it with impunity. Silent reading is then no longer guided.

The very best readers in the class can tolerate this—they'll set their own purpose for reading (even if it's only to get through the assignment) and slog on—but most of the others cannot. The good readers will give it a try—they'll at least come up with the gist of the assignment; average readers will run their eyes over print and take what they can get (about half); the not-so-good readers will flounder through paragraphs and pages of text and construct little, if any, meaning; and the really-not-so-good readers will give up—they're the ones sleeping, heads on desks, while the rest of the class works. Purpose-setting statements that are followed up as opening-discussion questions teach students how to enter text with focused intent and increase the possibility that all students will construct purposeful meaning from text.

Following response to the purpose-setting question, discussion then should be focused on exploration of many aspects of the reading and application of that information to students' lives (middle school, junior, and senior high students always want to know, "What's in this for me?") At this point, the questions you use to guide discussion are critical; they can and *should* be complex, interesting, and directly related both to textual information and the lives of the students in the class. They *should not* be concerned solely with literal-level questions designed to "check" to see if students read the chapter. You will discover soon enough, in response to complex questions, whether students understand literal information (and, incidentally, whether they read the chapter). If student responses indicate noncomprehension, *then* it is time to back up, see where the problem lies, resolve it, and continue on at the interpretive and applied levels. If students already *do* understand the literal information (i.e., have constructed meaning that accurately reflects the author's intended meaning), then point-by-point reiteration of it in question-answer "discussion" is nothing more than a poorly disguised, boring (let's be honest) test. Unfortunately, these tests are all too common in secondary classrooms. Recall Goodlad's observation that ". . . teachers [rarely] give students a chance to romp with an open-ended question. . . ." (1984), and our 30 years' worth of documentation that literal questions are teachers' questions of choice 75% of the time (Guszak, 1967; Mehan, 1979; Goodlad, 1984).

So, it is here, during discussion, that much of the quality of the DRA is established, and it is the teacher who determines the tone and content of that discussion. The following guidelines are intended to help you move toward the goal of becoming an accomplished question-asker and discussion leader:

1. *Take the time to articulate clearly your instructional objectives for units of study and lesson plans.* Determine what you want students to know or to be able to do when they are through with this lesson; these are your instructional objectives. Evaluate them: How useful/important are they? Do they reflect what you really want students to learn? Then choose the very best, and write questions that relate directly to them.

2. *Focus your time and energy on higher-level questions and initiate discussion with them.* Do not believe that in order to ask higher-level questions, you have to lead up to them with lower-level questions. It is simply not true. In fact, Martin Haberman (1991) calls the notion of basic-level thinking before higher-level thinking "the pedagogy of poverty," not only because it is so predominant in schools with large populations of low-SES students, but because the practice of beginning always with literal information gets in the way of real learning. *Start* with the higher-level questions; trust that your students can think abstractly and deeply and *want* to think abstractly and deeply, that they really *like* latching on to a problem and having to use intellectual power to solve it. They do.

Ask questions that allow students' minds to "click." As students grapple with larger questions, they will use and learn facts and figures (the bits and pieces of subject matter). If you find that you need to ask literal-level questions, they will come to you with little effort; you do not need to have these questions written out in advance. You do need to have higher-level questions thought out and written out, however; it is well to focus your energy on them.

3. *Constantly seek to connect subject matter content to students' lives.* Build on what students *know*, rather than trying to "catch" them unable to recite what they don't know. Design questions that link the known with the new, and help students see that carbon-dating tables, Ping-Pong tables, multiplication tables, and water tables all have bearing on their lives.

4. *Write and ask questions that you find interesting, intriguing, and provocative.* Chances are, your students will feel the same way. Certainly, if you find writing the questions to be boring, class discussion will be correspondingly dull.

5. *Don't be afraid to let students learn from one another.* Teacher-led discussions need not be limited to the one-person-response model. Put students in groups or let them work with partners. Ask big-picture questions and receive group consensus responses. Students will teach one another and learn from one another. They will cover main points and use details and facts to support their group response; they will also assist and help those students who need either. After all groups have contributed, give students time to reflect and comment on variations in the original responses. This has a way of chaining into wonderfully satisfying, rich discussion. When that happens, comprehension is correspondingly satisfying and rich.

6. *After writing your questions, check to see what comprehension levels you've addressed.* Check to see how many of your questions require:

- *Reader understanding of ideas directly stated in text*—Literal-Level Comprehension.

- *Reader conclusions drawn from text elements not directly stated (unstated relationships or comparisons, nuance, symbolic language)*—Interpretive-Level Comprehension.

- *Reader integration of new information with world knowledge from which new relationships emerge*—Applied-Level Comprehension.

Step 4   Skill Development and Application   Skill development and application should follow logically and reasonably from discussion that has taken place and from the lesson objectives. It may, in fact, occur as part of the discussion during and immediately following reading. The intent of this part of the DRA is to give students opportunity to practice doing what they've just learned to do, whether it's observing and recording weather conditions, solving arithmetic equations, reading and interpreting Shakespeare, playing basketball, or understanding the historical forces that led to the Vietnam War. Obviously, some activities are "skillsier" than others. The questions are: How *important* are they? And how significantly do they contribute to your students' ability to function in your content area? Answers to these questions allow you to decide if your skill development and application activity should be some sort of drill, vocabulary study, expository/narrative writing, group mapping with discussion and analysis, individual or group projects, or some combination of the above.

Step 5   Extension and Follow-up Activities   Sometimes it is difficult to decide where skill development and application ends and lesson extension and follow-up activities begin. That's all right. In real life, step-by-step procedures have a way of getting blurred at the edges. What is important is that extension and follow-up activities allow both *closure*—bringing a lesson to a satisfying end—and *extension*—pursuing an exciting idea well beyond immediate lesson boundaries. So, these "5th-Step Activities" (Davidson, 1989) may be small or large, a Big Deal or a Little Deal, short and sweet, or long and involved. The larger ones tend to be easily identifiable: major course projects; skits, plays, and productions; science fairs; completed furniture, paintings, clothing, and meals; research papers; and any number of more or less elaborate activities.

It's the small, nonspectacular follow-up activities that are sometimes difficult to design. One that I recommend for all subject areas is the Three-Minute Write (which some people refer to as a "Quick Write"), an activity we'll explore further in Chapter 6. Very simply, the Three-Minute Write is 3 minutes of time, at the end of a lesson or class, in which students are asked to write about what they learned, what they didn't learn, what they liked about class, what they didn't understand, what they want more of, and what bothered them—in short, to write about their immediate impressions of the class period. These may be signed or anonymous and are turned in to the teacher (also sometimes called "exit slips"—the students' passports for leaving class). The wise teacher reads these writings carefully, noting where confusion/noncomprehension occurred; looking to see what should be repeated and what should not; checking to see if damage-control efforts need to be launched; and facing honestly his/her own strengths and weaknesses as perceived by the students. I have no doubt that both my students and I have benefitted from Three-Minute Writes. Certainly, they are an informative and satisfying end to a lesson.

DRA LESSON PLAN—9TH GRADE SOCIAL STUDIES

The following DRA lesson plan was written to guide reading and study of a chapter in the text, *Civics Government and Citizenship* (Fraenkel, Kane, & Wolf, 1990). The chapter is titled "Urban Problems" and is divided into two major sections: "City Planning" and "Problems That Cities Face." The lesson plan covers the 2-day period allotted for the first half of the chapter. The first two pages of the chapter text are reproduced below; following it is the lesson plan.

LESSON PLAN   *DRA*

1   CITY PLANNING

To plan something is to think about how you want it to turn out. A **city planner** is a person who thinks about how a city should be. He or she suggests ways to make a city a better place in which to live. Many cities have a city planning commission whose job is to think about the city's future.

CITY PLANNING IN COLONIAL TIMES

Some of the early cities in the colonies were designed with great care. In 1688, William Penn, the Founder of Pennsylvania, revealed his plan for the city of Philadelphia. One part of the plan provided for five large squares, or civic centers.

Washington, D.C., our nation's capital, also began as a planned city. Congress gave the job to a French engineer, Pierre L'Enfant. He submitted his plans to Congress in 1791. L'Enfant designed Washington so that there would be plenty of open space. Some of the streets were 46 meters (150 feet) wide, with 3 meters (10 feet) of sidewalk on either side. L'Enfant's plan provided for the planting of trees and a number of circles and beautiful parks.

Over the years, L'Enfant's original design has been followed fairly closely. Today, the National Capital Planning Commission supervises further developments and improvements in the city.

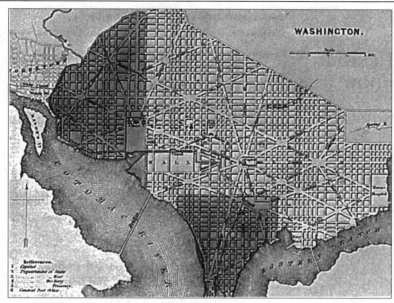

Above is Washington, D.C., as planned by the French engineer, Pierre L'Enfant.

LESSON PLAN *City Planning*

LESSON OBJECTIVES

Upon completion of this lesson, students will:

1. Be able to identify ways that city planning affects urban (and other community) life.
2. Be able to identify current issues related to city planning, both in the local community and across the nation.
3. Understand the impact of city planning on their own lives, both current and future.

DAY ONE

Step 1   Preparation for Reading

A. Vocabulary Presentation: Write the following on the board.
   1. Many cities have a city planning *commission* whose job is to think about the city's future. (Context.)
   2. . . . a French engineer, Pierre *L'Enfant* (Pronunciation only—"Lahn-fahn.")

3. . . . poor sewage and sanitation led to dangerous *epidemics*. (Context: Spot check "sewage" and "sanitation.")

4. Each zone is divided into *subzones*. (Context, structure.)

Read sentences/phrases aloud, and ask students what they think the underlined word means. (#2. Just give pronunciation.) Continue discussion until reasonable definitions are developed.

B. Focusing Event: Say something like the following:

"Today we're going to read about city and community planning. What parts of our community do you think were planned?" (List on board as students respond.)

"What do you think are current 'hot topics' of planning in the community today?" (List on board.)

(NOTE: Chapter title/focus is urban. Include suburban and rural communities in discussion; many problems/issues have spread to them.)

Step 2   Guided Silent Reading

Purpose-Setting Statement: "Read pages 291 through 295 to find out how city and community planning affect city and community life."

Step 3   Comprehension Development Discussion Questions

A. How do city and community planning affect city and community life? Why?

B. Let's go back to our list of planned parts of our community. Now that we've read, what additions might we make? (Have students justify responses.)

C. What are some possible areas of controversy inherent in the concept of city planning? How might these affect a community? Do you think city/community planning will become more or less predominant in the future? Why or why not?

Step 4   Skill Development and Application

A. Direct students' attention to the class list of current "hot topics" in community planning for this area. Make the following assignment:

"Working with your group, you are to develop a list of what the group believes to be the *top five priority planning issues for our community*. For each item, develop a written rationale giving reasons for your choice, and identify the person or agency you think will be responsible for the planning. In order to do this assignment, you will need to:

1. Brainstorm with your group a wide variety of issues; you have time to do that now. You are not limited to the list we have on the board.

2. Seek information from a variety of sources: newspapers, parents, community leaders, your own experiences, etc.

3. Gather reasons with issues; read or ask more to get at underlying information.

4. Come to class tomorrow with a written list of issues and rationales in rough priority order. Be prepared to share these with other group members and work toward a consensus list."

DAY TWO

Step 4   Skill Development and Application *(cont.)*
   B. Allow first half of period for groups to arrive at consensus priority lists. Circulate, and assist as needed.
   C. Initiate discussion by having groups report on priority lists and reasons for their choices. Compare. Develop a class consensus list by allowing students to negotiate by choosing, debating, extending arguments, persuading one another, and (if necessary) voting.

Step 5   Extension and Follow-up

   A. Ask students to speculate regarding the outcome of their priority choices for community planning. What problems might be solved and what problems are created by the planning they envision?
   B. Assign Three Minute Write.

How to do . . . .

A DRA

The DRA has been criticized in the past as being too focused on teacher talk and not focused enough on student thinking (Stauffer, 1969) and as being too closely connected with direct reading instruction rather than emphasizing content learning (Herber, 1970). I think at least some of this criticism is misplaced. The biggest problem with the DRA is that teachers *misuse* it (such as when questions do not get beyond the literal level or when an entire class discussion is suspended while the teacher searches for the word "clever" or when discussion ignores the content and focuses solely on so-called reading skills). The strategy is not at fault here. The fact is, the DRA is a solid, useful instructional strategy when it is used intelligently and appropriately. It is particularly useful for teachers who feel a need for a bit of structure to support them as they negotiate the complex classroom culture. Use the following guidelines to develop scintillating and subject-matter-rich DRA lessons:

1. Select the reading assignment, and estimate number of class periods needed to complete prereading, reading, skills development, and follow-up activities. Establish homework assignment(s), if any.

2. Choose vocabulary words to be presented prior to reading. Determine how they will be presented in context: on the board, a duplicated handout, or in the text. Note probable means for defining (i.e., context, structure, sound, and dictionary).

continued

How to do   continued

3. Write the purpose-setting statement and accompanying question for initiating discussion.

4. Write probable discussion questions.

5. Identify skills to be developed and practiced and the activities to be used for that purpose. Prepare any needed handouts, materials, equipment, etc.

6. Identify extension and follow-up activities. Prepare needed materials/ equipment, make any necessary special arrangements, and establish time-lines and assignment dates, if appropriate.

REQUEST

ReQuest was designed by Anthony Manzo (1969a, 1969b) for the purpose of increasing students' comprehension through a process of reciprocal questioning between teacher and student. It is based on two important notions about constructing meaning from text: first, that asking the right question is equally important as (and possibly more important than) knowing the right answer, especially when one's purpose for reading includes learning the information in text (recall Frank Smith's belief that the real "stuff" of comprehension is getting answers to questions one poses); and second, that teachers serve as powerful models for student behavior—if students are repeatedly exposed to teachers asking good questions about text, students will adopt similar strategies and begin doing the same thing.

The point of ReQuest is to use student-to-teacher/teacher-to-student questioning interactions to engage students in the same type of purposeful reading and rich comprehension processing as is found with DR-TA. In fact, Manzo considers ReQuest to be a DR-TA-like instructional strategy (Manzo, personal communication, 1974). Originally intended for one-to-one instructional settings, ReQuest is equally adaptable to small-group and large-group instruction. It is, in fact, one of my favorite ways of teaching, which I used extensively during my last 2 years in the public schools. I will describe its use for group instruction here; later, in Chapter 10, I'll show you how it can be used when working with individuals. For ease of presentation, I have divided ReQuest into sequential steps.

STEPS FOR USING REQUEST

Step 1

The teacher and students silently read a segment of text (the amount of text is predetermined and announced by the teacher). After reading, the teacher closes her/his book, and students are invited to ask as many questions as they wish about the text. They are encouraged to ask "teacher-type" questions. The teacher answers all questions as fully as possible.

Step 2

After students have finished questioning, they close their books and the teacher asks questions, following up on items/ideas students raised, raising new issues, and/or calling students' attention to other important information. The teacher is responsible for asking good questions and for asking questions at all levels of comprehension; Manzo (1969a) recommends seven categories of questions, which are identified and demonstrated immediately following this discussion.

Step 3

The next segment of text is read, and the reciprocal questioning between students and teacher continues. By the second segment, and continuing throughout the procedure, the teacher's questions should include those that explicitly integrate information from one reading segment into discussion of another: for example, "In the last paragraph, we found out that there is a direct relationship between wind and wave. What effect do you think prevailing winds have on ocean currents?" This step ensures that students will perceive the importance of this kind of integration and accumulation of knowledge.

Step 4

The procedure continues until students can reasonably predict what is going to happen, what further information they are going to get, or what they need to do to complete activities and/or exercises. At that point, the teacher asks, "Based upon what we have read so far, what do you think the rest of the chapter will be about? What question can we ask that you think the chapter/story will answer?" (Alternatively, ". . . what do you think you'll be asked to do in the exercises/activity following the reading? What will you need to know to do them/it? What question(s) can we ask that will help us complete the exercises/activity?")

Because of the clear focus on question-asking in the ReQuest Procedure, it is critical that teachers help students turn their prediction statements into questions (e.g., "What question can we ask that you think the chapter will answer?"). It is not important that the final purpose-setting question be "perfect" or match the question the teacher has in his/her head. Imperfect questions can be dealt with in follow-up discussion and are themselves vehicles for developing a sense of what constitutes a "good" question.

Step 5

Students write the purpose-setting question and complete the reading/activity assignment. To initiate discussion, the teacher begins by asking the purpose-setting question and allowing students to answer and evaluate it. (As with the DRA, it is important for this to be the first question addressed; afterward, discussion broadens to include many other topics and areas.) A purpose-setting question the class formulated that was not answered by the text (i.e., an "imperfect" question) is identified as such at the onset of discussion when the teacher asks it. That is, when the teacher asks, "What is the relationship between color and light in oil painting?", if the text did not address this topic, students will likely answer, "We don't know. The chapter wasn't about that." The teacher then can say, "All right. If the chapter didn't answer our question, what question did it answer?", and allow students to ask a question that leads into the content discussion that needs to occur.

Later, the teacher should go back to the "imperfect" question and let students analyze how they came to ask it; e.g., "What was it that led us toward this question? Was it something in the book? Something we already knew about the topic? A combination of both?" In this way, students can engage in metacognitive thought by examining and reexamining their own logic and line of reasoning in comparison with the logic of the text. Following discussion, the teacher assigns or guides follow-up activities as appropriate.

CATEGORIES OF QUESTIONS FOR REQUEST

As mentioned earlier, Manzo (1969a) suggests seven categories of questions teachers should ask during a ReQuest interaction. You will see readily that his category list includes all three levels of comprehension (literal, interpretive and applied); however, these are implicit within his categories and are not addressed directly as such. I like his list because it adopts a slightly different perspective toward questioning than standard categories do and can be helpful in formulating questions, especially if you're new at the game of question-asking. It's a rather nice alternative to the traditional, hierarchical comprehension-level model. The category explications below were taken very nearly verbatim from Manzo (1969a); sample questions for each category were written for the text excerpt immediately following the category list—junior high mathematics (Davidson, Landau, McCracken, & Thompson, 1995). The following types of questions should be asked during a ReQuest interaction:

1. Questions for which there is an immediate reference; questions that can be answered by looking at the text: "How do you read $m\angle ABC$?" "What does 'vertex' mean?"

2. Questions that relate to common knowledge and for which answers can be reasonably expected: "If you hadn't seen the illustration here, how would you expect a right angle to look? Why?"

3. Questions for which the teacher does not expect a "correct" response but for which she or he can provide related information: "Have you ever seen a quilt made from angled pieces? Let me show you one my grandmother made . . ."

4. Questions for which neither the teacher nor the selection is likely to supply a "right" answer but that are nonetheless worth pondering or discussing: "I wonder how any of us could use comparison of angles in our daily lives?"

5. Questions of a personalized type that only the students can answer: "What do you find hardest about using a compass or protractor?"

6. Questions that are answerable but are not answered by the selection being read; further reference is needed: "I wonder how sophisticated computers and computer programs are in generating and measuring geometric figures these days?"

7. Questions requiring translation, e.g., from one level of abstraction to another, from one symbolic form to another, from one verbal form to another: "In your own words, how do we tell an obtuse angle from a right angle? From an acute angle?"

Lead-in for developing the final purpose-setting question, "Based upon what we've done so far, what do you think the practice exercises will require you to do? What information will you need to have in order to do them? What questions will you be answering in completing the exercises?"

I think you can see how the reading lead-in questions follow naturally from questions asked during the teacher-student question exchange. Notice that all seven categories of questions are not needed at each stop-point during the discussion; however, in the course of any complete ReQuest lesson, you should ask the full range of question types. It is the teacher's responsibility to see that this occurs. When I first started using ReQuest, I kept a small file card in my book with the category types jotted on it to remind myself of them; I found that I very quickly internalized the question categories and was easily able to keep mental track so that all types of questions were asked in each lesson.

Text Excerpt: Junior High Mathematics

9–2   ANGLES

OBJECTIVE:
To investigate angle measures and relationships.

When lines or parts of lines intersect, they form angles. Different angles contribute to designs on quilts, tile floors, stained glass windows, and other forms of art and architecture.

You can name an angle by the vertex and points on the sides, by a number, or by the vertex alone. When using three letters, the middle letter always names the vertex.

Angle   Two rays with a common endpoint form an angle.

Example 1 Name the angle shown in four different ways.

Solution $\angle ABC$, $\angle 1$, $\angle B$, $\angle CBA$

We classify angles by their measure in degrees (°). The notation $m\angle ABC$ means *the measure of angle ABC.*

FLASHBACK:
The symbol ∟ indicates a right angle. Perpendicular lines form right angles.

acute
less than 90°
$m\angle 2 < 90°$

obtuse
between 90° and 180°
$90° < m\angle 3 < 180°$

right
equals 90°
$m\angle PQR = 90°$

straight
equals 180°
$m\angle AOR = 180°$

We use a protractor to measure and draw angles.

Example 2   Use a protractor to measure $\angle XYZ$.
  1.   Place the center point of the protractor on Y, the vertex of the angle.
  2.   Position the protractor so that $\overrightarrow{YZ}$ passes through zero on the protractor scale. Estimate to decide which scale to read. Is $\angle XYZ$ acute or obtuse?
  3.   Read the angle measure at the point where $\overrightarrow{YX}$ passes through the protractor scale.

Solution $m\angle XYZ = 29°$

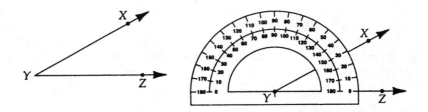

USING REQUEST

During ReQuest, it is critical that the teacher listen carefully to the questions students ask, not only to monitor the kinds and quality of those questions, but because often students "beat you to the punch" by asking all the questions you'd planned. That's all right (in fact, it's wonderful!) as long as you don't plow forward and ask the same questions anyway. As in so many other situations, you've got to be light on your feet and able to conjure up new questions (or have the presence of mind to say you don't have any questions, compliment the class on a job well done, and move right along).

ReQuest is a powerful strategy for increasing students' comprehension, teaching lesson content, and developing students' reading/learning skills. After using ReQuest for only half a semester, I was more than a little surprised to find my own words coming right back at me from my students. (I discovered I asked "What do you suppose . . ." questions a lot!) Not only that, students even modeled my manner of speech, body language, and strategies for gaining clarification. Once, after I had asked a really muddled question (I was trying to think and ask a question at the same time—not an easy task) the most unlikely student—a painfully shy, never-assertive young man who had been in special reading classes most of his 10 years in school—responded to my muddled question by asking me, "Would you *rephrase* that question please?" with the most *teacherly* intonation. It was wonderful. I could have jumped for joy. Instead, I thanked him for giving me the opportunity to start over and asked him a crisp and articulate question. I wanted to make sure he felt rewarded for daring to use the strategy of asking me to rephrase my question and encourage him to continue using it and other information-getting strategies in the future. He did, on both counts. He answered the question quite nicely, and, in fact, proceeded to become rather bold in my classroom. I've seen many students nurtured toward intellectual curiosity and increased classroom proficiency with ReQuest. I know that it does, indeed, foster the kind of reading and learning we've been talking about through this entire chapter.

How to do . . . .

REQUEST

ReQuest is rather easily learned by teachers and students alike. It is particularly useful in short vignettes that stimulate activation of students' prior knowledge base. It serves as a marvelous mechanism for students to obtain information *without having to admit ignorance* (they treat your answers as responses to known-information questions they've asked!). As such, it allows students to fill missing slots in their prior knowledge base, gain access to key language to express half-known or emerging concepts, and enter text with a richer sense of the content knowledge itself. The following steps are useful for preparing and teaching ReQuest:

1. Select the reading assignment, and determine length and number of reading/questioning segments.

2. Preread material, making note of areas you consider to be important enough for questioning (correlate these with already-stated lesson objectives).

3. Determine lead-in question for eliciting student-generated purpose-setting question.

4. Identify follow-up activities and/or assignments.

SOME CONCLUDING THOUGHTS ON COMPREHENSION

At the opening of this chapter, I stated that the ultimate goal of reading is comprehension: constructing meaning that is in some way congruent with the author's intended meaning. The instructional practices presented here—DR-TA, Group Mapping, DRA, ReQuest—share a clear focus on guiding student comprehension of text. They are, however, valuable resources for doing much more. Certainly, they address the three other goals associated with secondary school reading: learning, increasing reading skill, and applying new knowledge. But more importantly, they accomplish all three of these goals in such a way as to differ significantly from the frontal teaching John Goodlad found to be the unrelenting staple of the secondary school day. They do, indeed, let students "romp with open-ended questions," and allow them to "turn things around by asking questions [themselves]."

What Goodlad found, and what we must acknowledge, is that all too many secondary classrooms offer little in the way of intellectual stimulation and challenge for students. DR-TA, Group Mapping, DRA, and ReQuest help change that. They are not the only ways to develop students' comprehension, teach subject matter, increase students' reading skills, or guide application of new information, but they are productive and generative ways. Further, each of these instructional strategies provides for students with diverse cultural, linguistic, and academic backgrounds. Diversity of viewpoints and perspectives is encouraged by each and every one of the strategies: They allow many voices to be heard in the classroom and opportunities for students to validate their own experience while learning content. These methods immerse students in extended, full discussion of content; at the very least, students who feel constrained to participate have access to important subject matter information. As students gain increasing mastery of the language of that content—which can come only from consistent, repeated exposure to it—they will increasingly participate in class discussion and learn the content itself. And finally, they create opportunity for all students to become thoughtful, strategic readers of content text. As you review the characteristics of thoughtful readers that I listed earlier in this chapter, you will notice that the instructional strategies presented here guide students in developing such characteristics. All of this is important, both for you and for your students. I firmly believe that if you used nothing more than these four instructional approaches in your classroom, you would be a good teacher. You need not, however, be limited to these. There are many other equally productive and useful tools, which will be discussed in the upcoming chapters.

DOUBLE ENTRY JOURNAL

What new ideas do you now have to add to or revise your definition of reading comprehension? What role can you see for comprehension instructional strategies for your subject area and for your own teaching? How can you use or adapt instructional strategies from this chapter to avoid frontal teaching practices and to help students who find your subject area their most difficult? Share your ideas with someone who teaches a subject area different from yours. How do your conclusions compare?

REFERENCES

Betts, E. A. (1946). *Foundations of reading instruction.* New York: American Book Company.

Bloom, B. S. (1956). *Taxonomy of educational objectives: Handbook I, cognitive domain.* New York: Longman, Green, and Co.

Boorstin, D. J., & Kelley, B. M. (1996). *A history of the United States.* Boston: Ginn.

Davidson, D. M., Landau, M., McCracken, L., & Thompson, L. (1995). *Mathematics: Explorations and applications.* Needham, MA: Prentice-Hall.

Davidson, J. L. (1982). The group mapping activity for instruction in reading and thinking. *Journal of Reading, 26,* 52–56.

Davidson, J. L. (1989). *The DR-TA reading series.* Monroe, NY: Trillium Press.

Durkin, D. (1978–1979). What classroom observations reveal about reading comprehension instruction. *Reading Research Quarterly, 14,* 481–533.

Fraenkel, J. R., Kane, F. T., & Wolf, A. (1990). *Civics government and citizenship.* Boston: Allyn & Bacon.

Gillet, J. W., & Temple, C. (1994). *Understanding reading problems* (4th ed.). New York: HarperCollins.

Gillotte, H. (1991, April). *The examination of literature-based series: Potential problems for minority students.* Paper presented at the annual meeting of the American Educational Research Association, Chicago, IL.

Goodlad, J. I. (1984). *A place called school.* New York: McGraw-Hill.

Gray, W. S. (1946). *On their own in reading.* Chicago: Scott Foresman.

Guszak, F. J. (1967). Teacher questioning and reading. *Reading Teacher, 21,* 227–234.

Haberman, M. (1991). The pedagogy of poverty versus good teaching. *Phi Delta Kappan, 73,* 290–294.

Haggard, M. R. (1988). Developing critical thinking with the directed reading-thinking activity. *Reading Teacher, 41,* 526–533.

Hampf, M. B. (1971). Mapping: A technique for translating reading into thinking. *Journal of Reading, 14,* (pp. 225–230, 270).

Harste, J., & Short, K., with Burke, C. (1988). *Creating classrooms for authors.* Portsmouth, NH: Heinemann.

Heath, S. B. (1982). Questioning at home and at school: A comparative study. In G. Spindler (Ed.), *Doing the ethnography of schooling: Educational anthropology in action* (pp. 102–131). New York: Holt.

Herber, H. L. (1978). *Teaching reading in the content areas* (2nd ed). Englewood Cliffs, NJ: Prentice-Hall.

Manzo, A. V. (1969a). The ReQuest procedure. *Journal of Reading, 13,* 123–126.

Manzo, A. V. (1969b). *Improving reading comprehension through reciprocal questioning.* Doctoral dissertation, Syracuse University. (University Microfilms No. 70–10, 364).

Markham, B. (1987). The splendid outcast. In M. S. Lovell (Ed.), *The splendid outcast: Beryl Markham's African stories* (pp. 33–47). San Francisco: North Point Press.

Mehan, H. (1979). "What time is it, Denise?"; Asking known information questions in classroom discourse. In *Theory into Practice* (Vol. 18, pp. 285–294). Columbus, OH: College of Education, The Ohio State University.

Paris, S. G., Lipson, M. Y., & Wixon, K. K. (1994). Becoming a strategic reader. In R. B. Ruddell, M. R. Ruddell, & H. Singer (Eds.) *Theoretical models and processes of reading* (4th ed.) (pp. 788–810). Newark, DE: International Reading Association.

Pearson, P. D., Roehler, L. R., Dole, J. A., & Duffy, G. G. (1990). *Developing expertise in reading comprehension: What should be taught? How should it be taught?* (Tech. Rep. No. 512). Champaign, IL: University of Illinois at Urbana-Champaign, Center for the Study of Reading.

Readence, J. E., Bean, T. W., & Baldwin, R. S. (1989). *Content area reading: An integrated approach* (3rd ed.). Dubuque, IA: Kendall/Hunt.

Roe, B. D., Stoodt, B. D., & Burns, P. C. (1995). *Secondary school reading instruction* (5th ed.). Boston: Houghton Mifflin.

Ruddell, R. B., & Harris, P. (1991). A study of the relationship between influential teachers' prior knowledge and teaching effectiveness: Developing higher order thinking in content areas. In S. McCormick & J. Zutell (Eds.), *Cognition and Social Perspectives for Literacy Research and Instruction,* 38th Yearbook of the National Reading Conference (pp. 461–472). Chicago: National Reading Conference.

Siegel, M. (In press). More than words: The generative power of transmediation in learning. *Canadian Journal of Education*.

Smith, F. (1994). *Understanding reading* (5th ed.). Hillsdale, NJ: Lawrence Erlbaum Associates.

Stauffer, R. G. (1969). *Directing reading maturity as a cognitive process*. New York: Harper & Row.

Stauffer, R. G. (1980). *The Language-Experience approach to teaching reading* (2nd ed.). New York: Harper & Row.

Suhor, C. (1984). Towards a semiotics-based curriculum. *Journal of Curriculum Studies, 16*, 247–257.

Taffel, A. (1992). *Physics: Its methods and meanings* (6th ed.). Needham, MA: Prentice-Hall.

Tierney, R. J., & Pearson, P. D. (1992). Learning to learn from text: A framework for improving classroom practice. In E. K. Dishner, T. W. Bean, J. E. Readence, & D. W. Moore (Eds.), *Reading in the content areas: Improving classroom instruction* (3rd ed.), (pp. 87–103). Dubuque, IA: Kendall/Hunt.

Tierney, R. J., Readence, J. E., & Dishner, E. K. (1995). *Reading strategies and practices: A compendium* (4th ed.). Boston: Allyn & Bacon.

Vacca, R. T., & Vacca, J. L. (1996). *Content area reading* (5th ed.). New York: HarperCollins.

BUILDING TABLE

CHAPTER 3	DR-TA	GMA	DRA	REQUEST
FOCUS ON	Content reading and discussion	Content reading and organization	Content reading and discussion	Content reading and discussion
GUIDES STUDENTS	Before and during reading	After reading and before writing	Before, during and after reading	Before and during reading
USE TO PLAN	Lessons	Lessons	Lessons	Lessons
MAY BE USED	Whole class, small groups	Whole class, cooperative groups, partnerships	Whole class, small groups	Whole class, small groups, individuals
MAY BE COMBINED WITH (known strategies)	GMA	DR-TA, DRA	GMA	GMA
MATERIALS PREPARATION	Light	None to light	Moderate to extensive	Light
OTHER PREPARATION	Moderate	Moderate	Moderate to extensive	Light
OUTSIDE RESOURCES	Not needed	Not needed	Useful	Useful
HOW TO DO	Page 60	Page 67	Page 79–80	Page 85

VOCABULARY LEARNING IN CONTENT AREAS

D O U B L E   E N T R Y   J O U R N A L

Can you remember an incident when you were elementary-school age in which you learned a new word or incorporated a word into your speaking vocabulary? In your journal, write the word, and describe the incident as fully as possible. Can you remember an incident when you were junior-high or high-school age in which you learned a new word or incorporated a word into your speaking vocabulary? Write the word, and describe the incident as fully as possible.

Vocabulary knowledge has long been accepted as a critical component of text comprehension and learning in all subject areas (Davis, 1945; Singer, 1964; Herber, 1978; Nagy, 1988; Ruddell, 1994). Virtually everyone agrees that learning the language of a subject area is an important aspect of learning the subject itself. Robert Ruddell (1986) states,

> The comprehension of written text, as well as speech, directly involves the use of language and thought—language in the sense that the reader's meaning store and linguistic structures provide currency for idea representation; and thought, as the student cognitively manipulates ideas based on reading purpose which in turns leads to meaning. (p. 581)

The important relationship between vocabulary, comprehension, and learning is, however, more universally proclaimed than it is operationalized in the classroom. All too often, vocabulary instruction is isolated: contiguous in time, perhaps, but not connected to the true point of the classroom and almost never connected to the lives of the students themselves. We all have memories of such vocabulary lessons: Definitions dictated by the teacher at the beginning of each reading assignment, words on the chalkboard to be written down, looked up, and defined verbatim from the dictionary, and the Dreaded Word Lists. Such instruction is contrary to much of what we know about vocabulary learning (Ruddell, 1994):

1. Words are known on a variety of levels and in gradients of understanding; similarly, words are learned not in one fell swoop, but in a more or less gradual way over time. Word learning involves a constellation of learning resources and abilities.

2. By adulthood, individuals have well-developed, personalized strategies for learning new words; instruction directed toward teaching students how to apply various word-learning strategies are, by and large, highly successful.

3. We know that students acquire strategies for learning and remembering new words, but we have almost no understanding of how, or whether, students systematically and selectively apply these strategies while reading and learning.

4. Much and varied information resides in text, and it is this information that makes up the context that readers use to construct meaning while reading.

5. The general consensus is that context does, indeed, facilitate meaning construction.

6. Substantial evidence suggests that readers spontaneously use context to construct meaning for new words.

7. We have little knowledge of how readers transact with words in text and the stances they adopt for understanding new words, learning new words, remembering word meanings, and applying that knowledge in everyday reading, writing, and learning events.

8. We are just beginning to explore the influence of social interactions on word learning. The limited evidence we have suggests that positive effects occur as the result of social interactions during word learning. (pp. 436–437)

Figure 4.1 shows a word list I picked up from the floor of an area high school at the end of school one day. Notice how it marches, shall we say, "inexorably," through the alphabet, context-less and forbidding; notice also that this student has decided that it only takes a synonym or two to define some pretty powerful words. This list, and other similar materials, actually encourage the kind of definition-by-synonym we see in Figure 4.1; no context, or text of any kind, is present to aid in meaning construction, add depth, suggest nuance, or indicate any connections with one's prior knowledge base. Further, long and context-less word lists typify precisely Bill Nagy's charge (1988) that much vocabulary instruction is ineffective because

1. Most instruction fails to produce in-depth word knowledge.

2. Most instruction is targeted toward a set of words considered to be "difficult," when, in fact, the difficulty of a given word lies not in the word itself, but rather in the word *in relationship to* the context within which it is used.

FIGURE 4.1   *The Dreaded Word List*

203. immutable
not changeable
204. impalle
to torture
205. impasse
deadlock
206. impeccable
without error
207. impediment
an obstruction
208. impervious
not capable of being influenced
209. implacable
unforgiving
210. impunity

211. inadvertent
unintentional
212. inane
lacking sense, foolish
213. inarticulate
not clearly defined

214. incarcerate
to imprison, jail
215. incessant
ceaseless
216. incipient
beginning

217. inclement
rough, stormy, harsh
218. incognito
(something-adj?) hidden, disguised
219. incongruous
not in keeping, unsuitable
220. incorrigible
beyond control
221. incredible
difficult ot believe
222. incubus
an evil spirit, nightmare
223. indigent
poor, impoverished
224. indomitable
undefeatable
225. inert
not moving, active (sic)
226. inexorable
relentless. unyielding, inflexible
227. inexplicable
cannot be accounted for,
unexplainable
228. inference
educated guess based on info
229. ingenious
very clever
230. ingenuous
naive

EFFECTIVE CONTENT VOCABULARY INSTRUCTION

Effective content vocabulary instruction must, if nothing else, *connect*. It must connect with reading/writing assignments, class topics, and the content to be learned; it must connect with students' prior knowledge and previous experience, with their interests and needs for learning content, and with their daily lives; and it must connect with all that goes on in the classroom, the "whole fabric" of classroom life (Ruddell, 1992). Nagy (1988) suggests that effective vocabulary instruction must include the properties of *integration, repetition*, and *meaningful use*, which all imply connectedness. Graves and Prenn (1986) highlight yet another type of connecting: the teacher's awareness of and sensitivity to varying task needs and levels of word knowledge that influence how words should be taught. Graves and Prenn identify three vocabulary-learning tasks associated with reading, each with its own distinct instructional implications:

1. learning to read words already in students' listening or speaking vocabularies, but not in their reading or writing vocabularies

2. learning to read words that are not in students' listening, speaking, reading, or writing vocabularies but for which a concept is available

3. learning to read words for which students do not yet have a concept

Instruction for these different tasks may range from simply pronouncing a word that students already have in their listening/speaking vocabularies, to telling what a word means and linking it to a known concept, to providing extended definitions and conducting detailed discussion to illustrate new words and concepts. But whatever form instruction takes, it must *connect*.

PURPOSES FOR CONTENT VOCABULARY INSTRUCTION

Integration, repetition, meaningful use, connectedness—all of these are critical components of effective vocabulary instruction. An equally important, but often overlooked, instructional component is that teachers need to understand the different *goals*, or purposes, for vocabulary instruction, and know when and how to use various instructional strategies and activities to achieve them. I find, for example, that very few people distinguish between two different purposes for teaching content vocabulary.

The first purpose is to *remove barriers to comprehension of text*. This is the instruction we do prior to reading, as we did in the DRA in Chapter 3, to preteach vocabulary. Preteaching vocabulary before reading is a traditionally recommended practice; however, it is currently receiving renewed attention because of its usefulness in assisting ESL students' acquisition of both the language and the content knowledge in subject area classrooms. For the most part, this instruction focuses on key words and concepts central to the content of the immediate text, so that both the words and their meanings are often specialized, technical, and lesson- or context-specific. In this instruction, multiple meanings, nuance, and meaning extensions generally are less important than the goal of building meaning and developing concepts pertaining to a particular topic or text. *Immediate*, specific use predominates in prereading vocabulary instruction and generally includes periodic review of words and terms as they occur across topics and texts. The task needs Graves and Prenn (1986) describe (e.g., learning to read words already partially known; learning to read words for which a concept is available; and learning to read words for which no concept is available) are pertinent to and influence the form this instruction will take.

A second purpose for content vocabulary instruction is to *promote long-term acquisition and development of the language of an academic discipline*. The rationale for this instruction is based, in part, on the conviction we all hold that increased command of the language will deepen and enrich students' understanding of the subject itself, and also because we know (whether intuitively or through our own study and observation) that the mark of an educated person in any discipline is his or her ability to function easily in the language of that field. We want our students to acquire this proficiency and to have the depth of understanding that signifies real learning. Further, we want them to become independent word learners and active knowledge seekers as well. Instruction designed to achieve this goal focuses on extending, refining, adding to, and changing schemata; developing multiple meanings, making connections within and across academic disciplines, and adding nuance and subtlety to word meaning and constructions of knowledge. This instruction is primarily directed toward in-depth understanding and requires exploration of words in relationship to the context in which they are embedded—and I would extend Nagy's notion of written context to include the context of the discipline as a whole.

To summarize, then, one goal of content vocabulary instruction is focused clearly on immediate, short-term learning needs, with emphasis on identifying what students know and preparing them for the reading and learning to follow. The other goal involves development and extension of students' mastery of a discipline through integration of new ideas into their existing knowledge base and assimilation of new words into working vocabularies. One occurs immediately prior to reading text, whereas the other is most reasonably accomplished after reading. One is short, sweet, and to the point; the other is extended, exploratory, and wide-ranging.

PROBLEMS ASSOCIATED WITH CONTENT VOCABULARY INSTRUCTION

Problems occur in teaching content vocabulary when we confuse instruction intended to remove barriers to comprehension with instruction aimed at long-term vocabulary acquisition and development and/or when we attempt to combine instruction to achieve both goals at once. Certainly, there is some overlap between the two; words taught prior to reading may eventually become words targeted for long-term development, and learning that occurs in the prereading period feeds into and strengthens instruction that follows. *When instruction is designed for one purpose* (preparing students to read, for example), *however, and teachers expect outcomes associated with the other* (long-term retention), *expectations are rarely realized and everyone believes that time spent teaching content vocabulary actually impedes subject learning by taking time away from teaching the content itself.*

Attempts to combine purposes are just as problematic: It is not until *after* reading that we really know what words need to be pursued for long-term acquisition. Students' prior knowledge and previous experience in relationship to text determine that, and more often than not, the "real" list is considerably shorter than the list of potential words that any book chapter or other text selection would yield. Consequently, if we attempt to preteach all the words that could interfere with comprehension of a passage in combination with all the words that we predict are important for long-term acquisition, the list becomes so long that vocabulary lessons in fact *do* delay or derail completely the content lesson itself.

So it is important for teachers to distinguish between these two related, but different, content vocabulary instructional goals. One is aimed at removing barriers to comprehension (instruction that should occur *before* reading); the other is intended to encourage long-term acquisition and development of the language of an academic discipline (instruction that should occur *after* reading). This chapter considers both prereading and postreading content vocabulary instruction; activities adaptable for vocabulary instruction in either condition are presented in each section.

Content Vocabulary Instruction: Removing Barriers to Comprehension

As content area teachers, we have two major responsibilities regarding vocabulary instruction and comprehension of text. First, we are responsible for ensuring that our students will experience some level of success in constructing meaning from text; this frequently is accomplished, in part, during prereading instruction by direct teaching of selected vocabulary words. We do this to remove barriers to comprehension and to "boost" students' understanding of key concepts and ideas they will encounter as they read. This is the kind of vocabulary instruction that most frequently occurs in secondary classrooms and is commonly referred to as "direct vocabulary instruction." It usually combines some degree of lecture, questioning, explanation, and discussion as teachers determine students' prior knowledge levels.

A second responsibility teachers have in prereading vocabulary instruction is to provide students with the means for dealing *independently* with unknown words. That is, we must make sure students have a *functional system* for learning new words, an effective answer for the question, "What do you do when you come to a word you do not know?" Further, we must ensure that students have instruction and practice using this system (Jenkins, Matlock, & Slocum, 1989) *in the classroom of every subject area in which they are expected to read, write, think, and learn.* This is much more far-reaching than direct vocabulary instruction, and it takes a little more *time* than direct vocabulary instruction; but we cannot ignore the responsibility for it by limiting instruction to teaching simply a selected set of words.

Jenkins and colleagues (1989) refer to these two responsibilities as: (1) instruction in individual meanings, and (2) instruction in deriving meaning. Consider for a moment the futility of attempting to teach *every* new word students need to learn in the course of one school year in your class. It simply cannot be done; part of your instructional time must therefore focus on teaching and reinforcing students' ability to handle unknown words on their own. (Sorry. The elementary teachers can't do this one for you. You can't teach a third-grader how to construct meaning for words in an advanced chemistry text, a woodworking manual, or one of Shakespeare's plays.) It is middle school and secondary teachers, then, who must assume the responsibility both for direct vocabulary instruction and instruction to assist students in developing a functional system for learning the language of middle school and secondary texts.

PREREADING INSTRUCTION: DIRECT VOCABULARY TEACHING

Recall the vocabulary portion of our sample DRA lesson in Chapter 3 (reproduced below).

A. *Vocabulary Presentation:* Write the following on the board.
1. Many cities have a city planning <u>commission</u> whose job is to think about the city's future. (Context.)
2. . . . a French engineer, Pierre <u>L'Enfant</u> (Pronunciation only: "Lahn-fahn.")
3. . . . poor sewage and sanitation led to dangerous <u>epidemics</u>. (Context: Spot check "sewage" and "sanitation.")
4. Each zone is divided into <u>subzones</u>. (Context, structure.) Read sentences/phrases aloud and ask students what they think the underlined word means (#2—just give pronunciation). Continue discussion until reasonable definitions are developed.

This is an example of direct prereading vocabulary instruction, and it is representative of a fair amount of the direct instruction that teachers do; however, any number of other activities may be used in addition to, or instead of, the "What do you think this word means?" discussion used in this lesson. Herber (1978) and Nelson-Herber (1986) suggest clustering vocabulary words around critical lesson concepts and teaching them with a Structured Overview model to introduce both the words and important lesson concepts prior to reading (see Figure 4.2). Nelson-Herber (1986) emphasizes the importance of extended class discussion of the structured overview and its usefulness for:

1. teaching content words and concepts;
2. refining and extending meanings of words previously learned; and
3. introducing the reading itself.

Many of the vocabulary activities presented in this section and later in the chapter are also good substitutes for the straightforward discussion we used with the DRA and may be adapted according to students' needs; that is, instruction may

1. *provide pronunciation* for a word that is in students' speaking/listening vocabularies.
2. *tell what a word means and link it* to known concepts.
3. *provide extended definition and discussion* of words for which concepts are incomplete or not available (Graves & Prenn, 1986).

FIGURE 4.2   *Structured Overview: Fungi*

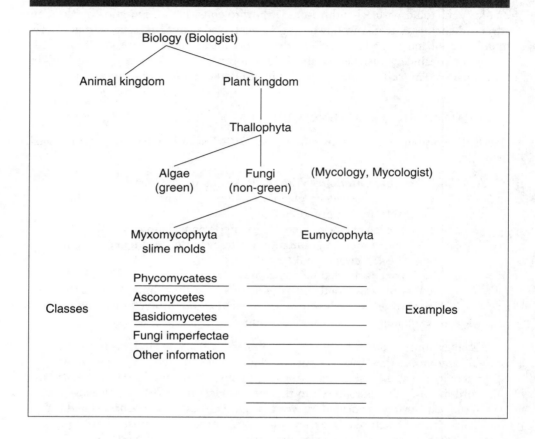

SEMANTIC MAPPING

Semantic mapping (Dyer, 1985; Heimlich & Pittelman, 1986; Johnson, Toms-Bronowski, & Pittelman, 1981) is a whole-class, small-group, or individual activity that develops associations and encourages personal response to targeted vocabulary words. Semantic mapping is particularly useful for prereading instruction because it assists in activating students' prior knowledge of key concepts to be encountered in text.

As a whole-class activity, semantic mapping begins with the teacher writing one of the selected vocabulary words on the board: e.g., "measurement." Students free-associate words, terms, or phrases they associate with the word ("inches," "precision," "testing," "numbers"); these are written on the board around the targeted word in random order as they are suggested. When students are finished suggesting ideas, they work in small groups or pairs or individually to categorize associations and label the categories. Students then produce their own maps for the word and the newly developed categories. Further discussion takes place as appropriate. Figure 4.3 shows a semantic map for the word *advantage* to be taught as part of a unit on tennis.

Heimlich and Pittelman (1986) recommend a slightly different procedure for semantic mapping in which the teacher

1. writes the word or term on the chalkboard.

2. asks students to list as many related words as they can and categorize their lists.

3. conducts discussion in which students share the prepared lists orally and write these on the class map.

4. asks students to label the categories.

5. continues discussion as appropriate.

Heimlich and Pittelman emphasize the importance of discussion in semantic mapping to provide much opportunity for students to connect prior knowledge with content concepts and terminology, thus increasing students' comprehension of text. Dyer's research with seventh-grade students (1985) supports this view, as does her subsequent work with college students in basic skills classes (Dyer, personal communication, 1991). I agree. Semantic mapping is particularly well-suited as a prereading activity precisely because it teaches content vocabulary and enhances text comprehension at the same time.

FIGURE 4.3   *Semantic Map: Tennis*

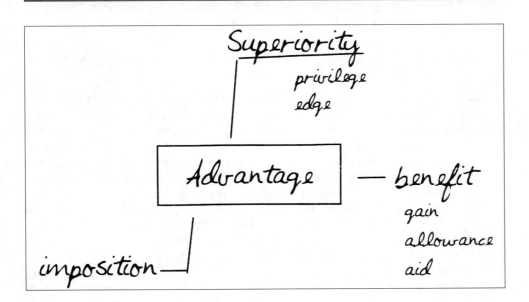

LIST-GROUP-LABEL

Moore, Readence, & Rickelman (1989) suggest List-Group-Label, a vocabulary-development strategy designed originally for social studies and science. List-Group-Label is similar to semantic mapping. It begins with students generating a List of all the words and terms they associate with a targeted vocabulary word; words are listed in random order. After no more associated words and terms are forthcoming, students then Group the words into categories and Label each. This part of List-Group-Label is best done in small student groups or pairs and should include a requirement that students provide a rationale for their category labels. List-Group-Label can be productively combined with semantic mapping.

CHARACTERISTICS OF DIRECT VOCABULARY TEACHING

One characteristic of effective direct vocabulary instruction is that it is *short*. It is, in other words, limited to a few, critical words and concepts (time constraints, alone, prohibit in-depth instruction for all possible unknown words). Recall Nagy's charge (1988) that most vocabulary instruction fails to produce in-depth word knowledge; more often than not, this results from teachers' attempts to preteach 10 or 15 words before reading instead of five. A realistic solution here is to adopt the position that it is far better to teach a few words well rather than many words poorly. Careful preselection of targeted words is therefore vital.

A second characteristic of direct content vocabulary instruction is that it is *connected explicitly to the actual text* students are to read so that no one can miss the connection; it must begin and/or end with target words embedded in sentences and paragraphs directly from the text to be read. This connection is strengthened when direct content vocabulary instruction involves opportunity for students to reconcile prior knowledge with new information acquired during discussion, allows students to predict meanings and generate informed guesses, and encourages students to support their predictions and guesses by personal experience and accounts.

PREREADING INSTRUCTION: DEVELOPING A FUNCTIONAL SYSTEM FOR LEARNING NEW WORDS

When I was a junior in high school, one of my teachers said to our class, "Good readers read with the dictionary by their sides. When they come to a word they do not know, they look it up." This statement confused me and made me feel more than a little guilty. I knew I was a good reader, but I also knew that I rarely did what she said good readers do. "Looking it up" was bothersome and disruptive; it interrupted the flow of text and interfered with my reading. So, I just got the general meaning from context and went right on; sometimes, I'd stop and work on a word, if I felt like I needed to; on *very rare* occasions, I'd check a reference if it was handy; sometimes, I'd just skip the word and go on reading. What I didn't know then (but do today) is that I had a very effective, functional system for learning new words.

For mature readers, the most efficient approach for constructing meaning of new words is the four-step interactive process Gray (1946) labeled CSSD (this was briefly discussed in Chapter 3): Step One, arriving at a gist of the meaning through *context*; Step Two, examining the *structure* of the word (prefixes, suffixes, roots, etc.) and combining that information with context; Step Three, pronouncing a word (identifying its *sound*); and Step Four, checking an outside *reference* by looking the word up or asking someone. (Gray limited this to Dictionary. I have expanded it to include any reference resource; I therefore refer to it as "CSSR.")

This system is functional and efficient because it uses steps in a sequence of descending probability of success. It begins with context, which has the highest probability of payoff, and moves through structural analysis to phonic analysis, which has the lowest; it leaves the most disruptive, but generally surest activity (looking it up), for last. It is, in fact, a system commonly used by good readers almost unconsciously and deserves mention in your classroom, if for no other reason than to encourage its continued use. I can't describe how good it felt when I discovered that what I was doing was right instead of wrong; I've seen the faces of high-achieving students and teachers alike when I describe the system to them. Their eyes reflect the same pleasure and relief I felt.

For less-able readers and writers, it is even more important that we teach a functional system to provide access to high-payoff strategies and to release them from the laborious, often futile, sound-it-out approach they typically use for every word they do not know. Sounding-it-out is time-consuming and difficult; further, in the world of middle school and secondary content reading, it is often impossible and/or nonproductive (try, for example to "sound out" *parabola*, *stare decisis*, *inveigle* [from the Figure 4.1 Word List], *per se*). Even when less-able readers use high-payoff sources of information (context, for example) they seem to do so nonsystematically and thus ineffectively (Stanovich, 1991); that is, either they don't know what to do with the information they get from context or where to go if context does not assist them in constructing meaning. For students learning English as a second language, gaining access to this system gives them more information about how English works and gives them one more way to manipulate and use the language effectively. Teaching the system requires that we (1) reveal the system to students, (2) provide instruction and practice using the parts of the system, and (3) demonstrate how to put the system together.

REVEALING THE SYSTEM

The easiest, most direct way to reveal the Context, Structure, Sound, Reference approach is simply to tell students about it. You may wish to use a schematic to illustrate and remind students of CSSR such as the one in Figure 4.4 developed by Peter Santucci in MaryEllen Vogt's content area reading class. Begin instruction by saying, "When you come to a word you do not know, here's what to do":

1.   Read to the end of the sentence. Can you guess the meaning? Are there any clues in the surrounding sentences or paragraphs that help you? Now do you have a pretty good idea of the meaning? Does it make sense? If so, keep right on reading.

If not,

2.   Look at the parts of the word. Are there prefixes or roots that you know? Do the suffixes or inflections (plurals, past tense, etc.) help you? Combine this information with context information to arrive at a meaning. Does it make sense? If so, go right on reading.

FIGURE 4.4   *CSSR: What to Do When You Come to a Word You Don't Know*

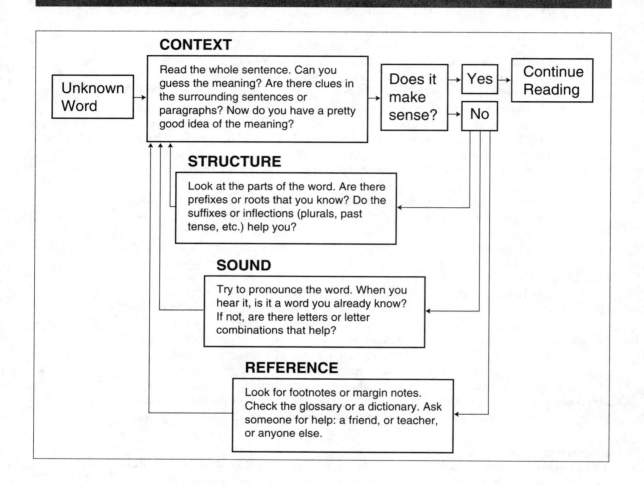

If not,

3. Try to pronounce the word. When you hear it, does it sound like a word you already know? If not, are there letters or letter combinations that help (e.g., the 'ct' in 'tract' as opposed to the 'ck' in 'track')? Combine this information with information from context. Does it make sense? If so, go right on reading.

If not,

4. Look for footnotes or margin notes. Check the glossary or a dictionary. Ask someone for help: a friend, or me, or anyone else. Combine this information with information from context. Does it make sense?

Notice the refrain of "Does it make sense?" in this procedure. This reminder is deliberate and highly critical to the process of constructing meaning for new words.

"Making sense" is what reading is all about, and the most proficient word-pronouncers are powerless if they do not achieve some modicum of meaning. It is particularly important to stress "making sense" with less-able readers because they often consider reading to be nothing more than correct pronunciation of words. Whether they use context information or enter the system by trying to sound out the word, if the attempt is unsuccessful, or if pronunciation does not reveal meaning, they have no place to go. So, they go on "reading" sentences, paragraphs, and whole chapters for which they have constructed little, if any, meaning. They are, in effect, unaware that the system has broken down. The focus on making sense—on constructing meaning—serves as a metacognitive alarm that alerts students when something has gone wrong; choices within the CSSR sequence provide functional alternatives that allow minimal disruption and high probability of recovery when something does.

Notice also the recursive nature of the CSSR procedure. While there is a generally sequential movement from context through reference, in actuality, the movement is circular and cumulative. On entering the system, the reader looks in surrounding text for meaning; then the reader checks structure and combines structural clues with any contextual information obtained earlier or that became available in light of the structural information; then the reader goes on to sound clues, adding this information to structural and contextual knowledge, and so forth, until enough sense is made to continue reading. Proficiency with the system increases to the extent that students (1) use previously obtained information at each new point in the sequence and (2) exit the system *as soon as useful meaning is constructed.* The parts of the system are not clearly separate and distinct; they blend together as information from one part influences how other types of information are used and reader decisions for exiting the system are made.

In order for students to acquire proficiency using the parts of the CSSR system, they need instruction and practice *in content areas*. All of the recommendations given below assume this condition: that activities will be developed from texts used in the class so that students will be learning the language of the discipline as they are learning a functional system for acquiring new vocabulary in that discipline. Keep in mind also that the activities recommended here are *not* intended to be full-blown, class-long lessons; rather, they are lesson *parts*, which occur during the class period in the course of teaching content. It is strange but true that occasionally it takes longer for me to tell you about these instructional strategies and activities than it will take you to teach them.

USING THE PARTS OF THE SYSTEM: CONTEXT

Context is an important source of information for learning new content words. By context, we mean the semantic and syntactic information contained in the words, sentences, and paragraphs of text. Jenkins et al. (1989) conclude from the results of a number of studies that ". . . students can learn word meanings from context, but the probability that they actually will learn a word meaning from context is low" (pp. 218–219). Their study suggests further, however, that instruction in how to use context increases students' ability to do so effectively. The purpose of such instruction is to make students aware of contextual information—the *context clues*—and to demonstrate how such information may be used to determine the meaning of an unknown word. Text conventions and types of context clues vary from subject area to subject area; therefore, a general "knowledge of context clues" does not transfer automatically from one text to another. Students need instruction and practice in using context that is specific to text in each subject area.

One versatile and effective way to do this is through the use of the Cloze teaching technique (Jongsma, 1971). Cloze is a teaching activity based on the Gestalt notion of "closure": the mind's ability to complete incomplete stimuli (Taylor, 1953). A Cloze activity consists of a reproduced passage from text (the class textbook or other subject text) in which certain words are deleted and replaced with a blank line. The purpose of the task is for students to use information in the passage (context clues) to replace the deleted words.

Interactive Cloze   Meeks and Morgan (1978) describe the Interactive Cloze activity, which is particularly good for subject area instruction. It begins with the preparation of a Cloze passage using a text students have not previously read. (This may be any reading material you're using or it may be taken directly from the class text. I find that students generally do not read ahead in their regular textbooks.) The passage should be rather short, and the deletions should not exceed 10 to 15 words; a good portion of the first and last sentences of the passage should be left intact. When using Cloze as a teaching technique, there is no set rule for deciding which words to delete; a good rule of thumb is to delete words/terms that would appear to stimulate lots of discussion about possible replacements. Figure 4.5 shows a science passage prepared for Interactive Cloze (Miller & Levine, 1995, p. 516).

Students are allowed to work singly or in pairs to replace the deleted words. They then meet in groups of four or five to compare their responses and to arrive at group consensus on the best replacement for each deletion. Final choices can be selected

FIGURE 4.5   *Interactive Cloze Passage: Science*

PLANT GROWTH AND DEVELOPMENT

You have probably heard the old saying: "Mighty oaks from tiny acorns grow." But have you ever thought about the amazing _____ that take place during the long life of such a _____? A tiny embryo oak plant sits _____ an acorn for months, maybe even years. Then one spring, it sprouts. Its roots grow deep into the soil in search of water and _____. Its leaves reach toward the sun—toward the light _____ that powers the life of the plant. In autumn, growth _____. The oak's leaves turn color and fall to the ground. The entire plant undergoes the _____ _____ to survive the approaching cold winter weather.

   Many years later the tree _____. Suddenly it produces hundreds, perhaps even thousands, of flowers. Some of the flowers produce _____ that mature into acorns. When the acorns ripen, they fall to the ground, where they may be buried or eaten by squirrels. With luck, the _____ of growth begins again.

from individual responses or from suggestions made during the course of small-group discussion. After all groups have finished, group answers are compared in whole-class discussion, along with the reasons for each choice, and class agreement for replacements is reached. Following this, the original intact passage is read to determine how close class replacement came to it; students are then given an opportunity to decide which they like best—their own replacements or the original. The entire procedure should take no longer than 8 to 10 minutes.

From this simple instructional strategy, an extraordinary amount of instruction and practice in using context occurs. Individual replacement choices are made on the basis of meaning each student constructs for the passage, including his or her prior knowledge base and experience with the topic. Reasons for replacement choices are then shared, debated, and challenged in small-group discussion. It should be emphasized that much of the learning occurs during these small-group discussions, so it is unnecessary to go over every explanation in whole group. In all probability, discussion there will center around three or four key words or issues, ranging from consideration of "best fit," to topic knowledge, to synonym distinctions, and beyond.

To understand the type and kind of information exchanged during such a lesson, use the passage in Figure 4.5 to do an Interactive Cloze with a group of friends or classmates. During the small-group stage, you may wish to ask one member to observe and take notes for your analysis of the process at its completion. (The intact passage follows the DEJ at the end of the chapter.)

Once students become experienced with this technique, any number of variations and adaptations may be used. Passages may be longer or the number of deletions increased. Interactive Cloze may be used for direct prereading instruction by deleting target words, rather than presenting and discussing them, and allowing students to discover the words as they discuss constructed meaning of the passage. Alternatively, the element of "deletion systems" may be introduced.

Yossarian's Game   Yossarian's Game is for students who have become competent at Interactive Cloze (I named this activity after the main character in *Catch 22* [Heller, 1955] who worked as a censor during wartime and used his own "systems" for censoring mail; his ultimate system was born the day he deleted everything except *a, an,* and *the*). The class is divided into groups, and each group is given a different intact passage. (*Remember:* These are passages from the classroom text or other content-focused material—students will be learning and discussing content as they consider and manipulate words.) Each group is to decide on its own system for deleting words and prepare the passage accordingly. I strongly advise some ground rules here. For example, you may require that the first and last sentences remain intact, or you may limit the number of deletions that may be made. The deleted passages are duplicated and distributed to the other groups. Groups then work together to complete the passages prepared by the other groups and to figure out the deletion criteria. Group decisions are shared with the whole class and compared to original-group criteria; general discussion follows.

Yossarian's Game is particularly well suited for use with computers and word processing software. You should prepare the intact passages on a computer, if possible, for ease of preparation of deleted passages; it's even better if students have computer access and can prepare deleted passages themselves.

The value of Yossarian's Game is that, in their efforts to make solving the passage difficult, students will first have to explore a variety of deletions systems to find one that will not be immediately apparent to others. To do this requires *lots* of brainstorming and exchange of ideas and information. Students may key on anything from initial letters (words beginning with "g"), to word counts (every eighth word), to content (words associated with water), to any combination of the above (every third word beginning with "t"; every second word referring to government services, etc.). The possibilities are endless. What is important is that students use substantial word, text, and content knowledge to develop their deletion criterion. In addition, once the system is selected, students analyze and evaluate undeleted parts of the passage to determine how difficult the solution will be for the rest of the class. In doing this, they will decide what information is given by the intact part to suggest replacement possibilities for the naive reader, dredging every clue they can from the context provided—including much that comes from their knowledge of the content and topic itself. That summarizes the *point* of these activities: Students are involved in acquiring content reading skills *as they learn content.*

Using the Parts of the System: Structure

Structural features of words that provide information for analysis are *roots, affixes* (prefixes and suffixes), *inflections* (plurals, past tense endings, possessives, etc.), and *compounds.* Of these, roots, prefixes, and compounds generally yield the most information directly tied to meaning. Suffixes and inflections do carry meaning (e.g., *i-s-t* meaning "one who"; *s, e-s* denoting plural; *e-d,* past tense), but it is general rather than specific. For example, in the word *geologists,* knowledge that *i-s-t* means "one who" and *s* indicates "more than one" is relatively useless unless we understand that *g-e-o* means "of or having to do with the earth," and that *o-l-o-g-y* is a combining form meaning "the science or study of." That is not to say that suffixes and inflections are unimportant to teach, but only that much of the instruction in structural analysis should probably concentrate on roots, prefixes, and compound words.

One approach for teaching structural analysis is to identify a structural element contained in a critical word of the reading assignment or chapter. For example, in a social studies chapter dealing with international trade, the element *p-o-r-t* in the words *import* and *export* might be chosen. Begin instruction by writing a known word containing that element on the board—*portable* or *transportation,* for example—underlining the targeted element (<u>port</u>able). Ask students to determine the meaning of the root *p-o-r-t* based upon what they know about the word *portable.* Once the meaning of "to carry" has been established, ask students to name other words with the *p-o-r-t* root and to carry meaning.

As words are generated, list them on the board, explore and discuss meanings, and give specific attention to the way in which each word is *similar to* and *different from* the original word *portable.* After a few words are discussed, allow students to work in pairs or groups to list as many words as they can with the element *p-o-r-t.* (Have dictionaries handy to settle disputes.) Group words are presented to class with appropriate discussion. Then, if they have not already been mentioned, the vocabulary words from the reading, *import* and *export*, are introduced in context by having students locate them in the textbook. Discussion now centers on the specific meaning of these words and their relationship to the content of the lesson at hand. If other important words in the chapter contain *p-o-r-t*, these should likewise be located and discussed.

Several significant features are part of this instructional approach. First, as emphasized in Chapters 2 and 3, this approach uses a learning pattern that moves from what students already know to what is to be learned. We began with a known word and concept, allowed students to explore and verify that knowledge, and then applied that information to a new situation.

Second, and perhaps even more important, we gave students the *means for making the transfer*. We walked them through the process of expanding their knowledge base and articulated the process to them. With continued instruction and practice, the process itself will become internalized and available to students in any number of situations.

Third, we increased student knowledge of words and word structure in an exponential, rather than additive, way. We could have effectively added to their knowledge by direct teaching of the words *import* and *export*; instead, we taught the generic *p-o-r-t*, thus making many new associated words available to students. In addition, this approach has a way of spiraling out in other directions as well. In the course of discussing the word *portable*, the suffix *a-b-l-e*, meaning "capable of being", is also defined. The same thing happens with the words *transportation*, *deportment*, *porter*, *important*, and, finally, *import* and *export*, so that what we really teach is a constellation of structural elements and forms with emphasis on a particular one.

Fourth, and finally, we used the students' own text and immediate assignment in a subject area as the medium for teaching a functional skill. Just as importantly, we demonstrated to students the value of this knowledge for learning the content of that subject area. Most disciplines contain at least some critical language that contains structural elements worth learning: equals, equation, equivalent; judge, judicial, prejudice, adjudicate; isobars, isostasy, isotherms, isotopes; dermis, dermatology, epiderm; *piano*, *pianissimo*, *forte*, *fortissimo*. It's worth some time to show students how to make connections between such words when they occur as part of the content being studied.

USING THE PARTS OF THE SYSTEM: SOUND

For all intents and purposes, the sound part of the CSSR is outside the purview of middle and secondary classrooms for at least two important reasons. First, most secondary teachers have little knowledge or training in "phonics" or pronunciation rules, and very few have any interest in gaining such. Rightfully so: The days of attempting to teach adolescents to "Crack the Code" thankfully are long past. So it is unreasonable to expect that middle school and secondary teachers are equipped to, or *should*, teach pronunciation rules and the like in their classrooms. Contrary to media assertions, all students have been taught "phonics rules"; in fact, we have evidence to suggest that the least-accomplished students have been taught the *most* phonics and other basic skills (Allington, 1978; Eder, 1986; Cazden, 1985; Collins, 1986). What must be understood, however, is that these rules were initially taught at a time when they were most useful, when the pool of new words encountered in text was relatively small and generally well within the students' listening and speaking vocabularies.

Second, beginning at about fourth grade and increasing rapidly, students read a wide variety of texts, both for study and pleasure, which include an extraordinary range of new and difficult words. Not only do many of these words not conform to the pronunciation rules (remember *parabola*, *stare decisis* and *per se*; consider *schedule*, *placebo*, and *lagniappe*), but even when they do, they frequently are so far removed from student experience and knowledge that pronunciation alone does not bring meaning (try, for example, "pixel," "egregious," "chancre," or define "contact sheet conference" taken from a senior-high photography-class course syllabus). The point here is that for middle and secondary students, phonic analysis has low utility, and it is therefore inefficient to continue spending large amounts of time teaching or reteaching phonics rules (Nelson-Herber, 1986). Rather, the goal should be to guide students as they apply and extend what they already know and place pronunciation rules appropriately within the functional system so that they are useful to students.

USING THE PARTS OF THE SYSTEM: REFERENCE

Learning to use reference sources—whether they are part of the class text, housed in a dictionary or the reference section of the library, on a CD-ROM, or another person— is of great importance as students move toward independence in reading, writing, and learning. This is particularly true for middle and secondary students who encounter new, and often highly abstract, concepts in their daily reading. To be sure, there are so-called basic skills associated with using reference sources: knowledge and application of diacritical markings; use of indices and tables of contents; first-, second-, third-, and fourth-letter alphabetizing; use of head words; and selection of contextually appropriate definitions, to name a few. Like phonics, these skills have been taught in elementary school; middle school and secondary teachers are responsible for demonstrating how such skills are applied to text and other materials used in their classes.

Much can be done toward this end by filling your classroom with all sorts of reference materials, thus signifying that you consider these books, objects, and software to be important and worthwhile for your own and students' use. Collecting reference materials is most inexpensively done by scavenging. Check the book-storage room for outdated sets of dictionaries and encyclopedias (in fact, make it a point to ask where the old books are stored in your school or district, and do a reconnaissance trip; you'll find all sorts of good stuff in there); respond immediately to librarians' offers to give away worn copies of materials (with the availability of interactive, three-dimensional illustrated encyclopedias on CD-ROM, there should be more and more relatively new encyclopedia sets floating around); haunt used bookstores and hurt-book sales; and, by all means, use the "squeaking wheel" approach. Take every opportunity to tell anyone who controls book requisitions just exactly what you want—in writing. Even when funds are tight, end-of-year surpluses do occur; money that must be spent immediately most often goes to the teacher whose written book order, complete with publisher names and ISBN numbers, is on the principal's desk at the end of the fiscal year. (Trust me on this one; it doesn't work every time, but it does work sometimes—it did for me.)

Effective instruction and practice in using reference sources occur as opportunities arise in the classroom to reinforce, extend, and apply what students already know about using reference skills. First, tell students about the availability of reference information in their textbooks and other materials: footnotes, margin notes, glossaries, and so forth. Take every opportunity to direct their attention to these reference sources, and encourage use of the sources. Second, become a model of good reference-using behavior by allowing students to watch as you demonstrate how accomplished learners get information about what they need to know. Critical to this is that you *think out loud* as you demonstrate so that students have access to the process. Consider the following scene:

The word *regimen* is encountered in a health class discussion of a newspaper editorial about new discoveries regarding fatty acids in margarine. The teacher might say, "Hmm. It says here 'Spartan regimen'—I'm not sure I know exactly what 'regimen' means. I think it has to do with a routine or daily schedule. Does anyone know? [a few tentative guesses] Let's check." Opening the dictionary (Garulnik, 1978), the teacher uses headwords to locate "regimen," continuing to think aloud. " 'Rainstorm,' [turning pages] 'rebellion,' 'red wing,' 'refloat,' 'refuse' [moves finger down page] 'regent,' 'reggae,' 'regime,' here it is, 'regimen'. It's pronounced *REJ a men* [writing the pronunciation on the board] and has two definitions: '1. the act of governing; government; rule; a particular system of government. 2. a regulated system of diet, exercise, etc. for therapy or the maintenance or improvement of health.' Okay, the sentence we read was, 'Those cholesterol-counters among us who dutifully adhere to a Spartan regimen in pursuit of that ever-glimmering Holy Grail—the clean and vibrant artery—have been dealt yet another underhanded blow (*San Francisco Chronicle*, August 17, 1990).' So, it's more than just a routine or schedule, it's actually directly related to diet and health—'regulated system of diet for maintenance or improved health.' I wonder why the editor considered this a 'Spartan' regimen? . . . What do you suppose they're going to do to margarine next?

The scene ends. Notice what happened. The students saw an active, inquisitive mind at work and watched as a whole set of skills were integrated in the search for understanding through the use of headwords, entry words, diacritical markings, and applying definition to context. Notice also the *positive* approach to "not knowing," rather than its negative counterpart. The teacher acknowledged that she didn't know the precise meaning of the word and offered some possibilities ("schedule" or "routine"), read the two dictionary definitions, and went back to sentence context to adjust meaning. The end result is a much more refined understanding of the word and the sentence, and nobody appeared dumb. In fact, somebody appeared very bright indeed.

Two postscripts are in order. First, consider the possibilities of the class discussion that might follow the teacher's heuristic questions, "I wonder why the editor considered this a 'Spartan' regimen?" and, "What do you suppose they'll do to margarine next?" Second, in the sentence immediately following the one we just discussed, the word *pallid* appears. It would seem entirely reasonable for a teacher now to direct students as they practice using the model (just presented) of how-to-get-the-meaning-of-a-word-when-all-other-attempts-fail. Here, as with the other parts of the CSSR system, instruction and practice in a functional skill are paired with meaningful discussion of content. Each reinforces the other, and not-knowing becomes a springboard for learning rather than a source of embarrassment. This very same sequence of events could occur to model effective use of a textbook glossary, a thesaurus (hard copy or computer-based), page footnotes or other written and graphic text aids, and any or all informational computer software.

PUTTING THE PARTS TOGETHER

Earlier, I stated that the easiest, most direct way to let students know about the CSSR system was simply to tell them about it and demonstrate it. The same principle applies to teaching them how to put the parts together. Tell students how to use the system, and give them practice doing it. When new words are introduced in context, ask students, "Can we tell from context what this word means? Does it make sense?" If not, ask, "Where do we look now?" and so on, until meaning is developed.

It is important to remember that the main purpose of the system is to be functionally efficient; that is, it has to work, and it has to work in the least possible time. Therefore, a major goal of instruction should be to teach students to exit the system *as soon as meaning is achieved.* This means you must not continue through predetermined lessons if students short-circuit your plans. You may have *planned* to use "pallid" as a means for teaching and practicing reference skills, but during discussion someone figured it out by combining previous experience and context. If this happens, stop the lesson, compliment the students on their skill, and go on to whatever is next. In this case, meeting the immediate goal of teaching reference skills is counterproductive to the overall goal of providing a functional system for learning new content vocabulary words—the students have done exactly what you wanted them to do. It's now up to you to be perceptive and flexible enough to reward their accomplishment.

How to do . . . .

PREREADING CONTENT VOCABULARY DEVELOPMENT

Let me reiterate: Prereading content vocabulary instruction should be short, sweet, and to the point. It should focus on a few key words that have been carefully preselected by the teacher and should use actual content text as the basis for instruction. Whenever possible, prereading vocabulary instruction should combine teaching words, teaching content, and teaching a functional system for learning unknown words. Use the following guidelines to develop prereading content vocabulary lessons:

1. Preview the material to be read and select five or six words to be taught.

2. Determine the type of instruction most appropriate for these words: (a) Direct Instruction—telling, linking to known concepts, or conducting elaborated definition and discussion; (b) Instruction About or Within the CSSR System—using the system or using one or more parts of the system.

3. Prepare for instruction: e.g., duplicate Cloze passage, write sentences on the board, determine stimulus word(s) for semantic mapping or structural analysis, establish groups, etc.

4. Identify link from vocabulary discussion to the reading and content topic.

Content Vocabulary Instruction: Long-Term Acquisition and Development

Content vocabulary instruction directed toward long-term acquisition of words may be seen as both an extension of prereading vocabulary study and an entity in and of itself. It extends prereading instruction because many of the words presented prior to reading are chosen for further discussion and study after reading; it may be used, however, whether or not prereading instruction was provided. (It also does not necessarily need to be linked with reading. It may follow any type of instruction: lecture, discussion, media presentations, writing, etc.)

POSTREADING INSTRUCTION: THE VOCABULARY SELF-COLLECTION STRATEGY (VSS)

The Vocabulary Self-Collection Strategy (VSS) (Haggard, 1982, 1985, 1986a, 1986b; Ruddell, 1992) is an instructional strategy intended to foster long-term acquisition and development of the vocabulary of academic disciplines. It has as its primary goal incorporation of new content words into students' working vocabularies (Haggard, 1982). VSS focuses on content words that students need to know, words that are important to them and for which they have expressed interest and curiosity; further, VSS gives students the skills necessary for continued, independent content vocabulary growth by simulating natural word-learning processes. I developed VSS some years ago (when my surname was Haggard) and used it in my own classrooms with students ranging from seventh grade, to high school sophomores and juniors, to college freshmen, to first-year pharmacy students in graduate school. I know firsthand how powerful it can be and how easy it is to do.

Using VSS
The Vocabulary Self-Collection Strategy (VSS) begins following reading and discussion of text (or any learning event) and is initiated by the teacher asking students to nominate one word or term that they would like to learn or to know more about and that they think should appear on a class vocabulary list. The teacher also nominates one word. Students are encouraged to find words/terms that are important to the topic at hand and are required to tell:

1. *Where they found the word.* (Read the sentence if in text or recall the context if from discussion or other learning event.)

2. *What they think the word means in this context.*
3. *Why they think the class should learn it* (e.g., identify the word's importance to the content topic).

In most classrooms, this part of VSS is most efficiently done with students in nominating teams of two to five people, depending on the number of words the teacher wishes to have in the nominated pool. (A good rule of thumb is 8 to 10 words, with a target of 5 to 6 words for the final class list.) Don't forget that the teacher nominates one of the original pool words as well. Generally, 3 to 5 minutes is sufficient time for groups to re-examine text and find words, prepare their definitions from text, and develop a rationale for learning each word; it is often useful to rush students a bit, keeping them on task and leaving little time for extraneous discussion and then extending the time if it is really needed. The teacher also is wise to predetermine his or her selection (and, in fact, have two or three on deck in the event of duplication with student choices) in order to be free to monitor group functioning and answer any questions that might arise.

As soon as groups are ready, a spokesperson from each group presents a nominated word, tells where it was found, what the group believes it means, and why it was chosen. The teacher writes the words on the board and leads discussion to define each, first from context as nominators tell what they think their word means, and then, if needed, from any references available in the room. Discussion should include contributions from other class members as well, so that definitions are extended and personalized.

The focus is always on the meaning of the word in the specific context of the immediate content topic or text; however, conversation is likely to range across other meanings or contexts that are part of students' prior knowledge and experience. These other meanings serve as useful comparisons and contrasts to the topic-specific meaning under discussion. After all words/terms have been nominated, a final class list is established by eliminating duplicates, any words or terms the class feels it already knows, and any that do not appear to be appropriate. (At this time, the teacher spot-checks to see if any content words introduced prior to the reading appear, or should appear, on the final class list.)

During this process, words chosen for the class list are circled (or identified in some way), and eliminated words simply left alone so that nothing is erased from the board. Chosen words are then redefined and written with definitions in vocabulary journals or any ongoing unit or lesson documents (e.g., entered in appropriate places on study maps [Haggard, 1985]). Words not chosen for class study may be recorded by students who wish to include them on their own personal vocabulary lists.

A SAMPLE VSS LESSON

The partial transcript below will give you a sense of what happens in VSS lessons, although it's difficult to capture the energy and spontaneity of the discussion. This lesson followed the DR–TA and mapping for "The Splendid Outcast" (Markham, 1987) presented in Chapter 3.

LESSON PLAN   *VSS Lesson*

Students in groups of three to five

T: I want you to find two words or terms that you think should be on our vocabulary list for this story—two words or terms that you think we should know, or study, or know more about. Listen carefully: I want you, as a group, to locate the words and be prepared to tell where the words are in the story, what you as a group think those words mean, and why you as a group think we should learn them. Got it? You have about 4 minutes.

Overheard as groups discuss:

Here are two that I had questions about . . .

Go ahead, influence me.

Weren't there a couple words you wanted to know? (Laughter.)

Second paragraph . . . okay, that's one, there's another one here . . . (Silence as students search text.)

Yeah, that's a good one.

Something interesting . . .

I know that there's one in here.

Where did you find one?

That's a good word. I missed it; I wonder what it means?

There on page 39 . . .

Of course, we have to tell why we're choosing them—the importance to the story . . .

Okay, we know that encomiums is, uh, it says here, "He listened to the encomiums" so you can tell it's a noun.

Yeah, okay, do you suppose that's a particular speech pattern . . . [do you] suppose it's a term that auctioneers use?

It just has a gorgeous sound. It does. That's a good reason.

That doesn't really tell *why* we're going to use that word.

Where was "Lilliputian"? Do you remember?

T: Ready, got your words?

(Continued discussion.)

T: Table 1, have you got your words? What about you, Table 2? Table 3, got your words? Okay, quickly.

(Waits.)

T: Okay, ready? Table 4?

(In background, "Who used "Lilliputians"? Where was "Lilliputian" used?" Continued discussion in groups.)

T: Who'd like to nominate a word? Okay, we're ready. (Murmurs continue.)

S1:   Encomiums.

T: (Writing word on board.) All right. Is that e-n?

S1:   e-n-c-o-m-i-u-m-s

(Continued murmurs and discussion in groups.)

T: Where did you find "encomiums"? Okay, everybody, stay with us . . . Read the sentence for us.

S1:   "He stared down upon the arena as each horse was led into it, and he listened to the dignified encomiums of the auctioneer with the humble attention of a parishioner at mass (Markham, 1987, p. 36)."

T: What do you think "encomiums" means?

S1:   Something as simple as "words" or "sayings."

T: Okay, it could be that. Anything else?

S2:   We thought it was peculiar to the auctioneer—language that an auctioneer uses.

S3:   Flattery, praises, related to money.

T: Descriptions that he was giving of the horses. . . .Why did you choose this one, group?

S1:   Because we didn't know what it meant.

(Much laughter.)

T: That's as good a reason as any to choose one. Okay, another one.

- -

S1:   "Lilliputian."

T: "Lilliputian." Did they have that capitalized?

S1:   Yes. Page 46.

T: (Writing on board.) L-i-l-l?

S1:   Yes. i-p-u-t-i-a-n.

T: Lilliputian, which means?

S1:   Very, very small. (In a very, very small voice.)

T: Very small. Why did you choose "Lilliputian"?

S1:   Do we have to be honest? (Laughter.)

T: Yes! (Laughs.)

S1:   Partially, because you just like to hear yourself say it. It's such a colorful word.

T: *Perfect* reason to learn a word—that it sounds wonderful, "Lilliputian."

- -

T: Table 1: Did you guys have one?

S1:   Those two. (Laughter.)

T: Are there any others that we haven't given?

S1:   Oh yeah, we wanted to know what "guineas" were for sure.

T: All right, spell "guineas."

S1:   g-u-i-n-e-a-s.

T: (Writing word on board.) Okay, we know it's part of the monetary system, we don't know what part of the monetary system, but was a part, okay? So your purpose here, your reason for choosing it is . . . you by gosh want to know what it is. Fine.

I have a word. It's "votary." (Writing word on board.) Page 36, "They were the cultists, he the votary, and there were, in fact, about his grey eyes and his slender lips, the deep, tense lines so often etched in the faces of zealots and of lonely men." I think "votary" must be connected to, or synonymous with, zealotry. I'm not sure of the exact meaning, but I chose it because I don't think I've ever heard it before. Okay, who has got another one? Any others?

- -

T: Everybody like these words? ("Um hmms" around.)

T: Go back to your map, and for right now—we'll do other things with them later—enter the words on your map in an appropriate place, and put an asterisk by them so that you remember they are our vocabulary words. You may already have them on your map. If you don't, find a place to enter the words on your map. (Waits.) If you can't find a place that feels good for each word, then simply list those words that you can't put on the map at the top, or bottom, or someplace on that piece of paper.

S1:   (Interrupting work silence.) I wonder if guineas and pounds are interchangeable. She said she had 500 pounds, but she started bidding in guineas.

T: (Trying to bring lesson to close.) Right.

S2:   Yeah, it does later, I remember, uh, you know, reading later, it said 500 pounds. So they are the same.

T: You think they're the same?

S2:   I think so. (General conversation and agreement.)

T: I don't think so.

S1:   Well, then why would she start bidding in guineas? I mean she'd gotten . . .

T: Well, the English, the old British system. See, we're so used to a decimal system: 10 pennies make a dime; 10 dimes make a dollar. It was not based on a decimal system back then, and so a guinea could be any given part of a pound.

S1:   It must be *close*, though, because she said she'd bid 450, hoping he wouldn't know there was so little to follow. So she knew she didn't have much left of her 500 pounds.

T: Right. Well, we'll find out. (Trying *again* to bring lesson to a close.)

S3:   Maybe pounds is a more formal way of referring to money. And I could see the "cultists" using pounds and not reverting to guineas, whereas people who are more blue collar . . .

T: Ah. So it'd be equivalent to saying, uh, a "quarter" versus "two-bits."

S3:   Right.

T: All right, that may be it. Well, we'll find out. Has everybody got your words on your map?

This lesson is typical of a VSS discussion. Notice the diversity of words chosen—"encomiums," "Lilliputian," "guinea," and "votary"—and the equally diverse reasons for choosing them—new words, partially known words, old words, interesting-sounding words. But the most important aspect of this lesson—and what makes it typical of a VSS lesson—is the intensity with which students participated. They had to be *pulled* into whole-class discussion to share choices because they did not want to stop their in-progress small-group discussions. And these groups were on task! Then, they were not about to turn loose of the discussion of "guineas"; recall that this discussion began during the initial story reading. Each time the teacher attempted to close the VSS lesson, beginning with her directions for students to enter the words on their maps, students brought the subject up again and simply conducted their own discussion. The teacher was constrained to yield the floor and allow time for the discussion to take place. This is not typical of classroom vocabulary lessons; it is, however, not in the least unusual for VSS discussion.

ACTIVITIES FOR LONG-TERM CONTENT VOCABULARY LEARNING

VSS is not complete without follow-up activities to reinforce initial content word learning. After the selection process, it is necessary for the teacher to design activities for extended study and practice so that students will attend to, use, and manipulate words sufficiently to incorporate them into working vocabularies. It must be empha-sized that *without planned opportunity for students to use new content vocabulary, it is un-likely that many students will be very successful learning the words, and, in fact, learning the content itself.*

Activities intended to promote content vocabulary acquisition and development must be adapted to and integrated with content instruction, if for no other reason than efficient use of time, but more importantly, because of the vital role language plays in the construction of content knowledge. Keep in mind that only the teacher needs to know what part of a follow-up lesson is directed toward "vocabulary" and what part is focused on content.

PRINCIPLES FOR DESIGNING VSS LESSON ACTIVITIES

A wide variety of activities may be used to assist students in the process of integrating new content words into their working vocabularies; ideas for vocabulary activities are available in any number of texts, teacher guides, and methods books. It is important, however, that these activities contain the properties we have already discussed—integration, repetition, meaningful use, and connectedness—because these properties are critical to the process of developing in-depth understanding and integrating new content words and concepts into one's prior knowledge base. Further, the assumption here is that VSS activities, just as prereading vocabulary study, will extend and reinforce content learning itself. The following principles (Haggard, 1986a; 1986b; Ruddell, 1992) are important standards for designing and adapting activities for use in VSS lessons:

1. *Activities should allow students to use content words in a meaningful way.* Meaningful use of words is a form of repetition and connectedness. It is important that, whatever activities teachers assign following identification of new words, these assignments must be a form of repetition that makes sense to students and genuinely involves them in the learning event. Repetition for repetition's sake (writing words or sentences over and over) or rote word practice (writing formulaic sentences or filling in blanks mindlessly) are of little value here; further, implausible use is just as valueless (writing sentences using high-flown words inappropriately; e.g., "I'd like to continue the redundance of my 'problem' and further segregate the crux of the issue."). Meaningful use of newly acquired content vocabulary requires that students write or speak reasonably, exploring new ideas and language, making connections, and reinforcing what they have just learned.

2. *Activities should allow students opportunities to associate new content words and concepts with their own experience.* As in so many areas of learning, and as schema theory suggests, making connections between what students already know and what they are to learn is one of the single most powerful learning tools available to teachers. Activities that reflect this principle are usually generative—students speaking or writing from their own experience—and often reveal students' logic and thinking as well as their prior knowledge base. Because they are generative, they generally require time for students to interact with one another, to explore ideas in writing, and to refine and extend meaning.

3. *Activities should develop associations with other content words.* Related somewhat to the previous principle, this one reminds us to provide activities that connect explicitly new content words with other, related, words and terms. This is important for all students learning the language of a content discipline and is particularly necessary for ESL students who are learning English, content, and the language of the content concurrently. Learning associated words thus boosts learning the language associated with literary elements (plot, theme, characterization, irony, satire), or key elements of the U.S. Constitution (legislative, judicial, executive branches of government; individual versus state and federal rights), or the language of baseball (ERA, ground-rule double, blooper, RBI, 6 to 4 to 3). Important here also are associations and distinctions made for multiple-meaning words both within and across disciplines (oil-base paint, third base, base verses acid, base numbers, base word, the base of a triangle, etc.). These associations and distinctions are usually developed through activities that invite comparison and contrast and allow students to articulate their thinking and line of reasoning.

4. *Activities should encourage higher-order thinking.* Higher-order thinking requires "deep processing," in which students make more cognitive connections between new and known information or spend more mental effort to learn something than they would if information were processed more shallowly (Stahl, 1986). Higher-order thinking, by definition, goes beyond the surface, the quick response, the easily accomplished. Activities that promote higher-order thinking therefore are extended and often are, themselves, extensions and elaborations of work that has gone before.

5. *Activities should lead students to many different resources.* One of the most pervasive preadolescent and adolescent tendencies in response to assigned questions is to look no further than the first answer they get, especially if that answer is in the one resource they typically use for getting answers. (This tendency does not necessarily hold when the question is, "May I use the car tonight?" and the first answer is, "No.") In the area of vocabulary study, a text glossary or class dictionary is the usual single resource. Rarely do students use the many other resources for vocabulary information available to them, including text notes and marginalia, computer software, encyclopedias, journals and magazines, on-line resources, newspapers, friends, parents, neighbors, experts, visual media, and so on. The first requirement for activities that encourage use of various resources is that some variety of resources be available in classrooms and schools; the second is that teachers actively seek opportunities to direct students to diverse, and often unusual, sources for information.

6. *Activities should acknowledge and capitalize on the social nature of learning.* We have discussed previously the Vygotskian argument (Bayer, 1990; McCaslin, 1989; Vygotsky, 1986) that there is a strong interrelationship between language, thinking, learning, and the social world of the individual. Much of what students learn, they can and do learn from one another through discussion, shared experience, and exchange of ideas and information; and, while we're just beginning to explore the effect of social interactions on vocabulary learning, preliminary research evidence suggests a strong positive relationship between the two (Berk, McKeown, & Omanson, 1987; Stahl & Vancil, 1986). Cooperative and collaborative grouping in content classrooms encourages social interaction, and every vocabulary/content activity presented in this chapter is readily adaptable to any variety of small-group and partnership configurations. (We will explore various collaborative learning approaches in Chapter 9.) None is nearly as effective when assigned as individual student homework or seatwork and left undiscussed. *Much* of the power of VSS comes from the discussion that occurs from the very beginning of the learning episode; that same power operates in the follow-up activities that reinforce initial learning.

SPECIFIC VSS LESSON ACTIVITIES

The following activities are particularly well-suited for developing understanding and knowledge of new content words. All of them meet at least one of the principles listed above; most satisfy two or more. These activities also may be adapted for prereading vocabulary introduction.

Semantic Feature Analysis (SFA)   Semantic Feature Analysis (SFA) (Anders & Bos, 1986; Johnson, Toms-Bronowski, & Pittelman, 1981; Pittelman, Heimlich, Bergland,

& French, 1991) is useful both for developing word associations and extending content knowledge. To do SFA, the teacher prepares a grid (see Figure 4.6) in which words listed vertically and features listed horizontally are related to a given category; one or more of the words and features are taken from the VSS list. Working in pairs or small groups, students indicate which features are associated with each word by marking a plus (+) in intersecting squares for those that are and a minus (–) for those that are not. Group decisions are then shared in whole-class discussion, generally to the tune of lively debate and disagreement. After the initial SFA, student groups are invited to add to the "words" and "features" lists and continue the exercise with these additions. Further exploration of ideas may be introduced by replacing the "yes-no" (+/-) coding with "always," "sometimes," or "never" criteria using additional coding symbols.

Numerous other extensions and elaborations of this activity are possible. For example, discussion about relationships between specific words and features may lead to re-analysis of text information or further research; or, such discussion may stimulate extended writing and/or formal essays supporting a position or point of view, particularly when issues remain unresolved. Paragraph summaries or analyses of the topic category are useful follow-up study aids or supplements to class notes. At some point, student groups should be encouraged to create their own SFA grids using their choice of VSS words; these may be duplicated and distributed to other groups, and then they may serve as the basis for a discussion comparing responses.

FIGURE 4.6   *Semantic Feature Analysis: Mathematics*

	Distributive Property	Number	Unknown	Addition	Subtraction	Multiplication	Division		
*Variable									
*Equation									
Solution									
*Operation									

*VSS Word

Semantic Mapping and List-Group-Label Activities   Semantic mapping is just as appropriate for use with VSS content words as it is for prereading instruction. The procedure is essentially the same; however, discussions may be more elaborated because students will have encountered the words in text and discussed them during the VSS nomination process.

List-Group-Label activities also work well. Semantic maps may be used independently of or in conjunction with text maps students have constructed (e.g., maps following reading). Semantic maps and List-Group-Label exercises also are useful beginning points for developing formal outlines or summary notes for topic study and as the basis for further writing.

Extended Writing   As already mentioned, open-ended or focused writing assignments, in which students are encouraged to use their VSS content words in written elaborations of lesson ideas, are extremely valuable for in-depth word learning. We know that writing itself is a powerful means for construction and clarification of knowledge (Calkins, 1986; Freedman, 1987; Squire, 1989) and highly useful for combined content/vocabulary learning. In the very act of meaningful writing using new content vocabulary, students will arrive at new insights and understanding. It is important that we provide numerous opportunities for them to do so. A partial list of activities follows. (We will discuss these and other writing activities in Chapter 6.)

> *Journal writing* is a means for students to elaborate their personal response to the lesson or a reading assignment; journals may or may not be read by the teacher.
>
> *Response group summaries* require that a working group of students decide on a group response to a given lesson or text and produce a written summary of that response.
>
> *Lab reports* require students to summarize steps of an experiment, report and analyze results, compare results with pre-experimental expectations, draw conclusions, and evaluate the experience.
>
> *Quick-Writes, Three-Minute Writes, Exit Slips* (as discussed in Chapter 3) interspersed during or at the end of class, allow students to identify what they learned, what is problematic, what they liked about the lesson, and what they didn't like.
>
> *Extended narrative and expository writing* include all manner of stories, poetry, drama, essays, or reports that have direct bearing on and relationship to content lesson goals.

Any number of other written responses to text and/or a content lesson may be used to provide opportunity for students to practice using new words, *as long as they do not involve requirements for students to copy definitions from the dictionary or write a series of unrelated, non-content-specific sentences for the express purpose of using and underlining targeted vocabulary words.*

Word Treasure Hunts   *Word treasure hunts* (Haggard, 1989) direct students to "Find out everything anyone would want to know" about one of the chosen VSS content words or terms. Students are encouraged to ask people they know; look the word up in various dictionaries, encyclopedias, and other reference books, and add their own knowledge and ideas. Students record information and report back to class. Ideas are put on the board in much the same way semantic maps are made, discussed, and used for other categorizing, mapping, and writing activities. Word treasure hunts are well suited for out-of-class and homework assignments.

Categorizing/Re-categorizing   *Categorizing* occurs in a number of the activities already discussed (e.g., semantic mapping); however, it may be used effectively to demonstrate word relationships and the effect of differing categorical criteria. In categorizing, the teacher prepares a series of words taken from the reading, including as many VSS words as possible. Students, in pairs or groups, are asked to categorize the words in any way they choose (similar to List-Group-Label). Group solutions are then presented to other groups, either with explanation or with directions for other groups to determine the group criteria. Following this, students may be asked to recategorize the words using a new criterion.

Davidson (1984) suggests the activity, "Which One Doesn't Belong?" (see Figure 4.7), in which students are given an ambiguously defined series of words (the "series" may be defined either horizontally or vertically) and asked to identify one word in each series that does not belong and state the reason for their choices. Which One Doesn't Belong? works best in small groups in which students can spend some time debating their choices for vertical or horizontal series definition and for word elimination. A great deal of prior knowledge and text information is used in making these choices. As a follow-up, teachers may then direct students to re-do the exercise by choosing different words or using a different series configuration.

The activities just presented are not the only effective ways for encouraging long-term acquisition and development of content vocabulary. They are, however, remarkably generative: You can design many different lessons from one or more of these activities. Consider also ways to adapt prereading activities to VSS lessons; the

FIGURE 4.7   *Which One Doesn't Belong?: Science*

DIRECTIONS TO STUDENTS:

Look at each series of words and think about how the words are related to one another. For each series, find one word that doesn't belong with the others. Be prepared to explain why the word doesn't belong and what the others have in common.

MAGNITUDE	TEMBLOR	FAULT	SEISMIC
TECTONIC	AFTERSHOCKS	TREMOR	COMPRESSIONAL WAVE
LOVE WAVE	ENERGY	MAGNITUDE	RAYLEIGH WAVE

structural analysis activity is well suited to that end, and Interactive Cloze, with some thought and planning, could be adapted as well.

BENEFITS OF USING VSS

Two of the most obvious benefits of VSS are its versatility and ease of use. VSS can be used in any subject area, with any size class, and following any type of lesson. It requires nothing in the way of new materials or equipment and makes no demand that text from which words are to be chosen meet any particular form or standard. VSS words can be collected from a videotape, a lecture, or a filmstrip just as readily as they can from a textbook, magazine, or primary source. It only takes a little planning, willingness to spend a portion of class time on content vocabulary study, and some time and effort developing reinforcement activities to implement VSS very effectively. A third benefit is that words and language become a vital part of classroom discussion and students' lives. That statement may sound hyperbolic, but it is not; my experience with VSS has been that *everybody* gets excited about words, and the biggest problem the teacher has is moving the lesson on to other important topics. It happened in "The Splendid Outcast" lesson, and it will happen in your class. The value here is that students become active, independent word learners. They become attuned to words in textbooks and the subject discipline itself, alert to new and increasingly difficult words, and eager to satisfy their curiosity. Students themselves express their preference for finding vocabulary words for study (Alvermann et al., 1995):

> Yet, when [the teacher] asked the students if they would prefer that she preteach the vocabulary that would likely present some trouble, they said "no." Laura explained, "When you tell me, I don't want to know. If I come across it on my own, I have a reason to find it." Jason and Mark agreed, while Jonathon noted, "If you tell us, it might focus more attention on the word than it really deserves." (p. 29)

Years ago, I once demonstrated VSS to a secondary reading methods class by having students bring words for our class to learn. One man brought the word *pottle* to class and defined it as a container that holds 1-1/2 quarts liquid. I was intrigued. I'd never heard the word before, so I began questioning him. For further clarification, he compared "pottle" to "hottle," the container used for one serving of coffee or tea by hotel room service. He said that a hottle is half a pottle. I was now enchanted; I'd been using hottles for years but had never known they had a name. A year or so later, I wanted to tell this story and give accurate definitions for "pottle" and "hottle." To my surprise, I could only find "pottle" (container for holding 1/2 gallon liquid) in my Webster's *Second College Edition* dictionary (Garulnik, 1978). No "hottle." I called the main library and neither the reference librarian nor the science librarian could find anything. I recounted this to a group of teachers a year or so later, and a district curriculum supervisor told me that I could have gotten accurate definitions from a restaurant-supply house because they are "container" terms: "pottle" is a combined word meaning "pot-bottle," and "hottle" comes from and means "hot-bottle." Interesting.

Then, *five years later,* on my very first trip to Europe, I visited the museum home of Thomas Nash, who married William Shakespeare's granddaughter, at Stratford-upon-Avon, England. Here is what I saw displayed from an account book [sic]:

Chamberlain's Accounts
   Jan 31, 1582
   Paid for a pottell (half a gallon) of sacke, a pottell of clarett wyne and half a pownde of sugar geven to Sir Thomas Lucy and Sir ffoulke Grevill at theire sitting at the Beare.
   S/C

I was thrilled because I'd discovered a seventeenth-century source for "pottle." Just recently, I read a hotel room-service menu that listed a "hoddel" of coffee or tea. I'm still on the look-out for any more information.

I'm perfectly aware that I have an already well-developed, natural interest in words and language, and that my experience does not necessarily signify when it comes to seventh-graders or high school sophomores. Nevertheless, this kind of interest and pursuit of information is common with VSS. Further, students become quite skilled at figuring out what words are important for learning content. When I used VSS in a seventh-grade English class in which students were allowed to bring any words they wanted for our weekly vocabulary/spelling words, I discovered two related and important things: (1) I could easily keep track of what was going on in all the other seventh-grade classes because students brought words important to the topics of study in them (U.S. Constitution, planets, fractions, etc.); and (2) students didn't bring "easy" words—just the opposite, in fact. They brought words that were important, complex, and interesting.

With VSS, students really do get excited about learning and actively seek knowledge. *They* nominate the pool of words and determine the final list, and, because they invest so much of themselves in the word- and list-selection processes, they develop abiding interest in the learning that follows. Their interest and involvement grow from one powerful source: These words touch them in some special way—a sound, an association, a need to know—and the impact of that internal motivating force is exceptionally strong.

In my research on the conditions that precipitate word learning (Haggard, 1979; 1986a), I found that adolescents enjoy playing with the sound of words and with the words themselves. Thus, an entire population of high school students adopted the catchword *behooves* after hearing an assistant principal tell them in an all-school assembly, "It behooves you not to show affection in public." *Four years later,* students were still saying to one another, "It *behooves* you not to hold hands in the hall." "It *behooves* you to study for the test!" Clearly, these students enjoyed playing with and using that word. VSS encourages this response and playfulness, and so, such words as *gymnosperm*, *ignominy*, and *behooves* find their way onto word lists. These words are just as difficult as the ones on the Dreaded Word List, but VSS words belong to students in a way no word list can ever duplicate. My own earlier research (Haggard, 1986) and current work in progress (Stewart, 1991; Stewart & Ruddell, 1992) confirm the long-lasting learning benefits of VSS. In the VSS classroom, word list definition-by-synonym yields to elaborated discussion in which exploration of content word meanings, connections with students' prior knowledge, and increased depth of understanding and learning are common. VSS words are content words students *need to know*, words that lead to independent, active learning, and which, in turn, develop and support content learning.

How to do . . . .

VSS

Student teachers' and teachers' first concern about VSS is the feature that allows students to select the words to be learned. My most frequent question about VSS is, "Won't they (the students) choose the simplest words?" The answer is a resounding "No." The simplest words are *not* the most interesting or useful or important to learning content. Students quickly discern the value word study has *and* see that by choosing interesting and important words they (1) make classroom learning more fun, and (2) serve their own goal of learning the subject matter (and getting good grades). Students love VSS; so do teachers who have tried it. The following guidelines will be helpful as you adapt VSS for your subject area:

1. After reading (or other learning event), ask student groups to find a word or term that they would like to study or learn more about. Students are to be prepared to
   a. Identify the word/term in context.
   b. Tell where they found it in the text.
   c. Tell what they think the word/term means.
   d. Tell why they think the word/term is important to the topic and should be on the class vocabulary list.

2. Accept word nominations with discussion of possible meanings and reasons for learning (*a* through *d* above). Encourage extension and refinement of meanings through collaboration and pooling of information.

3. Nominate the word you wish to have on the list and supply all of the requisite information (*a* through *d* above).

4. Narrow class list to predetermined number (if needed).

5. Refine definitions as needed for each word/term.

6. Direct students to record final list words and definitions (as developed in class discussion) in vocabulary journals, on maps, or wherever you wish.

7. Develop VSS lesson activities for reinforcement (e.g., SFA grid).

8. Provide time for students to complete lesson activities (e.g., semantic mapping) and/or make out-of-class assignments.

9. Incorporate vocabulary items into end-of-chapter/unit test, as appropriate.

D O U B L E   E N T R Y   J O U R N A L

_____

_____

_____

_____

_____

In my vocabulary research, I found that I could categorize people's responses to questions about word learning. I called these categories Precipitating Conditions for vocabulary learning. I also found that the categories were different for elementary and secondary learners. Here are the categories I found in descending order of frequency:

Elementary

The word was appealing because of its *sound* or *adultness*.

The word was learned as the result of an incident involving *strong emotions*.

The word was learned as the result of an incident of *immediate usefulness*.

The word was learned as the result of *peer usage*.

Secondary

The word was learned as a result of *peer usage*.

The word was learned because of *immediate usefulness*.

The word was learned as the result of an incident involving *strong emotions*.

The word was appealing because of its *sound* or *adultness*.

_____

_____

_____

_____

Where in these categories do your words and incidents fit? What conclusions can you draw about how middle and secondary students respond to words? What are some ways you can encourage students to acquire and develop their vocabularies in your subject area? Share your ideas with your group.

FIGURE 4.5 *Intact Passage (See page 104)*

PLANT GROWTH AND DEVELOPMENT

You have probably heard the old saying: "Mighty oaks from tiny acorns grow." But have you ever thought about the amazing *changes* that take place during the long life of such a *tree?* A tiny embryo oak plant sits *within* an acorn for months, maybe even years. Then one spring, it sprouts. Its roots grow deep into the soil in search of water and *nutrients.* Its leaves reach toward the sun—toward the light *energy* that powers the life of the plant. In autumn, growth *slows.* The oak's leaves turn color and fall to the ground. The entire plant undergoes the *changes necessary* to survive the approaching cold winter weather.

Many years later the tree *matures.* Suddenly it produces hundreds, perhaps even thousands, of flowers. Some of the flowers produce *seeds* that mature into acorns. When the acorns ripen, they fall to the ground, where they may be buried or eaten by squirrels. With luck, the *process* of growth begins again.

REFERENCES

Allington, R. L. (1978). *Are good and poor readers taught differently? Is that why poor readers are poor readers?* Paper presented at the meeting of The American Educational Research Association, Toronto, ONT.

Alvermann, D. E., Weaver, D., Hinchman, R. A., Moore, D., Phelps, S. F., Thrach, E. C., Zalewski, P. (1995). *Middle- and High-School students' perceptions of how they experience text-based discussion: A multicase study.* (Reading Research Report No. 36). Athens, GA: National Reading Research Center.

Anders, P. L., & Bos, C. S. (1986). Semantic feature analysis: An interactive strategy for vocabulary development and text comprehension. *Journal of Reading, 29*(7), 610–616.

Bayer, A. S. (1990). *Collaborative-apprenticeship learning.* Mountain View, CA: Mayfield Publishing Company.

Beck, I. L., McKeown, M. G., & Omanson, R. C. (1987). The effects and uses of diverse vocabulary techniques. In M. G. McKeown & M. E. Curtis (Eds.), *The nature of vocabulary acquisition* (pp. 147–163). Hillsdale, NJ: Erlbaum.

Calkins, L. M. (1986). *The art of teaching writing.* Portsmouth, NH: Heinemann.

Collins, J. (1986). Differential instruction in reading groups. In J. Cook-Gumperz (Ed.), *The social construction of literacy* (pp. 117–137). New York: Cambridge University Press.

Davidson, J. L. (1984). *Inquiry approaches to content learning.* Paper presented at the meeting of the International Reading Association, Atlanta, GA.

Davis, F. B. (1944). Fundamental factors of comprehension in reading. *Psychometrika, 9,* 185–197.

Dyer, P. A. (1985). *A study of the effect of prereading mapping on comprehension and transfer of learning.* Doctoral dissertation, University of California, Berkeley.

Eder, D. (1986). Organizational constraints on reading group mobility. In J. Cook-Gumperz (Ed.), *The social construction of literacy* (pp. 138–155). New York: Cambridge University Press.

Freedman, S. W. (1987). *Peer response groups in two ninth-grade classrooms* (Technical Report No. 12). Berkeley, CA: Center for the Study of Writing.

Garulnik, D. B. (Ed.) (1978). *Webster's new world dictionary of the American language* (2nd ed.). Cleveland: William Collins.

Graves, M. F., & Prenn, M. C. (1986). Costs and benefits of various methods of teaching vocabulary. *Journal of Reading, 29*(7), 596–602.

Gray, W. S. (1946). *On their own in reading*. Chicago: Scott-Foresman.

Haggard, M. R. (1982). The vocabulary self-collection strategy: An active approach to word learning. *Journal of Reading*, 26(4), 203–207.

Haggard, M. R. (1985). An interactive strategies approach to content learning. *Journal of Reading*, 29(3), 204–210.

Haggard, M. R. (1986a). The vocabulary self-collection strategy: Using student interest and world knowledge to enhance vocabulary growth. *Journal of Reading*, 29(7), 634–642.

Haggard, M. R. (1986b). The vocabulary self-collection strategy: Implications from classroom practice and research. In M. P. Douglass (Ed.), *Reading: The quest for meaning, 50th Yearbook of the Claremont Reading Conference* (pp. 340–351). Claremont, CA: The Claremont Reading Conference.

Haggard, M. R. (1989). Instructional strategies for developing student interest in content area subjects. In D. Lapp, J. Flood, & N. Farnan (Eds.), *Content area reading and learning: Instructional strategies* (pp. 70–80). Englewood Cliffs, NJ: Prentice-Hall.

Heimlich, J. E., & Pittelman, S. D. (1986). *Semantic mapping: Classroom applications*. Newark, DE: International Reading Association.

Heller, J. (1955). *Catch-22*. New York: Simon & Schuster.

Herber, H. L. (1978). *Teaching reading in content areas* (2nd ed.). Englewood Cliffs, NJ: Prentice-Hall.

Jenkins, J. R., Matlock, B., & Slocum, T. A. (1989). Two approaches to vocabulary instruction: The teaching of individual word meanings and practice in deriving word meaning from context. *Reading Research Quarterly*, 24, 215–235.

Johnson, D. D., Toms-Bronowski, S., & Pittelman, S. D. (1981). *A review of trends in vocabulary research and the effects of prior knowledge in instructional strategies for vocabulary acquisition* (Theoretical Paper No. 95). Madison, WI: Wisconsin Center for Education Research.

Jongsma, E. (1971). *The Cloze procedure as a teaching technique*. Newark, DE: International Reading Association.

McCaslin, M. M. (1989, December). *Motivated literacy*. Paper presented at the meeting of the National Reading Conference, Austin, TX.

Meeks, J. W., & Morgan, R. F. (1978). Classroom and the Cloze procedure: Interaction in imagery. *Reading Horizons*, 18, 261–264.

Miller, K. R., & Levine, J. (1995). *Biology*. Englewood Cliffs, NJ: Prentice-Hall.

Moore, D. W., Readence, J. E., & Rickelman, R. J. (1989). *Prereading activities for content area reading and learning* (2nd ed.). Newark, DE: International Reading Association.

Nagy, W. E. (1988). *Teaching vocabulary to improve reading comprehension*. Newark, DE: International Reading Association.

Nelson-Herber, J. (1986). Expanding and refining vocabulary in content areas. *Journal of Reading*, 29(7), 626–633.

Pittelman, S. D., Heimlich, J. E., Bergland, R. L., & French, M. P. (1991). *Semantic feature analysis: Classroom applications*. Newark, DE: International Reading Association.

Ruddell, M. R. -H. (1992). Integrated content and long-term vocabulary learning with the Vocabulary Self-Collection Strategy (VSS). In E. K. Dishner, T. W. Bean, J. E. Readence, & D. W. Moore (Eds.), *Reading in the content areas: Improving classroom instruction* (3rd ed.) (pp. 190–196). Dubuque, IA: Kendall/Hunt.

Ruddell, M. R. (1994). Vocabulary knowledge and comprehension: A comprehension-process view of complex literacy relationships. In R. B. Ruddell, M. R. Ruddell, & H. Singer (Eds.) *Theoretical models and processes of reading* (4th ed.) (pp. 414–447). Newark, DE: International Reading Association.

Ruddell, R. B. (1986). Vocabulary learning: A process model and criteria for evaluating instructional strategies. *Journal of Reading*, 29(7), 581–587.

Singer, H. (1964). Substrata-factor patterns accompanying development in power of reading, elementary through college levels. In E. Thurston & L. Hafner (Eds.), *The philosophical and sociological bases of education. Fourteenth Yearbook of the National Reading Conference*. Marquette, WI: National Reading Conference.

Squire, J. R. (1989). *Research on reader response and the national literature initiative*. Paper presented at the annual convention of the International Reading Association, New Orleans, LA.

Stahl, S. A. (1986). Three principles of effective vocabulary instruction. *Journal of Reading*, 29(7), 662–668.

Stahl, S. A., & Vancil, S. J. (1986). Discussion is what makes semantic maps work in vocabulary instruction. *The Reading Teacher, 40,* 62–67.

Stanovich, K. E. (1991). Word recognition: Changing perspectives. In R. Barr, M. L. Kamil, P. Mosenthal, & P. D. Pearson (Eds.), *Handbook of reading research: Volume II* (pp. 418–452). New York: Longman.

Stewart, J. (1991). *Vocabulary learning of high school sophomores: A comparison of traditional list instruction with VSS.* Unpublished Master's program paper, Sonoma State University.

Stewart, J. & Ruddell, M. R. (1992). *Vocabulary learning using VSS with high school sophomores.* Unpublished manuscript.

Taylor, W. L. (1953). Cloze procedures: A new tool for measuring readability. *Journalism Quarterly, 30,* 360–368.

Vygotsky, L. S. (1986). *Thought and language* (A. Kozulin, Ed. & Trans.). Cambridge, MA: MIT Press.

BUILDING TABLE

CHAPTER 4	SEMANTIC MAPPING	LIST GROUP LABEL	INTERACTIVE CLOZE	VSS
FOCUS ON	Content vocabulary and concept learning	Content vocabulary and concept learning	Contextual analysis of content vocabulary	Content vocabulary and concept learning
GUIDES STUDENTS	Before and after reading	Before or after reading	Before reading	After reading
USE TO PLAN	Lessons	Lessons	Lessons	Lessons, units, semester
MAY BE USED	Whole class, cooperative groups, partnerships, individuals	Whole class, cooperative groups, partnerships, individuals	Cooperative groups	Whole class, cooperative groups
MAY BE COMBINED WITH (known strategies)	VSS, GMA, DR–TA, DRA	DR-TA, DRA, VSS, GMA	DRA	DR-TA, GMA, Semantic Mapping, DRA, Re-Quest
MATERIALS PREPARATION	None	None	Moderate	Moderate
OTHER PREPARATION	Light	Light	None to light	Moderate
OUTSIDE RESOURCES	Useful	Useful	Not needed	Necessary
HOW TO DO				Page 124

READING ACROSS THE CURRICULUM

D O U B L E E N T R Y J O U R N A L

Think for a moment about the reading your students

do in the class where you student teach or teach. Make

a list of those reading events, being as specific as you

can. Then categorize your list items or create a map

with them. How do these reading events contribute to

your students' knowledge and skills in your subject

area? How do they contribute to students' interest and

active participation in the class?

"Reading across the curriculum" and "reading in the content areas" are phrases we use to suggest the fundamental importance of reading in middle and secondary schools. Starting at third or fourth grade, subject area textbooks, primary sources, and other written materials assume increasing prominence in the classroom and, by senior high school, become major sources of information for classroom learning.

If you reflect a moment on your own schooling, you'll probably find that your school book experience follows the same general pattern that most of us remember: moderate-sized books in the elementary grades that were relatively easy to read (lots of open space, fairly large print, rather extensive use of visuals such as artwork, pictures, and figures, and relatively readable chapters). These books were used as part of teacher-directed lessons and often were assigned for reading only after considerable topic introduction and discussion had occurred. Somewhere between fourth and ninth grade, this began to change. Books got larger and longer, visuals decreased noticeably (or disappeared altogether), print got smaller, chapters and reading assignments got longer, and two-column pages of text appeared. In some texts (mathematics, for example), prose may have disappeared altogether. Increasingly, textbooks and other reading were assigned as homework, accompanied by little or no introduction or explanation. Such assignments were often followed the next day by teacher-led "discussions" that were little more than accuracy tests or question-answer sessions in which teachers checked to see that students understood the reading.

Significant here, in our traditional approach to subject area reading, is the similarly traditional view of the relationship between reading and learning. Where once we viewed reading as an important but essentially technical adjunct to learning—that is, a "skill" or "tool" or something learners *do* or *use* in the process of learning—we now understand that reading is an integral part of the learning process itself (Ruddell & Ruddell, 1995).

For over 50 years, reading has been viewed as a study skill of major importance in learning. This study skills perspective is based on the belief that certain reading behaviors—e.g., identifying main ideas, separating main ideas from significant details, using graphs and charts—contribute significantly to study-type reading ability and thus to learning from subject area texts. The causal relationship is thought to be that the greater the reading-study skills, the more one can read and learn from text.

The study skills perspective of literacy and subject area learning, however, does not, in and of itself, account for the full complexity of reader-text interactions. It is not sufficient for understanding (or promoting) strategic reading of subject area text. Certainly, having the right "tools" or "skills" for reading subject area texts is important, but current theories of reading and learning suggest that learners do far more than apply reading study skills to text. Rather, readers construct (or create) meaning *in the very act of reading*—extending their prior knowledge base, arriving at insights, integrating new information, and constructing new subject area knowledge. These constructions of meaning, both during and after reading, are influenced not only by application of reading-study "skills," but, more importantly, by the myriad interactions and transactions that occur in reading events: transactions involving readers' prior knowledge base, reader intent or stance, social interactions, reading and learning goals, instructional decisions, and so forth (Ruddell & Ruddell, 1995; Ruddell & Unrau, 1994). Thus it is that meanings students construct during and after reading, while certainly influenced by reading study skills, are fundamentally shaped by the complex interactions and transactions that characterize the comprehension process itself, and these constructions of knowledge form the basis for subject area learning.

The importance of reader-text transactions and the prominent place of textbooks and other materials in middle school and secondary classrooms, then, requires that we, as teachers, examine the assumptions we make about what students need to do to be successful in using classroom texts, as well as what we expect students to do—both with the texts and the information learned from them. To make those assumptions and expectations explicit reveals our responsibilities for assisting students in reading and learning from text and for promoting their continued growth in each.

CONTENT READING NEEDS OF MIDDLE SCHOOL AND SECONDARY STUDENTS

In previous chapters, we discussed various aspects of thinking, reading, comprehension, and content vocabulary development. What we talked about in those chapters applies to this chapter, with one new wrinkle: Where we focused earlier on general issues—comprehension, for example—with an emphasis on content learning, here we focus directly on content learning itself, and we will address this issue from the perspective of reader-text transactions in subject area learning rather than from a study skills approach. Central to the demands of academic learning is that students:

1. develop the ability to learn from text;

2. satisfy an external criterion of knowledge acquisition, whether this criterion takes the form of an end-of-unit test, a research paper, some other group or individually prepared product, a general achievement test administered by the school or district, or materials collected in a portfolio;

3. become increasingly competent strategic readers of content text.

In addition, content learning often requires more than schema activation (as we discussed in earlier chapters), but schema construction as well; that is, students must not only articulate what they already know but also construct and acquire new knowledge (Bransford, 1985, p. 394). Requirements for academic achievement (the construction and acquisition of new knowledge) increase as students progress through school; in the face of these incremental criteria and task requirements, students' literacy needs become proportionately more precise and more demanding.

AUTHENTIC ACHIEVEMENT

Let us look now at what resources students must marshal in order to be successful in learning from text and learning the subject matter of academic classes. To do this, we must consider for a moment what is meant by "successful student achievement." Fred Newmann (1991) identifies "authentic achievement" as an important goal of subject matter instruction. Authentic achievement is different from conventional school learning by its emphasis on what Newmann calls "substantive discourse" in the classroom, in which students create or produce things rather than name and discuss what others have produced and in which students perform by writing, building physical objects, talking, participating in artistic performance, etc. (1991, p. 460). Newmann's idea is not revolutionary; in fact, it follows a line of reasoning and thinking long embraced and recommended by educational theorists (Dewey, 1910, 1933; Bruner, 1960; Stauffer, 1969, 1980; Goodlad, 1984; Cohen, 1986).

Authentic achievement requires *production*—rather than *re*production—of knowledge. Newmann proposes "disciplined inquiry" as a means for arriving at authentic achievement. He defines "disciplined inquiry" as classroom inquiry that involves:

1. students' prior knowledge base

2. in-depth understanding
3. integration of knowledge and information (this definition is not at all unlike our discussion of "disciplined inquiry" in Chapter 3)

What, then, will students need to do if they are to achieve in the manner Newmann proposes? Certainly, they will need to know how to apply what they already know to each new learning event (that is, use their prior knowledge base); then, they will need to go beyond the surface of new—and old—ideas, to contemplate, inquire, manipulate, and construct new meaning (that is, develop in-depth understanding); finally, they will need to blend the new with the known, to change previous ways of thinking, and construct new, or change existing, schemata (that is, increase their content knowledge base). Students will need to be able to do these things in many different classroom activities, including reading and writing, and in different subject areas.

I said earlier that what we discussed in previous sections of this book about thinking, reading, and writing (Chapter 2) and about reading comprehension and content vocabulary learning (Chapters 3 and 4) all applies to the notion of reading (and learning) across the curriculum. It does. In fact, the ideas and instructional strategies we discussed—DR-TA, GMA, ReQuest, VSS, etc.—promote learning that is highly congruent with the authentic achievement Newmann describes as a learning ideal. Of real importance is that if students are to acquire the cognitive and learning resources that allow authentic achievement, then teachers must provide experiences that direct students' learning beyond the trivial, and ultimately mind-dulling, level that John Goodlad found to be all too pervasive in U.S. junior and senior high schools (1984) and that Fred Newmann and others propose we should change (Eeds, 1988; Goodlad, 1984; Haggard, 1989; Newmann, 1991).

LEARNING FROM TEXT

In content classrooms, learning from text occurs as the result of a variety of transactions, including (but not limited to) the transactions between teacher and students, between students and students, between students and text, and between teacher and text (Haggard, 1985). These transactions produce conditions that help or hinder student learning and that do or do not lead students toward authentic achievement. To become strategic readers and learners (recall from Chapter 3 that strategic readers know *what* to do in reading/learning events, *how* to do what they need to do, and *when* to do what), students need guidance before, during, and after reading (Herber, 1978) to assist them in constructing useful meaning for the immediate understanding of text, to increase their general knowledge base, and to develop strategic reading/learning abilities. It follows that teachers are responsible for providing that guidance. Figures 5.1 and 5.2 summarize what students and teachers need to do.

The instructional strategies presented in the rest of this chapter reflect the student needs and teacher responsibilities I have just outlined. (Incidentally, they are also quite compatible with instructional strategies from previous chapters and, in fact, are in many cases easily combined with them.) This chapter extends discussion initiated in previous chapters and demonstrates additional means for increasing student learning and application of content knowledge by focusing on teaching and learning from text.

FIGURE 5.1 *What Students Need to Do When Learning from Text*

Students need to:

1. *Recall prior knowledge and previous experience*—Identify what they know; raise questions about what they do not know; predict what text will be about.

2. *Organize information while reading*—Predict what information will be found; confirm/adjust predictions; relate new information to prior knowledge.

3. *Organize information after reading*—Respond to text in some important way; identify major concepts and ideas; perceive relationships between concepts and ideas; perceive relationships with prior knowledge; understand relative importance of ideas.

4. *Synthesize and articulate new learning*—Arrive at new understanding and insights; integrate new understandings into prior knowledge base; find out how much was learned; establish base for further learning.

5. *Learn vocabulary that labels important concepts, elements and relationships*—Identify new words and terms; identify known words and terms in new contexts; use new words and terms in meaningful ways; relate new vocabulary to prior knowledge base.

6. *Produce or create something new and apply new information*—Work through new ideas in writing; build, make, or create something new; perform.

GUIDING STUDENTS BEFORE, DURING, AND AFTER READING

Each of the strategies presented next is useful for guiding students before, during, or after reading, and, in some cases, the strategy incorporates useful guidance for two, or even three, of these reading/study stages. We'll begin with a short reprise of strategies already presented to show how they may be adapted and combined; following that, a number of other instructional strategies will be developed. As I present each, I'll demonstrate how it may be used and combined with other strategies for developing students' content knowledge and their ability to read and learn from text. In addition, I'll discuss how each meets students' academic needs.

CONTENT DR-TA, GMA, AND VSS

The Content DR-TA (Haggard, 1985, 1989) is an alternative form of the basic DR-TA we discussed earlier. The Content DR-TA requires students to be in partnerships or small-group teams (generally consisting of no more than three people per team). Each team has paper, pencils, and text (textbooks, primary source, literature, or whatever). Instruction begins when the teacher directs the teams to work together to jot down everything they know about the general topic within which the lesson topic fits. So, for example, in a lesson to teach the rules and regulations for playing field hockey,

FIGURE 5.2   *What Teachers Need to Do to Guide Students' Learning from Text*

Teachers need to

1. *Determine students' prior knowledge and previous experience concerning the topic at hand*—Provide means for students to articulate their prior knowledge base; find out what students already know; determine the magnitude of difference between what students know and what is to be learned.

2. *Provide means for students to organize information while reading*—Focus students' attention; engage students in the cycle of predicting/reading/adjusting predictions/reading some more; develop linkages between prior knowledge and new information.

3. *Provide a means for students to organize information after reading*—Establish various means for students to respond to text; engage students in elaborative discussion and follow-up activities; encourage and teach various organizational structures for recording information.

4. *Provide means for students to synthesize and articulate new learning*—Allow opportunities for students to talk and write about what they have learned; further develop linkages between prior knowledge and new information; identify linkages between new information and what is yet to come.

5. *Identify and teach vocabulary that labels important concepts, elements, and relationships*—Allow students to identify words and terms they need to know; find out what words and terms students already know; develop linkages between new words and terms and prior knowledge base; develop activities for students to use new words and terms in meaningful ways.

6. *Provide opportunity for students to produce or create something new*—Promote elaborative projects and activities; find out what students have learned; evaluate degree of teaching/learning success.

students might be asked at this point to list everything they know about *field hockey;* if the topic is state government, they may begin by listing everything they know about *government;* or if the lesson is stringed musical instruments, students would list everything they know about *musical instruments.* Students should be given about 6 to 8 minutes for working while the teacher observes and listens in from a distance and/or assists any teams that appear to be having trouble. It is not unusual for the noise level in the room to reduce at some point well before the end of the 6 to 8 minutes, signaling that students have exhausted their immediate, top-of-the-head ideas and are searching memory for more. Generally, it's best to allow time for those additional ideas to surface; by about 8 minutes, teams should be ready to move on.

The teacher next announces the *specific topic* the reading is to be about and focuses student attention: For example, "Today we're going to read and learn the rules and regulations for playing field hockey. Go back to your list and put a check mark (✓) beside anything you listed that you think might be in our reading. Add any new ideas that occur to you." Students review their lists for 2 to 3 minutes, checking and adding ideas. Then to initiate the reading, the teacher directs, "As you read, put an asterisk (*) beside any item on your list that appears in the text."

Students then read the assignment individually; however, even though students are reading individually, the room is by no means silent. You can expect to hear a low buzz of conversation as students read—partners and teams will talk to each other and comment about information found in the text. (I once heard someone call this "mumble reading"—an apt description.) Students will read to each other to support a point they made ("Listen, it says right here . . . "), exclaim over words or ideas in the text ("*'breaching,'* that's it!"), or simply respond to text ("I didn't know *that.*"). The teacher observes, "tuning in" to different groups' discussions to monitor how well students are doing; when the reading is completed, the teacher leads a short discussion of content.

Planning and teaching a Content DR-TA is simple. Below are the Content DR-TA instructions used for a *National Geographic* article on whales.

(classroom partnerships already established)

Teacher: You and your partner will need a piece of paper and a pencil. Working together, you are to list everything you know about *whales.* Do that now.

(6 to 8 minutes later)

Today we're going to read about the *feeding habits of the humpbacked whale.* Go back to your list and put a check mark by anything on your list that you think might be in the reading. Add any new ideas you have.

(2 minutes later)

I'm handing out the article. As you read, put a mark of some kind—an asterisk or something—by anything on your list that appears in the article.

Following the Content DR-TA, Group Mapping and VSS, provide further opportunity for students to organize information after reading. Since we have already discussed the basic structure for both the GMA and VSS in previous chapters, the discussion here will be short and will focus on specific ways to extend the content uses of GMA and VSS by converting maps into clearly designated study aids.

GROUP MAPPING (GMA) AS A STUDY AID

As a combined idea organizer and study aid, I like to use mapping in a slightly more structured way than the very open-ended way described in Chapter 3. To do so, instructions for the initial mapping activity should be something like the following:

Without looking back at the book and without talking to anyone, map your perceptions of the reading you just did on the rules and regulations for playing field hockey (or about state governments or stringed instruments). (Add explanatory information ["a map is a diagram of what you think the reading was about . . . "] if mapping is new; otherwise, such information is generally unnecessary.) You are going to use this map to record important information as we go through the field hockey unit; at the end of the unit, you'll find it a useful study aid in preparing for our field hockey test. Be sure to include on your map all of the information you consider to be important.

After completing the maps, students are directed to share their maps with their partner by telling them *what* they considered important, *how* they chose to organize the information, and *why* they made the choices they made. Partners are to respond by eliciting elaboration about important information (e.g., "What made you choose that point?") and by looking to see what relationships are shown on the map.

Emphasis is placed on the value of the maps as the basis for further study or as starting points for individual and group projects throughout the unit. Further, students are reminded that their and their partner's maps *do not have to look alike;* rather, whatever the information and organization scheme used, the map must be complete. After one map is discussed, partners then exchange roles. During this discussion, the original text is consulted repeatedly to verify information and add details and ideas missed in the original mapping. Full group discussion may then be initiated, in much the same way as discussed in Chapter 3.

Study maps are marvelously expansive and can continue to grow as new ideas are encountered. They also may be used to teach students how to do more formal organization of information: summary writing, précis writing, single-idea development and elaboration, and (The Really Big One) outlining. One caution I would give: If you decide to use maps as study aids, which gives added weight and permanence to their content, you must be prepared to accept varying map structures and constructions of meaning. Harry Singer said it best:

> . . . different cultural backgrounds and perspectives are likely to result in a range of acceptable variations in interpreting texts and events . . . [the teacher should be willing to] accept as accurate a whole band of interpretations (1985, p. 13).

Your willingness to accept a "band of interpretations" need not in any way reduce your requirement for precision or understanding of specific information, including formulas, theories, core knowledge, and/or facts in any subject area. Rather, use discussion to clarify and define these elements within the context of students' constructions of meaning; this will allow students to elaborate further on their own understanding. Following such discussion, either with a peer or in whole class, students may decide to restructure their maps for added precision or the inclusion of other ideas. Figures 5.3 and 5.4 show study maps developed from the Content DR-TA lesson on the feeding habits of humpbacked whales. These maps are original conceptualizations that have been shared with a partner. The maps are now ready to be reconsidered and/or redrawn to reflect that discussion and in preparation for use throughout the whale unit.

VOCABULARY SELF-COLLECTION STRATEGY (VSS) AS A STUDY AID

As with mapping, VSS may be used essentially as described earlier (see Chapter 4). To be useful study aids, however, VSS words must be recorded in such a way as to give context to the words themselves; for example, the teacher may direct students to enter their VSS words on their study maps "where the words make sense." VSS words should be marked in some way on the map (with an asterisk, or by underlining, high-

FIGURE 5.3   *Study Map Derived from Content DR-TA Lesson: Biology*

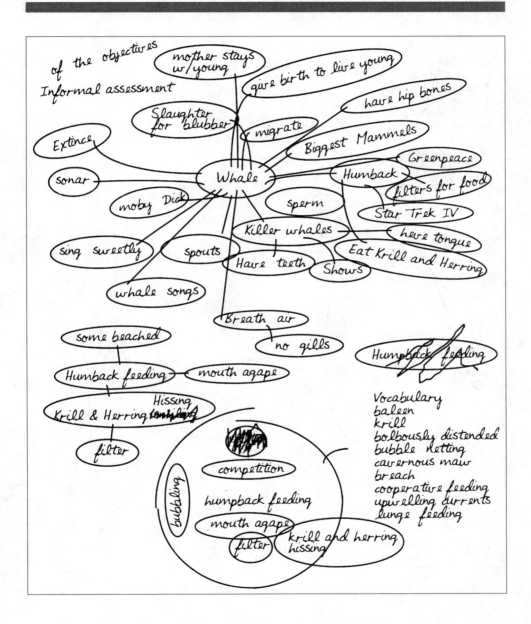

lighting, or circling) and should be given attention through follow-up activities just as general vocabulary words are. Figure 5.5 shows a Semantic Feature Analysis grid for the VSS words chosen as part of the lesson on whales (Ruddell, 1992).

FIGURE 5.4   *Study Map Derived from Content DR-TA Lesson: Biology*

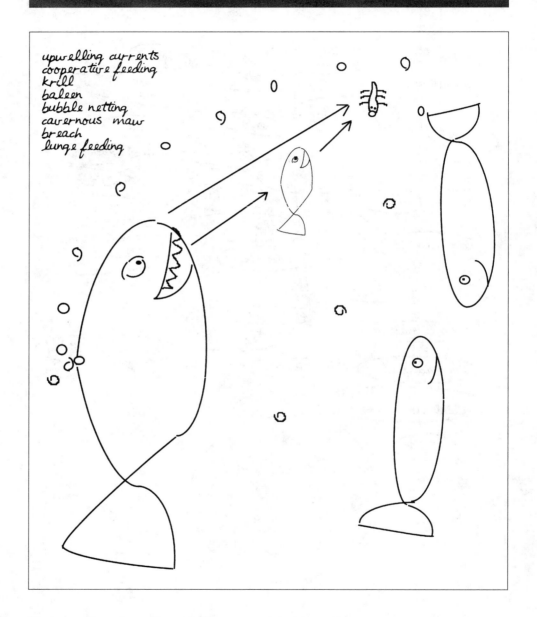

Guiding Students Before, During, and After Reading with the Combined Content DR-TA, GMA, and VSS

Notice that this progression of events—Content DR-TA, GMA, and VSS—provides ample opportunity for students to do all the things we said earlier they need to do: re-

FIGURE 5.5   *Semantic Feature Analysis: VSS Words from the Whale Lesson: Biology*

Humpbacked Whales	Characteristic	Behavior	Learned	Unlearned				
*Baleen								
*Lunge feeding								
*Bubble netting								
*Breaching								
Cavernous maw								
Cooperative feeding								
Competitive feeding								
*VSS word/term								

call prior knowledge and previous experience, organize information during and after reading, synthesize and articulate new learning, learn the content vocabulary, and create something new. Notice also that students are given a great deal of support in the three reading/study stages (before, during, and after reading), as well as practice in strategic reading. Of particular importance is that this progression—Content DR-TA, GMA, VSS—provides a context for reading and learning that assists students in seeing the *significance* of the text with which they are engaged. If students do *not* perceive that significance, then ideas in text become an arbitrary list of things that make little sense and are easily forgotten (Bransford, 1985). The Content DR-TA, GMA, and VSS, then, develop important linkages between the known and the new, prepare students to extend learning, and develop students' strategic reading/learning abilities.

How to do . . . .

THE COMBINED CONTENT DR-TA, GROUP MAPPING, AND VSS

One of the nicest things about the Content DR-TA is how easy it is to use with just about any text or other learning medium. It requires no special materials or equipment, no elaborate preparations, and no alteration of text or textbooks.

continued

How to do   *continued*

What *is* critical is that you define *explicitly* the lesson topic and goals you wish to address so that you can establish clear focus for what the students respond to in the two stages of idea-listing. The first stage is always focused on the *general topic:* the prior knowledge and previous experience students have *related to* the actual topic of study. This is followed in the second stage by attention to the *specific topic*, which is made fuller because of the associations triggered by the previous exploration of related information. The following steps will lead sequentially through the Content DR-TA, GMA, and the VSS.

CONTENT DR-TA

1. Ask student teams to list everything they know about a *general topic* (for example, "whales," "baking," "algebra," or "baseball"). 6 to 8 minutes.

2. Announce *specific topic* (for example, "feeding habits of humpbacked whales," "yeast bread baking," "factoring," or "fielding").

3. Ask students to predict what information on their lists might appear in the reading (✓); add any new predictions they have. 2 to 3 minutes.

4. Ask students to read the assignment; note how well they predicted (*).

5. Lead short discussion about the predictions and the reading (for example "How well did you predict?" "How many of your ideas appeared in the reading?" or "What new ideas appeared?").

GMA STUDY AIDS

6. Ask students to map their perceptions of the reading without talking to anybody and without looking back at the reading. Remind them that the maps will be used as study aids and should include all information they consider important.

7. Ask partners to share their maps with one another and to assist each other in elaborating what they considered important, how they chose to organize it, and why they made the choices they made. Allow students to refer to the reading as they wish.

8. Lead whole-class display and discussion of selected study maps.

VSS STUDY AIDS

9. Have student teams choose a word or term that students believe to be important to the chapter. Teams should be prepared to tell where they found the word, what they think it means, and why they think it is important. (You also nominate a word.)

10. Lead discussion as words are nominated and defined; write all nominated words on the board.

11. Lead discussion for students to choose the final class vocabulary list; review and refine definitions of words on the list.

12. Have students enter vocabulary words on their study maps where the words fit the map. Mark vocabulary words with an asterisk.

13. Develop follow-up activities for using the vocabulary words meaningfully.

14. Provide opportunities for students to elaborate on what was learned.

THE DIRECTED INQUIRY ACTIVITY (DIA)

Another DR-TA-like reading and learning strategy is Keith Thomas's Directed Inquiry Activity (Thomas, 1986). Thomas developed the DIA to apply the predicting elements of a DR-TA to meet the expressed needs of middle school and secondary students and teachers. The point of the DIA is to allow student involvement in learning while at the same time preserving the teacher's prerogative to determine what information is to be learned. Thomas sees this strategy as one that directs students through text with specific emphasis on inquiry directed to Who? What? When? Where? Why? and How? (1986, p. 279).

The DIA begins with the teacher presenting five or six inquiry questions about the chapter or material to be read. These may be listed on the board, leaving plenty of space for recording predictions, or they may be duplicated on a handout. Students are then asked to survey a portion of the material to be read: the title and some introductory paragraphs; the headings listed in the table of contents; the introduction and the summary; or even just the title alone for a very short selection. Students then predict responses to the inquiry questions using information from the survey and any background information they have. The teacher records predictions on the chalkboard or has students record them on their handouts.

Important here is that the teacher probe student responses to find out how students arrived at the predictions they are making. Such questions as, "What makes you say that?" and, "How did you arrive at that prediction?" are highly useful. When no more predictions are forthcoming, students read the material to confirm, adjust, or reject predictions made. Further discussion leads to refinement and clarification of responses, analysis of predictions, and addition of related ideas and information not found in the text.

GUIDING STUDENTS BEFORE, DURING, AND AFTER READING WITH THE DIA

Notice that this instructional strategy guides and assists students in organizing information before, during, and after reading as students make and discuss predictions for how the inquiry questions will be answered in text, read to confirm or adjust their predictions, and then clarify responses in follow-up discussion. Furthermore, the DIA helps students understand the significance of text and make the all-important linkages between the known and the new, as well as make the cognitive accommodations necessary for constructing new schemata or changing existing ones.

DIA is particularly useful when you feel the need to focus student attention a bit more than you might with other strategies on specific aspects of text and the information to be learned. While it has a stronger emphasis on teacher direction than other strategies, it does retain the significant elements of student generation of ideas and knowledge, provision for capitalizing on students' prior knowledge and previous experience, and guidance throughout the reading/learning episode. It is also quite amenable to adaptation. For example, DIA can be used very easily in a small-group or partnership-class structure. Simply have groups or partners work together to do the original predicting. After allowing sufficient time for teams to work, have teams share their predictions with the whole class. This has the advantage of giving students the support that comes with cooperative work and the opportunity for additional insight that often occurs when individuals build on one another's knowledge base (Bayer, 1990).

There are also possible combinations of homework/in-class work with the DIA. Initial surveying and predicting may be done in class and the reading assigned for homework; or, students may do the surveying in class, generate predictions at home, and return to class for sharing predictions, completing the reading, and doing the follow-up activities.

SAMPLE INQUIRY QUESTIONS FOR A DIA

Figure 5.6 shows possible DIA inquiry questions for the first seven pages of a chapter section from a seventh grade physical science text (Maton, 1994). If these were used on a student handout, room should be left for students' predictions; used on the chalkboard, they should similarly be arranged so that predictions can be recorded under each.

How to do . . . .

A DIA

The DIA, like the Content DR-TA, is relatively easy to use. Once again, the key is establishing well-articulated lesson objectives in order to write clear, use-

FIGURE 5.6   *DIA Inquiry Questions: Forms of Energy: Physical Science*

1. What are the different forms of energy?

2. How do we use energy, and what are the implications of energy use?

3. Why is it important to consider issues related to energy resources?

4. How do we distinguish between "kinetic" and "potential" energy resources?

5. What are some important questions we need to explore?

ful inquiry questions. Your inquiry questions should meet two criteria: First, they should stem directly from and explicitly reflect your lesson objectives; and second, they should be generative, rich questions that stimulate the "substantive discourse" Newmann promotes (1991). A reasonable extension of the DIA is group mapping or VSS, or both. Use the following steps to do a DIA:

1. Determine your lesson objectives.

2. Write five or six inquiry questions reflecting your lesson objectives.

3. Determine what portions of the text you wish to have students survey.

4. Write questions on the board or reproduce them on an individual sheet for distribution. Be sure to leave room for recording responses to each question.

5. Ask students to survey the reading assignment, and make predictions about how the text will answer the inquiry questions listed.

6. Lead the discussion as students make predictions; ask probe questions that emphasize students' elaboration of the logic and background knowledge that led to their responses.

7. When all predictions are made, ask students to read the material.

8. Lead discussion to reexamine responses to each inquiry question in light of information gained from text. Help students refine, add to, modify, and revise responses.

9. Lead or assign any follow-up activities for reinforcing and extending the lesson.

THREE LEVEL READING GUIDES

Three level reading guides are part of the functional, indirect teaching of reading approach introduced by Harold Herber (1970) as the most useful means for teaching reading in the content areas. Herber's instructional strategies and approaches—which include graphic organizers, reaction guides, reasoning guides, structured overviews, and others, as well as the three-level guide (1970, 1978)—have been enormously popular and appear in a number of textbooks on middle and secondary school reading instruction (Herber, 1978; Readence, Bean, & Baldwin, 1995; Roe, Stoodt, & Burns, 1995; Vacca & Vacca, 1996; and others).

The three level guide is a direct outgrowth of the three levels of comprehension—literal, interpretive, and applied—that Herber identifies and that we discussed in Chapter 3. Herber (1978) emphasizes that the intent of the guide is, first, to maintain a classroom focus on subject matter while teaching reading and study strategies indirectly, as they are needed for learning content; second, to " . . . show students how to do what they are required to do" (1978, p. 6); and finally, to provide a structure that will assist students before, during, and after reading.

As with the DR-TA, the easiest way to describe the three level guide is to demonstrate one. We will use text from an Algebra I text (Fair & Bragg, 1993). If possible, you should do this activity in a group with two or more other people since it is not as effective if done alone.

SAMPLE GUIDE SHEET *Three Level Guide*

I. ***Directions.***   Read the statements below; then read the following selection to see if it has the information contained in each statement. Put a check beside each statement that you believe can be supported by the text. Provide evidence for why you mark each statement as you do.

_____ *Outcomes* are the result of specific events.

_____ When we talk about *probability*, all possible outcomes have an equal chance of occurring.

_____ The number of ways an outcome can happen in relationship to the total possible outcomes determines the probability of an outcome's happening.

FIGURE 5.7 *Probability : Algebra I*

SIMPLE PROBABILITY

Objectives: To determine the probability of an event and of the complementary event for a random experiment. To solve problems involving probability.

The Italian mathematician Girolamo Cardano (1501–1576) helped to develop the field of *probability*. **Probability** measures the likelihood that a particular event will occur. The measures are expressed as ratios.

CAPSULE REVIEW

EXAMPLE   Write the ratio 4 out of 10 as a fraction in simplest form and as a percent.

$\frac{4}{10} = \frac{2}{5}$ *Write as a fraction. Simplify.*

$= 0.40$ or 40%.   *Divide to find the percent.*

Write each ratio as a fraction in simplest form and as a percent.

1. 15 to 25   **2.** 18 out of 48   **3.** 28 to 49   **4.** 48 to 64

In probability, each repetition of an experiment is a **trial.** A possible result of each trial is called an **outcome.** When you toss a fair coin, the two possible outcomes are *heads* (*H*) or *tails* (*T*). The probability of tossing heads is 1 out of 2 possible outcomes.

$$\text{Probability (heads)} = \frac{1}{2} \quad \text{or} \quad P(\text{H}) = \frac{1}{2}$$

$$\text{Probability (of an event)} = \frac{\text{number of favorable outcomes}}{\text{total number of possible outcomes}}$$

When the possible outcomes have the same chance of occurring, they are described as **equally likely;** they occur at *random*. The set of all possible outcomes is called the **sample space.** The sample space for tossing a coin is heads or tails. An **event** is any of the possible outcomes, including all or none.

EXAMPLE 1   A box contains 12 buttons, identical in size and shape but not in color. There are 2 blue, 3 yellow, 6 black, and 1 white. Find the probability of selecting:

    a. a blue button   **b.** a blue or yellow button

    c. a green button   **d.** a blue, yellow, black, or white button

    a. $P(\text{blue}) = \frac{2}{12}$ ⟵ ———————— number of blue buttons

                    ⟵ ———————— total number of buttons

           $= \frac{1}{6}$ *Simplify.*

    b. $P(\text{blue or yellow}) = \frac{5}{12}$ ⟵ ———————— *There are 2 blues and 3 yellows*

    c. $P(\text{green}) = 0$. There are no green buttons.

    d. $P(\text{blue, yellow, black, or white}) = \frac{12}{12} = 1$

The probability of an event that is impossible is 0. The probability of an event that is certain to happen is 1. All other probabilities are between 0 and 1. In general, for any probability $P(E)$,

$$0 \le P(E) \le 1$$

In a random experiment, the two situations—that an event does occur and that the event does not occur—are **complementary events.**

In Example 1, $P(\text{blue})$ and $P(\text{not blue})$ are complementary events.

$$P(\text{blue}) = \frac{1}{6} \qquad P(\text{not blue}) = \frac{5}{6} \qquad \text{Note: } \frac{1}{6} + \frac{5}{6} = 1$$

The sum of the probability of an event $P(E)$ and the probability of its complement written as $P(\bar{E})$, is 1. $P(E) + P(\bar{E}) = 1$

Odds are a ratio that compares the probability of an event to the probability of its complement. *Odds of 2 to 1 for* means that the probability of the event occurring is $\frac{2}{3}$. *Odds of 2 to 1 against* means that the probability of the event not occurring is $\frac{2}{3}$.

EXAMPLE 2   The table below shows the SAT math scores for 186 seniors at Garrison High School. If one senior is chosen at random, find

    a. the probability that the student had a score between 501 and 600

    b. the odds that the student scored between 301 and 500

Score	201–300	301–400	401–500	501–600	601–700	701–800
Students	2	15	35	62	42	30

II. **_Directions_**   Read the following statements and consider how they relate to the information you just discussed. Put a check beside the statements below which you believe to be logical inferences from your reading. Be prepared to support your choices. Discuss this section before going on to Section III.

_____ Probability is a type of ratio.

_____ Outcomes are lawfully related to probabilities.

_____ Probability is associated with common events.

III. **_Directions_**   Read through the following statements and consider how they relate to information in your text, inferences you have drawn, and ideas from your discussion. Check the statements below which you believe are reasonable conclusions from your reading, discussion, and any other information you have. Be prepared to support your choices.

_____ Knowledge about probability can be useful when playing card, dice and spinner games.

_____ You can make better "educated guesses" if you know something about probability.

_____ _Probability_ and _possibility_ are terms that have a special relationship.

GUIDING STUDENTS BEFORE, DURING, AND AFTER READING WITH THE THREE LEVEL READING GUIDE

Three level reading guides, used as Herber intended (1978), provide the structure and stimulus for individual learning within the context of small-group discussion and exploration of ideas associated with written text. Each section of guide lessons allows students to read and respond to text, support their response choices through the combination of previous experience and information in the text, and compare their responses with those of the group. Specifically, three level guide lessons progress as follows:

Part I (Literal Comprehension)
1. Students individually read the written directions and statements for Part I of the three level guide.
2. Students read the assigned section of text.
3. Students reread statements in Part I marking those that they believe to be supported by the text and deciding how the text supports their choices.
4. Small groups meet for students to identify, support, compare, debate, and discuss individual responses to Part I statements.

Part II (Interpretive Comprehension)
5. Students individually read and respond to Part II statements.
6. Small groups meet for students to identify, support, compare, debate, and discuss these responses.

Part III (Applied Comprehension)
7. Students individually read and respond to Part III statements.
8. Small groups meet for students to identify, support, compare, debate, and discuss these responses.

9.   The teacher leads a short whole-class discussion for students to share the nature of the exchange in each group, to summarize discoveries/insights achieved from the reading, and/or to clarify or elaborate ideas from the reading and small-group discussions.

10. The teacher makes follow-up assignments for elaboration of information, continuation of the lesson, or reinforcement of lesson ideas or skills.

As you can see, the three level guide lesson is rich with active participation and student exchange of ideas. It does all the things we've talked about throughout this chapter: guides students before, during, and after reading; assists students in organizing information; demonstrates the significance of the text by linking it to student prior knowledge and by showing relationships; engages students in "substantive discourse" about text, and promotes strategic reading of text. What is critical to understand about three level guides, however, is that to use them *without* the small-group discussion, without stopping periodically to discuss student responses and reasoning, is to *misuse the guides.* Many of you may well remember making your way through long lists of reading guide statements in high school classes: 25 to 50 statements for each reading assignment, to be done on your own and brought to class for discussion. That was three level guides at their worst. Three level guides at their best stimulate lively, animated discussion and debate. To achieve this, you will need to attend to several critical aspects while writing the guides and directing the lesson.

WRITING AND USING THREE LEVEL READING GUIDES
<u>When writing three level reading guides,</u> use the following principles to guide your work:

1.   *Establish clear lesson objectives.* You simply cannot write statements for guiding students through the reading without knowing what the learning objectives are. Ask yourself, "What do I want my students to know or be able to do when they are through with this lesson?" Using whatever format works for you, write these objectives down.

2.   *Read the selection to:* (a) identify essential information and main ideas, (b) determine relationships between ideas, (c) determine generalizations or conclusions that can be drawn from the ideas and their relationships, and (d) decide how the text information does (and does not) meet your lesson objectives.

3.   *Write declarative statements* (not questions) for each level of the guide. *Literal* statements should answer the questions, "What is the essential information contained in this assignment? What are the important ideas here?" *Interpretive* statements reflect the questions, "What relationships can be seen from this information? What inferences might be drawn? What important point is the author trying to make here?" *Applied* statements should answer the questions, "What conclusions can be drawn by combining what students already know with what information is here (or implied)? How does all of this relate to students' lives or to what they know of the world?"

Keep in mind that you do not need to write "foils" (statements that are misleading or deliberately incorrect); rather, write statements that are reasonable, defendable, and reflective of a variety of perspectives and interpretations.

4. *Monitor the number and quality of the statements.* For a number of reasons, it is far better to have too few rather than too many statements. Important among these reasons is that too many statements will overwhelm the very students you're trying to assist. A few well-chosen statements will serve to launch the interesting, animated small-group discussions you're attempting to stimulate and should reflect rather directly the lesson objectives you've established. If you have trouble winnowing your list of statements down to that few well-chosen number, you may not have real clarity about the lesson objectives themselves. In that case, go back to the objectives, rewrite as necessary, and get that clarity; then look at your statements again.

5. *Double-check* to see that the applied statements (Level III) show relevance of information to students' lives. These statements should clearly allow for students to apply new insights to their lives and to the world at large. They should *broaden* students' knowledge so that students, and the lesson, go beyond the text. This is one of the ways that teachers increase the power of text.

6. *Write directions to assist students in working through the guide.* These directions must be adjusted to students' grade level. Mine were written for adults and would probably be appropriate for older high school students. They can easily be modified for younger students.

<u>When directing the lesson</u>, actually using the three level reading guide, the following principles should guide you:

1. *Make sure instructions for each discussion include specific, explicit directions for students to support their choices.* It is not enough for students simply to compare who agreed with what statements. Monitor small-group discussions to make sure students are looking at rationale, individual reasoning, and logic. Model with them the kind of probe questions that lead to such discussion if you find they are not doing it.

2. *Have students do something with the information discussed.* Go back to your objectives, and see what you want students to know or be able to do that goes beyond the text. Have students map (or add to their maps), write position statements, do practice problems, summarize group response to the text, write summary-response logs, identify vocabulary words, complete an experiment, or play a game of volleyball: in other words, *use the new information meaningfully.*

How to do . . . .

A THREE LEVEL READING GUIDE LESSON

I think you can see that three level guides require considerably more teacher preparation than do Content DR-TAs and DIAs. They do, but they're worth it, especially when the reading material is particularly difficult or the topic unwieldy. Three level guides help *you* organize your thinking and lesson planning and so help students also. One cautionary note: While it is important that *you* understand and can differentiate between literal, interpretive, and applied levels of comprehension and then write corresponding declarative statements, it is not important for your *students* to be able to do so. *You do not need to teach the three comprehension levels to students or refer to the statements by their comprehension-level names* (Herber, 1978). As with any other instructional strategy, three level guides are not to be used with every lesson or assignment. I recommend that you build a "library" of guides over time, writing several new ones each year and adapting old ones to meet the needs of subsequent units, lessons, and students. Further, I recommend that you use any and all word processing facilities available to you in developing your three level guide library. With guides stored on disks, updating, changing, and rearranging is relatively easy. The following steps will assist you in writing and directing a three level guide lesson:

1. Identify lesson objectives.

2. Read the selection to identify important ideas, relationships, and conclusions that may be drawn from it.

3. Write declarative statements to correspond to the three levels of comprehension: literal, interpretive, applied.

4. Write directions for students to follow for reading the text and discussing statement responses at each level.

5. Direct students as they work individually and in small groups to read and discuss the lesson. Activities should alternate between individual response and small-group discussion of responses to each section of the guide.

6. Upon completion of individual/small group activities, lead whole-class discussion to compare small-group experiences, summarize responses, or clarify information.

7. Assign follow-up activities for elaboration of information, continuation of the lesson, or reinforcement of lesson skills.

READING RESPONSE GROUPS

Reading response groups are beginning to get considerable attention and acceptance in middle school and secondary classrooms. Referred to variously as "Conversational Discussion Groups" (O'Flahavan, 1989), "Reading-Writing Workbench" (Tierney et al., 1989), and Reading Response Groups, most activities involving reading response groups center around transforming classroom discussion of text from "gentle inquisitions" to "grand conversations" (Eeds & Wells, 1989). The point of the activity is to engage students in gently directed small-group discussion of text that has all the characteristics of the spontaneous discussions that occur when an idea captures, sparks, and excites a group. Fundamental to reading response group instruction are two major assumptions (Ruddell, 1990):

1. Meaning derived from text is highly individualized and is constructed from personal transaction between reader and text (Rosenblatt, 1978).

2. *R*eader understanding is deepened through social transactions between peers for the purpose of sharing personal constructions of meaning, asking questions, and building group meaning (Golden, 1986; Probst, 1989; Vygotsky, 1968, 1986).

GUIDING STUDENTS BEFORE, DURING, AND AFTER READING WITH READING RESPONSE GROUPS

Reading response groups generally are considered to be productive additions to the classroom. They are not without some difficulties, however, most of which are usually associated with the quality of group discussion and participation by group members (Eeds & Wells, 1989; Ruddell, 1990). Despite these drawbacks, reading response groups offer important opportunities for students to work together to generate and construct meaning. Much of the support for students before and during reading comes from clear instruction and guidance for the group discussion that follows reading. In addition, teacher-written prompts focus student attention through all phases of the reading.

Although current designs for reading response groups are most frequently tied to literature study, I see no reason why the benefits for understanding literature would not apply equally as well to reading and understanding subject matter texts. When using reading response groups, the teacher should do the following (Bleich, 1978; O'Flahavan, 1989; Tierney et al., 1989):

1. Establish heterogeneous (nonability grouped) reading response groups, generally consisting of four to five persons per group.

2. Develop and teach guidelines for groups to function effectively. (We will discuss these at some length in Chapter 9.)

3. Focus student attention on specific kinds of responses they are to construct from the text.

4. Monitor student groups as they develop and discuss responses. (More about this in Chapter 9 as well.)

5. Design follow-up activities for students to apply responses and elaborate further on them.

PROMPTS FOR CONTENT READING RESPONSE GROUPS

Focusing response group discussion (the third item in the list above) is critical to the success of reading response group activity. The following sections present various ways for focusing student response in a unit on weightlifting; the reading assignment was a section of the book *Getting Stronger* (Pearl & Moran, 1986) titled, "The Elements of Fitness" (see Figure 5.8).

Prior Knowledge, Text Meaning, and Reaction Response Prompts   O'Flahavan (1989) suggests that the teacher leave three questions with each group that address the following areas: (1) background knowledge—how student experiences relate to the text; (2) ideas derived from the text—how students construct text meaning; and

(3) ideas that go beyond the text—how students interpret or react to the text. For our fitness unit and reading assignment, these questions might be as follows:

1. "What fitness needs do you see in your own life? What might you like to be able to do (or do better) that you can't do now?"
2. "Based on what you read, how would you define 'fitness'? Support your definition."
3. "If you were to design a fitness program for your own needs, what element or elements would be your first priority? Why?"

These three types of questions loosely reflect the three comprehension levels (literal, interpretive, applied) we've discussed previously. The difference here is that the focus of the first question is more on students' prior knowledge base than on information available in text.

FIGURE 5.8   *The Elements of Fitness: Physical Education/Health*

What does it take to be in shape? What are the basic qualities of fitness? Just as a farmer needs the four elements for his crops to grow—water, sun, soil and air—*you* need the following four elements to be in good shape:

- Strength
- Muscular endurance
- Cardiovascular endurance
- Flexibility

Understanding these elements of fitness, especially how you train to achieve each one, is very important if you are to get the most out of your weight training.

STRENGTH

Strength is the ability of a muscle to produce force. It is measured by the amount of weight you can lift in one repetition; for example, the most amount of weight you can bench press or lift in the squat.

Pure strength is the most important ingredient in many sports: shot-putting, discus-throwing, jumping high in basketball, having a powerful tennis serve, driving a golf ball, throwing a baseball, etc. Strength is also the key to sports where you have to meet an opponent with a lot of force, such as wrestling or football.

Power = Strength + Speed

A person may have a lot of strength at the bench press, but not be able to put the shot well. He doesn't have the speed of movement that, combined with strength, generates the necessary power for a long toss.

MUSCULAR ENDURANCE

Muscular endurance is the ability of a muscle to produce force repeatedly *over a period of time.* It is measured by the number of repetitions of the movement or skill.

FIGURE 5.8 *continued*

If you can do only one or two push-ups, then for you it's a strength movement. If you can do 35 push-ups, then for you it's a muscular endurance exercise. Sports requiring muscular endurance are wrestling, hurdling, rowing, sprinting and sprint swimming. These sports differ from strength sports in that you have to apply force for a longer period of time.

An athlete can continue to produce muscular force for only a limited period of time before the energy stores in the muscle are depleted. In movements that apply maximum force (strength), such as lifting a heavy weight, the energy stores are quickly depleted. If less than maximum force is required, and the athlete must ration strength (as in a wrestling match or sprint), energy stores are depleted more gradually and the movement can continue for a longer period (muscular endurance).

CARDIOVASCULAR ENDURANCE

Cardiovascular endurance is the capacity of the respiratory system (lungs and blood vessels) and the circulatory system (heart, arteries, capillaries and veins) to supply oxygen and nutrients to the muscle cells so an activity can continue for a long period of time.

This type of fitness is necessary for sports like distance running, cross-country skiing, cycling, distance swimming, triathlons, rowing and soccer. (These sports are also the best exercises for *improving* cardiovascular endurance.) Here the amount of force required of a particular muscle or muscle group is low and the movement is rhythmic. This means that one muscle group is resting while another takes over. For example, in rowing you pull with your back muscles in the power stroke and push with chest muscles on the return stroke: while one group is resting, the blood stream is bringing in nutrients and whisking away waste products. These alternating rest periods allow the movement to continue for a long time.

FLEXIBILITY

Flexibility, the fourth element of fitness, refers to the range of motion possible in the joints. This is controlled by muscles, tendons and ligaments.

It is well known that flexibility can be increased by stretching. However, there are two important factors to keep in mind:

1. *Every individual differs in flexibility.* Some are loose-jointed, some tight. A loose-jointed person is obviously well-suited for gymnastics, but is liable to get injured in contact sports. A tight-jointed person can better withstand the impact stresses of contact sports, but tends to have great difficulty at gymnastics. Most people are somewhere in between and can modify their flexibility to coincide with the demands of the sport and their body type.

2. *Each sport has different flexibility requirements.* You don't always want *maximum* flexibility in every direction. Example: football players are susceptible to blows from the side of the knee, and skiers often fall and twist their knees. These ath-

FIGURE 5.8

---

letes should do quadriceps exercises to provide stability for the knee, and make themselves *less* flexible in side-to-side knee motion. On the other hand, gymnasts need full body flexibility, since good-performance involves going to the extreme range of motion for the joints.

As a general rule, *you need enough flexibility to go through the range of motion required in your sport without restrictions in movement.*

Many people think that weight lifters are inflexible or "muscle-bound." On the contrary, weight training improves flexibility. In a study that compared flexibility for champion college gymnasts, champion college wrestlers, and average 16-year-old boys along with national champion weight lifters and bodybuilders, the weight lifters were slightly more flexible (in measurements of 30 different joint movements) than the gymnasts and much more flexible than the wrestlers or 16-year-olds.*

---

*Flexibility Characteristics of Three Specialized Skill Groups of Champion Athletes. Jack Leighton, Ph.D. *Archives of Physical Medicine,* 1957, Vol 38, No. 9.

Perception, Reaction, and Feelings Response Prompts   Bleich (1978) asks students to react *in writing* to slightly different focusing categories: (1) text perceptions—how students "see" (or construct meaning from) the text; (2) reactions to the text—how students respond to the text; and (3) associations with the text—feelings and thoughts students have in relationship to their perceptions of the text. So students are asked to write about, and then discuss, what they think the text theme is (for example, "In your own words, what do you think the authors are saying about fitness?"), how they respond to it (for example, "Do you accept the authors' definitions of fitness? Why or why not?"), and how they feel about it (for example, "What is your attitude toward fitness? Would [do] you work out? Why or why not?"). Following discussion, students then may develop a fitness program for themselves, with teacher guidance, or pursue further an exploration and study of fitness and health.

Stages of Understanding Response Prompts   The Reading-Writing Workbench approach (Tierney et al., 1989) begins at a thematic level and progresses in three general stages. In our unit, for example, groups might begin by exploring the large question, "What is fitness?" (Stage One). From this discussion, students read the central assignment, as well as other resources, to explore many aspects of the notion of "fitness." During this exploration, they are encouraged to experiment with various reading and writing activities to get more information, express what they are learning, and share information with one another. Some type of culminating activity occurs: development of one's own fitness program with written rationale; group dramatization of "From Fragile to Fit"; compilation of various low-impact methods for achieving fitness (Stage Two). Finally, students are asked to reflect and assess what they have learned and what meaning this learning will have in their lives (Stage Three).

How to do . . . .

READING RESPONSE GROUPS

As you can see, reading response groups may be used in daily, short-term classroom activities, or they may be the central organizational foundation for major units of study. However you wish to use them, teacher planning is critical to their success. First and foremost, you must define your unit and lesson objectives. Second, you must decide how extensively you wish to use response groups. Many new teachers start on a small scale and gradually lead in to major response group projects. Finally, you need to develop useful focusing activities that promote the response and interaction you are intending. The following steps are appropriate for using reading response groups:

1. Determine unit/lesson objectives.

2. Establish response groups (four to five students per group).

3. Decide how you want groups to function, develop guidelines for group behaviors, and teach students how to do what you want them to do in their groups (see Chapter 9).

4. Prepare focusing questions or statements, and develop necessary directions for students' guided responses.

5. Observe groups as they work, troubleshoot when necessary, and provide access to resources students need.

6. Lead reflection and follow-up discussion for students to evaluate response group functioning.

K-W-L PLUS

K-W-L Plus (Carr & Ogle, 1987) is a combination of Ogle's original K-W-L (1986) with mapping. K, W, and L stand for *Know, Want to Know,* and *Learned,* respectively, and are used to guide students through text in much the same manner that the Content DR-TA does. Students begin by brainstorming everything they Know about a topic and then categorizing their knowledge and listing it on a K-W-L worksheet (see Figure 5.9) under K. Following this, students generate a list of questions about what they Want to Know and anticipate learning from the text. Want to Know questions are listed under W. Additional questions may be listed as the reading progresses. After reading, students summarize what they have Learned by listing that information under L. The worksheet then is used as the basis for mapping; students categorize the in-

FIGURE 5.9   *Ninth-Grade Student's K-W-L Worksheet for a Lesson on Killer Whales*

K (Know)	W (Want to know)	L (Learned)
They live in oceans.	Why do they attack people?	D—They are the biggest member of the dolphin family.
They are vicious.	How fast can they swim?	D—They weigh 10,000 pounds and get 30 feet long.
They eat each other.	What kind of fish do they eat?	F—They eat squids, seals, and other dolphins.
They are mammals.	What is their description?	A—They have good vision under water.
	How long do they live?	F—They are carnivorous (meat eaters).
	How do they breathe?	A—They are the second smartest animal on earth.
		D—They breathe through blow holes.
		A—They do not attack unless they are hungry.
Description		D—Warm blooded
Food		A—They have echo-location (sonar).
Location		L—They are found in the oceans.

Final category designations developed for Column L, information Learned about killer whales:

  A = abilities, D = description, F = food, L = location.

formation under L on the worksheet and develop their own maps using those categories and content. Carr and Ogle recommend alternatively that written summaries may be used to extend K-W-L learning. Figure 5.10 (Carr & Ogle, 1987) shows a map developed from the ninth-grader's K-W-L worksheet shown earlier.

K-W-L Plus is clearly designed to assist students throughout the learning from text episode (before, during, and after reading). As with other, similar strategies, K-W-L Plus builds on what students already know, engages them in prediction and anticipation of the reading, and then leads them through organization, reorganization, and development of information after reading.

K-W-L Plus seems perfectly suited to partnership and small group work. Just as the Content DR-TA, DIA, and Three Level Guide lessons are made more powerful through group interaction, so is K-W-L Plus. I also would recommend the kind of

FIGURE 5.10   *Ninth-Grade Student's Map Generated from K-W-L Worksheet*

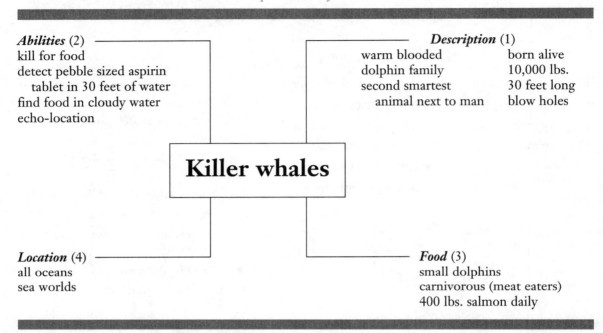

(1) through (4) indicate the order of categories the student chose later for writing a summary.

follow-up discussion Davidson built into the GMA (1982) for the mapping part of K-W-L Plus to give students the advantages such interaction yields.

How to do . . . .

K-W-L PLUS

You may want to prepare a K-W-L Plus in worksheet form, with the "K," "W" and "L" columns labeled and defined, which you then print and distribute to students. This gives the work at each stage of the reading an official air that adds to its appeal and importance. These worksheets would also be ideal for placement in students' portfolios or whatever you use to document student progress. The following steps are useful in developing K-W-L Plus lessons:

1. Ask students or student teams to brainstorm what they know about the topic of the lesson.

2. Direct students to organize and categorize their knowledge and list it under *K* on their worksheets.

3. Ask students to anticipate what they will read as they list questions they would like to have answered under *W*.

4. Ask students to read the assignment, adding questions to their list as needed.

5. Have students list the information they got from the text under *L* on their worksheets.

6. Ask students to generate categories for the information they learned and to develop individual maps.

7. Lead a discussion in which students display and explain their maps.

8. Assign further writing and idea development as desired.

REAP PROCEDURE

REAP—*R*ead, *E*ncode into your own words, *A*nnotate, *P*onder (Eanet & Manzo, 1976)—is a study strategy in which students respond to reading by writing different types of annotations, or notes, designed to cast various perspectives on the text. REAP may be used with students working independently or with groups. Critical to its success are teacher and student understanding of the different types of annotations. Eanet and Manzo suggest the following categories of annotations; I have added illustrative annotations from a health class handout of a newspaper editorial on blood pressure:

1. *Heuristic.* Using the author's words to stimulate a reaction: for example, "The author of this article states that 'High sodium may not be the villain of high blood pressure; rather, low calcium may be more at fault.' I wonder what this will do to advertising and food companies who are currently making a bundle on low-sodium products."

2. *Summary.* Highlighting the main ideas of the text: for example, "The main idea of this article is that we don't know as much about high blood pressure as we thought. Elements and factors other than sodium—calcium, for example—may affect high blood pressure."

3. *Thesis.* Stating the theme of the text: for example, "I think the theme here is cautionary: let's not be so quick to jump on solutions when we may not really understand the full extent of the question. Remember oat bran?"

4. *Question.* Asking a question related to major ideas in the selection: for example, "If low calcium rather than high sodium could be the real culprit in high blood pressure, what and how many other unexplored or unresearched variables might be involved?"

5. *Intention.* Speculating on the author's intent in writing the text: for example, "I think that the intent here is to inform the public so reasonable personal decisions may be made about one's health. Dire warnings over a number of years about the effects of high sodium may have been overstated and caused inappropriate actions. At the very least, the article appears to be intended to get people to look at this issue."

6. *Motivation.* Identifying or considering the author's motivations: for example, "This article was probably motivated by two things: (1) the occurrence of research results that run counter to accepted knowledge and previous research, a sort of 'shock' factor; and (2) the prominence of high blood pressure as a threat to health in a country where a substantial portion of the population is above middle-age or at risk for developing high blood pressure."

7. *Critical.* Examining the author's point of view and the annotator's reaction: for example, "I don't see a heavy 'point of view' in this article except that by its presence it suggests alternative viewpoints to current beliefs about high blood pressure. I was glad to see someone presenting such a possibility. I've never understood how high sodium could be so harmful to some people and not to others (I eat lots of salt, and my blood pressure is 110/80) unless some other factor or factors were at work."

The Ponder step of REAP is usually best done in a group setting, perhaps a Reading Response Group, so that students have the opportunity to interact with one another, comparing and elaborating on their original annotations.

The REAP procedure may be adapted in many ways for use with various students and classes. Its focus is guiding students after reading (rather than before or during), and it may be most easily used, at least initially, in an informal way: by having students work in pairs or groups to do their first few annotations, for example. Another possibility is to have students annotate after mapping and map sharing. The procedure allows students to respond to text in ways other than simply retelling or identifying main ideas. Further, the annotations themselves are useful as springboards to extended discussion or other major activities.

THE PREREADING PLAN (PREP)

Judith Langer's PReP strategy (1982) provides students with a means for organizing information before reading. It begins with the teacher saying, "Tell me anything that comes to your mind when I say _____ ('electricity' or 'sculpture' or 'human needs', etc.)." The students' free associations are recorded on the board. The teacher then asks, "What made you think of _____ (each student's response to the first statement)?" pointing to the response on the board. After responses have been discussed, the teacher says, "Based on our discussion, have you any new ideas about _____ ('electricity,' 'sculpture,' 'human needs,' etc.)?" Students then read the assignment to see how their old and new ideas apply. PReP is a useful introductory activity that may be done on a whole-class basis or directed in small-group discussions. You may wish to have students make a prediction or two after new ideas are discussed to give them immediate reasons for doing the reading. Any number of discussion/elaboration activities or instructional strategies may be used to follow the reading.

STUDY SKILLS AND SUBJECT AREA READING

Because I made such a point earlier in this chapter that the study skills perspective was not sufficient for developing strategic subject area readers and learners, I think it is important to address the rightful place of study skills in content learning. Certainly, there are definable reading/study skills, for example:

1. Understanding and using book parts (tables of contents, indices, marginalia, glossaries, etc.).
2. Alphabetizing, using head notes and pronunciation guides, understanding abbreviations in reference sources (dictionaries, encyclopedias, atlases, etc.).
3. Using other references (telephone directories, newspapers, etc.).
4. Using the library (card files, data bases, Dewey Decimal System, etc.).
5. Adjusting reading to purpose (skimming, scanning, intensive reading).
6. Reading graphs, charts, maps, globes, and other pictorial information.
7. Notetaking.
8. Finding main ideas; separating main ideas from important details.
9. Outlining.
10. Summarizing.

My point here is that instruction and guidance in these skills is embedded in the instructional approaches in this chapter in such a way that using the skills became a natural and useful part of the total learning event.

SQ3R and *notetaking/underlining* are two instructional practices that have been used traditionally to develop students' study skills. I present them here because of their wide popularity; however, for each I raise questions regarding the usefulness of teaching the strategy to students.

SURVEY, QUESTION, READ, RECITE, REVIEW (SQ3R)

SQ3R (Robinson, 1946), if not the oldest study strategy around, is certainly one of the oldest, and one of the most frequently cited study techniques. The SQ3R is intended to guide students before, during, and after reading; further, it is meant to be used independently by students after they become adept at its use. Steps in this activity are:

1. *Survey the text* by skimming the assignment, looking at headings and subheadings, and examining illustrations, charts, etc.
2. *Ask Questions* about what you are to read by converting subheads to questions.
3. *Read the text* to answer the questions.
4. *Recite* by stating answers to the questions.
5. *Review* by going back over the information, filling in details to your answers, and recalling answers over time.

SQ3R contains provisions for guiding students through all stages of reading and meaning construction; however, we have little evidence that it is particularly useful (Caverly & Orlando, 1991). More importantly, my experience suggests that, however solid a technique it is, students don't like doing SQ3R. It's more than a little bit cumbersome and requires substantial instruction for students to understand; unfortunately, it does not stick with students very long, no matter how carefully it is taught. My experience is supported by Caverly and Orlando's review of the SQ3R literature (1991), in which they suggest that students will need to be made aware of " . . . the effort required in using this strategy" (p. 149). I suggest an informal use of SQ3R: that is, getting students into the habit of looking through what they're going to read before reading it, developing questions or predictions about what they think they'll be reading, and looking back and making sense of what they've read when finished. Selective and thoughtful use of reading study guides also may be helpful. (See the guides mentioned in Wood, Lapp & Flood [1992], *Guiding Readers Through Text: A Review of Study Guides*.) Teacher-guided practice at effective study reading, particularly with the DIA, but also using the Content DR–TA or K-W-L, appears to be most effective in promoting students' independence in guiding their own progress before, during, and after reading text.

UNDERLINING AND NOTETAKING

Underlining (or highlighting) and *taking notes* while reading are two independent study skills that nearly every student is expected at one time or another to use, especially in college and beyond. Caverly and Orlando (1991) identify underlining as having " . . . grown in popularity to become one of the most ubiquitous strategies used in postsecondary schools" (p. 107).

The most striking thing we can say about underlining and notetaking from text is that those students who underline or take notes spontaneously (generally average readers and above) tend to do them well: Their underlining and notes capture ideas central to the major points of the text and eliminate the least-significant detail. Students taught or induced to underline or take notes (generally low-average readers and below) do not: Their underlining and notes are random, with little differentiation between important ideas and insignificant detail (Brown, 1985; Caverly & Orlando, 1991 summary of 31 studies on underlining and 30 studies on notetaking from text). Caverly and Orlando conclude that attempts to teach underlining and notetaking, especially to students who are having difficulty with the text, are not likely to be effective (1991).

So, it appears that, while notetaking and underlining are popular study techniques, they are not easily taught. It seems far more reasonable, therefore, to spend class time engaging students in the complex, elaborative activities recommended in this chapter, and throughout this text, rather than attempting to teach underlining and notetaking directly. Using maps as study aids, with provision for map sharing and reconstructing, and adding VSS words to the maps appear to be highly useful here; other strategies—K-W-L, reading response groups, REAP, etc.—have components equally valuable for teaching students how to summarize and record important information, insights, and concepts constructed as the result of reading content texts. As students become sophisticated in using these strategies, they are more fully prepared to move spontaneously into underlining and notetaking practices.

CONCLUDING THOUGHTS

If I were to identify the single-most-voiced complaint about middle school and secondary students, it is undoubtedly, "The kids can't read and write." You'll hear it often. You may even be tempted to say it. I hope, instead, that you'll say what needs to be said: *"The kids can't read and write in my classroom if I do not support their literacy progress* (in science, or math, or physical education, etc.) *and provide for its growth."* That's a pretty weighty statement, but it is true—in each and every subject area. If teachers are to support students' literacy progress and provide for its growth, they need to use the kind of instructional approaches we've discussed in this and other chapters, to teach content. Teachers must remember how much more they know about their subject than students do: Teachers need only concentrate on *activating* their schemata; students are *constructing* theirs. Teachers are *remembering* and *recalling* formulas, principles, ideas, and concepts; students are *learning* them. Now consider the extraordinary increase in difficulty we add if we attach "in a second language" to what students are required to do. Teachers therefore need to center their classrooms around *real* learning and literacy, engaging students in activities that have meaning and substance and promoting the disciplined inquiry that stimulates activation of students' prior knowledge base, in-depth learning, and integration of knowledge and information. Newmann's powerful notion of "substantive discourse" alludes to classroom interactions that are full, rich, and meaning-laden; it suggests exchanging ideas in an environment of diversity and open inquiry by involved, active learners; it sounds complex, exciting, demanding, and rewarding. I can't think of any better way to conduct school.

D O U B L E   E N T R Y   J O U R N A L

Using ideas from this chapter, and combining them with as many ideas as you want from Chapters 3 and 4, what are some instructional activities and strategies you can use to make content reading and learning easier, more interesting, and more productive for your students? Which instructional strategies look most promising for your subject area? Why? Compare your ideas and conclusions with a partner or group.

REFERENCES

Bayer, A. S. (1990). *Collaborative-apprenticeship learning.* Mountain View, CA: Mayfield.

Bleich, D. (1978). *Subjective criticism.* Baltimore: Johns Hopkins University Press.

Bransford, J. D. (1985). Schema activation and schema acquisition: Comments on Richard C. Anderson's remarks. In H. Singer & R. B. Ruddell (Eds.), *Theoretical models and processes of read-*

ing (3rd ed.), (pp. 385–397). Newark, DE: International Reading Association.

Brown, A. (1985). Metacognition: The development of selective attention strategies for learning from texts. In H. Singer & R. B. Ruddell (Eds.), *Theoretical models and processes of reading* (3rd ed.), (pp. 501–526). Newark, DE: International Reading Association.

Bruner, J. (1960). *The process of education.* Cambridge, MA: Harvard University Press.

Carr, E., & Ogle, D. (1987). K-W-L Plus: A strategy for comprehension and summarization. *Journal of Reading*, 30, 626–631.

Caverly, D. C., & Orlando, V. P. (1991). Textbook study strategies. In R. Flippo & D. C. Caverly (Eds.), *Teaching reading & study strategies at the college level* (pp. 86–165). Newark, DE: International Reading Association.

Cohen, E. G. (1986). *Designing groupwork.* New York: Teachers College Press.

Davidson, J. L. (1982). The group mapping activity for instruction in reading and thinking. *Journal of Reading*, 26, 52–56.

Dewey, J. (1910). *How we think.* Boston: Heath.

Dewey, J. (1933). *How we think* (2nd ed.). Boston: Heath.

Eanet, M. G., & Manzo, A. V. (1976). REAP—a strategy for improving reading/writing study skills. *Journal of Reading*, 19, 647–652.

Eeds, M., & Wells, D. (1989). Grand conversations: An exploration of meaning construction in literature study groups. *Research in the Teaching of English*, 23, 4–29.

Fair, J., & Bragg, S. C. (1993). *Algebra I.* Englewood Cliffs, NJ: Prentice-Hall.

Golden, J. M. (1986). Reader-text interaction. *Theory into Practice*, 25, 92–96.

Goodlad, J. I. (1984). *A place called school.* New York: McGraw-Hill.

Haggard, M. R. (1985). An interactive strategies approach to content reading. *Journal of Reading*, 29, 204–210.

Haggard, M. R. (1989). Instructional strategies for developing student interest in content area subjects. In D. Lapp, J. Flood, & N. Farnan (Eds.), *Content area reading/learning: Instructional strategies* (pp. 70–80). Englewood Cliffs, NJ: Prentice-Hall.

Herber, H. L. (1970). *Teaching reading in content areas.* Englewood Cliffs, NJ: Prentice-Hall.

Herber, H. L. (1978). *Teaching reading in content areas* (2nd ed.). Englewood Cliffs, NJ: Prentice-Hall.

Hirsch, E. D. (1986). *Cultural literacy.* Boston: Houghton Mifflin.

Langer, J. (1982). Facilitating text processing: The elaboration of prior knowledge. In J. A. Langer & M. T. Smith-Burke (Eds.), *Reader meets author/bridging the gap* (pp. 149–162). Newark, DE: International Reading Association.

Maton, A., Hopkins, J., Johnson, S., LaHart, D., Warner, M. O., & Wright, J. D. (1994). *Motion, forces, and energy.* Needham, MA: Prentice-Hall.

Newmann, F. M. (1991). Linking restructuring to authentic student achievement. *Phi Delta Kappan*, 72, 458–463.

O'Flahavan, J. (1989). *An exploration of the effects of participant structure upon literacy development in reading group discussion.* (Doctoral dissertation, University of Illinois–Champaign).

Ogle, D. (1986). K-W-L: A teaching model that develops active reading of expository text. *The Reading Teacher*, 39, 564–570.

Pearl, B., & Moran, G. T. (1986). *The elements of fitness: Getting stronger.* Bolinas, CA: Shelter Publications.

Probst, R. (1989). Teaching the reading of literature. In D. Lapp, J. Flood, & N. Farnan (Eds.), *Content area reading and learning: Instructional strategies* (pp. 179–186). Englewood Cliffs, NJ: Prentice-Hall.

Readence, J. E., Bean, T. W., & Baldwin, R. S. (1995). *Content area literacy: An integrated approach* (5th ed.). Dubuque, IA: Kendall/Hunt.

Robinson, F. P. (1946). *Effective study* (2nd ed.). New York: Harper & Row.

Roe, B. D., Stoodt, B. D., & Burns, P. C. (1995). *Secondary reading instruction: The content areas* (5th ed.). Boston: Houghton Mifflin.

Rosenblatt, L. (1978). *The reader, the text, the poem: The transactional theory of the literary work.* Carbondale, IL: Southern Illinois University Press.

Ruddell, M. R.-H. (1990, December). *The year of silence: An analysis of high achieving readers' nonparticipation in a reading response group.* Paper presented at the National Reading Conference, Miami Beach, FL.

Ruddell, M. R.-H. (1992). Integrated content and long-term vocabulary learning with the Vocabulary Self-Collection Strategy. In E. K. Dishner, T. W. Bean, J. E. Readence, & D. W. Moore (Eds.), *Reading in the content areas* (3rd ed.), (pp. 190–196). Dubuque, IA: Kendall/Hunt.

Ruddell, R. B., & Ruddell, M. R. (1995). *Teaching children to read and write: Becoming an influential teacher.* Boston: Allyn & Bacon.

Ruddell, R. B., & Unrau, N. J. (1994). Reading as a meaning-construction process: The reader, the text, and the teacher. In R. B. Ruddell, M. R. Ruddell, & H. Singer (Eds.), *Theoretical models and processes of reading* (4th ed.) (pp. 996–1056). Newark, DE: International Reading Association.

Singer, H. (1985). A century of landmarks in reading research. In H. Singer & R. B. Ruddell (Eds.), *Theoretical models and processes of reading* (3rd ed.), (pp. 8–20). Newark, DE: International Reading Association.

Stauffer, R. G. (1969). *Directing reading maturity as a cognitive process.* New York: Harper & Row.

Stauffer, R. G. (1980). *The language-experience approach to teaching* (2nd ed.). New York: Harper & Row.

Thomas, K. J. (1986). The Directed Inquiry Activity: An instructional procedure for content reading. In E. K. Dishner, T. W. Bean, J. E. Readence, & D. W. Moore (Eds.), *Reading in the content areas* (2nd ed.), (pp. 278–281). Dubuque, IA: Kendall/Hunt.

Tierney, R. J., Caplan, R., Ehri, L., Healy, M., & Hurdlow, M. (1989). Writing and reading working together. In A. H. Dyson (Ed.), *Writing and reading: Collaboration in the classroom?* Urbana, IL: NCTE.

Vacca, R. T., & Vacca, J. A. L. (1996). *Content area reading* (5th ed.). New York: HarperCollins.

Vygotsky, L. S. (1968). *Mind in society.* Cambridge, MA: MIT Press.

Vygotsky, L. S. (1986). *Thought and language* (A. Kozulin, Ed. & Trans.). Cambridge, MA: MIT Press.

Wood, K. D., Lapp, D., & Flood, J. (1992). *Guiding readers through text: A review of study guides.* Newark, DE: International Reading Association.

Building Table

Chapter 5	Content DR-TA, GMA and VSS	DIA	Three Level Guides	Reading Response Groups
Focus On	Content reading and discussion; information organization	Content reading and discussion; information organization	Content reading and discussion; information organization	Content reading and discussion; information organization
Guides Students	Before, during, and after reading Before writing	Before, during, and after reading	Before, during, and after reading	Before, during, and after reading
Use to Plan	Lessons, units	Lessons, units	Lessons, units	Lessons, units
May Be Used	Partnerships, cooperative groups	Whole groups, cooperative groups, partnerships	Cooperative groups	Cooperative groups
May Be Combined With (known strategies)	Reading Response Groups	GMA, VSS, REAP	GMA, VSS, K-W-L Plus, REAP	GMA, VSS, K-W-L Plus, REAP
Materials Preparation	Light to moderate	Light	Extensive	Light to moderate
Other Preparation	Moderate	Moderate	Moderate	Light
Outside Resources	Necessary	Useful	Useful	Necessary
How to Do	Page 141–143	Page 145	Page 150–151	Page 156

CHAPTER 5	K-W-L PLUS	REAP	PREP
FOCUS ON	Content reading and discussion; information organization	Content information organization	Content reading and concept learning
GUIDES STUDENTS	Before, during, and after reading	After reading; during writing	Before reading
USE TO PLAN	Lessons, units	Lessons	Lessons
MAY BE USED	Whole class, cooperative groups, partnerships	Cooperative groups, partnerships	Whole class, cooperative groups, partnerships
MAY BE COMBINED WITH (known strategies)	VSS, REAP, reading response groups	DR-TA, DRA, GMA, DIA, Content DR-TA	DRA, VSS, DIA
MATERIALS PREPARATION	Moderate	Light	None
OTHER PREPARATION	Light	Light	Light
OUTSIDE RESOURCES	Necessary	Useful	Not needed
HOW TO DO	Page 157–159		

WRITING ACROSS THE CURRICULUM

Consider your most recent observation(s) of middle school, junior high, or senior high classes in your subject area. What amount and kind of writing were students doing? List what writing activities you observed. How does this recent observation compare with your own junior high/senior high school writing experiences in your subject area?

"Writing across the curriculum" is our newest misunderstood slogan in the world of literacy development and instruction. It is misunderstood because some people construct meaning for writing across the curriculum that conjures up 500-word essays, grammar and punctuation exercises, research papers, creative writing, and all the other aspects of writing instruction generally associated with the English curriculum. Some people in the field of middle and secondary school literacy instruction have even begun avoiding the phrase because of this misunderstanding and the resulting confusion (Atwell, 1990).

What then, *is* writing across the curriculum? Very simply, it is the opportunity *in each and every class* for students to work through ideas in writing, to articulate their thinking by writing, and to polish and refine ideas in written form. Writing across the curriculum may, indeed, involve themes and essays, but more likely it will be accomplished primarily in jottings, learning logs, lab books, journals, reading/viewing response statements, notebooks, quick writes, and all manner of places and ways that are vastly different from the written essay that typifies writing in English classes.

Further, writing across the curriculum is concerned mainly with *process*—writing as a medium for learning—rather than writing as a polished product. That is, the *act* of writing assumes greater importance here—when students jot down everything they know about a topic, list questions they have about an idea or an assigned reading, write their reaction to an experiment or performance, or respond to a classmate's idea in writing—than the actual writing that is produced. (In fact, the term *process writing* is frequently used to designate content and writing instruction with this focus.) Sometimes, the product of that writing will be developed further into a polished piece; often, it will not. The value of the kind of writing we are focusing on here is the deep processing required by the act of writing itself and the very real phenomenon of people achieving insight and developing concepts *as writing progresses*, as opposed to merely writing down what they have already understood or perceived. When students elect (or are assigned) to develop a piece of their writing into a polished product, that value is increased through the elaboration and refinement processes that are required for such development.

WRITING IN SUBJECT AREA CLASSROOMS

TRADITIONAL WRITING INSTRUCTION

Until very recently, almost everyone viewed writing in the secondary school to be a sort of academic dance—a stylized task in which a teacher assigns "topics" that students "write about" and submit for the teacher to "grade." This notion of writing was focused almost exclusively on students recording and documenting their learning rather than gaining insight or elaborating knowledge through the writing process itself. The point of writing from this traditional perspective was for students to "show what you know," even if they used others' words to do it (Ruddell & Ruddell, 1995).

Arthur Applebee (1981) captured such a view of secondary writing in his national study, *Writing in the Secondary School*. As part of the study, Applebee, over a two-year period, visited 15 students' classes unannounced to see what was going on when students were writing. He found the following:

1. A lot of writing went on outside English classes (about 60% of what he observed).

2. Almost half of all writing tasks required only that students write or respond to words or sentences; almost none (about 3%) required response to or development of full-bodied text beyond the word/sentence level.

3. On the average, only 3 minutes were devoted to thinking time for writing assignments (the time from the moment students realized writing was to happen to the moment they began to write).

4. Teachers typically abandoned students during the time when students were actually writing. The general practice was, as we suggested earlier, that teachers assigned topics, students wrote (often outside the class), and teachers evaluated.

5. Most writing assignments asked students to demonstrate knowledge rather than encouraging them to speculate, question, or explore ideas.

6. Many writing assignments centered around what Applebee (1983) called "Impossible topics": for example, "Describe the social, political, cultural, and religious changes Europe was going through at the Reformation."

7. Most assignments required students to give knowledge to someone who knew more about the topic than they *and who could therefore make sense out of nonsensical writing*. The entire exercise—the dance [my language]—consisted of students writing on topics they knew very little about in an attempt to demonstrate what it was they did know, followed by teachers using their greater experience and knowledge of the topic to construct meaning from students' less-well-constructed writing attempts.

NEW VIEWPOINTS ABOUT WRITING

Applebee's picture is a pretty discouraging one, and, I think, a fairly accurate reflection of the writing experiences we all had in secondary school. Happily, the picture is changing, and this about-face change in teachers' thinking is typified in Susan Mauney's teaching experience:

> I realized that reading science references and writing up reports was a very limited use of the written word in my classroom. I believed I had missed opportunities to use language—particularly writing—for years because I used writing primarily as an end-product exercise. We would do lab and write about it or conduct research and write about it. Writing was used at the end of an activity as a summative evaluation rather than as a tool for use during all stages of learning. I knew that writing things down helps me learn, but I had not given my students the most beneficial kinds of writing tasks. They had not had much opportunity to put their understandings about science into their own words (Mauney, Lalik, & Glasson, 1995, p. 193).

What Mauney, and others, now recognize is that students need to write daily in all their classes for the purposes of what James Moffett (1989) has categorized as "NOTING DOWN (Notation), LOOKING BACK (Recollection), LOOKING INTO (Investigation), THINKING UP (Imagination), and THINKING OVER/THINKING THROUGH (Cogitation)" (p. 3).

THINKING WITH A PENCIL IN HAND

Lucy Calkins (1986) calls such writing "thinking with a pencil in hand." It's worth a paragraph or two from Lucy Calkins (in fact, it's *always* worth a paragraph or two from Lucy Calkins) to get a real sense of the value of writing for thinking, learning, and manipulating ideas.

> I think with pencil in hand. Writing gives me awareness and control of my thoughts, it allows me to hold onto ideas long enough to scrutinize them, to think about my thinking. When a student comes to my office to talk to me, I

often say, "Wait, let me get a pencil." The pencil allows me to listen, to structure what I hear. My fingers itch for that pencil. I carry pencils in my car, and when I plan speeches or rehearse chapters, I sometimes jot a word or two down on nearby scraps of paper. I do not care about neatness or word choice; I am not writing to produce but, instead, to think. Fulweiler, one of the influential scholars on this topic . . . writes, "Scientists, artists, mathematicians, lawyers, and engineers all 'think' with pen on paper, chalk on blackboard, hands on terminal keys" (1982, p. 19). Like these people, I think by writing and I want my students to do likewise (p. 262).

Calkins continues about teachers' roles in developing students' thinking abilities:

It often seems that students watch our classes as I watch television. With glazed eyes, they wait for information to come to them. We see their glazed eyes and think, "I've got to be more stimulating." Our lessons become more animated, more varied, anything for a flicker of interest. Of course, we fooled ourselves. We've bought into the notion that we can "learn them." This is not only bad grammar, it is impossible. Learning isn't something we can do for or to our students. Learning requires an act of initiative on their part. We can only create conditions in which learning can happen (p. 265).

One way we can create facilitative learning conditions for students is to provide many opportunities for them to write: in Calkins's words, to "think with pencil in hand." Specifically, we must allow students to connect with their prior knowledge base, articulate and integrate new information, and ask questions about what they know and don't know about a given topic; in short, we must engage students in precisely the same "substantive discourse" discussed in Chapter 5 (Newmann, 1991).

William Zinsser, in his book *Writing to Learn* (1988), echoes Calkins in his explanation of the "why" of writing across the curriculum and adds a new twist or two:

Writing is a tool that enables people in every discipline to wrestle with facts and ideas. It's a physical activity, unlike reading. Writing requires us to operate some kind of mechanism—pencil, pen, typewriter, word processor—for getting our thoughts on paper. It compels us by the repeated effort of language to go after those thoughts and to organize them and present them clearly. It forces us to keep asking, "Am I saying what I want to say?" Very often, the answer is "No." It's a useful piece of information (p. 49).

THE WRITING REPERTORY

Moffett's (1989) categories of student writing are useful for reminding us of the many kinds of writing experiences available for classroom use. He calls this the "writing repertory" and suggests various types of writing in each category. I would like to focus on three of his categories—NOTING DOWN, LOOKING INTO, and THINKING OVER/THINKING THROUGH—because they are the most appropriate to all subject areas. The following discussion extends Moffett's (1989) analysis to explore ways in which writing activities are applicable across the curriculum.

Noting Down   Noting Down is often the foundation for a variety of writing, reading, thinking, and learning events. This category includes:

Journals	Jottings
Logs	Speculations
Lists	Predictions
Diaries	Forecasts
Maps	

Consider how we began the content DR–TA in Chapter 5 by asking students to list "everything you know about whales" and the topic brainstorming used in Carr & Ogles's (1987) K–W–L Plus. That's Noting Down. We extended the Content DR–TA listing and transformed it into prediction by focusing attention on the topic for the reading—feeding habits of humpbacked whales—and asking students to mark anything on their list they believed would be in the reading. K–W–L Plus extends similarly by requiring students to list what they want to learn before reading. That's also Noting Down. Every bit of this is Noting Down with a purpose—the purpose being to activate prior knowledge and set the stage for substantive discourse and integration of the new information with what students already know.

Noting Down activities are a major way for us to hear students' voices, to find out what students know and do not know about a given topic, and to learn the different perspectives and content knowledge bases afforded by various cultural and experiential backgrounds. Clearly, this kind of activity need not be confined to preparation for reading. It can, and should, be used to prepare students for discussion, film/video viewing, experimentation, action, and many other classroom events. What is important is that we keep firmly in mind that what we're doing here is using writing as a medium for learning (we are, indeed, engaging students in "writing across the curriculum activities") *as we teach content* and consider ways that we can extend this writing with activities that are authentic to our discipline.

Looking Into   Looking Into activities are frequently the very thing to extend Noting Down. This category includes:

Biography	Experiments
Investigations	Research
Review	Analysis

Looking Into extends Noting Down as students create a new text from what they have read, seen, done, thought about, or examined. Nancy Spivey (1989) describes this process as one in which the reader (or observer) constructs knowledge through interaction with the text (or event), transforms that knowledge through organizing, selecting, and connecting ideas, and then, in turn, constructs new meaning in a new written text. Sometimes this process is highly structured, as in formal laboratory reports or major research papers; other kinds of writing such as biographies, reviews and informal analyses are less so.

In the content DR–TA lesson on humpbacked whales, the issue of cooperation verses competition during feeding was raised as students discussed the article. The following Looking Into activity is appropriate for accompanying this reading:

> In our reading, an issue was raised about whether humpbacked whales' feeding habits are cooperative or competitive. Consult at least three (3) other sources and gather as much information as you can about the cooperative/competitive nature of humpbacked whales' feeding habits and list your conclusions. Bring your conclusions and outside information to class on Monday.

There are many other authentic Looking Into writing activities for all academic disciplines. High on the list are student surveys and analyses of their own and others' ideas, actions, attitudes, knowledge, and beliefs in relationship to whatever topic is being studied.

Thinking Over/Thinking Through   Thinking Over/Thinking Through is conceived by Moffett (1989) as the highest level of writing. It is, in fact, an important means for bringing about the integration of new knowledge that is so critical for learning. Thinking Over/Thinking Through includes:

Editorials	Musings
Personal essays	Reactions/responses
Position papers	Evaluations
Comparative analyses	Conclusions

Thinking over/thinking through involves many of the same cognitive and writing processes we described in Looking Into. The difference is that, in Thinking Over/Thinking Through, students are truly transforming information and incorporating it into their own knowledge base. According to Spivey (1989), "They dismantle source texts and reconfigure content they generate from stored knowledge." *This is where students make knowledge their own*, and we increase substantially the probability they will do so when we give them many opportunities for Thinking Over/Thinking Through *in writing*.

Recall our content DR-TA on the feeding habits of humpbacked whales. We have already done noting down writing in the preparation for reading. Students have read and constructed knowledge about the article and done some Looking Into writing. We can now transform that newly constructed knowledge with the following writing assignment:

> Consider the issue raised in our reading about whether humpbacked whale feeding habits are truly cooperative: There is some evidence to suggest they are competitive instead, and we have gathered evidence that supports one or both positions. Discuss this issue with your partner, using conclusions you have drawn both from the original article and from other sources. Agree on a position with your partner and draft a position statement (length is your choice) of your conclusions with reasons. You may consult additional sources.

As you can see, this writing activity is appropriate for in-class writing, an overnight homework assignment, a full-blown research project, or some combination of the three. How it is used should be determined by student and curriculum needs. Most likely, you'll use such assignments more in the course of daily work than you will as full-blown research projects. Keep in mind that your choice to use extended writing such as this does not mean that you will now have to grade 75 to 90 papers (one-half of the 150 to 180 students you'll have in your classroom daily). Instead, the position statements may simply be recorded as completed and then used as the basis for a full-scale class debate over the issue of cooperative verses competitive feeding habits of humpbacked whales. Grades may be assigned on the combined basis of completed papers and contribution to the debate.

This brings us back to our original point: that writing across the curriculum writing is not part of the traditional academic dance; it does not include teachers assigning topics, students writing essays to fit those topics, and teachers putting grades at the top and notes/corrections in the margins of the paper indicating how successful students were in achieving that fit. Writing across the curriculum becomes something students do for themselves and each other rather than simply for the teacher. Its focus, once again, is process—the opportunity for students literally to *write their way through* knowledge construction and articulation. This process benefits all students, particularly those learning and writing in a second language, and gives everyone advantages and assistance in learning content. More importantly, perhaps, is that writing evolves into a natural, integral part of learning and of the classroom environment itself. The Writing Workshop (Calkins, 1986) is gaining great national popularity as a means for implementing writing across the curriculum.

WRITING WORKSHOP

Writing workshop is a term Lucy Calkins (1986) and others (Atwell, 1987, 1990; Graves, 1983) use to describe a time set aside each day for students to write in classrooms. Much of the impetus for the writing workshop came from the National Writing Project, and to date, writing workshop procedures have been mainly the purview of English teachers in middle school and junior/senior high schools. Those of you in English are probably familiar with Nancie Atwell's *In the Middle* (1987) and/or *Coming to Know* (1990), and Lucy Calkins's *The Art of Teaching Writing* (1995) and *Living Between the Lines* (1991). All of these books provide vivid and useful guides for implementing fully developed writing workshops in elementary classrooms and middle and junior/senior high English classes. Writing workshop ideas, however, are too rich to be confined solely to select classrooms; they are easily transportable to all content areas at all levels. Glenellen Pace's exquisite text, *Whole Learning in the Middle School: Evolution and Transition* (1995), illustrates this, as do others. The following discussion focuses on how writing workshop can be used in all middle school and secondary subject area classrooms.

WRITING WORKSHOP IN SUBJECT AREA CLASSROOMS

The essential notion of writing workshop is that in every classroom there is a time set aside, daily if possible, when everyone in the room is immersed in writing. This time is established and maintained consistently, so that students can depend on its daily (or alternating-day or three-times-a-week) occurrence. The purpose of the workshop is to give students frequent, regularly scheduled opportunities to write about the subject matter of that class and their relationship to it. Calkins (1986) states:

> The content of the writing workshop is the content of real life, for the workshop begins with what each student thinks, feels and experiences, and with *the human urge to articulate and understand experience* [emphasis mine]. The structure of the workshop is kept simple so that teachers and [students] are free from choreography and able to respond to the human surprises, to the small discoveries, to the moth as it pokes its antennae over the top of the desk (p. 8).

The point of the writing workshop is to write and to use writing as a means for making sense of the world; in subject area classrooms, the world we are talking about is the world of content disciplines: physics, government, art, physical education, trigonometry, family living, accounting, auto mechanics, and so forth. Part of the point of the writing workshop is that we are not attempting to "motivate" students to write; we are *turning them into writers* in our subject area. There is a major difference between the two. The reason a regular schedule is so important, the reason everyone must be able to depend on the workshop regularity, stems from a wonderful tendency of the human mind. When students know that they will be writing at a certain time and place, their minds begin to rehearse (during class, out of school, in the middle of lectures and reading and experiments) gathering information, ideas, and ways of saying things to fill the writing time (Calkins, 1986). This is an important event, for it means that students are thinking, analyzing, and *processing* content information; it also means that they are internalizing information and ideas that are part of the class. That, I believe, is precisely what we want them to do.

WRITING WORKSHOP APPLIED

How, then, do we make writing workshop happen in a middle school or junior/senior high classroom and still have time to teach content? To begin with, *let us keep firmly in mind that we are teaching content in the writing workshop.* Perhaps a better way to say this is that students are learning content as they do writing workshop activities.

I recommend setting aside 10 to 15 minutes at either the beginning of class or end of class daily for writing workshop. Both of those times are frequently used for routine tasks or are not particularly productive anyway—when the teacher is taking roll and doing other record-keeping tasks at the beginning of the period, and when everyone is sitting books-in-arms ready to leave at the end of the period. Combine an already-lost 5 minutes with 10 more, and you have a solid 15-minute block of time for writing workshop. To open class with writing workshop, the rule can be, "When the tardy bell rings, you are to be in your seat and writing." To end class with writing workshop, the rule can be, "Everyone writes until you hear the dismissal bell."

Critical to the success of writing workshop is how the teacher interacts with students and perceives his or her role as students write. Remember, I said earlier that the writing we're talking about here is different from the traditional academic dance; the teacher doesn't simply assign, abandon, and grade. Instead, the teacher *guides*. He or she designs writing "prompts" and ideas, rather than assigns topics; consults with writers and teaches mini-lessons (Calkins, 1986) to develop writing skills, rather than abandons; and gives feedback, response, and focusing direction, rather than merely affixes grades. All of this is done with the goal of enhancing students' understanding of class content and developing their ability to become independent, competent learners and writers in the subject area.

GUIDING SUBJECT AREA WRITING

Any number of instructional materials, activities, and strategies are available for guiding student writing. Some are more structured than others; some are "quick and easy" whereas others require more in the way of planning and teaching; and some adapt more easily to certain subject areas than they do to others. Each of the ideas presented here for guiding students' writing is usable in the writing workshop; each is just as adaptable to be used on its own or in some other manner. These ideas also contain critical elements of Noting Down, Looking Into, and Thinking Over/Thinking Through, which we discussed earlier.

WRITING FROM MAPS

Let us go back to the final exercise from our "Splendid Outcast" story in Chapter 3. After the students had entered the VSS words on their maps, the teacher gave the following directions for a sequence of events:

T: Now I want you to go back to your map, and I want you—without talking to anybody and without looking at your story—to find something on your map that really speaks to you, and I want you to write about it in any way you choose. Find something on your map—an idea, a concept, whatever—that really capsulizes the story or makes it more meaningful to you or stands out, and simply write in any form you choose about that part of your map. I'm going to give you several minutes to begin your writing.

(After several minutes.)

T: I'm going to ask you now to share your writing at your table with your group. Everyone understands that this is first draft, the first time pencil hits paper. But I want you to read what you've written to the people at your table and then begin making plans for what you could do with this piece of writing—what you *will* do with this piece of writing for developing what it is you've started. OK? Do that now, please.

(Students read responses to groups.)

(Heard during the group discussions.)

S1:   I'll read mine first—it's very short. First of all, I'll tell you where I'm coming from. I see Rigel as [parallel] to many people in society . . . "reverence and hatred rival attention—the reverence we have for the unattainable . . ."

(Various students talking.)

S2:   The thing that struck me was that it's not easy to be free.

S3:   It's symbolism between Rigel and much of society in the way that a person or a group of people can be viewed in such different ways.

S4:   That story gives you so much to think about.

T: [To one group] Begin planning what you will do with this piece.

Notice how these writing events grow naturally and logically from the other lesson activities. Students have already discussed many aspects of the story and its relationship to their own experience and prior knowledge, organized their thinking about the story with maps (Noting Down), and explored various words and concepts connected with the story during vocabulary discussion. Now they are extending all of this with their written response to the text (Looking Into; Thinking Over/Thinking Through).

EXTENDING SUBJECT KNOWLEDGE WITH WRITING FROM MAPPING

This open-ended "ideas that speak to you" assignment is utterly appropriate for curriculum goals and writing in an English class. In your subject area, however, you may wish to focus student attention more directly. Our previous assignment for students to draw conclusions about whether humpbacked whales' feeding habits are cooperative or competitive is one way, although it was not directly stemming from individual students' maps. Here's another possible assignment from that same reading that achieves both goals of focusing student attention and requiring them to write directly from their maps:

> Go back to your map and decide what you believe to be the key (or critical) event, concept, or interaction associated with the feeding habits of the humpbacked whales. Write a description of that event, concept, or interaction and tell why you believe it is so important. When you have finished, exchange your write-up with your partner. Read what your partner has written, and write a response.

Following this, partners can discuss their respective choices and responses, and these can then be shared with the class as a whole. A final activity could be a teacher-led discussion in which a final class statement is developed to prioritize and summarize important events, concepts, and interactions of the feeding habits of humpbacked whales. Students would be invited to add to their written descriptions and rationale statements in the course of this discussion.

ADVANTAGES OF WRITING FROM MAPS

Writing from mapping is relatively easy. Mapping, by definition, is an organizational activity; it therefore precedes writing naturally by providing visual representation of students' constructions and organizations of knowledge from a learning event (reading or some other). While writing from maps, students can focus on one or more aspect of this organizational scheme and then elaborate their knowledge construction with written text.

Recall Spivey's (1989) notion that writers transform knowledge from reading (or other learning events) through the processes of organizing, selecting, and connecting ideas. Maps literally *are* each student's preliminary organizational plan; they show what ideas the student selected as most meaningful, how these ideas are connected, and the supporting details for each. Through the process of transmediation (Siegel, in press), students are able to "reconfigure" content (Spivey, 1989)—that is, construct new information, with mapping as the primary vehicle for organizing, selecting, and connecting information. Mapping therefore serves as a productive foundation for student writing to extend knowledge constructed from reading.

How to do . . . .

WRITING FROM MAPS

When you have students write from maps, keep in mind that the fullness of the mapping activity itself is critical to successful writing; specifically, writing will be easier and more fluent when students have had sufficient time to develop their maps fully and share and discuss their maps with other students. Since much of the organizing, selecting, and connecting of ideas goes on during the mapping and sharing, student energy can subsequently be directed toward the writing itself.

Important also are the kind of directions you use to initiate the writing. These directions need to combine two seemingly disparate elements: (1) They must grow from and relate directly to your content curriculum objectives; they need to reflect what you want students to know or be able to do when they've finished this lesson; (2) at the same time, they must be sufficiently open-ended to allow for diversity in students' responses related to perspective, stance, cultural and linguistic background, prior knowledge base, and various other cognitive, affective, and social aspects of learning. Your role—the true essence of the art of teaching—is to facilitate and direct the writing and discussion so that instructional objectives are achieved without stepping on or invalidating diverse viewpoints. The key to that is focusing on students' logic, support, and rationale for decisions rather than the decisions themselves. The following steps are useful for implementing writing from maps:

1. Identify instructional objectives.
2. Plan the lesson activity (reading, etc.) and follow-up group mapping activity.

continued

How to do   *continued*

3. Develop writing directions that lead students from important ideas on their maps to decisions, conclusions, or evaluations. Include attention to logic and rationale in the directions.

4. Develop procedures for partnership, small-group, or whole-class sharing of writing; include written responses, if possible.

5. Decide how writing will be used: for example, notes for class discussion, base for revision and further development, or idea for research paper focus.

JOURNALS

Writing journals are beginning to be seen as standard operating equipment in all secondary classrooms. They've been around a long time in English classes and just recently have begun to find their way into mathematics, physical education, social studies, science, and other subject area classrooms. Journals are particularly useful in the writing workshop because they lend themselves well to regular, systematized writing times. Spiral-bound, 8½ " by 11" notebooks are the most commonly used journals.

EXTENDING SUBJECT KNOWLEDGE WITH JOURNAL WRITING

The purpose of journals in subject area classes is to allow students to keep a running account of their progress and knowledge in a class (Zinsser, 1988) and to explore ideas and issues in relationship to what they know and what they are learning. Usually, journal writing is content-specific but open-ended: Students write about their reactions to ideas, grapple with new concepts or skills, ask questions, call for help, or pass judgment on ideas or class events. Other times, teachers focus students' writing with prompts or directions; this may take the form of asking students to describe the meaning of an algebraic sentence, for example (Zinsser, 1988, p. 157), or some other task.

It is important that journals be subject-focused so that they perform the function for which they are intended. Everyone must understand that content area journals are not totally free-form; they are not diaries or chronicles of students' personal lives. Rather, they are a forum for students to express honestly their constructions of knowledge and attitudes in a subject area, to ask questions, and to state what they do and do not know. This requires that journal writing become a regular part of classroom routine and, if possible, a daily procedure. If journal writing opportunities are infrequent, students rarely get past their initial tendency to cover their feelings of inadequacy and/or mask honest responses and cannot develop the fluency of expression that allows them to explore areas that baffle or frustrate them. Several authors (Atwell, 1987; Thompson, 1990; Zinsser, 1988) recommend a "letter to the teacher" format to give focus to student writing about their current progress in class. Whatever the format, journals are universally considered to be "private talk" between teacher and students; any sharing or public revelation of journal content must be done only with express consent from both.

Journals offer two major advantages to students in learning content. First, they constitute a written record of students' ideas and steps in learning. As such, they allow students to return to their ideas, concerns, insights, and so forth so that elaboration of barely formed ideas may occur after a time of reflection or as the result of other new learning. Second, because initial ideas and jottings are kept intact in the bound journal (and not lost in the jumble of notebooks and lockers), they remain available to be mined by the students at a later date when major projects or extended elaborations of class content are to be completed.

RESPONDING TO JOURNAL WRITING

Generally, teachers collect, read, and respond to journals on a regular basis. (Smart teachers learn to establish a staggered schedule for collection so that they don't face the daunting prospect of reading 150 journals in the same weekend! Transportation issues alone suggest careful planning and discretion here.) Most teachers do not grade the journals per se but, rather, respond and react to student entries. If grading does occur, it is usually associated with whether or not the journal writing has been done.

The issue of how one finds time to respond to student journals deserves to be addressed here. One easily overlooked aspect of this issue is that when journals are used daily, *responses to students' writing must be done overnight or over the weekend so that journals are back in students' hands and available for more writing on the next school day.* This means that there is very little slack in whatever submission schedule you choose; there is some slack if you use journals on alternate-day schedules.

I recall that when I had freshman, sophomore, and junior English class journals to read, I very quickly became overwhelmed by the sheer volume of students' writing and the amount of time it took to read and respond to each entry. I learned I couldn't read and respond to *everything* students wrote. I learned I didn't want 120 journals at the same time (I couldn't even carry them to the car!) because it made the job of responding seem so much more overwhelming. So, I set staggered due dates for journals by class (two classes each Friday on alternating weeks) and asked students to designate one entry each week (total of two) for me to read and respond to. I could then spot-check other entries as time permitted, but was, at the very least, responsible for reading and responding to the designated entries. There are other alternatives and options for responding to journals that are equally useful; decisions about them are usually based on a combination of personal, pedagogical, and curricular variables in combination with a certain amount of trial and error adjustment.

JOURNALS IN SUBJECT AREA CLASSROOMS

Because journals are becoming much more common in middle and junior/senior high classes other than English, various alternatives for using journals are appearing in the literature (Zinsser, 1988) and in classrooms themselves. A common pattern in mathematics seems to be that on arrival in the classroom, students get their journals from the teacher's desk and write for a designated time. Often, students use the journals to describe their experiences (problems and successes) in completing the homework from the night before. Other mathematics teachers use journals at the end of class for students to state in their own words what it was they learned that day, what questions they have, and what they felt they didn't understand. It is heartening to note that my physical education students report journals being used in a middle school physical education program for the same kind of reflection on progress in physical education and health. Social studies and English teachers often use a "Quote of the Day" writing prompt as a means for opening class each day. Famous quotes, current-day quotes, quotes from popular television shows, or others are used for students to respond to in writing and share their responses for the purpose of connecting the quote both with their own experiences and the current class topic.

I think you will find it possible to include journal writing of some type in your classroom, whatever your subject area. Keep in mind that you are not limited to written prompts for student journaling; cartoons, pictures, music, art, and other media are perfectly good resources. Below is one approach for journaling using excerpts from a *Smithsonian* article (Daniloff, 1991) that might be part of a world history, English, or humanities course. The article is about Russian Decembrists forced into exile in Siberia and their wives who followed them. Following the article excerpts are two writing prompts that could be used following the reading.

FIGURE 6.1   *Excerpts from* Smithsonian *Article*

I first became aware of the wives of the "Decembrists," as the conspirators are called, through my husband's research on his great-great-grandfather Alexander Frolov, a young lieutenant who received 30 years' hard labor and eternal exile for a negligible role in that ill-fated plan to eliminate the czar. In his memoirs, Frolov referred to the women as "guardian angels," crediting them with the prisoners' survival. As I learned more about these courageous women, who undertook a 4,000-mile journey into the icy wastelands of Siberia to save their men, I became convinced that without their wives, the rebels would have disappeared from history, just as the czar had wanted. Certainly they would not have become the legendary figures they are today in the Soviet Union . . .

In 1855 Maria Volkonskaya recalled a Siberian day in 1827: "I heard the clanging of iron on the stone floor, then my husband stood before me and I saw his legs were held in heavy chains," she noted in her memoirs upon returning to Russia after 28 years in exile. "Only then did I fully realize the sacrifices required to fight for liberty in our country." To the amazement of the guards, the princess dropped to her knees and kissed the prince's iron shackles.

When she had left Moscow for Siberia, Maria was only 20, the daughter of a hero of the Napoleonic Wars. Growing up on a huge estate in the Ukraine, she had been dubbed "Princess of the Ganges" because of her dark eyes and hair. Her thick locks, according to Pushkin, were "more lustrous than daylight and darker than night." He was so attracted to the young Maria that he immortalized her in several of his works, and many biographers believe he was secretly in love with her until his death.

In 1827, the emaciated convict in vermin-infested rags who shuffled out of the bowels of the Nerchinsk prison to greet Maria was His Highness Maj. Gen. Prince Sergei Volkonsky,

FIGURE 6.1

scion of one of Russia's most illustrious families. Her father had encouraged her marriage to a Volkonsky—the family was immensely wealthy, with close ties to the imperial court. The prince was one of 121 men banished to Siberia for his role in the plot to destroy the monarchy, free the serfs and bring constitutional government to Russia.

The confrontation between Nicholas and the wives began soon after the sentencing of their husbands, in July 1826. When the czar learned that several of the women, including the Princesses Volkonskaya and Trubetskaya, wanted to follow their men to Siberia, he resolved to stop them. Since travel documents were required for moving around the empire, the women needed government permission. Normally, Nicholas encouraged families to accompany prisoners to Siberia. It was a way of settling the periphery of his huge empire. But the Decembrists' wives were a different matter. He feared they "would see to it that their husbands were enshrined as martyrs." He was determined to eradicate the "traitors" from history so they could not "poison the minds of other Russians with their liberal heresies."

Nicholas hesitated to ban outright the women's departure, since he would have appeared heartless in the eyes of some of the most powerful families in Russia. Instead, he created obstacles to force the women to change their minds. He made it known that children would not be allowed to accompany their mothers into exile. When Maria Volkonskaya, who had given birth to a son a few weeks after the rebellion, learned of this, she dispatched a letter to the czar pleading for permission to join her husband. "My son is happy," she argued, "but my husband is unhappy and needs me more." Nicholas relented—Maria, yes; the baby, no—but not without an underlying threat. "You are undoubtedly aware of the particular interest I have always taken in your personal welfare," he wrote her in December 1826, "and . . . I feel it is my duty to warn you against the extreme danger that awaits you once you have traveled beyond Irkutsk." . . .

The two princesses' adjustment to conditions in the penal colony was surprising, considering that they had been raised in households with large retinues of servants. At first, they slept on the floor of a peasant shack, so cramped that when they lay down, their heads touched one wall and their feet the other. Small windows covered with fish skin barely let in the light; the stove smoked continually. The wives' first task was to learn to prepare food—a struggle, since most had never done it. They made a great effort to keep up appearances, especially Ekaterina, who insisted on donning a fashionable fur coat and plumed hat even when driving around the village in a peasant cart. Dressing like a lady was not only good for morale, it also reinforced the women's social status with the prison personnel . . .

Maria and Ekaterina had been at the penal colony for only a few weeks when they experienced their first major confrontation with the prison authorities, triggered when the prisoners went on a hunger strike to protest the confiscation of candles from their cells. The commandant accused the men of mutiny, a crime punishable by death. When the women learned of it, they dressed in their finery and took up positions on a boulder outside the prison, where they shouted words of encouragement to their men and gleaned information from the guards. Their vigil lasted two days and three nights. In the end, the commandant returned the candles. A drunken sadist, he raged against the restrictions placed on him both by the czar, who decreed that the "state criminals be occupied, but not worked to the detriment of their health," and the women, who didn't hesitate to complain to their influential families back home. "The Devil

continued

FIGURE 6.1   *continued*

take the prisoners!" he told Maria when she reminded him of his responsibility. "What stupid instructions! If it wasn't for this laughable stipulation I would have shot them long ago." Without the women as witnesses, it would have been easy to do so, passing a death off as an accident.

Writing Prompts   Choose one of the prompts below and write your response in your journal:

1. You are Maria Volkonskaya, wife of Decembrist Prince Sergei Volkonsky, ready to join your husband in exile in Siberia. Write a letter explaining why you will leave your infant son to make this 4000-mile trip.
2. How do you think you would respond to the conditions of life in Siberia? Write a letter describing how the conditions of your exile affect you. What hope do you see?

How to do . . . .

JOURNAL WRITING

Structure is probably the most important element of successful journal writing ventures. I don't think it is an exaggeration to say that most unsuccessful ones have, in all likelihood, been lost for want of structure. It is not enough simply to decide to have your classes do writing workshop journal writing. Planning must go considerably beyond that and include the following steps:

1. *Decide why you're doing journal writing and how it reflects instructional goals.* Consider carefully your reasons, and have them ready to explain to students.

2. *Determine and state explicitly what the daily, weekly and semester-long policies and procedures are for the journal writing.* Consider and make decisions about all of the following:

    What effect, if any, will journal writing have on students' grades?
    When is the best time to write—beginning or end of class?
    How often shall we write?
    Shall we simply *write*, or shall we use a letter to the teacher format, or do I want to develop daily prompts?
    What is a reasonable timeline and routine for reading and responding to students' journals?

3. *Develop and list expectations for student behavior.* Consider and make decisions about all of the following:

> Where will I locate journals? Will students bring them or will I store them? (Many teachers keep journals in their room if they don't have to change rooms. This eliminates many hassles.)
>
> How will students get journals kept in the classroom? What is the consequence if students forget to bring their journals from their lockers?
>
> What is the signal to start writing? What is the signal to stop?

4. *Develop and list expectations for teacher behavior.* Consider and make decisions about the following:

> What will I be doing while students are writing?
>
> Will I write and share my writing with students?
>
> What will be the focus of my response to students' writing?
>
> How much of each student's writing will I read and respond to?
>
> What is my commitment for returning journals after I've collected them?

LEARNING LOGS

Learning Logs are special kinds of journals that accompany students through units of study. They are the repository for students' thinking, ideas, plans, accomplishments, procedures, and products during that unit (Blake, 1990; Chard, 1990; Thompson, 1990). Teacher-written prompts are used to guide student writing before, during, and after the unit of study and are directed toward the cognitive tasks of focusing, gathering, remembering, organizing, predicting, elaborating, integrating, and evaluating (Thompson, 1990, p. 36). Frequently, the unit-opening prompt is what you and I recognize as the beginning of a Content DR–TA or a K–W–L Plus: "List everything you know about _____." Instead of students recording their list on a piece of scrap paper or a K–W–L form, though, they record it in their spiral-bound learning log and have access to it throughout the unit of study. In this sense, learning logs offer the same advantages as journals by preserving students' thinking for later consideration.

Occasionally, teachers use learning logs additionally to deal with procedural issues in the classroom. Nancy Chard (1990) describes a situation in which a group activity was not progressing well: Students were not on task; groups were dysfunctional; and so on. Chard asked students to make two lists in their learning logs under the headings "What Is Working?" and "What Needs More Work?" These lists then served as a springboard for class discussion and decision making regarding continuation of the group project. The project continued.

Learning logs are business; they are filled with all manner of writing, all of which has something to do with the progress of the unit under study. Teacher-developed directions, or prompts, help students focus on important aspects of the unit and guide them in planning their participation in it. The key here for teachers is developing generative prompts. You may wish to use Moffett's (1989) Noting Down, Looking Into, Looking

Back, Thinking Up, Thinking Over/Thinking Through categories to guide your development of prompts. Or, you may use Thompson's (1990) focusing, gathering, remembering, organizing, predicting, elaborating, integrating, and evaluating categories. Recall, also, O'Flahaven's (1989) categories for reading response discussion groups:

1. background knowledge
2. ideas derived from text
3. ideas that go beyond text

These are just as useful guidelines for designing writing prompts as are Bleich's (1978) categories of:

1. text perceptions
2. reactions to text
3. associations with text.

Or you may wish to use categories of thinking that are particularly associated with your subject area. The key is to write prompts that require thoughtful, elaborated responses. Below is an example of how learning log writing prompts guide students through a lesson. The subject area is Civics (Fraenkel, Kane & Wolf, 1990), and the topic is "The Right to Vote."

SAMPLE GUIDESHEET   *Learning Log Prompts for Reading and Writing: Government*

Learning log prompts for reading and writing follow.

WRITING PROMPT 1 (BEFORE READING).
What do you believe the qualifications for voting should be? Why? How are your qualifications alike/different from those we currently have? Share your qualifications with your group.

Students read Section 1: The Electorate

FIGURE 6.2   *The Bill of Rights Expanded*

THE BILL OF RIGHTS EXPANDED

The Bill of Rights does not contain all of the rights that we are guaranteed by law. Attempts have been made to increase the people's rights throughout the history of our country. The Constitution has been amended 16 times since the Bill of Rights was added. Eight of the 16 other amendments involve rights.

EQUAL TREATMENT
Several million black people in the United States were slaves for 69 years after the Constitution was approved. In a case that challenged slavery in 1857, the Supreme Court ruled that the Constitution

did not view black people as citizens. The Chief Justice of the Supreme Court stated that blacks were not included in the phrase "people" in either the Declaration of Independence or the Constitution. At that time, although the practice was unjust, black people's right to citizenship was not recognized.

Slaves had to wait until the Thirteenth and Fourteenth Amendments were passed to have some of their rights recognized. The Thirteenth Amendment ended slavery. The Fourteenth Amendment made black people citizens. It states that:

- All people born or naturalized in the United States and subject to its laws are citizens. (A **naturalized citizen** is one who was not born a citizen but became one later.)
- No state may take away a citizen's Constitutional rights.
- The states must treat all citizens equally.

The Fourteenth Amendment is important because it guarantees full Constitutional rights to all of us, no matter what our race, color, national background, or religious belief.

THE RIGHT TO VOTE

In the early years of our nation, the states did not permit women to vote. In many states, only white males over 21 who owned property valued at a given amount could vote. For years less than half the adult population was eligible to vote.

Today, all born or naturalized citizens 18 or over may vote. Aliens may not vote, nor may inmates of mental institutions or any persons who have been legally found to be mentally incompetent. In nearly all states, persons convicted of serious crimes may not vote. Two qualifications for voting in all states are that a person must be a citizen of the United States and must live in that state. The states are allowed to decide voting qualifications with certain restrictions. For example, voting qualifications may not conflict with the Constitution or other laws that protect the right to vote. The right to vote has been given to all citizens of the United States through the passage of the following six amendments.

The Fifteenth Amendment (added in 1870).   No person may have the right to vote taken away because of race, color, or having been a slave. This amendment removed many voting restrictions (limits) against blacks. Some states, however, found ways to limit black people's voting rights. In 1965, Congress passed the Voting Rights Act to make sure that no qualified citizen would be denied the right to vote.

The Seventeenth Amendment (added in 1913).   Senators are to be elected by the people. The Constitution originally stated that Senators were to be chosen by their state legislatures, rather than by the vote of the people. As a result, powerful groups in a state often picked candidates whom they wanted elected, and the legislature then chose them. The amendment guarantees that the interests of all the people will be better represented.

The Nineteenth Amendment (added in 1920).   No citizen may be prevented from voting because of sex. This amendment brought to a happy ending a long campaign to secure the right to vote for women.

The Twenty-third Amendment (added in l961).   The people of Washington, D.C., may vote for President. Before this amendment passed, they could not vote for President. The city was given the number of electoral votes it would have if it were a small state. Currently it has three electoral votes.

The Twenty-fourth Amendment (added in 1964).   No person may be denied the right to vote because he or she cannot pay taxes. Previously, some states had used a poll tax to prevent black people from voting. A **poll tax** is a sum of money a person must pay in order to vote. Since many blacks were poor and could not pay this tax, they could not vote before the Twenty-fourth Amendment was passed.

The Twenty-sixth Amendment (added in 1971).   No citizen 18 years of age or older may be denied the right to vote because of age. Previously, the voting age in most states had been 21.

Unratified Amendments.   A total of seven amendments have been approved by Congress but have failed to be ratified by the states. If ratification does not occur within a specific time period, the amendment "dies." One example is the Equal Rights Amendment (ERA) of 1972, which died in 1982. It proposed: "Equality of rights shall not be denied or abridged by the United States or by any state on account of sex." Supporters of the original ERA are working toward another ratification attempt.

In 1978, Congress sent to the states a proposed amendment to give the people of Washington, D.C., the same voting representation they would have if the city were a state. Currently the people of that city have no representation in Congress. The proposal must be ratified by the states before it can become an amendment to the Constitution.

WRITING PROMPT 2 (AFTER READING).
Do a survey of the voting habits of your family and friends. Find out how often they vote, why they choose to vote or not, whether they know where their voting place is, and how they arrived at their attitudes, beliefs, and practices. As a "bonus question," ask if they can name their local, state, and national representatives. Write a summary of what you found, and be prepared to share it with your group.

WRITING PROMPT 3 (AFTER GROUP DISCUSSION).
Why do you think states have the right to pass their own voter qualification laws? What issues might enter into state laws regulating voting qualifications? What do you think might be the hottest issue today? What are the voting laws in our state?

DOUBLE ENTRY JOURNALS (DEJ)

By now, you're experienced DEJ users, or, at the very least, you've had opportunity to see a number of prereading and postreading DEJ prompts. The Double Entry Journal (Berthoff, 1981; Vaughan, 1990) is yet another special kind of journal. In the DEJ, the left-hand page of a spiral notebook is for notes, drawings, observations, ideas, word clusters, and maps; the right-hand page is for what Vaughan (1990) calls "cooking" those ideas and observations (p. 69). Writing prompts for the right-hand (postreading) page writing are used with the clear intent to integrate and construct new knowledge from information contained on the left-hand (prereading) page. The same writing prompts illustrated in the section on learning logs are appropriate for use in DEJs. DEJs may also be used to develop or reinforce procedural knowledge, particularly when the class is starting new kinds of research, investigation, or learning. Below are writing prompts for use with DEJs in a music class.

WRITING PROMPT 1: PREREADING; LEFT-HAND PAGE
As you listen to the folk opera *Porgy and Bess*, write down feelings and associations the music and words create for you. Jot them down in any order and any way.

After listening to the opera and recording feelings/associations, the class then reads the prologue to *The Life and Times of Porgy and Bess* (Alpert, 1990) [Excerpted here; possible homework assignment].

FIGURE 6.3   *Excerpts from* The Life and Times of Porgy and Bess: *Music*

What was seen and heard that night after the strains of "Summertime," sung sweetly and winningly by Abby Mitchell, filled the theatre is now known throughout the world. The audience was stirred, moved (many brought to tears), by a musical event unlike any in previous Broadway history. Never had so many black singers of training and talent performed together on a Broadway stage. New stars were made: Todd Duncan, who sang Porgy in a stalwart baritone; Anne Brown, a classically trained and highly educated young singer, in the role of the wanton Bess; Ruby Elzy as the bereft Serena, whose husband is killed early on.

When the curtain fell after the last of the three acts, the tumultuous applause and cheering went on for half an hour. Gershwin was brought to the stage. So were Rouben Mamoulian, the director, and Alexander Smallens, the musical director, and, more reluctantly, the shy Heyward. The audience came to its feet and cheered and cheered.

THE RESPONSE by the New York-based critics to what would eventually be regarded as this country's greatest contribution to opera, and would later conquer many of Europe's most prestigious opera stages, was much more favorable than not, although the notion has persisted that it got a poor press. Only a very few took the work seriously to task. Mostly there seemed an air of puzzlement as to just what it was. Opera was supposed to be presented at an opera house. Porgy and Bess had been performed in a Broadway theatre, and the tendency was to judge it by the standards of Broadway.

Most of the drama critics were admiring. They hailed it as colorful, poignant, well sung and well acted . . . well, except for some pretty dull stretches of recitative. It was from the music critics that a more patronizing tone emerged. A few were sour indeed. Virgil Thomson called it "crooked folklore and half-way opera." Undoubtedly, the mix of opinions caused confusion among theatregoers.

The production, with its large cast and chorus and unusually large orchestra, was costly to run. The break-even point was barely reachable even with full houses night after night. Yet, in spite of its universal popular acceptance, it has generated a remarkable amount of controversy. For years, arguments continued over the merits of its music and whether or not it was truly opera, and, if not, what it should be called. Was it meant for the theatre or for the opera house? And what about the work's treatment of its black characters? Charges were flung that it

continued

FIGURE 6.3   *continued*

contained demeaning stereotypes of American black people. Some black singers, approached for roles, refused to appear in it.

Others have pointed to the fact that because of Porgy and Bess hundreds of black performers, over the years, found work on Broadway stages and in opera houses and thereby advanced their careers. Nowadays the demand for classically trained black singers sometimes exceeds their availability, and the Metropolitan Opera employs dozens in its permanent company. Porgy and Bess has had a great deal to do with this welcome change. The work and its gifted performers have proven to be of vast cultural importance during many travels abroad.

It is taken for granted now that Porgy and Bess represents an epochal event in American music, but in its many manifestations it can also be seen as a kind of mirror of social change in America. The opera's history has its curious aspects, and it has been regarded differently in the decades in which it has been played. It has also been played differently.

Writing Prompt 2: Right-Hand Page
Based on what you've heard and felt and read, how would you answer Gershwin's critics?

BEGINNING RESEARCHERS

Donna Maxim (1990) describes a process she used to guide her students away from the traditional informational report writing mode (in which plagiarism, tracing, and tedium predominated) and teach them how to become real researchers. Maxim used this approach with young children, but it is every bit as useful with students of all ages who have settled into the habit of copying researched information directly from primary and secondary resources and then patching together a "report" that is, essentially, a plagiarized piece of work. Maxim developed her instructional approach in three phases: First, she taught students how to take notes and develop research ideas from listening; second, she developed their ability to read without notetaking and subsequently construct notes; and third, she taught students how to initiate and carry through a research plan by actually doing so.

Phase One: Taking Notes and Developing Research Ideas from Listening
The program begins by teaching students how to take notes without copying ("reading and writing at the same time," as Maxim calls it) through the simple expedient of teaching notetaking by reading to students rather than having them do the reading themselves. The teacher reads a book or book section to the class. The book may be nonfiction or fiction, but it should have sufficient informational content for notetaking to be relatively easy. After the reading, students are asked to record in their logs (1) facts and information they recall from the reading, followed by (2) questions and

speculations these facts and information generate (a good idea the first time you use this might be to go through the process in a whole class discussion using chart paper to recall facts and write questions so that students can see how the notetaking is done). After each listening-notetaking experience, students share their individual notes and questions with the class, and the teacher leads discussion in which students speculate as to what research projects might grow out of the information and questions they've collected.

Any number of books, journals, or magazines are appropriate for this exercise. You may find that nonfiction informational pieces are particularly good for initiating notetaking, such as those found in such weekly or monthly popular magazines as *Newsweek*, *Time*, or *Sports Illustrated* or in topical journals such as *Smithsonian*, *Nature Conservancy*, or *National Geographic*. Don't limit the reading to nonfiction, however; any number of fiction books have social and/or scientific import and are highly useful for stimulating research projects. O'Dell's *Island of the Blue Dolphins* (1960), Jean Craighead George's *Julie of the Wolves* (1972) and *My Side of the Mountain* (1959), Harper Lee's *To Kill a Mockingbird* (1960), Clavell's *Shogun* (1975) and Anna Quindlan's *One True Thing* (1994) are certainly all reasonable choices. Many, many other books are available. I suggest that you gather lots of books, magazines, journals, primary sources, and other materials related to the area of study you're targeting the research projects for and that you read daily from this pool and have students do the notetaking and question generation at the end of each reading.

Phase Two: Reading and Taking Notes

After students become good at listening and taking notes, they're ready to learn reading and notetaking skills. This phase begins by distributing informational magazines to the students (back issues of anything you've collected will do). Students are told not to open their magazine but to look at the cover and generate questions they think they'll find answers to on the inside. Questions are recorded in students' logs. Then, students are asked to leave their desks and their lists and pencils, and go sit someplace else in the room to read their magazines for ten minutes. At the end of 10 minutes, they *leave their magazines at the place where they were reading*, return to their desks, and write out any answers they found to their list of questions.

Maxim reports that her students found this exercise very difficult; they wanted to be able to look back at their reading and do the kind of copy-notetaking they'd become so used to. I'm sure you're likely to encounter some resistance to the activity as well, and I further predict that the older your students and more entrenched their encyclopedia-copying habits are, the stronger the resistance will be. Stand firm here. It will take several repetitions of the exercise for students to realize that they can, indeed, take notes without copying. Keep the source material well within a range of reasonable difficulty (a good reason for using magazines) and repeat the activity frequently.

Phase Three: Initiating and Carrying out Research

It is useful for the class to be engaged in a unit of study concurrently with the exercises you use to teach and have students practice notetaking from listening and reading. It is also important that the students see how their newly learned notetaking skills might be applied to a project in that unit of study. As many resources as possible should be made available that are appropriate within the context of the unit—slide shows, speakers from educational organizations and governmental offices, field trips, movies and television documentaries on videotape, parents and other individuals from the community, library resources both at school and in the community, and so forth.

In the course of this study, and as students become acquainted with various materials and resources, they should begin recording in their logs ideas and questions that they deem worthy of further investigation. Through large class discussion and individual conferences, they will frame their research question, consider and list possible resources, and decide on their plan for the research itself. The students then launch their projects and carry them out.

Donna Maxim's approach for teaching students how to become researchers is, I think, a particularly sound practice. Essentially, it provides guided, sheltered simulation of a productive research process for students to engage in concurrent with a unit of study for which they will subsequently do research. Implementing this approach is not difficult, but it does require advance planning and thought.

QUICK WRITES

Quick writes were described earlier in this text (Chapter 3) as short, open-ended writing opportunities in which students reflect on their own immediate learning process. Quick writes are most commonly, but not always, used at the end of the instructional period. Many teachers use quick writes in mid-lesson if they suspect that students are struggling. Sometimes, the questions that surface in quick writes create breakthrough moments. Certainly, quick writes are appropriate for use in any kind of journal; saving them in the journal further serves to keep them in the context of the lesson for later reference. Quick writes are wonderfully easy to use and are illuminating glimpses into students' thinking. Use them liberally.

WHEN WRITING GOES BEYOND PROCESS

On any number of occasions, you will want your students to develop their process writing into polished products. These pieces will be graded for their final content and form, and students will be expected to follow all the conventions of formal writing. It is important to understand, however, that you cannot expect formal writing instruction and learning processes and conventions students learn in English classes to transfer automatically to your class. You are responsible for *guiding* that transfer by providing instruction and assistance in the kinds of writing appropriate to your subject area and your standards of quality (particularly for polished products).

To do this most effectively, you will need to teach, and the easiest way to do that is through what Calkins calls "mini-lessons" (1986). Mini-lessons are short, to-the-point instructional episodes in which one *something* is taught. For example, perhaps the major written product you want from your students is a formal laboratory report of a series of experiments in chemical reactions. You have noticed that students' learning logs reveal a certain laxness in their observational language, an imprecision of language that leads to ambiguity and murkiness. So, you conduct a mini-lesson on precision of observational language—nothing more. You deal with no other aspect of the laboratory report. The lesson is short (3 to 5 minutes long). The examples you use come from language samples you've gathered in this or other classes. You engage students in generating various ways to achieve precision.

Mini-lessons on library research procedures, report writing, editing strategies, and limitless other topics are useful in guiding students toward polished written products. In addition to mini-lessons, teacher conferences with individuals or groups are frequently helpful. Calkins (1986, p. 19) lists a set of questions that are useful in developing students' writing. Even if you do not view yourself as a "writing teacher," you may find these valuable when you want to assist students in moving from their journals or learning logs into more formal writing in your class. These questions (or something like them) might even be written on poster board and displayed in the room so that students can see them daily.

QUESTIONS FOR GUIDING MY WRITING

1. What have I said so far? What am I trying to say?
2. How do I like it? What's good here that I can build on? What's not so good that I can fix?
3. How does it sound? How does it look?
4. What will my reader think as he or she reads this? What questions will they ask? What will they notice? Feel? Think?
5. What am I going to do next?

A FEW FINAL WORDS ABOUT WRITING ACROSS THE CURRICULUM

In Chapter 2, I said that reading and writing are different sides of the same coin. Certainly, there are differences between them, but for the learner, both reading and writing yield constructions of knowledge that support learning. Very few people debate the importance of reading in a subject area as a potent means for learning; yet many people are skeptical about the potency of writing's influence on learning. I hope you no longer are. Your students will benefit enormously from the process writing they do in your class, and the extent to which you make writing a regular, daily part of classroom life is the extent to which you will increase that benefit.

Just as we want our students to be readers who learn more about calculus, world literature, economics, health and fitness, music, chemistry, and much more, from reading, so too do we want them to be writers who learn from writing. Joe Bob Briggs (1991), one of my favorite newspaper columnists, gives the quintessential advice for how one becomes a writer. His words resonate just as clearly for writing in subject areas:

The way you become a writer is you write. Every day. No exceptions.

Nobody believes this. Everybody wants to believe in something called "talent" or "inspiration" or "knack for it." Maybe there is such a thing, but it has nothing to do with becoming a writer. . . .

Nobody can tell you how to write, but there are certain things you can do to get to a place where you can write. There are three of them:

Write every day.

Write every day.

Write every day.

This is all I know.

D O U B L E E N T R Y J O U R N A L

List five different kinds of writing students could do in your subject area. Add a written description of how you can incorporate these into your daily instruction. How could these, or other writing strategies, be used in specific lessons you teach? Compare your ideas with your partner's or group's.

REFERENCES

Alpert, H. (1990). *The life and times of Porgy and Bess.* New York: Alfred A. Knopf.

Applebee, A. N. (1981). *A study of writing in the secondary school* (Research Report No. 21). Urbana, IL: National Council of Teachers of English.

Applebee, A. (1983, March). *Writing in the secondary school.* Paper presented at the San Diego State University Conference, "New Directions in Comprehension Research." San Diego, CA.

Atwell, N. (1987). *In the middle: Writing, reading and learning with adolescents.* Portsmouth, NH: Heinemann.

Atwell, N. (1990). *Coming to know: Writing to learn in the intermediate grades.* Portsmouth, NH: Heinemann.

Berthoff, A. E. (1981). *The making of meaning: Metaphors, models, and maxims for writing teachers.* Portsmouth, NH: Heinemann.

Blake, M. (1990). Learning logs in the upper elementary grades. In N. Atwell (Ed.), *Coming to know: Writing to learn in the intermediate grades* (pp. 53–60). Portsmouth, NH: Heinemann.

Bleich, D. (1978). *Subjective criticism.* Baltimore: John Hopkins University Press.

Briggs, J. B. (1991, June 9). Writers do it daily. *This World*, p. 4.

Calkins, L. M., with Shelley Harwayne (1991). *Living between the lines.* Portsmouth, NH: Heinemann.

Calkins, L. M. (1995). *The art of teaching writing* (2nd ed.). Portsmouth, NH: Heinemann.

Carr, E., & Ogle, D. (1987). K-W-L Plus: A strategy for comprehension and summarization. *Journal of Reading*, 30, 626–631.

Chard, N. (1990). How learning logs change teaching. In N. Atwell (Ed.), *Coming to know: Writing to learn in intermediate grades* (pp. 61–68). Portsmouth, NH: Heinemann.

Clavell, J. (1975). *Shogun*. New York: Atheneum.

Daniloff, R. (1991). How Czar Nicholas was outfoxed by the guardian angels. *Smithsonian*, 22 (3), 102–113.

Fraenkel, J. R., Kane, F. T., & Wolf, A. (1990). *Government and citizenship*. Needham, MA: Prentice-Hall.

Fulweiler, T. (1982). Writing: An act of cognition. In K. Erle & J. Noonan (Eds.), *Teaching writing in all disciplines*. San Francisco: Jossey Bass.

George, J. C. (1959). *My side of the mountain*. New York: E. P. Dutton.

George, J. C. (1972). *Julie of the Wolves*. New York: Harper & Row.

Graves, D. H. (1983). *Writing: Teachers and children at work*. Portsmouth, NH: Heinemann.

Lee, H. (1960). *To kill a mockingbird*. New York: Lippincott.

Mauney, S. W., Lalik, R. V., & Glasson, G. E. (1995). Looking forward: A science teacher incorporates whole language. In G. Pace (Ed.), *Whole learning in the middle school: Evolution and transition* (pp. 183–203). Norwood, MA: Christopher-Gordon.

Maxim, D. (1990). Beginning researchers. In N. Atwell (Ed.), *Coming to know: Writing to learn in intermediate grades* (pp. 3–16). Portsmouth, NH: Heinemann.

Moffett, J. (1989). *Bridges: From personal writing to the formal essay* (Occasional Paper No. 9). Berkeley, CA: Center for the Study of Writing.

Newmann, F. M. (1991). Linking restructuring to authentic student achievement. *Phi Delta Kappan*, 72 (6), 458–463.

O'Flahavan, J. (1989). *An exploration of the effects of participant structure upon literacy development in reading group discussion.* (Doctoral dissertation, University of Illinois-Champaign).

Pace, G. (1995). *Whole learning in middle school: Evolution and transition.* Norwood, MA: Christopher-Gordon.

Quindlen, A. (1995). *One true thing.* New York: Random House.

Siegel, M. (In press). More than words: The generative power of transmediation in learning. *Canadian Journal of Education.*

Spivey, N. N. (1989, November). *Composing from sources: Text and task.* Paper presented at the annual meeting of the National Reading Conference, Austin, TX.

Thompson, A. (1990). Thinking and writing in learning logs. In N. Atwell (Ed.), *Coming to know: Writing to learn in the intermediate grades* (pp. 35–51). Portsmouth, NH: Heinemann.

Vaughan, C. L. (1990). Knitting writing: The Double-Entry Journal. In N. Atwell (Ed.), *Coming to know: Writing to learn in the intermediate grades* (pp. 69–75). Portsmouth, NH: Heinemann.

Zinsser, W. (1988). *Writing to learn.* New York: Harper & Row.

BUILDING TABLE

CHAPTER 6	WRITING WORKSHOP	WRITING FROM MAPPING	JOURNALS, LEARNING LOGS, DEJ
FOCUS ON	Content information organization and articulation	Content information organization and articulation	Content information organization and articulation
GUIDES STUDENTS	Before, during, and after writing	Before, during, and after writing	Before, during, and after reading and writing
USE TO PLAN	Units, semesters	Lessons	Lessons, units, semesters
MAY BE USED	Whole class	Whole class, cooperative groups, partnerships	Whole class, cooperative groups
MAY BE COMBINED WITH (known strategies)	DR-TA, DRA, GMA, ReQuest, VSS, Content DR-TA, DIA, REAP, Three Level Guides, Reading Response Groups, K–W–L Plus, DEJ, Journals, Learning Logs	DR-TA, DRA, VSS, ReQuest, DIA, Content DR-TA, Three Level Guides, Reading Response Groups, K–W–L Plus, Journals, Learning Logs	DR-TA. DRA, GMA, ReQuest, VSS, Content DR-TA, DIA, REAP, Three Level Guides, Reading Response Groups, K–W–L Plus
MATERIALS PREPARATION	Light to moderate	Light to moderate	Moderate
OTHER PREPARATION	Moderate	Moderate	Moderate to extensive
OUTSIDE RESOURCES	Useful	Useful	Useful
HOW TO DO		Page 179–180	Page 184–185

ASSESSMENT OF STUDENT PROGRESS IN SUBJECT AREA READING AND WRITING

D O U B L E   E N T R Y   J O U R N A L

Draw a line down the center of your page. On the left side of the line list everything you know about assessment. On the right side list what you think you need to know about assessment in order to be a good teacher. Share your lists with a friend.

Evaluation and assessment of student abilities are long-standing issues in public education, especially at the middle school and junior/senior high levels. Few other aspects of secondary education get as much press as student achievement, and it is through evaluation and assessment programs that student achievement levels are measured and reported to the public. "A Dismal Report Card," trumpets a *Newsweek* feature article headline of a few years back (Krantrowitz & Wingert, 1991). (To be fair, the headline was not on the cover, and the story was the last feature article in the issue.) "Rich and poor, North and South, black, brown and white, eighth-graders flunked the national math test. What can be done about this scandal?" (Krantrowitz & Wingert, 1991), continues the story preview of the then-recent National Assessment of Educational Progress (NAEP) results. (I must admit that when I saw the story, my first thought was, "Oh good, they're leaving reading alone for a little while." My second thought was, "Oh dear, here we go again.")

Such headlines and stories are not new, they're not confined to one sector of the media (*Newsweek* is not working alone here), they're not confined to one part of the curriculum—reading seems to get the lion's share, with writing, mathematics, and science running close behind and physical education and foreign language education taking occasional lumps—and they're not likely to go away soon. Those of us who have been in education for a few years have learned to read the headlines and stories and to endure. What we know is that these reports, and the testing programs behind them, tell only part of the story; and, while we rejoice when that part is told reasonably accurately, we realize that media reports generally leave much of the complexity of student achievement undiscussed. Barbara Fox (1990) summarizes the situation well: "Like a barometer that registers air pressure but does not shed light on the reasons for pressure changes, the NAEP reports tell us only how well students are reading [or doing mathematics]; they do not illuminate the reasons for differences in levels of . . . competence" (p. 337).

Those of us in public education, and teacher education, know that no matter how well teachers teach, and no matter how difficult or complex their teaching circumstances, these reports will continue. MaryEllen Vogt (1995) expresses well the ongoing consternation and frustration we all feel as the targets of such reports:

> When Susan Estrich, a UCLA law professor, has a forum in *USA Today* in which she states, "The vast majority of public school students in California are unable to read, write, or compute," I feel defensive and angry. When, while quoting our new state superintendent, Estrich adds, "There are now three years' worth of recently trained teachers in our classrooms who've never been taught basic reading methodology," my blood pressure elevates to dangerously high levels. My temptation is to become an "expert" in tort reform . . . since it's obvious I know as much about legal issues as Susan Estrich knows about reading.

To counter the effects of negative press, *we* must assume responsibility for telling the rest of the story—for illuminating the reasons for differences in students' competence. And we must continue the daily work of teaching school, regardless of how accurately (or inaccurately or incompletely) the story was told in the first place. This means that teachers working in every level of education must be knowledgeable about all types of assessment programs and procedures—classroom, school, district, state, and national—so that we can communicate fully and openly with students, parents, other educators, and the community as a whole about how students (and we) are doing. Further, we must develop and maintain useful, accurate assessment and reporting mechanisms in our own classrooms while monitoring and using appropriately those assessment programs mandated by districts and states.

Our discussion of assessment and assessment programs begins with an overview of key concepts and issues central to various types of achievement evaluation. From there, we go to the focus of this chapter: ways for student progress in subject area reading and writing to be incorporated into classroom assessment. Finally, we will discuss briefly some of the issues and concepts important to understanding and interpreting formal testing programs.

EVALUATION AND ASSESSMENT IN CONTEXT

Let's start with some agreed-upon operational definitions of assessment language to lend clarity and precision to this discussion. Often, assessment words and terms are used slightly differently from text to text and person to person, even though there is a loosely agreed-upon usage standard for each. The definitions that follow represent common usage in the reading/language field; at the very least, these definitions establish mutually understood meanings for discussion in this text.

ASSESSMENT CONCEPTS AND TERMS

TESTING AND MEASUREMENT

Testing and *measurement* are ways we appraise students' reading and writing abilities using a set of oral or written questions, problems, or exercises. Testing and measurement involve some form of *quantification*; that is, when we give tests, or when we measure reading and writing abilities, we use numbers to express what we find. So, we say someone is reading at the "eighth-grade level," or that they scored "in the 75th percentile," or that their writing sample achieved a "5 on a scale of 6," or that their SAT verbal score was "563." All of these numbers have accrued rather stable meanings (both denotative and connotative) through years of common usage and reference; these meanings are used subsequently to interpret and make decisions about students' literacy abilities.

SAMPLING

Sampling is the act of using part of any given entity to tell us about the whole. When we give a reading test with 35 questions and use the results of that test to describe someone's reading abilities, we have *sampled*, not evaluated completely, that person's reading behavior. I always think of sampling as "one taste of the gravy," a little sip that allows you to judge, or predict, how the whole batch will taste. To the extent that we understand that the smaller and narrower the sample, the greater the probability for error (the fewer the tastes we take, the more likely we are to overlook a missing ingredient), we realize the need for broadly based, frequent samples of students' reading and writing behaviors if we are to have a full understanding of their literacy abilities.

ASSESSMENT AND EVALUATION

Assessment and *evaluation* are words generally used interchangeably to describe ongoing qualitative analysis of students' literacy behaviors. Assessment and evaluation may include testing, but are not limited to it; observation, interview, in-progress analyses, and various other evaluative methods are usually combined with test results for teachers to draw conclusions about students' reading and writing abilities. Assessment and evaluation occur over time, so that sampling yields a profile of reading and writing behaviors across that time. A great deal of assessment and evaluation go on in teachers' heads as they watch students in their classes, review and grade work, and consider individual and group academic effectiveness.

All of these analyses are added to the meanings attached to testing numbers to increase the depth of evaluative judgments. So, if we know that a student's language score on a test is the 93rd percentile *and* that the student routinely demonstrates well-constructed knowledge comprehension in written and oral work, we know that the student is functioning very well indeed; on the other hand, if the language score is the 93rd percentile and the student's oral and written work are consistently below adequate, then we know we need to find an explanation for the discrepancy between the test score and the student's response to academic tasks.

FORMAL ASSESSMENT

Formal assessment refers to the assessment program or programs usually carried out at the school or district level that typically focus on testing and measurement. It includes district-designated achievement test batteries—the Comprehensive Test of Basic Skills (CTBS) is a popular achievement test, as is the Stanford Achievement Test (SAT, not to be confused with *the* SAT), and some districts use the Stanford Diagnostic Reading Test (SDRT) as a special kind of achievement test—as well as state-mandated tests. There also may be district-written or district-designated minimum competency tests administered at specified grade levels (sixth, eighth, and tenth grade assessments are common). Tests used in formal assessment programs may be norm-referenced or criterion-referenced. (Definitions for these testing terms are given at the end of the chapter.)

Formal assessment programs in high schools generally also include the PSAT (Pre-Scholastic Aptitude Test), the SAT (Scholastic Aptitude Test, *the* SAT), and the ACT (American College Test). School-district assessment frequently includes statewide testing programs and may involve participation in the National Assessment of Educational Progress (NAEP) test administration as well; NAEP reports that 41 out of the 50 states and the District of Columbia participated in the 1994 NAEP reading testing (U.S. Department of Education, 1994). Formal assessment can involve more than tests, including formal observation (generally done by certified psychometrists or psychologists) and formal consultations, called "staffings," which are led by trained counselors or resource specialists. Counseling, Title I Reading, Special Education, and other programs carry out their own formal assessment programs and procedures in school districts.

Important to understand here is that, for most classroom teachers, actual involvement in the formal assessment program is minimal: At most, teachers may administer all or part of yearly achievement tests in their classrooms under the guidance of a testing coordinator, counselor, or principal. Generally, major decisions about formal assessment are made administratively or by faculty with special degrees and credentials (Counseling, Special Education, Title I Reading, Resource Specialists, etc.). Classroom teachers are, however, expected to understand and know how to interpret these tests.

INFORMAL ASSESSMENT

Informal assessment goes on in classrooms daily and includes all manner of teacher-made tests, structured and unstructured observations, grading procedures and standards, interviews, self-reports, and the myriad things we do to decide how students are progressing. Unit tests are informal assessments, as are teacher observations of students working in collaborative groups or playing a game of volleyball. Information that teachers gain about students' prior knowledge and experience during a guided discussion and information revealed on students' maps or written responses to text, likewise, are informal assessments, as is the information teachers extract from words and definitions students bring to a VSS discussion.

Central to informal assessment is that we are able to take many more, and more varied, samples of students' abilities and behaviors than formal assessment procedures allow; thus, we can have a richer, fuller understanding of what students can and cannot do in our classrooms. With the increased restructuring of middle schools, and some junior and senior high schools, informal conferencing among teacher teams regarding student progress is occurring more and more regularly, adding further to the pool of knowledge about students' academic performance. Informal assessment and informal conferencing are not to be confused with "incidental," or "chance," or "haphazard" assessment and conferencing; rather, informal assessment and conferences are planned, systematic, teacher-informed and -directed, and deliberately comprehensive.

Informal assessment is where classroom teacher responsibility predominates. Classroom teachers carry out the bulk of informal assessment that goes on in schools, although special-class teachers do some informal assessment. It is classroom teachers (not site or district administrators) who are responsible for knowing how to assess; what sampling procedures are most appropriate and useful; how to systematize assessment so that it is not random or arbitrary; and how to communicate results to students, parents, the school, and the community.

AUTHENTIC ASSESSMENT

Authentic assessment refers to systematic sampling of student behavior to see how well and in what ways students are able to do requisite tasks. (The focus in this text is literacy tasks; authentic assessment applies to all other academic areas as well.)

For formal assessment, this means movement away from test items that do not resemble real-life literacy tasks (e.g., reading 150-word paragraphs and answering main idea questions, or choosing correct usage responses in sentences and short paragraphs) toward tasks that do simulate real life experiences (e.g., reading extended complete or excerpted texts and responding to them, or writing extended text)—a movement that poses no small set of problems for test developers and administrators.

For the classroom teacher, authentic assessment is informal assessment made more thoughtful. That is, it is all of the assessment practices we discussed in the section on "Informal Assessment," but these are made authentic—and therefore more likely to reflect students' true abilities—by adherence to the following standards:

1. *Authentic assessment occurs at short intervals over time.* We get as many samples of students' literacy abilities, or tastes of the gravy, as we can. These intervals are planned and systematic, not left to chance or whim, and include assessment sampling during instruction as well as sampling of the products of that instruction.

2. *Authentic assessment requires information from a variety of sources.* Tests are considered only one source of information about how well and in what ways students are able to do what we want them to do. Other ways include daily, weekly, and unit work samples; observation during guided and independent class activities; conferences and interviews with students; student self-reports; and conferences with other teachers (e.g., in team teaching arrangements).

3. *Authentic assessment occurs while students are engaged in, or using products from, real reading and writing tasks.* Instead of giving isolated-word spelling/vocabulary tests, teachers note and keep systematic records of students' spelling/vocabulary behaviors in draft and polished written products. Teachers maintain systematic records evaluating and noting students' responses during DR-TA, three-level guide, journal writing, and other discussion and writing episodes. Teachers read and maintain records of students' quick writes on what the lesson was about and/or what problems were encountered; teachers note what students are able to say in their own words about lesson content or connections students make between the Quote of the Day and class content in journal entries and learning logs. Reading and writing tasks, themselves, are authentic to the subject area discipline rather than skill-and-drill, isolated, and/or artificial.

4. *Authentic assessment uses teacher observation as a major source of information about how well and in what ways students can articulate content knowledge,* rather than relying on test results, or any one other assessment procedure, as the sole criterion of academic achievement. To become skilled in authentic assessment, teachers learn to observe and analyze student behaviors as these behaviors occur in the course of regular classroom activities; they acquire record-keeping procedures that are efficient, informative, and unobtrusive; and they learn to trust their own judgment based on many samples over time, even when their judgment differs from test results.

ASSESSMENT TODAY AND IN THE FUTURE

The notion of authentic assessment represents a major shift of assessment focus and responsibility at every level of schooling and in every sector responsible for evaluation of academic performance. Traditionally, assessment in this country has focused on testing, and no two decades are more representative of this emphasis than the late 1970s and the 1980s, with their skill tests, and minimum competency tests, criterion-referenced tests, state-wide tests, and reemphasis on standardized achievement tests. During this time, the loud and clear message to teachers from every level of administration was, "Test, test and test some more, and don't bother us with judgments about what you see in front of your eyes on a day-to-day basis."

Also, traditionally, classroom assessment has had a negative, and sometimes even punitive, cast; unannounced "pop tests" have long been used to catch kids with their reading assignments down. (This is a blatant misuse of assessment. Teachers using pop tests are trying to encourage students to remain current and involved in class events, but there are many better ways to do this.) More than one or two teachers over the years have deliberately designed tests to be so difficult and arcane that students are baffled and defeated in just the taking of them.

NEW ASSESSMENT VIEWPOINTS

All of this is changing. Teacher evaluation and judgment, rather than tests, now predominate in authentic assessment practices. No one, however, is recommending that we do away with tests—far from it. In fact, coinciding with the authentic assessment movement is discussion and serious consideration about *national* testing mandates for secondary and college (and teacher education) graduates. The result is a resurgence of interest, as National Standards are formulated for subject areas and tests developed to determine how well students meet those standards (Lewis, 1995). Rather than advocate abolishing tests, educators concerned about authentic assessment recommend *changing the tests* (as we discussed earlier) so that tests more accurately represent what we want students to know and be able to do. In the course of this effort, formal tests will have to undergo some degree of transformation, as they are already beginning to do. Teacher-made tests, as well, will acquire new dimensions. By definition, if we turn our attention to writing tests that yield authentic information about how well and in what ways students are able to do certain things, we must abandon test formats directed toward other aims (e.g., punishment or defeat).

As tests become one of a number of important components of assessment, but not sufficient as a single criterion for evaluation, other kinds of assessment practices and skills are required for teachers to have an accurate view of what students can and cannot do. Progress in this area, too, is already beginning to occur, as evidenced by recent literature devoted to alternate authentic assessment practices (Camp, 1990; Howard, 1990; Murphy & Smith, 1990, 1991; Rief, 1990; Ruddell, 1991; Simmons, 1990); the "full house" attendance in sessions on new assessment practices that routinely occurs today at professional conferences in every subject area; and the number of middle, junior high, and senior high schools focusing exclusively on authentic assessment for a year or more of the professional development efforts in that school.

LITERACY ASSESSMENT IN SUBJECT AREAS

I think it is safe to say that you will be involved, in one way or another, in the development of alternative ways to assess and evaluate student progress, whether the language used to describe that effort is "authentic assessment" or some other new name. The goal of this chapter is to give you a thorough understanding of the full extent of what authentic assessment means and the infrastructure, or support, needed for implementing alternative assessment practices in your classroom. Our emphasis, as you would expect, is literacy assessment, but it is literacy assessment *in the context of subject area learning and teaching.* The rationale here is that knowledge of students' reading and writing abilities in your subject area yields much valuable information to you, including:

1. insight into the substance and extent of students' content knowledge
2. understanding of what literacy behaviors students need to learn in order to function effectively in your subject area

3. indication of what you need to do to assist or guide students' reading and writing in your classroom

4. identification of students who should be referred for additional evaluation and/or placement in other school programs.

AUTHENTIC ASSESSMENT OF SUBJECT AREA READING AND WRITING

Assessment in subject area reading and writing must be based on some set of principles, or guidelines, so that we have a means for determining what assessment procedures are and are not appropriate. The following discussion is based on principles adapted from the South Australian *Position Paper on Assessment* (Education Department of South Australia, 1989), which outlines comprehensive guidelines for assessment at all levels.

PRINCIPLES OF ASSESSMENT

1. Assessment should *focus on learning*. The goal here is to encourage, assist, and enhance learning—not to "catch" students unable to do what it is we expect or want them to do. Assessment procedures, therefore, should focus on what students know, rather than on what they don't know, and should occur only after students have been given adequate time to learn. Further, evaluation and assessment should, in some manner, reward students for taking risks and for coming close to a targeted goal. One of the most appealing viewpoints in current theory about language and language learning is that we need to *value approximation* (Cambourne & Turbill, 1987); in other words, we need to understand that "coming close" is a positive, rather than a negative, occurrence—instead of being "wrong," coming close means you are one step closer to being right.

I like the cast that gives assessment. With it, teachers' attitudes and approaches are, "Look how close you came," or "Here's how much my students know," rather than, "Look how many you missed," or "Here's how much my students don't know." This positive cast focuses us away from the old, punitive attitudes and behaviors and toward assessment practices that inform students honestly about what they can do, encourage students to increase the range of things they do well, and allow students to try to do things they have never done before.

2. Assessment should *be equitable*. Equity has to do with fairness, impartiality, and justice. Assessment equity means that evaluation procedures are not simply impartial, but fair and just as well—appropriate for all students, regardless of the range of diversity that these students represent. Whatever students' race, gender, abilities, culture, ethnicity, socioeconomic status, or language background, no assessment practices or procedures should systematically bias evaluative judgments for any individual or group. That's a big order, but it is an important one. Given the diversity of students in today's classrooms, and the probability that your students represent many different cultures, viewpoints, and language and experiential backgrounds, the most reasonable approach is to learn and use a variety of assessment practices so that all students can demonstrate their accomplishments as fully as possible. Further, for some students, equity may require that you use special facilities or services for assessment; if this is the case, do so. If appropriate facilities or services are not available, do whatever is necessary to get them, or make whatever adjustments are necessary to provide these students equal access to equitable evaluation.

3. Assessment should *be congruent with the aims of the system, the school, and the curriculum.* This sounds self-evident, but it really isn't. For years, we've talked about the importance of "critical thinking," "problem solving," and "higher-order thinking" in education, yet we continue to give teacher-made and published achievement tests that focus on literal-level knowledge. That's not congruent. We tell students we want them to "think for themselves" and "use their own judgment," but the minute their thinking or judgment differs from ours, we tell them they're wrong. That's not congruent, either. In fact, this whole area is a maze of misunderstanding.

If we are to move toward alignment between educational aims and assessment, we must first ascertain that the aims of the "system, the school, and the curriculum" themselves are congruent (and not so incidentally, you need to make sure your aims are congruent with those). Then, and only then, can we determine the degree to which assessment practices adhere. It is not unusual to find discrepancies between stated and real values; districts and schools can and do have statements of educational aims that are not fully, or even partially, reflected in the curriculum being taught, available textbooks and equipment, and teaching traditions in the school. When this is the case, serious and extended discussion is required to resolve a basic and crucial inconsistency. Once goals, curriculum, and instruction are in line, assessment strategies must be determined that reflect and support them; these assessment practices must represent what the system and school truly value and what expectations the school holds for students. *That's* congruent.

4. Assessment should *recognize limitations of assessment methods.* One of the frustrations of evaluation and assessment is that no one assessment procedure is perfect. No matter what means we use to evaluate student progress—giving tests, observing students as they work, grading written work, asking students to self-report, or devising elaborate point systems—error or bias may intrude. Of key importance, therefore, is that we understand how each procedure is vulnerable to error, recognize that limitation, and take steps to minimize it. As is so frequently the case, one of the best ways to reduce error is to use a variety of assessment practices because one procedure's weakness is often another's strength. (For example, multiple choice tests give us little information about why students responded as they did; learning logs and DR–TA-type discussions yield lots of information on the "why" of students' logic and reasoning.) Using two or more assessment procedures in tandem reveals a truer picture of what students know than any one procedure alone could.

5. Assessment should *reduce competition and increase cooperation in the classroom.* This sounds antithetical to commonly held beliefs about assessment. In fact, much of what occurs in the name of assessment, from elementary school all the way through college and beyond, is based on a competitive model of evaluation in which one "gets ahead" in the world by "beating" everyone else. I've heard all the arguments about competitive grades "toughening the kids up" and how we're doing a disservice to students by not getting them ready for the competition in the "real world." I don't buy the argument for several reasons. First, we have a substantial body of research (Aaronson, 1978; Cohen, 1986; Deutsch, 1949a, 1949b; Johnson, Maruyama, Johnson, & Nelson, 1981; Sharan, 1980; Slavin, 1980; Sherif, Harvey, White, Hood, & Sherif, 1961) documenting the negative effects of competition in the classroom (and beneficial effects of cooperation), particularly with regard to academic evaluation (Deutsch, 1949b; Johnson et al., 1981; Slavin, 1980).

Second, the argument in support of competitive assessment flies in the face of what real (that is, authentic) assessment is all about: *The purpose of assessment is to find out how well and in what ways students are able to do what we want them to do.* If that is true, then assessment should increase teacher-student and student-student communication; competition generally shuts communication down. Assessment should build feelings of self-worth and competence; for many students, competition destroys both. Finally, assessment should take place in an environment of mutual respect, openness, and trust; competition works against all three. I am not denying the presence of competition in middle and secondary schools (or in the "real world"), nor am I saying it should all go away; rather, I am proposing that assessment and grading are not the appropriate arena for competition to predominate.

6. Assessment should *include participation by students.* I suppose it sounds idealistic, and maybe even iconoclastic, to give some of our assessment "power" to students. Yet, this is an area in which a little yielding on our part as teachers can have major benefits for both our students and ourselves. Most teachers, at one time or another and to a greater or lesser extent, suffer frustration over students' seeming inability or lack of desire to take responsibility for their own learning. We bemoan students' passivity and apparent willingness to let us, or somebody else, do all the work, while we continue to do all the thinking and the work.

I think at least some of the reason students don't take more responsibility is that we control so completely the area of assessment and grading standards and practices. Perhaps if we would ask a bit more—*ask* students what they want to do, *ask* how they think they should do it, and *ask* what they think it's "worth"—perhaps if we would listen a little more closely to students' voices and feed what we hear from them into our own agenda and knowledge of what needs to go on in the classroom, students would willingly assume the responsibility. Whatever our goals and beliefs about grading, students need to have some say in how they are assessed.

7. Assessment should *include consistent and meaningful reporting*, which occurs in many ways and on many levels. First, we must give clear, honest appraisal to students frequently and regularly so that they know at all times where they stand in our class. Second, we need open, consistent communication with parents to give them the same clear, honest appraisal we give students; it is here, however, that communication frequently breaks down.

Many social and economic conditions have led to the widening gap between home and schools—for example, family working and commuting schedules that don't leave time for parents to visit schools; large, impersonal schools that are forbidding and frightening to all but the most secure parents; single-parent families for whom any visit to school requires special child care or work arrangements; immigrant parents who may feel overwhelmed and uncomfortable in schools; teachers and students who commute to schools outside of their living community; homeless students who may or may not even live with their parents. Nevertheless, we must continue our efforts to maintain contact with parents and reduce the barriers to parental participation in schools. Many schools have launched innovative programs to do just that. In addition to parents, school administrators, district governing boards, and local and state communities must remain informed of the results of assessment programs. It is from this widespread reporting of formal and informal assessment results that thoughtful, informed instructional decisions can be made.

AUTHENTIC INFORMAL ASSESSMENT PROCEDURES

One issue that surfaced earlier in this chapter in our discussions of informal and authentic assessment was the need for teachers to use various sources of information in the evaluation of students' subject area reading and writing abilities. This is because virtually all literacy testing devices, no matter how carefully conceived and developed, engage students in artificial literacy tasks unrelated to school tasks and everyday life reading and writing (Brozo, 1990; Elbow & Belanoff, 1986; Simmons, 1990; Sternberg, 1991; Valencia, McGinley & Pearson, 1990). Sternberg (1991) points to the short passages, immediate-recall tasks, multiple choice questions, and single-purpose nature of reading tests; Elbow and Belanoff (1986) note that writing tests lead students to believe that "proficient writing means having a serious topic sprung on you (with no chance for reading, reflection, or discussion) and writing one draft (with no chance for sharing or feedback or revising)" (p. 336). So if teachers want to know how students *really* read and write, specifically with regard to subject area materials, then teachers must have information that goes well beyond the results of reading and writing tests. Two of the most useful types of information are teacher observation and teacher-student interviews.

OBSERVATION AS AN ASSESSMENT TOOL

Observation is probably the single most useful means available for getting information about students' reading and writing abilities (or any other abilities, for that matter). I generally distinguish between "unstructured" and "structured" observation. By "unstructured" observation, I mean those times when you are observing students and are open to any information that may come your way: You are not looking for specific items or particular areas of learning/expertise, but you take note of important information as it is revealed. "Structured" observation, on the other hand, occurs when you have clearly identified purposes for observing: Perhaps you are wanting to see what students do when they come to a word they do not know, or how students preplan first-draft writing, or how well students are able to make and support predictions while reading the textbook. Both types of observation are useful and appropriate in the classroom. Generally, structured observation yields more systematic information, but unstructured observation may be equally productive—we often learn the most important details about students when we least expect it.

NOTETAKING AND RECORD KEEPING WITH OBSERVATION

Critical to the success of any type of observation is that teachers develop and maintain a system of notetaking to record information and impressions they have of students. This can be as simple and straightforward as keeping a spiral notebook in which notes are kept in a diary-like fashion by recording events/insights occurring daily, or each student is assigned to a page and dated notes are entered as observations occur. Or, perhaps a set of 4" by 6" or 5" by 8" file cards with each student listed on a separate card would be ideal. Some teachers keep Post-It note pads handy for jotting down information they observe during busy class time; later, they transfer the information to more permanent record sheets. Another possibility is using a database or word processing capabilities for establishing and maintaining observational records. Use whatever method suits your style.

This notion of maintaining notes and records of observations is not new to modern classrooms. Teachers used to keep all sorts of anecdotal records of students in the "cumulative folders" that followed students from grade to grade. Mostly, these notes and comments were focused on statements about students' behavior and represented teacher judgment and impressions from daily contact with students rather than so-called hard facts. Then two things happened to change this practice. First, the Buckley Amendment (Family Educational Rights and Privacy Act) was passed in the mid-1970s, a federal statute that decreed that all official school records must be open and available to parents—a condition heretofore unheard of in U.S. education. In no time, throughout the country, cumulative folders were denuded of all teacher and counselor comments, leaving nothing but test scores and attendance records. The second occurrence was the ascendancy of test scores over teacher judgment as *sine qua non* of student evaluation that occurred as a natural result of the heavy testing emphasis in the late 1970s and throughout the 1980s. Fear that teacher comments would be unsubstantiated (and vulnerable to legal action) and the availability of "hard data" in the form of test results led to an official stance that, for almost two decades, has been evaluation based on test results with almost no credence given to anecdotal, observational information.

NOTETAKING AND PURPOSES FOR OBSERVATION

With our renewed focus on observational data and teacher judgment, we must keep in mind our purpose for observation so that the notes we take and the records we keep reflect that purpose and not something else. (Otherwise, school administrators will get very, very nervous.) *The purpose for assessment (observation) is to determine how well and in what ways students are able to do what we want them to do in a given subject area:* that, and nothing more. (Our focus in this text is limited further to language and literacy abilities in subject areas.) So, the notes you take and the records you keep should focus on how well and in what ways students function with text in your classroom. I recommend that you begin by using some sort of structured observation to assist you in focusing your attention on specific aspects of literacy and to hone your observational skills. Later, as observation becomes second nature to you, you may want to use a more free-form, unstructured approach.

THE DEVELOPMENTAL INVENTORY

The *Developmental Inventory* is an observational instrument I wrote (Haggard, 1984; Ruddell, 1991) for use during routine classroom activities and/or with written products from these activities. The inventory can be used to evaluate all aspects of language, reading/listening, and writing/speaking. It is designed to guide teacher observation during any of the instructional activities we've discussed in this text—VSS, mapping, writing workshop, DR–TA discussion, Content DR–TA, DIA, learning logs—as well as other kinds of activities that routinely occur in classrooms, including, but not limited to, current-events presentations, chapter discussions, demonstrations, all manner of media activities, and so forth. In addition, the inventory is useful for guiding teacher evaluation of written work and other products of classroom instruction. It is called the *Developmental Inventory* to focus attention on a basic notion about literacy: that the literacy behavior students exhibit at any given time reflects their current theory of how language works (Ruddell & Ruddell, 1994; Ruddell, 1991); these theories, and behaviors, are expected to change over time (i.e., develop) so that language and literacy functioning becomes more proficient.

The *Developmental Inventory* is made up of two separate, but generally parallel, lists of language and literacy behaviors focusing on listening/reading (Figure 7.1) and speaking/writing (Figure 7.2). Within each list are four categories of language and literacy behaviors that contribute to students' ability to use subject area materials and generate text. These categories are:

1. Guides Self or Audience Through Text
2. Knows How Text Works
3. Understands Social Nature of Meaning Construction
4. Uses a Range of Strategies while Listening, Speaking, Reading, or Writing.

The purpose of the inventory is to guide teacher observation and analysis of students' language and literacy behaviors; it is one way to do structured observation in your classroom and as you grade student work. It is certainly not the only way—there are any number of alternative foci you could have, and just as many different criteria for assessment. Nevertheless, this inventory is a place to start. After you become comfortable with it, you can then adjust, add, or revise according to your own specific needs. Let's now look at the four categories of literacy behaviors that the inventory uses.

1. *Guides Self or Audience Through Text.* Whether students are reading with your guidance or independently, whether they are watching a demonstration narrated by you or on a film or videotape, or whether they are mapping or writing their response to a classroom event, their ability to generate guideposts for moving them through the text of that event is critical to the knowledge that they construct. It is, in fact, a major aspect of strategic reading and learning. So, we need to look closely at students' ability to generate these guideposts (Guides Self and Audience Through Text) to monitor their opportunities for arriving at well-constructed knowledge. While reading, listening to an oral presentation, or watching a demonstration or film, students guide themselves through text by making predictions or asking predictive questions.

FIGURE 7.1   *Developmental Inventory: Listening, Reading*

Student Name _____ Grade _____ Date _____

Observation and evaluation of:

LISTENING   READING
(circle one)

Instructions: Circle the appropriate letter to describe how each statement fits this student during your most recent period(s) of observation.

U = Usually   O = Occasionally   R = Rarely

Guides Self Through Text

1. Makes predictions   U O R
2. Supports predictions with logical explanations   U O R
3. Uses both prior knowledge and text information to support predictions   U O R
4. Changes and refines predictions as reading/discussion proceeds   U O R

Knows How Text Works

5. Demonstrates knowledge of common text elements and patterns   U O R
6. Draws inferences from spoken and written text   U O R
7. Understands how to use various source materials and events appropriate
   to age/grade level   U O R
8. Demonstrates fluency and confidence when engaged with text   U O R

Understands Social Aspects of Meaning Construction

9. Is aware and tolerant of others' interpretation of spoken
   language and written text   U O R
10. Supports and maintains own position in face of opposition   U O R
11. Participates in interactions to negotiate meaning construction   U O R

Uses Range of Strategies While Listening/Reading

12. Raises questions about unknown information   U O R
13. Uses illustrations and/or other graphic information to construct meaning   U O R
14. Relocates and uses specific information to support predictions, inferences,
    and conclusions   U O R
15. Revises meaning as new information is revealed   U O R
16. Uses a functional system to gain meaning for unknown words
    (e.g., context-structure-sound-reference)   U O R

A useful way for you to assess how well students do this independently is to observe the extent to which they do it during guided reading and other discussion events. The DR-TA, Content DR-TA, K-W-L, DRA, ReQuest, DIA, and similar instruc-

FIGURE 7.2   *Developmental Inventory—Speaking, Writing*

Student Name _____ Grade _____ Date _____

Observation and evaluation of:

SPEAKING   WRITING

(circle one)

Instructions: Circle the appropriate letter to describe how each statement fits this student during your most recent period(s) of observation.

U = Usually   O = Occasionally   R = Rarely

Guides Audience Through Text

1. Uses language markers to identify the beginning, middle, and end of spoken or written accounts   U   O   R
2. Develops and elaborates ideas   U   O   R
3. Uses descriptive names for objects and events   U   O   R
4. Provides adequate information for audience understanding of events, ideas, arguments, and accounts   U   O   R

Knows How Text Works

5. Demonstrates knowledge of common text elements and patterns   U   O   R
6. Relates information in a logical sequence   U   O   R
7. Uses language and sentence structures appropriate to text type and age/grade level   U   O   R
8. Demonstrates fluency and confidence while speaking and writing   U   O   R

Understands Social Aspects of Meaning Construction

9. Understands and appreciates various speech and writing styles   U   O   R
10. Adjusts language to clarify ideas (spontaneously or over time)   U   O   R
11. Participates in interactions to negotiate meaning construction and develop elements of text and style   U   O   R

Uses Range of Strategies While Speaking/Writing

12. Uses ideas and language effectively to show sequence of events, cause-effect relationships, and to support main ideas   U   O   R
13. Revises extemporaneous speech or first draft writing to arrive at a more polished product   U   O   R
14. Develops cohesion through idea organization and language use   U   O   R
15. Explores topics with some degree of breadth and depth   U   O   R
16. Develops graphic, spoken and written text that illuminates meaning   U   O   R

The Developmental Inventories may be reproduced for classroom use.

tional strategies are very revealing of students' predictive abilities and the extent to which students are able to support and refine predictions as reading progresses. Therefore, they are perfect opportunities for teachers to do structured observations. The DR–TA, especially, allows teachers to evaluate further the degree to which students are integrating prior knowledge with text information throughout the reading event. Remember, our goal here is not to see whether students' predictions are *right*. Rather, we're interested in whether or not students are able to:

1. Generate predictions that make sense based on the information students currently have.
2. Support their predictions with arguments that are logical and reasonable.
3. Connect what they already know with what they are learning.

Guideposts for moving through text are just as important in speaking and writing events as they are during listening and reading, but here, the individual must guide the audience, as well as the self, through text. We use any number of speaking and writing conventions to do this. Language markers are one kind of convention. Language markers are words and terms that signal certain text events. When you were young, the words, "Once upon a time" signaled the beginning of a story; that's a language marker. In middle grades, students use "The End" liberally to bring their writing to a close; that's a language marker, too.

What you want to observe in students' speaking and writing is their growing sophistication with such markers: opening accounts with statements of time and place ("Yesterday as I was driving to school"); itemizing major points ("First . . . second . . . and finally . . ."); summarizing and recapitulating major ideas ("In summary,"); and many other ways that speakers and writers guide their audience. Further, you want to look to see how well students decontextualize when writing and speaking; that is, the degree to which they develop and elaborate ideas, use descriptive names for objects and events ("legislative and judicial branches of government" versus "senators and judges"; "low, line drive into the right field corner" versus "a hit"), and provide sufficient detail so that the audience didn't have to *be there* in order to understand the event. Questions you can use to guide your analysis here are,

"Does the description or account make sense on its own?"

"Is it understandable without numerous probes for clarification, definitions, and further explanation?"

2. *Knows How Text Works.* One of the most important abilities your students can have is knowing how text and other materials commonly used in your subject area work: how they are organized, what kinds of information reside in them, what information margin notes and footnotes contain, how illustrations and other graphic materials add to or support written text, and so on. Mathematics books, for example, frequently use a format pattern like this:

Explanation and Example

Rule, Generalization, or Formula

Example

Example

(Example)

Exercises

Students who perceive this pattern know where to go when something doesn't make sense; students who don't know the pattern don't know how to get help when they need it. Other texts in other subject areas have different patterns, and some mathematics books have alternative patterns. Critical here is to determine whether your students know these patterns exist, know how to use them, and know how to switch from one to another.

Observing students as they use their texts and when they have questions gives you some understanding of their knowledge of how text works. Similarly, their ability to draw inferences (i.e., see the relationship between the explanation, the rule, the examples and the exercises), use various source materials (e.g., reference books, the card catalog, microfiche, computer software, etc.), and demonstrate fluency and confidence with all kinds of subject-specific text all indicate how well students are able to function in that subject area.

This same fluency and ease need to be established in students' production of spoken and written text in the subject area as well. In journal entries and quick writes, look to see whether students use the text conventions and patterns typical of your subject area, and how well they are able to relate information in logical sequence, use the language of the subject area and topic, and develop ideas fluently. Since those are typically first draft writing, look also to see how revised and polished efforts contrast with first draft speaking and writing. Use questions such as the following:

"Does rehearsal and revision increase the student's reading, writing or speaking fluency?"

"Does she or he demonstrate knowledge of how the text works?"

"Does the student's polished work demonstrate real knowledge of the text conventions of the subject area?"

3. *Understands Social Aspects of Meaning Construction.* We have already discussed at length the social nature of learning and the influence of "substantive discourse" (Newmann, 1991) on knowledge construction. Students need to understand the value of these interactions as well and to participate actively in many different kinds of small- and large-group events. Sophistication in this area requires students to be able both to "hold their own" (maintain own position in the face of opposition, and present ideas articulately and forcefully) and at the same time to understand and appreciate alternate views and perspectives (recognize the validity of other experiences and viewpoints, and appreciate the diversity of different voices and writing styles). Helpful questions include:

"Does the student listen to other points of view?"

"Is his/her response thoughtful, logical?"

"Is he/she willing to include other points of view in his/her own thinking?"

"Does the student achieve a balance between maintaining his/her own position and accepting others'?"

"Does the student understand, appreciate, and use various writing and speaking styles?"

"Does he/she participate willingly in classroom discussions and other events?"

4. *Uses a Range of Strategies during Language and Literacy Events.* Students need any number of "coping strategies" (Cambourne & Turbill, 1987) to be effective language users and strategic readers, writers, and learners. Not everyone agrees on the list of strategies that make students effective, and everyone's list reflects their own particular biases. My list is based on what I believe to be important parts of students' metacognitive strategies for processing language and texts in classrooms; these are things students do that serve to monitor their progress through text and tell them what to do if something goes wrong.

First on the list is raising questions. Next to making predictions, I can think of no other more important cognitive act than question-asking for monitoring learning and constructing knowledge; I am not alone in this belief (see Manzo, 1969a, 1969b; Manzo & Manzo, 1990; Palincsar & Brown, 1986; Paris, Cross & Lipson, 1984; Raphael & Pearson, 1985). Careful observation during ReQuest episodes reveals a great deal about students' question-asking abilities. Second on the list is students' ability to locate and use helpful information in text; using illustrations and graphics, relocating ideas and information to support predictions and conclusions, and reexamining and changing ideas as new information warrants. Finally, there is the all-important area of how students function *independently* with text when they come to a word they do not know. All of these coping strategies affect how well students learn the content itself. They are well worth observing while students read text or listen to lectures and demonstrations.

Coping strategies are just as important in speaking and writing. Here, as with other parts of the inventory, we distinguish between first draft and polished efforts; however, we begin by looking at how well students are able to marshal thoughts and language to do whatever it is they're trying to do. We also look to see progress during the year and how students' abilities to articulate subject knowledge develop in correspondence to instruction and activities occurring in the classroom. Useful questions related to literacy strategies include:

"Does the student raise questions? Are the questions pertinent and useful for arriving at new understandings?"

"Is the student able to show sequence of events, cause-effect relationships, and support main ideas?"

"Does he/she understand the importance of revising and drafting in speaking and writing, and engage willingly in revision efforts?"

"Is the student developing strategies to bring cohesion and organization to his/her work?"

"Does she/he have the knowledge base sufficient for exploring ideas with breadth and depth?"

"Can the student speak, write, and produce maps that illuminate rather than confuse or obscure ideas?"

Using the Developmental Inventory   The inventory is usable both during instruction and when you are reading or grading students' work. You can duplicate multiple blank copies and use one each time you observe a student in class or target that student for analysis of written work. You may want to begin by focusing on only one section of the inventory (Guides Self and Audience Through Text, for example), or you may want to use selected items from the entire instrument. I recommend that you choose a limited number of students to observe during any given class period, no more than two or three. Then, as class progresses, pay close attention to the response of those two or three students, keeping notes as you can.

Have a copy of the inventory near to consult periodically to remind yourself of what you're looking for in the students' behavior. Focus on what students *can* do, and not on what they can't do. Deliberately plan and lead instruction so that behaviors you want to look at are displayed: predicting, elaborating ideas, using graphic information, and so on. Don't forget to continue observing as students work independently or in groups—whether they are reading, writing, or discussing—so that you have a full range of behaviors to record. As unobtrusively and efficiently as possible, take notes and jot down impressions. *As soon as you can after class*, fill out the inventory and make additional notes. If you can do one targeted observation of each student during each grading period, you will have abundant information over the semester or year about your students' language and literacy abilities in your subject area. You will want to plan time to share with students what you observe so that they will have the same knowledge you have about their language and literacy abilities in relation to your subject area.

Notetaking and Record Keeping with the Developmental Inventory   Crucial to the success of observational assessment are the notes you take during your observations and the systematic recording of what you find. The Developmental Inventory is highly useful for recording your observations and additional notes. By recording information on the inventory and maintaining these records, you will be able to see students' progress over the semester or year they have in your class. That's the most useful knowledge of all; you will be able to see how each individual student progresses, how each class as a whole progresses, and how all of the students you teach in a given year develop as the result of your teaching.

A major value of maintaining systematic records of your observations is that such records legitimize the kind of informal assessment that observation represents. Recall my earlier comments about the demise of anecdotal records in students' cumulative folders and the heavy, almost sole, reliance on so-called hard data from tests in our recent past. Much of this change occurred because teachers did not always maintain observational records and notes to support the comments they made: the hard data, if you will. Contributing also was the fact that anecdotal records, for some students, became wholly focused on negative attributes and what students couldn't or didn't do rather than what they could do. (After the Buckley Amendment was passed, such records were abandoned, in part, because of this negative focus.)

If we are to make observation and informal assessment procedures successful now—as we must do if we really are committed to authentic assessment practices—we *must* keep careful records to demonstrate that we are not being arbitrary, capricious, or prejudicial in our assessment practices. These records will demonstrate that: (1) *we are assessing systematically,* in other words, we have specified behaviors that we are observing and goals for the number and kind of observations we make for each student; (2) *we can demonstrate a clear parallel between our instructional goals and the behaviors we are assessing,* in other words, our instructional strategies and classroom activities reinforce the very behaviors we are evaluating, and these behaviors increase and enhance content learning; and (3) *we can demonstrate student progress over time,* in other words, we have numerous samplings of literacy behaviors over semesters and academic years and can demonstrate what students can do at the end of the year that they were unable to do at the beginning.

From such careful record keeping, we put ourselves in a position to override hard data test results *when those samples of student abilities do not accurately reflect what students can and cannot* do. This is how, with informal, authentic assessment practices, teachers come to be able to *trust* their judgments and to become seen by others (parents, administrators, and the community as a whole) as experts on the issue of student achievement.

I think you can see how truly authentic this kind of observational assessment is and that it meets all of the standards for authentic assessment. Clearly, we are using standard, everyday classroom events and tasks as the basis for the evaluation, as opposed to artificially set-up, special tasks. Just as importantly, we increase authenticity by *not stopping class to "test" or "observe" how students are doing;* class is going right on. Students are reading, doing experiments, working problems, using their learning logs, working in small groups, and doing various other activities without interruption. Content learning is progressing. It's only the *teacher* who is stopping periodically to concentrate on students' subject area language and literacy abilities in the context of content learning.

If you choose not to use the Development Inventory for this kind of assessment, then it is to your benefit to devise a list of questions or items you will use to guide your observations and record your findings systematically on a checklist or response sheet. This keeps you honest, it reminds you consistently of what you're looking for, and it establishes your hard database.

INTERVIEWS AND STUDENT SELF-REPORTS

Probably one of the most overlooked methods we have for assessing student abilities is simply to ask them what they can and cannot do. Most of the time, especially if they feel reasonably secure with us, they'll tell us. Students have an amazingly accurate view of their own academic abilities; if anything, they tend to underestimate what they can do.

Interview Assessment   Interview assessment has been a recommended educational practice for many years, and yet it has never really caught on. Most classroom teachers I know would not consider interviewing to be an important part of their assessment practices. I think that's mainly because "interviewing" sounds so formal and time-consuming. Responsibility to conduct 150 interviews, even distributed over an entire semester, is more than a little daunting. Few teachers have the time, energy, or inclination to do anything like that.

Student interviews do not have to be drawn-out, however. We talk to students all the time, both in class and out. If we would use the same mind-set appropriate to observational assessment when we're talking to students, we could do interview assessment just as often and just as authentically as we observe. So, when a student asks for assistance while reading, we can ask, "What do you do when you come to a word you don't know?" (Strategies While Reading and Writing) and note his/her response. Or, we can ask, "When you can't remember how to do the problems in your math homework, what do you do?" (Knows How Text Works); or, "How do you find information in an encyclopedia?" (Knows How Text Works); or "When you're getting ready to write, what are the steps of your preplanning?" (Guides Audience Through Text; Knows How Text Works). You get the idea. The key here is:

1. Do this kind of questioning deliberately and systematically.
2. Write down students' responses.

Voila! Interview assessment.

Questionnaire Assessment   Questionnaire assessment is a form of indirect interview. Many teachers like to have students fill out questionnaires about various aspects of students' knowledge and interest in the subject area. Written questionnaires suffer somewhat from writing-fluency limitations, which may cause students to say less than they would orally, but, for the most part, this doesn't seem to constitute a major problem. Because questionnaires so often ask about interests and attitudes, many teachers like to use them as ice breakers and find that students respond readily to them. Figures 7.3 and 7.4 are questionnaire surveys you may wish to use or adapt for your class. You can, of course, use the questionnaire questions in an informal interview.

Portfolio Assessment   Part of the recent attention on authentic assessment has led to consideration of portfolios as the most useful means of gathering various kinds of evidence to use in the assessment process. *Portfolio* is defined as "1. a flat, portable case, usually of leather, for carrying loose sheets of paper, manuscripts, drawing, etc., . . . and 5. a selection of representative works, as of an artist." (Garulnik, 1978). Portfolio assessment in schools is actually a cross or combination of these two definitions (except for the "leather case" part). That is, in portfolio assessment, we use a specially designated folder or case to hold a representative sample of each student's work that is then used as the material to be examined for assessment of the student's progress. In subject area classrooms, portfolio assessment is focused on content learning but may include language and literacy elements as well. Certainly, it seems reasonable to incorporate some aspect of students' reading, writing, listening, and discussing abilities into evaluation of their subject area knowledge (Murphy & Smith, 1991; Tierney, Carter, & Desai, 1991).

Portfolio assessment can be used in many variations; consequently, teachers and schools considering a move to portfolio assessment from more traditional assessment

FIGURE 7.3   *Reading Questionnaire*

Student Name _____ Grade _____ Date _____

1. Are you a reader? _____ (If no, skip questions 2 and 3.)

2. What do you like to read? _____

   _____

3. What do you like most about reading? _____

   _____

4. How do you know if someone is a good reader? _____

   _____

5. How do you think teachers decide who is a good reader? _____

   _____

6. If you had your choice, what topics or type of books would you like to read for this class? _____

   _____

7. What books or other things have you read that you'd recommend for use with this class? _____

   _____

8. What advice would you give someone who wanted to get better at reading (subject area)? _____

   _____

9. What's the most recent thing you've read? _____

10. What did you think of it? _____

    _____

11. What else would you like to tell me about the reading you do for pleasure or for school? _____

    _____

FIGURE 7.4   *Writing Questionnaire*

Student Name _____ Date _____

1. Are you a writer? _____ (If no, skip questions 2 and 3.)

2. What do you write? _____

    _____

3. What do you like most about writing? _____

    _____

4. What do you think makes a good writer? _____

    _____

5. How do you think teachers decide who is a good writer? _____

    _____

6. What kind of writing do you think we will do in this class? _____

    _____

7. What kind of writing would you like to do in this class? _____

    _____

8. What advice would you give someone who wanted to become a better writer? _____

    _____

9. What have you written lately? _____

    _____

10. What did you think of it? _____

    _____

11. What else would you like to tell me about the writing you do for pleasure or for school? _____

    _____

procedures are immediately faced with a number of important decisions. Murphy and Smith (1990) suggest the range of decisions to be made:

> In a sense, coming up with a portfolio project is like choosing what to teach. The decision automatically creates possibilities and limitations. In the infinite scheme of what can be taught, teachers choose for their particular classroom communities. In the same way, they can make decisions about portfolios with themselves and their students in mind (p. 1).

Purposes for Portfolio Assessment   High on the list of decisions is determining what *purpose(s)* the portfolio assessment is to fulfill. The following potential purposes are adapted from the California Assessment Program Portfolio Project (1989):

1. To examine students' progress over time.
2. To involve students in a process of self-evaluation.
3. To chart and observe growth in second-language development.
4. To serve as an alternative to standardized testing.
5. To identify instructional strengths and areas needing improvement.
6. To assist students and teachers in setting goals.
7. To provide time for reflection about students' accomplishments.
8. To examine writing and other response modes in different disciplines.
9. To replace competency exams.
10. To serve as a college application vehicle.
11. To provide student ownership, motivation, sense of accomplishment, and participation.
12. To look at various stages of the writing process: planning, first draft, revision, rewrite, final revision, and final draft.
13. To serve as an end-of-semester/end-of-year culminating project.
14. To assess curriculum needs.
15. To connect reading, writing, and thinking.
16. To evaluate the kinds of assignments we give students.
17. To serve as a vehicle for publication.
18. To serve as a means for changing our conversations with parents and the public.
19. To supplement or substitute for state-mandated testing.
20. To serve as the basis for parent conferences.
21. To demonstrate to students their own progress and growth.
22. To give importance to daily writing and work.
23. Other _____ .

More than likely, you will find when you are ready to begin using portfolio assessment that several of these potential purposes, and others not listed here, will combine to constitute the full intention for portfolio assessment in your class. Because of the rather large differences between some of these goals (for example, number 9, to replace competency exams, and number 22, to give importance to daily writing and work), and the overlap between others (for example, number 2, to involve students in a process of self-evaluation, and number 11, to provide student ownership, motivation, sense of accomplishment, and participation), it is important to spend the time necessary for purposes and goals of portfolio assessment to be identified. In this way, you will know precisely what you want to do, which will then direct your other decisions.

Early Decisions for Portfolio Assessment   Several years ago, I decided to convert all of my university-course grading to portfolio assessment. I recall well the decision making I had to do. After I decided why I was doing it and what I wanted to accomplish with the portfolios, then came all the other important questions, the first of which was, "What will *be* our portfolio?" Leather cases weren't possible; common pocket folders (color-coded by class) were. I went to a discount office store and got them. I wanted the envelope kind with the elastic band, but those weren't in stock, so I got the less-desirable pocket type. They worked perfectly.

That settled, the other questions loomed:

1. *What will be the criteria for assessment?* What am I looking for? What do I want students to demonstrate? How will I make sure students know what needs to go into their portfolios? What kind of mix do I want between daily work, individual work, group work, tests, first draft and polished writing, and outside work?

2. *Whose responsibility is it to do what?* How directive should I be regarding portfolio contents? How much leeway should I give students to determine what they each want in their portfolio? Should I rule certain things out? Should I require certain things?

3. *What will the guidelines be?* How will students know or be able to judge the quality of their own work? By what standards will I judge the quality of their work?

4. *How shall materials be collected?* Where will the portfolios be housed? How shall materials be presented? What categories of work and what self-evaluations should be included? How many items should be presented for each category of work?

5. *What will the working procedures be?* When and how often will portfolios be evaluated? How will I report evaluation to students? What is my commitment for returning portfolios to students?

These, and many more, questions will need to be answered in the course of a portfolio assessment cycle. Because portfolio assessment is so recent in our notions about what should constitute assessment in schools, and actual implementation is rather scary, you will do well to have a firm grasp on what you want to accomplish with portfolio assessment (the purposes and goals) before you begin using them. More than once during this planning period and the first time you use portfolios, you'll ask yourself, "Why am I *doing* this?" Being able to answer that question keeps you focused and intent on bringing about this very significant change in assessment.

Possible Solutions for Portfolio Decisions   There are some very reasonable and relatively easy ways to answer all those critical decision questions. Linda Rief (1990) describes a portfolio project in her seventh and eighth grade English classes in which she chose to settle the question of who is responsible for what in this manner: She, the teacher, decided the *external* criteria for what goes into the portfolios:

> Each student's two best [written] pieces chosen during a six-week period from his or her working folder, trimester self-evaluations of process and product, and, at year's end, a reading/writing project (p. 24).

The students decided the *internal* criteria: that is, which pieces they wished to present and the reasons for their choices. I like that plan because it's workable and sufficiently directed by the teacher to guide student development. By no stretch of the imagination is it laissez-faire; nevertheless, it remains open to a significant amount of student choice in the assessment process. (Recall the assessment principle that students should have some say in how they're being assessed. This approach is one way to give students real power in their own evaluation.) I used this plan with my students: I identified the objectives for which they were to demonstrate knowledge and ability; they were free to demonstrate their knowledge and ability in any way they wished for each objective.

Determining the mix or range of things that can go into the portfolio is another issue. Here is a partial list of possible portfolio contents:

1. *Samples of student writing*, including idea development (brainstorming), first draft, revision and rewrite drafts, and final pieces. Writing samples should show work over time.

2. *Story maps* from in-class and out-of-class reading. Included also should be writing that grew from the mapping experience.

3. *Reading log*, a bibliography or dated list of books the student has read for pleasure and/or in response to class projects, topics, and issues. Writing done in relationship or response to books listed should also be included.

4. *Vocabulary journal or log* that shows words the student has collected and the definitions she/he has developed for them. Written vocabulary activity work should accompany the journal.

5. *Art work, project papers, photographs*, and other products of work completed.

6. *Group work papers, projects, and products*. A written explication of each member's contribution and self-evaluation of how well the group functioned may be included.

7. *Daily journal* of student's personal thoughts, reflections, ideas, and so forth.

8. *Writing ideas*, a list of things the student thinks would be interesting ongoing writing topics (never a "polished" product).

9. *Observational assessment results*, including, for example, the developmental inventory, interviews, questionnaires, or any other checklist or informal measurement used.

10. *Reading response log or writing from assigned reading* during the year (e.g., summaries, notes, feelings, reflections, evaluations, and other responses).

11. *Learning log/double-entry journal*, including notes, essays, social argument, imaginative writing, written responses, analyses and responses, explication, and writing done in a second (or third) language.

12. *Letters* exchanged with the teacher, pen pals, classroom visitors, and others in the school and community.

13. *Out-of-school writing and artwork* the student selects to include.

14. *Unit and lesson tests* collected over the grading period and/or academic year.

15. Other _____ .

In my opinion, students should be given a wide range of acceptable means for demonstrating their ability to meet standards or criteria. In fact, in my classes, I had to keep reminding students of the broad variety of choice they had; they tended to want to "write something up" for every criterion. You may find it useful to consider media in determining your external criteria; for example, you may require two pieces of writing, three tests, five representative homework assignments, and so forth.

Another possible dimension is the requirement for self-reflection and self-evaluation. Rief (1990, p. 28) required students to answer the following questions regarding their choices of "two best pieces":

- What makes this your best piece?
- How did you go about writing it?
- What problems did you encounter?
- How did you solve them?
- What makes your most effective piece different from your least effective piece?
- What goals did you set for yourself?
- How well did you accomplish them?
- What are your goals for the next 12 weeks?

MaryEllen Vogt and Maureen McLaughlin (in press) comment on the importance of self-reflection in portfolio evaluation:

Self-reflection is the heart of portfolio assessment. It encourages students to ponder what course goals mean and contemplate their ownership of the portfolio process. It tells students that we value their thinking and affords us access to information we've never had in the past (p. 47).

You may also want to consider other kinds of portfolio materials. For example, you may want to increase the depth of information from tests by allowing students to select *x* number of tests out of the total given during the grading period, rework/rewrite/redo the chosen test(s), and accompany that with a written self-reflection similar to what students produced from Rief's evaluation prompts. If nothing else, that certainly changes the role of tests in classrooms. I would expect, also, that first draft and polished writing, text responses, and other literacy artifacts would be included in just about any portfolio collection. These are authentic representations of students' reading and writing abilities in subject areas and are valuable means for evaluating subject area progress.

Making Portfolios Work   You must make several other decisions about portfolios. One is how the portfolio will figure in the grade to be assigned for the grade period. I chose in one class to split the final grade between three items—the portfolio, graded daily assignments, and a research project; in the other class, everything went into the portfolio—daily assignments, group work, and projects; the final portfolio grade constituted the grade for the class. I don't think either choice was particularly fairer to students, more valid, or more appropriate. I favored the everything-in-the-portfolio model at the time of actual grading because it seemed much less bulky and was, in fact, slightly less time-consuming. In that class, 2 out of 28 students misunderstood the point of the everything-in-one-portfolio, however, and believed their grade was based on "one assignment." (There were eight criteria for which students were to demonstrate knowledge and ability using daily work, projects, outside work, class reading responses, and so forth.) Many of the other 26 students were effusive in their praise of the process and felt it was the most thorough, and fair, evaluation they'd ever experienced.

Another set of decisions you will need to make is how and when you will evaluate the portfolios. I recommend that for each grade period, you do one or more "in-progress" evaluations prior to the final, grade-producing evaluation. The in-progress evaluations allow you to assess and give feedback to students about the quality of their work and the choices they are making while the consequence of risk-taking is low. Critical to the evaluation process is that there be a structure for carrying out the evaluation systematically and equitably. I use a combined rubric-narrative-letter grade response for my students' portfolios; the rubric used to evaluate each part of the portfolios ranges from "exceptional" to "thorough" to "adequate" to "inadequate." Then for each section, I write a narrative explanation of its placement on the rubric scale, I write a narrative statement of my overall evaluation of the portfolio, and assign a letter grade. There are any number of systems for evaluating portfolios; Tierney and associates (1991) recommend various alternative formats.

Rubrics assist both you and your students in defining how portfolios are to be assessed and what differentiates good work from not-so-good work. Below are the defining statements that my students and I developed for the rubric I used:

Exceptional:

Information is thoughtfully synthesized.

Information goes well beyond the required.

Information is presented imaginatively and creatively.

Artifacts and rationale statements demonstrate deep understanding.

Artifacts are rich, in-depth, and original.

Rationale statements are explicit, clearly stated, and full.

Rationale statements show clear linkages of artifacts to objectives.

Thorough:

Information is well thought out and organized.

Information is clearly presented.

Artifacts and rationale statements demonstrate clear understanding.

Rationale statements are clear, specific, and varied.

Rationale statements show linkages of artifacts to objectives.

Adequate:

Information is minimal and accurate.

Artifacts and rationale statements demonstrate understanding.

Rationale statements show some linkages of artifacts to objectives.

Every criterion is addressed.

Inadequate:

Information is missing, inaccurate, and/or muddled.

Artifacts and rationale statements are incomplete and/or lacking in breadth or depth.

Rationale statements show no or little linkages of artifacts to objectives.

Every criterion is not addressed.

Obviously, these are not the defining statements that everyone would use; they were, however, appropriate to my class and my students' portfolios. I recommend that you involve students in developing portfolio rubrics (this does, indeed, allow students to participate in their own evaluation), especially if the portfolio is to be awarded a letter grade. After determining the criteria for portfolio contents and explaining that to students, begin the discussion of grading by asking, "What would distinguish 'exceptional' work from 'inadequate' work?" Have students generate statements for the extreme points of the rubric scale, and from that discussion fill in the gradations between the extremes. (A really good idea is to do a "practice rubric-construction exercise" first using a nonacademic task—creating a rubric for "Cleaning Your Room"—and *then* do the portfolio rubric.) This process helps everyone gain clarity about what is to be evaluated and how it is to be evaluated. It also makes your job easier when it comes time for you to do the actual evaluation.

The issue of *time* needs to be addressed here. This kind of assessment, where you look at a variety of work students have done and where you respond in writing to each student, takes time. There is simply no glossing that over, and the only way a secondary teacher with five or six classes a day can possibly find the time is to establish staggered schedules for evaluating different classes. Time commitment is considerable. But even more problematic is figuring out how to get portfolios back and forth from school to home (a wagon, grocery cart, or luggage carrier helps!); portfolios can get bulky and heavy. An even better plan would be to use your planning period and some before- and after-school time, and any other at-school time you can find to eliminate the need to transport portfolios. You may find that you simply cannot evaluate five or six classes' portfolios each grade period. In that event, you may want to use portfolios for students to collect their best work over a semester or year, and, using criteria you establish, organize, write self-evaluations for, and present that work as a culminating project for the semester or year.

There are other time-saving and transportation alternatives. One is to have students evaluate their portfolios and submit a written analysis of their evaluation with attached selected work samples. You, then, would spot-check portfolios in class on an ongoing basis and collect students' self-evaluations at the end of the grade period for determination of final grades. By reducing the bulk of materials you collect (that is, collecting only selected samples of student work), problems associated with transporting portfolios for grading are eliminated and grading time itself is considerably reduced. Another alternative is to allot class periods for you to meet with each student, discuss and evaluate their portfolios in conference with them, and award the final evaluation (whether it is a grade or a written comment) at that time.

Having said all that, I must tell you that even with the time commitment and the scariness of doing something so different from what I'd done before (or seen anybody else do), I am *absolutely committed* to portfolio assessment in my classes. I have never felt so buoyed by grading and assessment; I have never felt I had so many different views of my students' work and learning; I have never felt my attention during assessment focused so clearly on *positive* aspects (what students knew, and could do, and had learned) rather than on the negative (what they didn't know or couldn't do or hadn't learned). In my experience, portfolio assessment has been worth all the planning time and effort and all the time it took to do the actual review and grading. I will continue to refine and use it. Furthermore, I heartily recommend that portfolios become at least a part of your own assessment practices.

You need not jump into portfolio assessment all at once as I did; after all, I had 25 years of teaching under my belt to support me in trying something so new. You may want to ease in. Find a way in your own classroom to incorporate portfolio assessment practices into your grading. Read professional journals to see how others in your field are doing it. (Artists and other performing professionals have used portfolios for years; there's a wealth of information and expertise out there.) Then you can gradually increase the presence and importance of portfolios in your classroom. This kind of assessment gives a means for reducing error, bias, and capriciousness in grading by encouraging us to use various test, measurement, and informal assessment procedures in the grading process. Along the way, we get valuable information about students' language and literacy abilities in our subject area.

FORMAL ASSESSMENT CONCEPTS AND PROCEDURES

Earlier, I said that teachers are much more involved in classroom grading and informal assessment than they are in the formal assessment program. That's why this chapter emphasizes informal assessment practices. Teachers are, however, responsible for knowing how to understand and interpret formal assessment results to students, parents, and the community at large.

It is not necessary for you to be a measurement expert to be able to read, under-stand, and interpret formal test results. You do, however, need a basic understanding of a limited number of measurement concepts. So I present a limited number of care-fully chosen measurement concepts here that will afford you a working knowledge of formal testing and the ability to understand the formal assessment instruments used in your school. The definitions below are based on information in the Test Service Notebook issued by the testing department of Harcourt-Brace-Jovanovich Publishing Company (Mitchell).

TESTING INSTRUMENTS

STANDARDIZED TEST/NORM-REFERENCED TEST

A *standardized test*, or *norm-referenced test*, is a test designed to measure individual per-formance as it compares to an identified "norm group." The norm group is the set of people, of like age and grade to the students being tested, whose performance set the standard against which the students being tested are measured. Standardized tests are supposed to be administered according to prescribed directions (so that the test group has the same conditions as the original norm group) and are scored by prescribed rules (so that the test group results are scored exactly as the original norm group re-sults). Most of the instruments used in formal testing programs are norm-referenced, standardized achievement tests; all standardized tests I'm aware of are commercially published.

TEST BATTERY

A *test battery* is a group of several tests standardized on the same norm group so that the test scores are comparable. Most of the achievement tests administered by school districts are test batteries that include sections on reading, writing, language, mathe-matics concepts, mathematics computation, social studies, and science. Some have fewer sections and cover fewer academic areas, while others are more comprehensive and include such areas as spelling, listening, and reference skills. The Stanford Achievement Test, the Comprehensive Test of Basic Skills, The California Achieve-ment Test, and the Metropolitan Achievement Test are the most widely used test bat-teries (Gillet & Temple, 1994). Some people refer to any group of tests administered at generally the same time as a "battery." That's technically incorrect because the tests do not fit the condition of having common norm groups; therefore, the results are not truly comparable.

SURVEY TEST/ACHIEVEMENT TEST

A *survey test*, or *achievement test*, is a test that measures general achievement in a given area. Survey tests are generally considered to be reasonable estimates of group achievement and not very good precise measures of individual achievement. Unfortu-nately, survey tests are commonly and routinely used to measure individual reading achievement and progress. Survey tests are found not only in batteries. In fact, there are a number of rather popular secondary survey reading tests: The Gates-McGinitie Reading Test and the Nelson-Denny Reading Test are two examples.

DIAGNOSTIC TEST

A *diagnostic test* is intended to locate and analyze specific strengths and weaknesses. For the most part, teachers of special classes and counselors are the primary users of diagnostic tests. Generally, these special teachers interpret results of diagnostic tests to teachers, students, and parents.

CRITERION-REFERENCED TEST

A *criterion-referenced test* is a test designed to provide information on specific skills a student has, rather than to compare the student to a norm group. Generally, criterion-referenced tests are limited in content and yield scores that have meaning in reference to what the student knows in relationship to a knowledge criterion. Most minimum-competency tests are criterion-referenced; students must score above a certain minimum score, or criterion, to pass. Spelling tests are one kind of criterion-referenced test. Some criterion-referenced tests are commercially published.

TEST SCORES

RAW SCORE

The *raw score* is generally the number of correct responses obtained by the student. On some tests, the raw score is the number of correct responses minus some fraction of incorrect responses. Virtually all raw scores are computed in relationship to the time allowed to complete the test. Raw scores are used to compute all other scores. You almost never see raw scores when you look at formal test results; rather, you see various converted scores that were obtained from the raw scores.

MEAN SCORE/MEDIAN SCORE/MODE SCORE

The *mean score* is the arithmetic average of raw or other scores. The mean is frequently used to compute converted scores. The *median score* is the middle score, the point that divides a set of scores into two equal parts. The median is the 50th percentile. Almost always, the mean and median scores of standardized tests are the same. The *mode* is the score that occurs most frequently; that is, it is the score obtained by the largest number of students.

GRADE EQUIVALENT (GE) SCORE

A *grade equivalent (GE) score* is a converted score expressed as a grade level for which the raw score is the real or estimated average. GE scores are expressed in terms of grade and month of grade, assuming a 10-month school year. A GE score of 10.7 is interpreted to mean tenth grade, seventh month; 7.2 is seventh grade, second month. Grade equivalent scores are not very useful, even though they are popularly used and often demanded by parents. Because GE scores are converted from raw scores by mathematical interpolation rather than actual comparison with the norm group, they're not very reliable. Just as importantly, they don't have useful meaning. "Tenth-grade, seventh-month" doesn't really tell us where a student stands, either in a real sense or in relation to other students; we have to infer meaning and/or that relationship by our knowledge of whether that student is a sixth-grader, a sophomore, or a senior in high school. And, even if we do know that relationship, a 10.7 score obtained by a sixth-grader does *not* mean that that student should be given reading material appropriate for the end of tenth grade.

PERCENTILE RANK

A *percentile rank*, on the other hand, is a converted score that tells the position of the obtained score within a group of 100 scores. Percentile ranks are computed using the norm group scores. For example, a 93rd percentile means that a student scored equal to or above 93% of the norm group and below 6% (99th %ile is the highest percentile rank). *Percentile ranks have nothing to do with percent of correct responses.* Percentile ranks are reasonably useful scores; in fact, I think they're the most useful scores for understanding students' achievement and for talking to students and parents. This is especially true if you place the percentile ranks into some sort of context. I use the context shown in Figure 7.5.

STANINE SCORES

Stanine scores are another way to compare a student's obtained score with the norm-group scores. Stanine scores are expressed on a nine-point scale of standard scores ("Stanine" is short for "standard nine"), with the number 5 corresponding to the mean. Since the mean is almost always the median as well, the 5th stanine is approximately the 50th percentile. Although stanines do not correspond exactly with percentile ranks, you can get a very good sense of how students compare with the norm group by looking at stanine scores. Generally, stanine scores are recommended by

FIGURE 7.5   *Scoring Grid*

90th to 99th %ile:	Superior
80th to 89th %ile:	
70th to 79th %ile:	Above Average
60th to 69th %ile:	High Average
50th to 59th %ile:	
40th to 49th %ile:	Average
30th to 39th %ile:	Low Average
20th to 29th %ile:	
10th to 19th %ile:	Below Average
0 to 9th %ile:	Very Below Average

measurement experts as the most useful score for comparing student progress from one test administration to another.

INTERPRETATION OF TESTS

In order to understand and interpret formal test results and the various converted scores, you need to know at least three more things.

Test Validity

Test validity refers to the degree the test measures what it says it measures. There are all kinds of validity expressions, but probably the most important of these are: (1) *content validity*, which is the extent to which the content of the test matches the content of the curriculum, and (2) *face validity*, which is the degree to which the test appears to measure real life skills and knowledge. There are validity computations available in every technical manual for every published test; if you have questions about a test's validity, talk to the test coordinator and get a copy of the technical manual to see the validity information.

Test Reliability

Test reliability refers to the extent to which the test is consistent in measuring whatever it does measure. Reliability concerns accuracy, stability, and dependability of test scores and the amount of confidence we can have that a student's obtained score is real. Reliability information also resides in the technical manual; you should know something about test reliability before you begin interpreting scores and using those interpretations for academic decision making.

Standard Error of Measurement

Standard Error of Measurement (SEM) is a statistic that provides an estimate of the possible magnitude of error present in an obtained score; it is the amount by which the student's obtained score may differ from his or her hypothetical true score due to errors of measurement. SEM is expressed ± X, which is read, "plus or minus X." So, if a test has an SEM of ± 4, and a student obtained a score of 32, this would be interpreted to mean that the student's true score is somewhere between 28 and 36. You can see that the higher the SEM, the less reliable the test.

Any movement within the SEM range (e.g., the student's score goes up or down one to four points), *is considered no movement at all*. Therefore, you cannot say the student has "improved" if his or her score is three points higher this year over last year; neither can you interpret a score as "falling" if it is three points lower. You can see that without knowledge of the SEM, *you cannot interpret test results* because you have no understanding of the amount of error present and the possible range of scores in which a true score resides. Further, you cannot determine the significance of repeated test scores, and therefore evaluate student progress, without this knowledge. As with validity and reliability, the SEM is provided in the technical manual of the test. Request that information from the counselor or test coordinator, and be sure to get information about: (1) what scores the SEM is in reference to (frequently, raw scores), and (2) printouts or lists of what those scores are for each student.

PUTTING FORMAL TESTING INTO PERSPECTIVE

Formal testing programs are a longstanding tradition in U.S. education; it's unlikely that anything will ever override their use. However, there are many problems associated with formal testing. Issues of test validity and reliability, and issues of test pollution or fraudulence, are serious and compelling; all of these issues have been discussed at length (Paris, Lawton, Turner, & Ross, 1991). Inappropriate use and interpretation of tests (recall the discussion of survey tests in which tests intended to measure *group* performance are commonly and routinely used to measure *individual* performance), difficulty in reporting the complexities associated with test performance (Fox, 1990), and a changing U.S. school population all contribute to educators' and others' concerns. These are exacerbated by the multimillion-dollar return publishers receive on yearly test sales and scoring services and the public's continuing demand for test results (Paris et al., 1991).

Major reform of testing practices and programs is occurring rapidly, however. For example, NAEP testing results are now reported and summarized according to Achievement Levels (Advanced, Proficient, Basic), each of which is defined and accompanied by an "anchoring description"; these achievement-level and anchoring descriptions are highly similar in nature to rubric statements. We've discussed authentic assessment as a means for changing classroom assessment practices, and I've alluded to changes in formal assessment several times throughout this chapter. Paris and his associates (1991) call for serious and concerted effort directed toward formal assessment reform based on important psychometric, political, and psychological issues that traditional testing has raised, and the results of a two-stage survey of test attitudes, beliefs, and practices that they administered to 1,000 students. What Paris and his associates found is disturbing, particularly with regard to middle school, junior high, and senior high students.

Student responses to the survey indicated that older students are more suspicious of the validity of test scores than are younger ones, have decreased motivation to excel on tests, and believe themselves not to have useful strategies for taking tests. Paris and associates concluded that yearly testing may have detrimental effects on students and actually depress scores artificially as students progress through school (1991, p. 15). They make the following recommendations:

1. Assessment should be collaborative and authentic to promote learning and motivation.
2. Assessment should be longitudinal.
3. Assessment should be multidimensional (1991, p. 18).

These recommendations are useful for instigating and supporting a major reform movement in the field of formal assessment, and they indicate the need for structural change in how we measure students' achievement. Further, these recommendations are not at all unlike the authentic assessment procedures that were discussed at length in this chapter and that are currently underway in middle and junior/senior high schools. The most valuable occurrence I can imagine would be parallel change toward authenticity in formal assessment practices with the result that our assessment agendas and practices, both formal and informal, will lead to real understanding of students' knowledge and ability.

D O U B L E   E N T R Y   J O U R N A L

_____

_____

_____

_____

_____

_____

_____

_____

Make a list of how you can use authentic assessment practices to learn about students' literacy abilities in your subject area. Beside your list or underneath it, note the problems or difficulties you foresee in using authentic assessment practices. Ask your partner or group to help you find ways to reduce or remove the problems. Spend time discussing how you can communicate to students and parents the results of your evaluations.

REFERENCES

Aaronson, E. (1978). *The jigsaw classroom.* Beverly Hills, CA: Sage.

Brozo, W. G. (1990). Learning how at-risk readers learn best: A case for interactive assessment. *Journal of Reading*, 33(7), 522–527.

California Assessment Program Portfolio Project (1989). Sacramento, CA: California Department of Education.

Cambourne, B., & Turbill, J. (1987). *Coping with chaos.* Portsmouth, NH: Heinemann.

Camp, R. (1990). Thinking together about portfolios. *The Quarterly of the National Writing Project and the Center for the Study of Writing*, 12(2), 8–14, 27.

Cohen, E. G. (1986). *Designing groupwork.* New York: Teachers College Press.

Deutsch, M. (1949a). A theory of cooperation and competition. *Human Relations*, 2, 129–152.

Deutsch, M. (1949b). An experimental study of the effects of cooperation and competition upon group process. *Human Relations*, 2, 196–231.

Education Department of South Australia. (1989). *Position paper on student assessment.* Adelaide, NSW, Australia: Education Department.

Elbow, P., & Belanoff, P. (1986). Portfolios as a substitute for proficiency examinations. *College Composition and Communication*, 37, 336–339.

Fox, B. J. (1990). Teaching reading in the 1990s: The strengthened focus on accountability. *Journal of Reading*, 33(5), 336–339.

Garulnik, D. B. (Ed. in Chief) (1978). *Webster's new world dictionary of the American language* (2nd ed.). Cleveland: William Collins.

Gillet, J. W., & Temple, C. (1994). *Understanding reading problems* (4th ed.). New York: HarperCollins.

Haggard, M. R. (1984, November). *Language-based strategies for assessing reading development.* Paper presented at the annual convention of the California Reading Association, Oakland, CA.

Howard, K. (1990). Making the writing portfolio real. *The Quarterly of the National Writing Project and the Center for the Study of Writing,* 12(2), 4–7, 27.

Johnson, D. W., Maruyama, G., Johnson, R., & Nelson, D. (1981). Effects of cooperative, competitive and individualistic goal structures on achievement: A meta-analysis. *Psychological Bulletin,* 89, 47–62.

Krantrowitz, B., & Wingert, P. (1991, June 17). A dismal report card. *Newsweek,* 64–65, 67.

Lewis, A. C. (1995). An overview of the standards movement. *Phi Delta Kappan,* 76(10), 744–750.

Manzo, A. V. (1969a). Improving reading comprehension through reciprocal questioning (Doctoral dissertation, Syracuse University, Syracuse, NY, 1968). *Dissertation Abstracts International,* 30, 5344A.

Manzo, A. V. (1969b). The ReQuest procedure. *Journal of Reading,* 13, 123–126.

Manzo, A. V., & Manzo, U. (1990). *Content area reading: A heuristic approach.* Columbus, OH: Merrill.

Mitchell, B. C. (1977). A glossary of measurement terms. *Test Service Notebook 13.* New York: Harcourt-Brace-Jovanovich.

Murphy, S., & Smith, M. A. (1990). Talking about portfolios. *The Quarterly of the National Writing Project and the Center for the Study of Writing,* 12(2), 1–3, 24–27.

Murphy, S., & Smith, M. A. (1991). *Writing portfolios: A bridge from teaching to assessment.* Markham, Ontario: Pippen Publishing.

Newmann, F. M. (1991). Linking restructuring to authentic student achievement. *Phi Delta Kappan,* 72(6), 458–463.

Palincsar, A. S., & Brown, A. L. (1984). Reciprocal teaching of comprehension-fostering and comprehension-monitoring activities. *Cognition and Instruction,* 1, 117–175.

Paris, S. G., Cross, D. R., & Lipson, M. Y. (1984). Informed strategies for learning: A program to improve children's awareness and comprehension. *Journal of Educational Psychology,* 76, 1239–1252.

Paris, S. G., Lawton, T. A., Turner, J. C., & Roth, J. L. (1991). A developmental perspective on standardized achievement testing. *Educational Researcher,* 20(5), 12–20, 40.

Raphael, T. E., & Pearson, P. D. (1985). Increasing students' awareness of sources of information for answering questions. *American Educational Research Journal,* 22, 217–236.

Rief, L. (1990). Finding the value in evaluation: Self-assessment in a middle school classroom. *Educational Leadership,* 47, 24–29.

Ruddell, M. R.-H. (1991). Authentic assessment: Focused observation as a means for evaluating language and literacy development. *The California Reader,* 24, 2–7.

Ruddell, R. B., & Ruddell, M. R. (1994). Language acquisition and literacy processes. In R. B. Ruddell, M. R. Ruddell, & H. Singer (Eds.), *Theoretical models and processes of reading* (4th ed.) (pp. 83–103). Newark, DE: International Reading Association.

Sharan, S. (1980). Cooperative learning in small groups: Recent methods and effects on achievement, attitudes and ethnic relations. *Review of Educational Research,* 50, 241–271.

Sherif, M., Harvey, O. J., White, B. J., Hood, W. E., & Sherif, C. W. (1961). *Intergroup conflict and cooperation: The Robber's Cave experiment.* Norman, OK: University of Oklahoma Book Exchange.

Simmons, J. (1990). Portfolios as large-scale assessment. *Language Arts,* 67(3), 262–268.

Slavin, R. E. (1980). Cooperative learning. *Review of Educational Research,* 50, 315–342.

Sternberg, R. J. (1991). Are we reading too much into reading comprehension tests? *Journal of Reading,* 34(7), 540–545.

Tierney, R. J., Carter, M. A., & Desai, L. E. (1991). *Portfolio assessment in the reading-writing classroom.* Norwood, MA: Christopher Gordon.

U.S. Department of Education (1994). *1994 NAEP reading: A first look.* Washington, DC: Office of Educational Resources and Improvement.

Valencia, S. W., McGinley, W., & Pearson, P. D. (1990). Assessing reading and writing. In G. G. Duffy (Ed.), *Reading in the middle school,* (pp. 124–153). Newark, DE: International Reading Association.

Vogt, M. E. (November, 1995). *CRA Research Institute: Introduction.* Paper presented at the annual conference of the California Reading Association, San Diego, CA.

Vogt, M. E., & McLaughlin, M. (In press). *Portfolios in teacher education: Theory, practice, and promise.* Newark, DE: International Reading Association.

EVALUATING INSTRUCTIONAL MATERIALS

In your journal, list the qualities you would look for in selecting texts and instructional materials for teaching your subject area. You may want to identify a specific grade, course, or level (e.g., "sophomores," "calculus," "middle school") to help you focus your thinking. How do the qualities you list assist student learning?

Evaluating instructional materials is the right and responsibility of every classroom teacher. As the people charged with teaching curriculum concepts; with meeting state, school, and district curriculum goals; and with guiding students in the acquisition of content knowledge, teachers must be thoroughly knowledgeable about instructional materials and involved actively in selecting materials. Since the bulk of materials selection focuses on textbooks and other texts, much of what we discuss here in relationship to selection of instructional materials is likewise focused.

Most schools and/or school districts that you're likely to be a part of already have in place standard policies and procedures for textbook selection. Generally, but not always, the larger districts and schools have more formalized procedures, whereas smaller schools and districts use less formalized procedures. Whatever the case, the process of textbook evaluation and selection is intricate and, while the prospect of getting state-of-the-art textbooks is exciting, the process itself can be volatile and difficult.

The reasons for this begin with the fact that textbooks represent an enormous district investment; consider the cost of changing texts in *just one subject area* for an entire district, K–12. (Then think about the cost of keeping textbooks current in all subject areas.) Districts can, and do, expect selection committee members and all teachers who will be using the new texts to spend time and energy in the decision-making process. For teachers, administrators, students, and parents serving on adoption committees and for all teachers affected by the process, time commitment for textbook selection is substantial. Added to the expense and time involved is the coordination that must occur for the adoption plan to be used, regardless of whether the plan is for new mathematics texts in grades K–12, new literature books for grades 7 and 8 in the middle school, or new health texts for grade 9 only.

Further, the process of textbook evaluation and selection is an exercise in compromise and accommodation. From the start, participants know that it will be impossible to find the one text that will please everyone, meet every teacher's needs, and be suitable for every student in the school/district. Yet, that's basically what the process attempts to do. The very makeup of the selection committee itself may be controversial, involving decisions of whether students, parents, school board, or other community groups should participate, and such issues as community values, beliefs, and rights. The upshot is, of course, that after the textbook evaluation and selection process is over, some teachers are inevitably unhappy and displeased, and others feel their agenda and needs haven't been addressed. In addition, there will likely be some students for whom the books are inappropriate as well as some parents or community groups disgruntled by the final choice.

The list of problems goes on. My point, however, is not to discourage you from participating in textbook evaluation and adoption processes. Far from it. You need to be very actively involved; the only alternative is simply to avoid the process and use whatever textbooks other people pick. Early in your teaching career, you will, in all likelihood, use textbooks that others have chosen. (Opportunity for serving on a textbook selection committee generally comes after you've been in a school or district for a while.) As soon as you can, you will want to have a voice in the textbook selection for your subject area. In the meantime, you will still need to evaluate the texts that others have chosen and that you are expected to teach with; you'll have any number of opportunities to choose or buy textbooks and other materials that do not require approval through the textbook selection process; and you'll need to be able to demonstrate to a department chair or principal in clear, crisp language why a given text should or should not be used with your students.

The purpose of this chapter is to give you information about traditional instruments for evaluation of instructional materials, demonstrate alternative approaches for looking at text difficulty and appropriateness, and suggest ways to increase the probability that the selection process—whether it involves you, alone, choosing some books for your classes, or a full-blown, district-directed textbook adoption—will result in well-chosen texts suited to curriculum goals and teacher and student needs.

TEXT AND TEXTBOOK ISSUES

If textbooks are not always boring, reading them is at least hard work. They tend to be impersonal, nonemotional presentations of facts; and, almost by definition, textbooks are difficult. Tremendous amounts of information and associated terminology are compressed into relatively few pages. . . . Add the fact that most secondary students choose neither the textbooks nor the courses in which they are used, and it is not hard to see why so many students consider so many textbooks to be so much drudgery (Baldwin, 1986, p. 323).

Scott Baldwin's description and analysis of how textbooks are viewed by students is, I think, eloquent and accurate. Most textbooks are boring and/or difficult, even now that textbook publishers are giving concerted attention to increasing the quality of their products. To test this theory, the next time you're in a college or university bookstore, go to a subject area that you know very little about or have very little interest in. Choose a course textbook from that subject area at random, and begin reading it. My guess is that you'll not find it easy to do nor very much fun. If you want to extend this experiment a bit further, next go over to the trade book (popular press) side of the store and try to find some fiction or nonfiction book in the same general subject area. Try reading it. Chances are, this book will at least be a little less difficult; chances are also that the experience will be a little more fun.

My point here is to support Baldwin's claim and to argue further (as he did) that we stand very little chance of turning students into lifelong readers and writers if the only thing they read and the only model of writing they see in classrooms is textbook text. This, however, appears to be pretty much the state of literacy use in middle school and secondary classrooms (Applebee, Langer, & Mullis, 1987; Alvermann & Moore, 1991; Tye, 1985; Weiss, 1977), where a single required textbook is frequently the only source for reading and writing activities. Baldwin recommends supplementing required textbooks with selections from the many trade books available in all content areas (1986); others (Atwell, 1987; Graves, 1990) recommend strongly that, when and wherever possible, trade books be used to replace textbooks completely.

COMPARING TRADE AND TEXTBOOK TEXT

To illustrate the contrast between textbooks and trade books, I reproduce an excerpt below from William Manchester's book, *Winston Spencer Churchill: Alone 1932–1940* (1988):

Often he was at his most dangerous when he seemed bored. Hunched over his seat below the gangway, within spitting distance of the Treasury Bench, he would appear to be inattentive to the business before the House. His eyes would close; he would breathe heavily. It was an ambush, of course, and twice MPs on the opposite side of the House lurched into it. The first asked loudly: "Must you fall asleep when I am speaking?" Winston replied: "No, it is purely voluntary." The second, more cautious, merely inquired whether he was asleep. Winston immediately answered: "I wish to God I were!" And he could stifle an effective jab with a sharper retort. As he finished a scathing attack on the cabinet, a backbencher called: "The Right Hon[orable] Gentleman, like a bad bridge player, blames his cards." Churchill snapped: "I blame the crooked deal" (p. 108).

To see how this writing compared with textbook representations of Winston Churchill, I searched a secondary world history textbook, sophomore/junior level, (Leinwand, 1994) to find all references to Churchill in the book. I found four. Of these, two were one-sentence statements in which Churchill's role in World War II was mentioned: for example, "Nevertheless, meetings involving the Big Three Allied leaders—Winston Churchill, Franklin D. Roosevelt, and Joseph Stalin—had taken place at several points during the course of the war" (p. 626). The two other references to Churchill were full paragraphs, one describing his "Iron Curtain" speech and the other telling of his fall from power as Prime Minister. The full text of the description of the Iron Curtain speech is as follows:

> In March 1946, in a speech made at Westminster College in Fulton, Missouri, British Prime Minister Winston Churchill stated: "From Stettin in the Baltic to Trieste in the Adriatic, an *iron curtain* has descended across the Continent." Churchill went on to say that on one side of that curtain, now known as Eastern Europe, was the Soviet Union and the Communist-dominated countries. On the other side, now known as Western Europe, were the democratic nations allied to the United States. Churchill urged that Great Britain and America work together against Soviet **expansionism,** or the the drive to increase territory (p. 635).

In my mind, there's little to compare between the Manchester and textbook text; I'll take Manchester any day.

Because of their very nature—the fact that trade books have the time and room to treat subjects in depth and the need for trade books to have broad-based and intrinsic appeal—trade books generally win hands down over textbooks when it comes to liveliness of text, depth of topic treatment, and interest. Textbooks are written for different purposes than trade books are and are held to standards of topic choice and coverage, pedagogical correctness, and information accuracy that do not affect tradebook publication. Furthermore, the people who select textbooks are not the audience for whom the books are intended. Alvermann and Moore state frankly, "A problem with textbook materials is that their contents are dictated by concerns other than appeal and comprehensibility to students" (p. 973).

RESOLVING THE ISSUES

I am not recommending here that we should do away with all textbooks; textbooks serve very useful purposes as outlines of subject area curricula, compendia of information and ideas, and resources for students and teachers alike. I do believe, however, that if we want to capture students' imagination and encourage them to become lifelong learners, we must give them large doses of the kind of writing exemplified by

Manchester's masterful three-volume biography of Winston Churchill (1983, 1988) (as of this writing, the final volume has not been published) and much smaller doses of the less vibrant, sanitized, and space-constricted standard textbook text. Well-written and well-produced trade books must be much more than simple adjuncts to classroom life; they must become central to the reading and writing that students do and perceived by students and teachers alike as essential materials for learning.

TRADITIONAL INSTRUMENTS FOR EVALUATION OF CLASSROOM TEXTS

Whenever we talk about evaluating texts, we quickly realize that no single factor describes text quality. That is, we can't fully evaluate a book by saying, "The illustrations and graphics are well done and useful for interpreting text"; neither can we use, "This textbook covers all facets of our curriculum"; nor is the statement "This text is at an appropriate difficulty level for our students" by itself useful. Clearly, each of the foregoing aspects of text evaluation is necessary and pertinent to any such discussion; nevertheless, none is sufficient in and of itself to give us reasoned assessment of a specific text. The point here is, all of these factors, and many others, must be considered in relationship to one another in order for valid and useful evaluation to occur. The following discussion looks at a number of traditional instruments for evaluating instructional texts.

READABILITY OF TEXT

Readability is probably the most well-known aspect of text evaluation. *Readability* refers to (1) the difficulty level of text materials, an area of continuing concern for teachers, students, textbook authors, and publishers; and (2) the degree to which texts are considered to be "readable" by a target population. Readability is expressed in terms of grade level; so, when a text is identified as having a readability level of seventh grade, the assumption is that to be able to read and construct meaning for that text, one would need to be reading at or above a seventh grade level.

Readability is also a major focus of discussion, both in the public media and in professional journals, regarding the quality of school texts. Cited in allegations first waged by former Secretary of Education Terrel Bell as the "dumbing down" of classroom texts (Farr & Tulley, 1985), the discussion centers on the efforts of publishers to produce textbooks written at levels so that all students, even those who are less proficient readers, will be able to read the text. Publishers and textbook authors are thought to be "writing to the [readability] formula" rather than producing well-constructed prose, thereby making textbooks "readable," but not very good (recall our earlier discussion) (Bernstein, 1985; Sewall, 1988). Concern exists over the appropriateness of this practice and the resulting quality, or lack of quality, of the textbooks produced.

READABILITY AND READABILITY FORMULAS
The notion of readability grew from reading research during the 1920s measuring the difficulty of content area textbooks and parallel research in vocabulary study (Chall,

1988). Essential to the notion of readability was the belief that if we could establish the level of competence required to read a particular text, we could then more accurately match texts with readers. This belief was the basis for early efforts to develop readability formulas to measure text difficulty (Dale & Chall, 1948; Dolch, 1928; Flesch, 1948; Gray & Leary, 1935; Lively & Pressey, 1923; Lorge, 1939) and continues so in more recent ones (Fry, 1968, 1977; McLaughlin, 1969).

Most readability formulas measure two dimensions of text difficulty: *semantic* (vocabulary) and *syntactic* (sentence) complexity. For each of these dimensions, the assumption of readability formulas is that longer = harder. Semantic complexity is therefore assumed to be associated with word length and multiple syllables; syntactic complexity is assumed to be associated with long sentences made so by modifiers and embedded phrases and clauses.

Clearly, these two dimensions do not account for all possible factors affecting text difficulty: The reader's prior knowledge and stance, text cohesion, and concept density, for example, influence textbook difficulty, along with such aspects as interestingness, understandability, and clarity (Irwin & Davis, 1980; Singer, 1992). Nor does the assumption behind the semantic and syntactic measures of complexity (longer = harder) always hold. "To be, or not to be; that is the question" is a relatively short compound sentence with only one two-syllable word; in all likelihood, it would register at first or second grade difficulty using a standard readability formula, yet any reasonable person would judge the concept level to be considerably above the second grade readability level. Conversely, we know that unusual, multisyllabic words, words that would increase the level of difficulty as measured by a readability formula— "neighborhood," for example—are readily learned by very young readers.

USEFULNESS OF READABILITY FORMULAS

Certainly, readability formulas have serious flaws that overlook important aspects of meaning construction; further, they may be (and, by the way, have been) improperly or inappropriately applied and interpreted. Nevertheless, readability formulas are one of the most researched and validated assessment tools in education; Fry (1989) states that over 1000 articles and reports on readability exist in the literature (p. 294). Furthermore, while various exceptions do exist ("To be or not to be"; "neighborhood"), Fry (1989) makes a strong case that, *on the average*, the longer = harder assumption does indeed hold. He and others (Chall, 1988; Fry, 1989; Klare, 1989) argue additionally that large numbers of studies suggest readability formulas to be valid tools for estimating the difficulty level of text.

In contrast, Weaver and Kintsch (1991) argue against the use of traditional readability formulas in light of recent knowledge regarding text structure, reader-text interactions, cognition, and knowledge construction. They conclude that ". . . these [readability] formulas provide a scandalous oversimplification, more frequently a serious distortion [of text difficulty]. Nevertheless, . . . they continue to be used" (p. 242). Weaver and Kintsch recommend that we refine old formulas or develop new ways to assess readability that reflect more completely our current understanding of knowledge construction, reading, and learning.

My own position is somewhere between fully advocating readability formulas and abolishing their use altogether. While I do understand and acknowledge all the limitations and problems associated with readability formulas as they are today, I must agree with Fry (1989, p. 295) that not using readability formulas is equally as limiting as the problems inherent in the formulas themselves. I am particularly wary of "throwing the baby out with the bathwater" here because I well remember when secondary subject area texts were written and published virtually without any regard for difficulty level. At that time (up until the mid to late 1970s, in fact), secondary teachers were not very able judges of how difficult a text was. This was not out of malice or neglect, but was related to the fact that until the 1970s, few secondary teachers took courses in content area reading. Therefore, they were not attuned to issues and concerns associated with content reading and writing.

Just as importantly, secondary teachers were, and remain, subject area *experts;* they have spent years vitally interested and immersed in the literature of their discipline, and have forgotten what it's like to be a novice: to know nothing of quarks, Wagner, sines and cosines, Chaucer's English, world political movements, and Impressionism, for example. Texts easy for the expert are not so for the novice, thereby leaving substantial room for error in their selection.

RECOMMENDATIONS FOR USING READABILITY FORMULAS

I recommend that we continue to use the readability formulas available to us today if for no other reason than to alert us to the *possibility* that a given text is not appropriate for our students. We must, however, be diligent to see that *we use the formulas appropriately and responsibly.* To do that, we must do the following:

1. Remember that readability formulas yield *estimates* (and imperfect estimates at that) of reading difficulty. Therefore, results should be interpreted cautiously and viewed in terms of grade-level *ranges*, rather than specific, immutable grade levels.

2. Also remember that readability formula estimates of difficulty level cannot be interpreted as evaluations of other text or reader elements: for example, concept difficulty, suitability, interestingness, reader prior knowledge, and so on (Irwin & Davis, 1980; Klare, 1989; Weaver & Kintsch, 1991; Zakaluk & Samuels, 1988).

3. Use as many samples as time allows when applying a formula to a given text to account for varying levels of difficulty within that text (Klare, 1989).

4. Use readability formula estimates *in conjunction with* a variety of other means for evaluating text materials. (We will explore various ways for doing this.)

TWO READABILITY FORMULAS

Let's look at the two most popular readability formulas that teachers use to evaluate middle school and junior/senior high texts. There are other, much more complex, formulas available on software for computer application; many schools and districts have these. The ones I'm presenting here are very easily applied and computed manually. After I've presented the two formulas, I'll suggest ways to help you understand and use them most effectively. Later in the chapter, we will explore text evaluation means that may be used as alternatives, or supplements, to readability formulas (see item 4 in the previous list).

FRY READABILITY GRAPH

The Fry Readability Graph (Fry, 1968, 1977) enjoys widespread use, especially for middle school, junior high, and senior high content texts. The graph and directions for its use are shown in Figure 8.1.

THE SMOG FORMULA

I've always liked the SMOG formula (McLaughlin, 1969), as much for its whimsical name—Simple Measure of Gobbledygook—as for its straightforward, easy procedures. The SMOG formula is applied using the following four steps:

1. Count 10 consecutive sentences near the beginning of the selection to be assessed, 10 in the middle, and 10 near the end. Count as a sentence any string of words ending with a period, question mark, or exclamation point.

2. In the 30 selected sentences, count every word of three or more syllables. Any string of letters or numerals beginning and ending with a space or punctuation mark should be counted if you can distinguish at least three syllables when you read it aloud in context. If a polysyllabic word is repeated, count each repetition.

3. Estimate the square root of the number of polysyllabic words counted. This is done by taking the square root of the nearest perfect square. For example, if the count is 95, the nearest perfect square is 100, which yields a square root of 10. If the count lies roughly between two perfect squares, choose the lower number. For instance, if the count is 110, take the square root of 100 rather than that of 121.

4. Add 3 to the approximate square root. This gives the SMOG grade, which is the minimal reading level needed to understand the selection assessed.

UNDERSTANDING AND USING READABILITY FORMULAS

Notice that with the Fry formula, you are locating three 100-word passages and counting number of sentences and number of syllables; in the SMOG formula, you are locating three 10-sentence passages and counting number of words with three or more syllables. Do you see how these are simply two different ways of getting at semantic and syntactic complexity? One involves the number of long sentences and number of syllables in 300 words (the more long sentences and more syllables in a limited number of words, the more difficult the text); the other involves the number of long words in 30 sentences (the more long words in a limited number of sentences, the more difficult the text). I have used both these formulas many times, and from using them, make the following suggestions for accurate use:

1. In the Fry formula, you are told to "randomly select" your three passages; the SMOG requires that sentence passages occur one at the beginning, one in the middle, and one toward the end of whatever material you are assessing. In both cases, random selection is appropriate so that you don't bias your choices; choosing passages from the beginning, middle, and end is equally useful with both formulas. The easiest way to do this is to close your eyes, open the book somewhere near the beginning, put your finger on one of the pages, open your eyes, find the nearest beginning sentence, and start counting (words or sentences). Do the same in the middle of the textbook and near the end for the other two passages.

FIGURE 8.1   *Graph for Estimating Readability—Extended*
by Edward Fry, Rutgers University Reading Center, New Brunswick, N.J. 08904

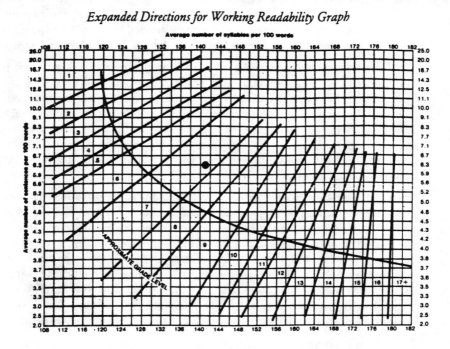

Expanded Directions for Working Readability Graph

1. Randomly select three (3) sample passages and count out exactly 100 words each, beginning with the beginning of a sentence. Do count proper nouns, initialization, and numerals.

2. Count the number of sentences in the hundred words, estimating length of the fraction of the last sentence to the nearest one-tenth.

3. Count the total number of syllables in the 100-word passage. If you don't have a hand counter available, an easy way is to simply put a mark above every syllable over one in each word, then when you get to the end of the passage, count the number of marks and add 100. Small calculators can also be used as counters by pushing numeral 1, then push the plus sign for each word or syllable when counting.

4. Enter graph with average sentence length and average number of syllables; plot dot where the two lines intersect. Area where dot is plotted will give you the approximate grade level.

5. If a great deal of variability is found in syllable count or sentence count, putting more samples into the average is desirable.

6. A word is defined as a group of symbols with a space on either side; thus, *Joe, IRA, 1945,* and *&* are each one word.

7. A syllable is defined as a phonetic syllable. Generally, there are as many syllables as vowel sounds. For example, *stopped* is one syllable and *wanted* is two syllables. When counting syllables for numerals and initializations, count one syllable for each symbol. For example, *1945* is four syllables, *IRA* is three syllables, and *&* is one syllable.

2. You *must* duplicate the passages so you can write on them. Contrary to what Ed Fry says in his directions, you really can't use a hand calculator for this job, regardless of which formula you're using, and you really can't work directly from the text. You have to stop periodically to consider and make decisions, and you will forget whether you had already counted one syllable for the word you're considering or two, or whether you've counted anything at all; you'll need to mark your progress when you stop and have a record of what you've counted how. Take my advice here: Make copies.

3. After counting your 100-word or 10-sentence passages, mark each passage's beginning and end with brackets or a block line so you will know precisely where to begin and end counting. To count the sentences for the Fry formula, circle each period or other sentence-ending punctuation. Write the number in a margin or on a worksheet. To count syllables for the Fry formula, put a tick mark above each syllable in each word (or put a mark above each syllable over the basic one syllable that every word has), as Fry suggested. If you use the SMOG formula, put one tick mark above each polysyllabic word.

4. *You will need to read these passages aloud* (or, at the very least, whisper); otherwise, you'll find yourself counting words such as *stopped* and *learned* as two syllables, or accepting *prepared* as polysyllabic. In addition, you'll need to make some decisions that reading aloud will help you make. For example, if you're using the Fry formula, you'll have to decide how many syllables to assign to words such as *interesting* (in-ter-es'-ting = 4; in'-tra-sting = 3) and *vague*. You will find more words than you expect that cause you to make decisions, whichever formula you use. Regional and other dialects (your own and ones in the area in which you teach) will enter into your deliberations here. The best rule of thumb is to say each word as naturally as possible and count whatever you hear.

5. Before you enter the Fry graph, make sure you have converted your sentence and syllable counts to *averages*. You only plot once using the average sentence and syllable counts. First, take the total number of sentences for each passage, and divide by the number of passages you used; do the same for the syllable count. Using the SMOG formula, add your counts of polysyllabic words from your three samples before finding the nearest perfect square. *If you choose to use more than three passages for the SMOG formula, you must use six or nine and make appropriate averaging adjustments.* The formula is based on the number of polysyllabic words in 30 sentences; if you use 40 or 50 sentences, you will distort the results. If you do use 60 or 90 sentences, you must total the polysyllabic words, divide by 2 or 3, respectively, to arrive at the "average number of polysyllabic words in 30 sentences." Then find the nearest square root. Alternatively, calculate the entire formula two or three times if you use 6 or 9 passages, and then compare results. Don't forget to add the "3" after finding the square root.

6. Handwrite or use your computer to create simple worksheets for your calculations. The two in Figure 8.2 are samples.

READER-TEXT INTERACTIONS

One of the most frequent disadvantages cited for readability formulas is that they evaluate text in isolation from the reader (Bruce, Rubin, & Starr, 1981; Duffy, 1985; Klare,

FIGURE 8.2   *Fry and SMOG Readability Graph Worksheets*

Worksheet: Fry Readability Graph

	Number of Sentences	Number of Syllables
Passage 1 (p. _____)	_____	_____
Passage 2 (p. _____)	_____	_____
Passage 3 (p. _____)	_____	_____
Total	_____	_____
Avg. (÷3)	_____	_____
Grade Level (Range)		_____

Worksheet: SMOG Readability Formula

Number of Polysyllabic Words

Passage 1 (p. _____)	_____
Passage 2 (p. _____)	_____
Passage 3 (p. _____)	_____
Total	_____
Nearest Square Root	_____
+3	_____ Grade Level (Range) _____

1976; Rankin & Culhane, 1969). The concern is that the estimates produced by readability formulas for given texts tell us nothing about what will happen when readers interact with that text and bring to it their own prior knowledge base, attitudes and interests, and knowledge about how text works. Neither do formulas inform us regarding the effect of social interactions and classroom instruction on knowledge construction. These are particularly important concerns with content textbooks because of the influence of subject area prior knowledge on reading and learning and because social interaction and class instruction change the interaction between reader and text. Concerns about the reader-text interaction gain even greater importance as grade levels and text difficulty increase (Klare, 1989).

Earl Rankin (personal communication, 1974) made the point that regardless of what the readability formula says, and regardless of how much we know about the student's reading ability, "If the kid can't read the book, the kid can't read the book." Rankin's point, and the point of other critics of readability testing, is that we need information about the interaction that occurs when reader and text meet in order to have a clear understanding of the usefulness of a given text.

CLOZE TESTING

One of the first attempts to include the reader in text evaluation was the cloze test introduced by Wilson Taylor in 1953. As we discussed in Chapter 4, cloze is based on the gestalt notion of "closure," which is the mind's ability to complete incomplete words, visual images, or thoughts. Closure depends, to a greater or lesser degree, on context. For example, if I wrote, "Happy _____," you might fill in the blank with "Halloween," "Thanksgiving," "Hanukkah," "New Year," "Valentine's Day," "birthday," "anniversary," or "trails to you," depending on the time of year, your immediate context, or any of a myriad of other personal proclivities. We all engage in closure events daily: for example, when we finish someone else's sentence, overlook typographical errors while proofreading, and deal with incomplete or disordered visual information.

Procedure for the Cloze Test   The cloze test Wilson Taylor proposed (1953) capitalizes on the mind's ability to create closure. In the test, the reader replaces systematically deleted words of a text passage; the percentage of correct replacements gives us information about how effectively a given reader handles a given text. Since the cloze test is a sample of its larger environment (i.e., the textbook itself) we then make some assumptions about how the reader will be able to read and construct meaning from that textbook as a whole.

Cloze testing and the percentage standards used for establishing levels of effectiveness with text have been subjects of considerable research over the past 30 years, particularly during the 1960s and 1970s, when the technique was relatively new. From that body of research, we have developed fairly standard administration and scoring procedures for cloze testing and percentage levels for evaluating reader effectiveness. Cloze testing differs in significant ways from cloze teaching strategies (see Chapter 4), and the two should not be confused. Cloze tests are carried out using much more rigid rules for word deletion and for determination of correctness of word replacement. To arrive at interpretable results of a cloze test, the following procedures should be used for constructing, administering, scoring, and interpreting the test:

Construction

1.   Select a passage by finding a section of relatively unbroken text from a portion of the textbook or selection to be evaluated that students have not yet read; you will need a passage of 275 to 300 words. It is not necessary that this passage be randomly chosen; in fact, it is best if you deliberately select a passage that typifies the text.

2.   Retype the passage double-spaced on your computer or typewriter. Leave the first sentence intact. Then, starting at a random spot in the second sentence, delete every fifth word using a standard 10- or 15-space underline to show the deletions. (Flexibility in deciding which words to delete is only appropriate when using cloze to teach; the "every fifth word" rule is standard for cloze testing.) Take care not to split deletion lines from one line of text to another. Number the deletions consecutively. When you have deleted 50 words, type the remainder of that sentence intact. Add one more intact sentence. It helps to mark all of this on a copy of the text, including space numbers, before beginning the typing.

3. Prepare an answer sheet by typing two columns of numbered blanks (1 to 50). *Be sure to include a place for students' names and any other information you want on the answer sheet.*

4. Prepare a scoring template with exact replacements written in the same formation as the answer sheet.

5. Duplicate sufficient copies of the test and answer sheets for your students. *Be sure that both the test and the answer sheet are cleanly duplicated so that smearing, smudges, and dark copies do not interfere with your results.*

Administration

1. Explain to students the purpose of the cloze test, and reassure them that it will have no effect on their grades in your class.

2. Demonstrate several examples of deletion replacement on the board or an overhead projector so students will know what they are expected to do. Be sure to demonstrate how to use the answer sheet.

3. Give students as much time as they need to complete the test.

Scoring

1. Count as correct exact replacements only. You will undoubtedly find synonym replacements that appear to be absolutely correct and others that are "sort of" correct; do not count these as correct. For purposes of evaluating text difficulty, synonym replacement increases the complexity of the scoring (e.g., where do you draw the line between "absolutely correct" and "sort of correct"?) but does not increase appreciably the precision or accuracy of the results. Percentage levels for interpretation are based on exact replacement scores.

2. Determine each student's total correct replacements; multiply by two (2). This product represents the student's percentage score.

Interpretation

1. Scores ranging between 61% and 100% represent the *Independent Reading Level.* Students who achieve these scores should be able to read this text with ease. If a number of students score in the upper ranges of this level, the text is probably not challenging enough for this class.

2. Scores ranging between 40% and 60% represent the *Instructional Reading Level.* Students achieving these scores should be able to read the text with *instruction*—that is, with guidance and assistance from the teacher. The most appropriate text for any group of students should have a relatively large majority of students scoring in or slightly above this level.

3. Scores ranging between 0% and 39% represent the *Frustration Reading Level.* Students achieving these scores will probably experience some degree of difficulty reading the text. If a significant number of students score within this level, the text is likely to be too difficult for this group.

Advantages and Disadvantages of Cloze Tests   Remember, the purpose of cloze testing is not to determine if students know the meaning of the words in the passage per se; rather, it is to tell whether they can read and construct meaning from text when these words are missing. Cloze tests, therefore, give us more information than do readability formulas: Instead of yielding an estimate of the reading grade-level ability needed for students to read a given text, the cloze test estimates how well each student functions when engaged with that text. To this extent, cloze tests have an advantage over readability formulas. In addition, cloze tests are easily constructed, administered, scored, and interpreted.

Unfortunately, cloze tests have one very significant disadvantage: They are difficult, and students generally do not like to do them. Cloze tests present students with a large number of unknowns in a small space, causing some students to become totally discouraged and unwilling to attempt completion, and even the best students to experience some level of irritation and discomfort. I recommend that cloze testing be used sparingly and that when you do use a cloze test, you take the time necessary to show students how to do it. Further, you will need to convince students that their course grades will not be affected by their cloze test results.

When Cloze Is Not Useful   There are at least two circumstances in which cloze testing is neither useful nor appropriate. The first is with texts in which there is not enough running text to allow for a 275- to 300-word sample. In such texts, clearly, construction of meaning does not depend on interpretation of prose text; a different symbol system entirely is used to develop meaning. Mathematics texts are often written in such a way. These, and other similar texts, must be evaluated using methods other than cloze testing.

The second circumstance in which cloze testing is not useful is in anthology texts and books of readings or articles in which several or many authors with varied writing styles, genres, and levels of difficulty are presented. Certainly, no one sample of such a text could represent the entire text. Literature texts and article collections are examples; however, even texts with a single author may vary in difficulty from chapter to chapter. These, too, must be evaluated alternatively.

THE GROUP READING INVENTORY (GRI)

The Group Reading Inventory (GRI) is yet another way to determine how students interact with text. GRIs go beyond cloze testing by focusing on students' abilities to understand and use book parts and study aids (such as tables of contents, indices, chapter titles, marginal notes, charts, maps, illustrations, tables, etc.) as well as to comprehend text content and vocabulary. Numerous forms and formats for GRIs have been recommended over the years, ranging from representative passages from the text accompanied by questions constructed to evaluate comprehension (Shepherd, 1982) to elaborate questionnaires that direct students to locate information in the text, use text graphics and aids, and answer multiple choice comprehension and vocabulary questions for one or more passages.

Usefulness of GRIs   GRIs require a considerable amount of time to construct, administer, and score. They are most useful for learning to what degree students perceive and can use the basic structure of the textbook, the written and visual aids, and the book parts. Information from GRIs is useful in determining how much assistance students will need to be successful in reading and learning from the text. I prefer short, open-ended inventories to the more elaborate ones generally recommended, and I like to evaluate students' comprehension with broad, open-ended questions rather than with multiple choice questions. Brevity has the advantage of time-efficiency, and open-endedness allows a richer view of students' abilities than do responses on multiple choice items.

Representative GRIs   The following are representative samples of what I think are useful GRIs:

Mathematics

1. In the lessons in our book, how can you tell the *examples* from the *explanations?*
2. What does the green highlighting signal in the text?
3. Where can you find the *generalizations* or *rules* in each lesson?
4. If you were doing your homework and forgot how to do the exercises, where would you look to get help?
5. List, in order, what steps you would take to figure out how to do the exercises.

Health

1. What are the Check Your Understanding sections for? How could you use them to guide your study?
2. What might you do with the information in the Chapter Summary and Do You Remember sections?
3. Where in this book would you look if you needed to know the meaning of a word?
4. How would you interpret Figure 23.9, Edith, on page 364?
5. Read Section 4, *Intoxication and Society* (pp. 250–252). In your own words, tell what you think that section is about.

Literature

1. Where would you look in the text to get information on the effect of T*he Enlightenment* on the English language?
2. What is the organizational scheme for the sequence of literature in this book?

3. How can you use the line notes and footnotes in this text?
4. Where in this book would you look to find definitions of literary terms?
5. Read the first chapter of Charles Dickens' *Great Expectations* (pp. 595–597). In your own words, tell what you think this chapter was about. What do you think it will lead to? (You may wish to read about Charles Dickens in the introduction to the Victorian period on the preceding two pages.)

Science

1. What is the significance of the white numerals in blue circles scattered through the chapters?
2. Look at the investigation into Solar Heating on p. 239. In your own words, list the steps you must take to carry out this investigation.
3. What is the relationship of the *dark black headings* to the *gold capitalized headings* in each chapter? How can you use these headings to help you study?
4. Where would you look in this text if you wanted to locate a particular topic? What is the name of that section? What pages does it cover?
5. List everything you know about tornadoes; draw a line after your last item. Then read the section on tornadoes (pp. 198–199). Go back to your list and add new information under the line you drew. Put an asterisk (*) beside anything you already knew that you found in the book.

ALTERNATIVE APPROACHES FOR EVALUATING CLASSROOM TEXTS

Much of our most recent efforts to find alternative means for evaluating text grew from widespread discontent with the limited focus of readability formulas (Irwin & Davis, 1980; Singer, 1986; Weaver & Kintsch, 1991). I suspect, that while Cloze Testing and GRIs do enlarge the scope of text evaluation to include the reader, even these measures do not account for some important aspects of the interaction between reader and text. In the past decade, we have increased considerably our understanding of the reading process and how knowledge is constructed from text. This new understanding must ultimately lead to parallel expansion of our definitions of what constitutes well-written text. We now know that what makes a text readable concerns not only the reader's prior knowledge but other attitudes, interests, beliefs, and predispositions as well; further, we are beginning to examine text in new ways to determine text elements that contribute, or do not contribute, to readers' constructions of meaning (Garner, Gillingham, & White, 1989; Goetz & Sadoski, 1995; Sadoski & Paivio, 1994). Therefore, variables other than semantic and syntactic complexity of text and readers' abilities to understand and use the text must be considered in our evaluations.

The following excerpts, some from textbooks and some from trade books, are all what I consider to be vibrant, exciting text appropriate for secondary classrooms (not included here but clearly illustrative of "vibrant, exciting [history] text" is the previously cited excerpt from William Manchester's *Winston Churchill: Alone 1932–1940*).

Health—*Health*, Chapter 2. *Emotional Development* (Kane et al., 1982):

> When Larry put pencil to paper in art class, he felt a surge of pleasure. He could even feel his heart beat faster. Then and there, he knew drawing was going to be very important to him. Sheila, on the other hand, felt bored and impatient in art class. She yawned a lot and hitched around in her seat. Drawing just wasn't for her. Next semester she would try to find an activity that felt better (p. 15).

English—*Love in the Time of Cholera*. Márquez, 1988:

> It was inevitable: the scent of bitter almonds always reminded him of the fate of unrequited love. Dr. Juvenal Urbino noticed it as soon as he entered the still darkened house where he had hurried on an urgent call to attend a case that for him had lost all urgency many years before. The Antillean refugee Jeremiah de Saint-Amour, disabled war veteran, photographer of children, and his most sympathetic opponent in chess, had escaped the torments of memory with the aromatic fumes of gold cyanide (p. 1).

Physical Education—*Getting Stronger*, Pearl & Moran, 1986:

> I'll never forget the day the circus came to town. The town was Yakima, Washington, the year was 1938 and I was an impressionable 8 years old. Fliers were posted throughout the town, showing the usual elephants, lions, clowns and best of all . . . the strongman! He was an impressive sight: handlebar mustache, leather wrist straps, powerful muscles and a seemingly immense barbell overhead at arm's length with one hand. From that time on, I wanted to be a bodybuilder. My friends dreamed of being policemen, firemen or baseball players, but not me (p. 8).

Art—"The Impressionists and Edouard Manet," Mallarmé, 1876:

> Without any preamble whatsoever, without even a word of explanation to the reader who may be ignorant of the meaning of the title which heads this article, I shall enter at once into its subject, reserving to myself either to draw my deductions, new from an art point of view, as the facts I relate present themselves, or leave them to ooze out when and as they may (in *The New Painting: Impressionism 1874–1886*, p. 28).

Integrated Curriculum (Science, Literature, Environmental Studies)—"The Island of the Endangered" (in *Zoo 2000: Twelve Stories of Science Fiction and Fantasy Beasts*, Ferguson, 1973):

> Once, of a morning, the sun rose on the island of the endangered and there was talk between the bison and the snow leopard.
>
> The bison grazed peacefully on the lush grasses and remembered, deep in his bison brain, when he and his kind had roamed in herds through the forests of Eastern Europe. The bison had been sent to the island of the endangered because he was presumed to be the last of his species, and he was both a little bit proud of this and a little bit sad (p. 139).

It seems self-evident that texts such as these cannot be evaluated simply by word and sentence counts, cloze tests, or questionnaires. Alternative approaches for evaluating instructional text seek to account for the vibrancy and strength of such texts and the interactions that occur when readers bring their prior knowledge, interests, and attitudes to those texts. The results of these efforts have yielded several instruments, each with its own signature focus on text, that can be used singly, or in tandem with other measures, to deepen our knowledge of textbooks under review. Irwin and Davis (1980) focus on the variables "understandability" and "learnability"; Singer (1986) adopts the computer-world notion of "user friendly" to discuss "friendly" text; and Pugh and Garcia (1990) explore the notion of cultural pluralism and its importance in school texts. These efforts are particularly timely in light of recent calls for a return to primary sources and unexcerpted text and a general upgrading of the quality of classroom texts (Sewall, 1988).

THE READABILITY CHECKLIST

Irwin and Davis (1980) developed the Readability Checklist with the express purpose of providing teachers both with the information about how readable a text is and the knowledge of what teacher aids may be supplied to make it more readable (pp. 124–125). The checklist has two main areas for analysis:

1. *Understandability.* Understandability refers to the degree to which the text accounts for reader prior knowledge and background experience; the ways in which concepts are developed in the text; various aspects of syntactic difficulty (sentence construction, main idea and detail arrangement, and explication of ideas); and resources for providing aids to comprehension.

2. *Learnability.* Learnability includes the clarity and usefulness of how the book, chapters, and special features (e.g., the index) are organized; included in the learnability analysis are *reinforcement* (the type and amount of practice provided) and *motivation* (the presence of features that interest readers). At the end of the checklist are questions designed to assist the evaluator in summarizing the text's strengths and weaknesses. The checklist includes provision for readability testing (*Understandability*, Item N). The Readability Checklist and directions for using it are shown in Figure 8.3 (Irwin & Davis, 1980, pp. 129–130).

THE FRIENDLY TEXT EVALUATION SCALE

Harry Singer (1992) developed the Friendly Text Evaluation Scale to be used along with readability formula evaluation in order to enable the evaluator to discern and specify what makes one text friendlier than another (p. 161). Singer organizes and categorizes items somewhat differently from Irwin and Davis, itemizes more in some areas (e.g., Instructional Devices), and offers examples and explanations right on the checklist itself; essentially, however, the two checklists are comparable. Singer emphasizes the importance of going beyond determining readability levels and friendliness of text:

> . . . if a prediction is to be made on how well students in a classroom situation are likely to comprehend a text, then a third step is to determine how a par-

FIGURE 8.3   *Readability Checklist*

This checklist is designed to help you evaluate the readability of our classroom texts. It can best be used if you rate your text while you are thinking of a specific class. Be sure to compare the textbook to a fictional ideal rather than to another text. Your goal is to find out what aspects of the text are or are not less than ideal. Finally, consider supplementary workbooks as part of the textbook and rate them together. Have fun!

Rate the questions below using the following rating system:

> 5 – Excellent
> 4 – Good
> 3 – Adequate
> 2 – Poor
> 1 – Unacceptable
> NA – Not applicable

Further comments may be written in the space provided.

Textbook Title: _____

Publisher: _____

Copyright date: _____

Understandability

   A. ____ Are the assumptions about students' vocabulary knowledge appropriate?

   B. ____ Are the assumptions about students' prior knowledge of this content area appropriate?

   C. ____ Are the assumptions about students' general experiential backgrounds appropriate?

   D. ____ Does the teacher's manual provide the teacher with ways to develop and review the students' conceptual and experiential backgrounds?

   E. ____ Are new concepts explicitly linked to the students' prior knowledge or to their experiential backgrounds?

   F. ____ Does the text introduce abstract concepts by accompanying them with many concrete examples?

   G. ____ Does the text introduce new concepts one at a time with a sufficient number of examples for each one?

   H. ____ Are definitions understandable and at a lower level of abstraction than the concept being defined?

   I. ____ Is the level of sentence complexity appropriate for the students?

   J. ____ Are the main ideas of paragraphs, chapters, and subsections clearly stated?

   K. ____ Does the text avoid irrelevant details?

   L. ____ Does the text explicitly state important complex relationships (e.g., causality, conditionality, etc.) rather than always expecting the reader to infer them from the context?

   M. ____ Does the teacher's manual provide lists of accessible resources containing alternative readings for the very poor or very advanced readers?

continued

FIGURE 8.3 *continued*

━━━

Learnability

Organization

   A. _____ Is an introduction provided for in in each chapter?

   B. _____ Is there a clear and simple organizational pattern relating the chapters to each other?

   C. _____ Does each chapter have a clear, explicit, and simple organizational structure?

   D. _____ Does the text include resources such as an index, glossary, and table of contents?

   E. _____ Do questions and activities draw attention to the organizational pattern of the material (e.g., chronological, cause and effect, spatial, topical, etc.)?

   F. _____ Do consumable materials interrelate well with the textbook?

Reinforcement

   A. _____ Does the text provide opportunities for students to practice using new concepts?

   B. _____ Are there summaries at appropriate intervals in the text?

   C. _____ Does the text provide adequate iconic aids such as maps, graphs, illustrations, etc., to reinforce concepts?

   D. _____ Are there adequate suggestions for usable supplementary activities?

   E. _____ Do these activities provide for a broad range of ability levels?

   F. _____ Are there literal recall questions provided for the students' self review?

   G. _____ Do some of the questions encourage the students to draw inferences?

   H. _____ Are there discussion questions which encourage creative thinking?

   I. _____ Are questions clearly worded?

Motivation

   A. _____ Does the teacher's manual provide introductory activities that will capture students' interest?

   B. _____ Are chapter titles and subheadings concrete, meaningful, or interesting?

   C. _____ Is the writing style of the text appealing to the students?

   D. _____ Are the activities motivating? Will they make the student want to pursue the topic further?

   E. _____ Does the book clearly show how the knowledge being learned might be used by the learner in the future?

   F. _____ Are the cover, format, print size, and pictures appealing to the students?

   G. _____ Does the text provide positive and motivating models for both sexes as well as for other racial, ethnic, and socioeconomic groups?

Readability analysis

Weaknesses

   1) On which items was the book rated the lowest?

   2) Did these items tend to fall in certain categories?

FIGURE 8.3   *continued*

3) Summarize the weaknesses of this text.
4) What can you do in class to compensate for the weaknesses of this text?

Assets
1) On which items was the book rated the highest?
2) Did these items fall in certain categories?
3) Summarize the assets of this text.
4) What can you do in class to take advantage of the assets of this text?

ticular teacher is likely to enhance the friendliness of a text, the readers' resources, and the interactions between the text and the reader (p. 161).

Singer concedes that no scale is available to predict teachers' responses to friendly and unfriendly text. The Friendly Text Evaluation Scale and directions for using it are shown in Figure 8.4 (Singer, 1992, pp. 162–163).

THE CARTER G. WOODSON BOOK AWARD CHECKLIST

More than ever before we are beginning in this country to become attuned to and acknowledge contributions of the many groups of people who comprise our population, whether these groups are identified by race, ethnicity, culture, gender, physical ability, social and economic status, or life experience. This change is beginning to be reflected in modern textbooks and other instructional materials and will increasingly be so. As classrooms become more diverse, and as textbooks begin to speak from the voices of many people to this new diversity, evaluation of instructional material needs to address issues related to pluralism.

FIGURE 8.4   *Friendly Text Evaluation Scale*

Directions: Read each criterion and judge the degree of agreement or disagreement between it and the text. Then circle the number to the right of the criterion that indicates your judgment.

1. SA = Strongly Agree
2. A = Agree
3. U = Uncertain
4. D = Disagree
5. SD = Strongly Disagree

continued

FIGURE 8.4 *continued*

	SA A U D SD
I. ORGANIZATION	
1. The introductions to the book and each chapter explain their purposes.	1 2 3 4 5
2. The introduction provides information on the sequence of the text's contents.	1 2 3 4 5
3. The introduction communicates how the reader should learn from the text.	1 2 3 4 5
4. The ideas presented in the text follow a unidirectional sequence. One idea leads to the next.	1 2 3 4 5
5. The type of paragraph structure organizes information to facilitate memory. For example, objects and their properties are grouped together so as to emphasize relationships.	1 2 3 4 5
6. Ideas are hierarchically structured either verbally or graphically.	1 2 3 4 5
7. The author provides cues to the way information will be presented. For example, the author states: "There are five points to consider."	1 2 3 4 5
8. Signal words (conjunctions, adverbs) and rhetorical devices (problem-solution, question-answer, cause-effect, comparison and contrast, argument-proof) interrelate sentences, paragraphs, and larger units of discourse.	1 2 3 4 5

Discourse consistency

9. The style of writing is consistent and coherent. For example, the paragraphs, sections, and chapters build to a conclusion. Or they begin with a general statement and then present supporting ideas. Or the text has a combination of these patterns. Any one of these patterns would fit this consistency criterion.	1 2 3 4 5

Cohesiveness

10. The text is cohesive. That is, the author ties ideas together from sentence to sentence, paragraph to paragraph, chapter to chapter.	1 2 3 4 5

II. EXPLICATION	
11. Some texts may be read at more than one level, e.g., descriptive vs. theoretical. The text orients students to a level that is appropriate for the students.	1 2 3 4 5
12. The text provides reasons for functions or events. For example, the text, if it is a biology text, not only lists the differences between arteries and veins, but also explains why they are different.	1 2 3 4 5
13. The text highlights or italicizes and defines new terms as they are introduced at a level that is familiar to the student.	1 2 3 4 5
14. The text provides necessary background knowledge. For example, the text introduces new ideas by reviewing or reminding readers of previously acquired knowledge or concepts.	1 2 3 4 5
15. The author uses examples, analogies, metaphors, similes, personifications, or allusions that clarify new ideas and make them vivid.	1 2 3 4 5
16. The author explains ideas in relatively short active sentences.	1 2 3 4 5

FIGURE 8.4   *continued*

		SA	A	U	D	SD
17.	The explanations or theories that underlie the text are made explicit. E.g., Keynesian theory in Samuelson's economic text, Skinner's theory in Bijou and Baer's *Child Development*, behavioristic or gestalt theories in psychology texts.	1	2	3	4	5

III. CONCEPTUAL DENSITY

		SA	A	U	D	SD
18.	Ideas are introduced, defined, or clarified, integrated with semantically related ideas previously presented in the text, and examples given before additional ideas are presented.	1	2	3	4	5
19.	The vocabulary load is appropriate. For example, usually only one new vocabulary item per paragraph occurs throughout the text.	1	2	3	4	5
20.	Content is accurate, up-to-date, and not biased.	1	2	3	4	5

IV. METADISCOURSE

		SA	A	U	D	SD
21.	The author talks directly to the reader to explain how to learn from the text. For example, the author states that some information in the text is more important than other information.	1	2	3	4	5
22.	The author establishes a purpose or goal for the text.	1	2	3	4	5
23.	The text supplies collateral information for putting events into context.	1	2	3	4	5
24.	The text points out relationships to ideas previously presented in the text or to the reader's prior knowledge.	1	2	3	4	5

V. INSTRUCTIONAL DEVICES

		SA	A	U	D	SD
25.	The text contains a logically organized table of contents.	1	2	3	4	5
26.	The text has a glossary that defines technical terms in understandable language.	1	2	3	4	5
27.	The index integrates concepts dispersed throughout the text.	1	2	3	4	5
28.	There are overviews, proposed questions, or graphic devices, such as diagrams, tables, and graphs throughout the text that emphasize what is to be learned in the chapters or sections.	1	2	3	4	5
29.	The text includes marginal annotations or footnotes that instruct the reader.	1	2	3	4	5
30.	The text contains chapter summaries that reflect its main points.	1	2	3	4	5
31.	The text has problems or questions at the literal, interpretive, applied, and evaluative levels at the end of each chapter that help the reader understand knowledge presented in the text.	1	2	3	4	5
32.	The text contains headings and subheadings that divide the text into categories that enable readers to perceive the major ideas.	1	2	3	4	5
33.	The author provides information in the text or at the end of the chapters or the text that enable the reader to apply the knowledge in the text to new situations.	1	2	3	4	5
34.	The author uses personal pronouns that makes the text more interesting to the reader.	1	2	3	4	5

continued

FIGURE 8.4   *continued*

Score   Total _____

Add the numbers circled.

Score range: 34 to 170 points

Interpretation of scores:

A score closer to 34 implies the text is friendly; scores closer to 170 suggest the text is unfriendly.

Sharon Pugh and Jesus Garcia (1990) present the checklist used for reviewing nonfiction texts nominated for the Carter G. Woodson Book Award, which ". . . recognizes authors who treat issues of race relations and minority and ethnic groups accurately and sensitively" (p. 21). This checklist is not only useful for looking at treatment of race and ethnicity, but appropriate for evaluating books treating other aspects of diversity as well, including gender, ability, life experience, and others. The checklist and directions for using it are presented in Figure 8.5.

SUMMARY OF ALTERNATIVE APPROACHES FOR EVALUATING TEXT

The three alternative approaches just discussed for evaluating instructional text represent real progress in how we select materials for classroom use. They build on and acknowledge traditional approaches and at the same time turn our attention to areas that traditional approaches do not address. These new approaches are demonstrably useful, even with the very short samples I used to illustrate vibrant text; selected items from the Readability Checklist Motivation section, the Friendly Text Evaluation Scale Metadiscourse section, and from the Carter G. Woodson Book Award checklist, when applied to those samples, reveal important information about the appropriateness of these texts for classroom instruction.

MAKING CLASSROOM TEXT EVALUATION AND SELECTION SUCCESSFUL

It should be apparent by now that text evaluation is multifaceted and complicated, as it should be. After all, our subject disciplines, the knowledge we want our students to acquire, and our students themselves are similarly complex. To the extent that current criticisms of textbooks persist (Sewall, 1988), as schools in the United States become increasingly diverse and pluralistic, and if textbooks continue to predominate as the focus of instruction in classrooms (Goodlad, 1984), textbook evaluation and selection processes will likely become even more complex and critical in the future than they are today.

Farr and Tulley (1985) outline many of the problems and complications of textbook adoption processes and even suggest the possibility that future efforts in textbook

FIGURE 8.5 *Checklist—Carter G. Woodson Nomination*

Title of book _____   Identification of evaluator _____

Author _____   Date _____

Publisher _____   *Place summary comments on reverse side

General guidelines	Superior	Acceptable	Unsatisfactory	Not applicable
1. Reflects respect for personal and cultural differences and the worth and importance of individual(s)/group(s) presented.				
2. Offers a factual, realistic, and balanced treatment of the past and present.				
3. Focuses on problems/issues that provide insight into the experience of racial and ethnic groups.				
4. Focuses on the interactions among racial/minority groups and the dominant culture.				
5. Avoids portraying the group(s) as "problem oriented"; stresses positives and negatives.				
6. Develops concepts related to cultural pluralism at a level appropriate for the intended audience.				

Guidelines—Illustrations				
7. Shows cultural diversity in illustrative materials.				
8. Avoids distortions and stereotyping.				
9. Presents the group(s)/individuals(s) in a variety of settings.				

Guidelines—Narrative				
10. Possesses a narrative theme that is believable, realistic, and unpatronizing of the targeted group(s).				
11. Describes narrative characters with feelings, emotions, and values equal to those of other individuals.				

2 = S = Superior Sum				
1 = A = Acceptable Points				
−1 = U = Unsatisfactory				
0 = NA = Not Applicable Total Points				

*The checklist should be used to evaluate the overall strengths and weaknesses of a book. Place a single value (2, 1, −1, 0) where appropriate, and note page reference. You need not place a value in each category.

adoption could have lasting influence on the quality of textbooks themselves. It becomes important, therefore, that whether teachers are working individually to select texts for their classes or participating in school- or district-mandated adoption committees, that the process be as orderly and thoughtfully planned as possible. Farr and Tulley offer the following suggestions (1985, p. 471):

1. *Do not confuse the textbook with the curriculum.* Finding one single textbook to cover all aspects of a curriculum is impossible and often leads to a choice of coverage over quality. Farr and Tulley state, "A single textbook series should be part of the curriculum, not the total curriculum" (p. 471).

2. *Limit the scope of the review to a few important features rather than attempting to cover every possible factor.* Long lists of features to review overwhelm and clutter the process; Farr and Tulley found criteria lists ranging from 42 items to 180 items. They recommend a list of no more than 12 items.

3. *Try procedures and instruments out and identify exemplars of excellence before launching the evaluation process itself.* These safeguards increase the validity and reliability of the procedures and the process and reduce confusion and/or mistakes. To their suggestions I add the following:

4. *Remember you are engaged in a process of accommodation and compromise to meet many teachers' and students' needs.* At some point in all adoption processes involving more than one person, comparative ranking occurs. The tendency is to focus attention on the top rankings, but don't forget the bottom rankings—the texts identified by teachers as the ones they least want to adopt. When making final decisions, it is sometimes best to choose a text from the top three that may not have gotten the most "first" rankings, but that did get the fewest "last" rankings. You have to live and work with the other teachers when this process is over.

5. *Carefully select several evaluative instruments to be used in conjunction with one another to show different facets of textbooks under review.* I recommend one (and only one) readability formula, one of the two readability checklists discussed (Readability, Friendly Text), the Carter G. Woodson checklist, and some spot checking with either a cloze test or a short GRI.

6. *Develop a summary sheet for final review of all texts under consideration.* I offer the one shown in Figure 8.6 as a prototype.

7. *Involve students in the textbook-selection process.* If at all possible, involve them from the very beginning; if not, get information from them at some point. At the very least, ask them what they like and don't like about the current text. Then listen to them. Students will give you insightful and important information about school texts.

COMPUTERS AND CLASSROOM TEXTS

It's highly likely that if you're not already using computer technology in your classroom you soon will be. Availability of computers and computer labs in middle and sec-

FIGURE 8.6   *Textbook Evaluation Summary*

Text: _____

Authors: _____

Publisher:_____   Date of Publication: _____

Final Evaluation:_____

Number of First ranks _____   Second _____   Third _____   Last _____

Readability Score: Formula _____   Score _____

Suitability (High, Medium, Low)
  Topics correspond to curriculum.   _____
  Information in text is rich, full, and accurate.   _____
  Contributions of ethnic, cultural, gender, and other groups to the discipline
    are included and treated honestly.   _____
  Nonsexist and nonstereotypical language and assumptions are
    used throughout.   _____

Results from other sources (Select one or more.)
  Readability Checklist _____

  _____

  Friendly Text Evaluation Scale _____

  _____

  Cloze Testing _____

  _____

  GRI _____

  _____

Results of the Carter G. Woodson Book Award Checklist _____

_____

Rank:_____   Reviewer: _____

Date: _____

ondary schools is rapidly increasing; many students have their own, or family, computers and are highly skilled at playing games, word processing, and surfing the internet (and, in fact, may have their own World Wide Web pages); and development of myriad kinds of software, CD-ROM, and hypertext products is booming. Most publishers of middle school and secondary textbooks are now advertising "make your own" texts in which districts/schools select from primary and other sources the materials they wish to have compiled for textbooks for any given class. And, much of the software available gives students (and you) the capability of creating extended, elaborated, and illustrated classroom texts.

You will undoubtedly have occasion to select software for your students' use, either with the computer(s) in your classroom or in a school lab. Any number of issues must be addressed here, ranging from the capabilities of the hardware to use recently developed, powerful software, to the examination of how specific software contributes to and enhances students' learning in your subject area, to the *intent* of the software and your purposes for using it (e.g., Is the purpose to provide practice in a specific skill? Is it to guide students in thinking critically about issues or ideas? Is it to challenge students in problem solving of some kind?). You may or may not have much experience or knowledge about computer technology and possibilities for your teaching; if you don't, I recommend that you find someone who does or participate in workshops that may be available in your district, county, local university, or at professional conferences. The checklist in Figure 8.7 is adapted from Haughlan and Shade's scale for rating developmental appropriateness for software for young children (1990, p. 21); the criteria as adapted are similarly useful for evaluating the quality of software for middle school and secondary students. To use the checklist, assign a rating to each of the criteria according to the descriptors listed below:

1.0 = The software reflects all the characteristics described.

.5 = The software reflects at least half of all the features described.

0 = The software reflects fewer than half of the features described.

Total the points assigned. Haughlan and Shade recommend a total score of 7 (out of a possible 10) for the software to be considered appropriate. You may not wish to hold to that standard always, but even when you don't, the value of the evaluation is clarifying the strengths and weaknesses of the program itself (Ruddell & Ruddell, 1995).

FINAL WORDS ABOUT EVALUATION OF INSTRUCTIONAL MATERIALS

Information about instructional texts—how difficult, interesting, useful, and appropriate they are—will be vital to you throughout your teaching career. You will use this information often in selecting texts and in deciding how those texts should be used in your classroom. Use one or more of the instruments demonstrated in this chapter to find out about the textbooks already chosen for the classes you teach. Consider how the results of the readability formula, checklist, or cloze test correspond to your initial impressions of the text. Don't forget to ask students what they like and don't like about it. Undoubtedly, you will discover some discrepancies between your prior impressions

FIGURE 8.7 *Developmental Scale for Rating Computer Software*

CRITERIA	RATING (1–.5–0)	CHARACTERISTICS
Age appropriate		Realistic presentation of concepts
Student control		Actors not reactors; students set pace; can escape
Clear instructions		Verbal instructions; simple and precise directions; picture choices
Expanding complexity		Low entry, high ceiling; learning sequence is clear; teaches powerful ideas
Independence		Adult supervision not needed after initial exposure
Process orientation		Process engages, product secondary; discovery learning, not skill drilling; intrinsic motivation
Real-world model		Simple, reliable model; concrete representations, objects function
Technical features		Colorful; uncluttered realistic graphics; animation; loads and runs quickly; corresponding sound effects or music; study disks
Trial and error		Students test alternative responses
Transformations		Objects and situations change; process highlighter

and results of your review; that's fine. It only demonstrates that those of us who are experts in any given field are sometimes not very good at choosing textbooks for novices in that same field. Armed with that knowledge, you are sensitized to many of the important issues involved in evaluating instructional materials and much more likely to consider those issues when you become responsible for that selection yourself.

REFERENCES

Alvermann, D. E., & Moore, D. W. (1991). Secondary school reading. In R. Barr, M. L. Kamil, P. Mosenthal, & P. D. Pearson (Eds.), *Handbook of reading research, volume II* (pp. 951–953). New York: Longman.

D O U B L E   E N T R Y   J O U R N A L

Get a copy of a textbook in your subject area actually being used in a middle school, junior high, or senior high school; find also a trade book, magazine or journal article, or some other text that contains information parallel to the information in the textbook. Compare these texts using knowledge and understanding you've gained from this chapter. Use one or more of the procedures described in the chapter to evaluate the texts. How does your analysis increase your awareness of each text's probable suitability for teaching and learning in your classroom? Share your findings with your group.

Applebee, A. N., Langer, J. A., & Mullis, I. V. S. (1987). _Literature and U.S. history: The instructional experience and factual knowledge of high school juniors._ Princeton, NJ: ETS.

Atwell, N. (1987). _In the middle: Writing, reading, and learning with adolescents._ Portsmouth, NH: Heinemann.

Baldwin, R. S. (1986). When was the last time you bought a textbook just for kicks? In E. K. Dishner, T. W. Bean, J. E. Readence, & D. W. Moore (Eds.), _Reading in the content areas_ (2nd ed.) (pp. 323–328). Dubuque, IA: Kendall/Hunt.

Bernstein, H. T. (1985). The new politics of textbook adoption. _Phi Delta Kappan, 66,_ 463–466.

Bruce, B., Rubin, A., & Starr, K. (1981). _Why readability formulas fail._ Champaign, IL: Center for the Study of Reading.

Chall, J. S. (1988). The beginning years. In B. L. Zakaluk & S. J. Samuels (Eds.), _Readability: Its past, present & future_ (pp. 2–13). Newark, DE: International Reading Association.

Dale, E., & Chall, J. S. (1948). A formula for predicting readability. _Educational Research Bulletin, 27,_ 11–20, 37–54.

Dolch, W. W. (1928). Vocabulary burden. _Journal of Educational Research, 17,_ 170–188.

Duffy, T. M. (1985). Readability formulas: What's the use? In T. M. Duffy & R. Waller (Eds.), _Designing usable texts._ New York: Academic Press.

Farr, R., & Tulley, M. A. (1985). Do adoption committees perpetuate mediocre textbooks? _Phi Delta Kappan, 66,_ 467–471.

Ferguson, D. (1973). The island of the endangered. In J. Yolen (Comp.), _Zoo 2000—Twelve stories of science fiction and fantasy beasts._ New York: Seabury Press.

Flesch, R. F. (1948). A new readability yardstick. _Journal of Applied Psychology, 32,_ 221–233.

Fry, E. B. (1968). A readability formula that saves time. *Journal of Reading, 11*, 513–516.

Fry, E. B. (1977). Fry's readability graph: Clarifications, validity, and extension to level 17. *Journal of Reading, 21*, 242–252.

Fry, E. B. (1989). Readability formulas—maligned but valid. *Journal of Reading, 32*, 292–296.

Garner, R., Gillingham, M. G., & White, C. S. (1989). Effects of "seductive details" on macroprocessing and microprocessing in adults and children. *Cognition and Instruction, 6*, 41–57.

Goetz, E. T., & Sadoski, M. (1995). The perils of seduction: Distracting details or incomprehensible abstractions? *Reading Research Quarterly, 30*(5), 500–511.

Goodlad, J. I. (1984). *A place called school*. New York: McGraw-Hill.

Graves, D. H. (1990). *Discover your own literacy*. Portsmouth, NH: Heinemann.

Gray, W. S., & Leary, B. E. (1935). *What makes a book readable*. Chicago: University of Chicago Press.

Haughlin, S. W., & Shade, D. D. (1990). *Developmental evaluations for software for young children*. Albany, NY: Delmar.

Irwin, J. W., & Davis, C. A. (1980). Assessing readability: the checklist approach. *Journal of Reading, 24*, 124–130.

Kane, W., Blake, P., & Frye, R. (1982). *Understanding health*. New York: Random House.

Klare, G. R. (1976). A second look at the validity of readability formulas. *Journal of Reading Behavior, 8*, 129–152.

Klare, G. R. (1989). Understanding the readability of content area texts. In D. Lapp, J. Flood, & N. Farnan (Eds.), *Content area reading and learning: Instructional strategies* (pp. 34–42). Englewood Cliffs, NJ: Prentice-Hall.

Leinwand, G. (1994). *The pageant of world history*. Needham, MA: Prentice-Hall.

Lively, B. A., & Pressey, S. L. (1923). A method for measuring the "vocabulary burden" of textbooks. *Educational Administration and Supervision, 9*, 389–398.

Lorge, I. (1939). Predicting reading difficulty of selections for children. *Elementary English Review, 16*, 229–233.

Mallarmé, S. (1986). The Impressionists and Edouard Manet. (Originally published, 1876).

In C. S. Moffett (Ed.), *The new painting Impressionism 1874–1886*. San Francisco: The Fine Arts Museums of San Francisco.

Manchester, W. (1988). *Winston Spencer Churchill: Alone: 1932–1940*. Boston: Little, Brown.

Márquez, G. G. (1988). *Love in the Time of Cholera* (Edith Grossman, trans.). New York: Alfred Knopf.

McLaughlin, G. H. (1969). SMOG grading—A new readability formula. *Journal of Reading, 12*, 639–646.

Pearl, B., & Moran, G. T. (1986). *Getting stronger*. Bolinas, CA: Shelter Publications.

Pugh, S. L., & Garcia, J. (1990). Portraits in Black: Establishing African American identity through nonfiction books. *Journal of Reading, 34*, 20–25.

Rankin, E. F., & Culhane, J. W. (1969). Comparable cloze and multiple-choice comprehension test scores. *Journal of Reading, 13*, 193–198.

Ruddell, R. B., & Ruddell, M. R. (1995). *Teaching children to read and write: Becoming an influential teacher*. Boston: Allyn & Bacon.

Sewall, G. T. (1988). American history textbooks: Where do we go from here? *Phi Delta Kappan, 69*, 552–558.

Shepherd, D. (1982). *Comprehensive high school reading methods*. Columbus, OH: Merrill.

Singer, H. (1992). Friendly texts: Description and criteria. In E. K. Dishner, T. W. Bean, J. E. Readence, & D. W. Moore (Eds.), *Reading in the content areas* (3rd ed.) (pp. 155–168). Dubuque, IA: Kendall/Hunt.

Tye, B. B. (1985). *Multiple realities: A study of 13 American high schools*. Lanham, MD: University Press of America.

Weaver, C. A. III, & Kintsch, W. (1991). Expository text. In R. Barr, M. L. Kamil, P. B. Mosenthal, & P. D. Pearson (Eds.), *Handbook of reading research* (Vol. II) (pp. 230–245). New York: Longman.

Weiss, I. R. (1978). *Report of the 1977 survey of science, mathematics, and the social studies education*. Washington, DC: U.S. Government Printing Office.

Zakaluk, B. L., & Samuels, S. J. (1988). Toward a new approach to predicting text comprehensibility. In B. L. Zakaluk & S. J. Samuels (Eds.), *Readability: Its past, present & future* (pp. 121–144). Newark, DE: IRA.

9

COOPERATIVE/COLLABORATIVE LEARNING, LITERACY INSTRUCTION, AND CONTENT LEARNING

DOUBLE ENTRY JOURNAL

What experience do you have working cooperatively or collaboratively with others toward a specific goal? How often is such work in your life associated with school—either in your role as teacher or as student? What do you like and not like about working collaboratively? What do you think makes cooperative or collaborative learning successful or not successful? Share your thoughts with a friend.

Cooperative and collaborative learning are now well entrenched in current educational literature, if not in the schools themselves. In all likelihood, you have read a great deal about cooperative learning, discussed it in many classes, and possibly observed or implemented such instruction in a middle, junior high, or senior high school. Cooperative learning has gained prominence and continues to be discussed because it appears to offer so much potential for enriching the middle school and junior/senior high school classroom. Recall our discussion in Chapter 1 of the national educational reform movement of the early 1980s. Much of the substance of that movement focused on the need for increased rigor and complexity of school tasks; critics called for a structural change in the content and procedures of classroom life with a dual emphasis on subject-knowledge acquisition and higher-order thinking skills.

To put all of this into perspective, consider again the description of U.S. classrooms developed by John Goodlad and his research team (1984) and the "frontal teaching" practices they found to dominate classrooms in the early 1980s:

The data from our observations in more than 1,000 classrooms support the popular image of a teacher standing or sitting in front of a class imparting knowledge to a group of students. Explaining and lecturing constituted the most frequent teaching activities, according to teachers, students, and our observations. And the frequency of these activities increased steadily from the primary to the senior high school years. Teachers also spent a substantial amount of time observing students at work or monitoring their seat-work, especially at the junior high level (p. 105).

Goodlad goes on to emphasize that seat-work activities were rarely focused on constructing or producing knowledge, ". . . students were not very often called upon to build, draw, perform, role play, or make things" (p. 105); and most independent work took the form of students working separately on identical tasks rather than individually working on tasks tailored to specific learning styles or circumstances. Mary-Ellen Vogt (1996) expands Goodlad's description of classroom life:

> In traditional classroom setting, . . . [t]he primary speaker is the teacher, the nature of the talk is questioning, and many interactions center around the correctness of student work, since school is traditionally viewed as a work place rather than a place of socialization. This classroom climate "creates teachers who interrogate rather than teach, who assess rather than assist" (Duffy, 1982, p. 6). The teacher is likely to ask as many as 80,000 questions each school year; her students will ask on average 10 questions apiece (Watson & Young, 1986). In fact, classroom interactions, when transcribed, frequently resemble the script of a play, with the teacher and students alternating their turns (pp. 181–182).

Using Friere's "banking" model analogy of schooling, Perry Marker (1993) completes the picture of traditional classrooms in U.S. secondary schools:

> Thus, we, as teachers, set ourselves up as omniscient and often infallible experts who have a huge cache of facts and information from which students can frequently make withdrawals. And, in most cases, we do not wait for students to make the withdrawal, we conveniently direct deposit the information into students' accounts through lectures, worksheets, and textbooks. Students are at the mercy of the banker, who creates all the rules as to how the bank and the information deposited therein shall be organized, managed and dispensed (p. 78).

It was this tradition that reformists sought to change in the 1980s and are continuing to challenge today. One outgrowth of the rhetoric of change in the 1980s was for educators to take a harder look at classrooms, and nowhere did those looks yield more action than with the middle school reform movement, which gathered considerable force during that decade.

INFLUENCE OF THE MIDDLE SCHOOL MOVEMENT

The middle school movement, which continues to grow and change, carries with it many important recommendations regarding appropriate content and practices for the schooling of young adolescents (Alexander, 1987; Atwell, 1987; *Caught in the Middle*, 1987; Moore & Stefanich, 1990; Pace, 1995a; *Phi Delta Kappan* special issue, February 1990). Two of these recommendations—interdisciplinary instruction and cooperative/collaborative learning—are particularly significant for subject area teachers.

INTERDISCIPLINARY INSTRUCTION

Interdisciplinary instruction may take the form of grade-level teachers sharing a planning period to coordinate learning experiences across academic areas; it may, instead, be team teaching in which several teachers (usually three) combine their skills and content knowledge to teach a given set of students; or it may be a combination of the two (MacIver, 1990). In many schools, interdisciplinary instruction takes the form of a full-blown Integrated Studies approach in which lines between disciplines are intentionally blurred through inquiry learning and project-based instruction (Pace, 1995a; Siu-Runyan & Faircloth, 1995; Stevenson & Carr, 1993). Middle schools are rapidly changing class configurations to arrive at some form of interdisciplinary instruction, and senior high schools are considering, or trying, similar alternatives. Many of the middle schools my students observe and teach in are moving to teacher teams for core subjects, combined class periods of 90–115 minutes (as opposed to the traditional 45- or 50-minute class period), and more and more middle school and junior/senior high schools and districts actively seek new teachers who have some experience working in such teams.

COOPERATIVE/COLLABORATIVE LEARNING

The second important middle school practice is focused on cooperative and collaborative learning strategies and other, varied instructional methodology which ". . . respect the diversity and the increasing sophistication of middle school students" (Moore & Stefanich, 1990, p. 8). Cooperative learning thus becomes a major component of exemplary instruction in middle schools and is appearing in some strength in junior high and senior high schools as well. New classroom configurations, changing demographics, extended class periods, and new values induced by the middle school reform movement all facilitate implementation of cooperative learning in schools (Braddock, 1990; Condon & Hoffman, 1990). It is from the "true" middle schools—those whose practices reflect the premises and recommended practices of the movement itself (Allington, 1990)—that we are beginning to see ever-widening circles of instructional change, especially in such areas as cooperative/collaborative learning.

This is happening to a significant enough extent that ideas and practices formerly associated solely with middle schools and below are now gaining widespread acceptance in junior and senior high schools as well, thus beginning the structural change Goodlad and others envisioned. Pertinent to our discussion at this point are the cooperative and collaborative learning models of instruction and their relationship to language, literacy, and subject area learning. Later, we'll discuss how interdisciplinary instruction serves as a useful vehicle for implementing cooperative and collaborative learning and for encouraging students' acquisition of subject area knowledge.

COOPERATIVE/COLLABORATIVE LEARNING IN CLASSROOMS

The literature that supports cooperative learning begins with pioneering work by social psychologists interested in the social effects of cooperative and competitive group environments (Lewin, Lippitt, & White, 1939; Sherif, Harvey, White, Hood, & Sherif, 1961) and, specifically, in school settings with academic goals (Aaronson, Blaney, Sikes, Stephan, & Snapp, 1975; Aaronson, Stephan, Sikes, Blaney, & Snapp, 1978). Later, educational psychologists and educators with specialties in various fields adopted cooperative learning as the focal point of study for developing effective instructional practice (Bayer, 1990; Cohen, 1986; Haggard, 1986; Johnson & Johnson, 1979; LittleSoldier, 1989; Mikulecky, 1986; Sharan, 1980; Sharan & Sharan, 1986, 1989–1990; Slavin, 1980, 1986). Their work in the past decade has been extensive and influential.

The foregoing list, which does not pretend to be inclusive of the entire literature of cooperative learning, indicates its broad appeal and current prominence in educational thought; included in the list is work representing the fields of social psychology, secondary education, reading education, elementary education, sociology, writing education, bilingual education, adult education, and educational psychology. It's not surprising, then, that the literature abounds with various names for cooperative learning, most of which are used synonymously; e.g., "group problem solving," "groupwork," and "group investigation." An important distinction does exist, however, between *cooperative learning* and *collaborative learning* (even though the terms are often used interchangeably); this distinction centers around who does what planning for whom. That is, *cooperative learning activities* are most often conceived and planned by the teacher and carried out by students in cooperative groups working from teacher direction and assistance. *Collaborative learning activities* are projects and ventures that are student-directed: projects planned, developed, and carried out by student groups in consultation with the teacher. This distinction gets fuzzy in both theory and practice when teacher-planned activities develop a life of their own and brand new direction as student work progresses, and/or when student-planned activities bog down and require greater amounts of structure and assistance from the teacher. Thus, cooperative activities can become collaborative, and collaborative student planning may require considerable teacher direction. So, I will continue using "cooperative/collaborative learning" as a general designation for learning that involves one or both; in those discussions where the literature is specific to one type of learning activity (cooperative or collaborative), I will use that terminology exclusively.

CHARACTERISTICS OF COOPERATIVE LEARNING

Cohen (1986) uses the term *groupwork* to refer to cooperative learning and suggests that cooperative learning has four key characteristics: (1) delegation of authority, (2) shared responsibility for learning, (3) mixed-ability grouping, and (4) complex academic tasks.

DELEGATION OF AUTHORITY
In cooperative learning classrooms, the teacher, rather than telling students how to solve problems and monitoring the work to prevent error or failures, must *delegate*

some of the work of problem solving and self-monitoring to students. That is, she or he allows students to ". . . make mistakes and struggle on their own . . ." toward solution of the problem with which the group is presented (p. 2). This means that cooperative learning activities change a major dynamic of the traditional classroom.

As we discussed earlier, the most common form of instruction in traditional classrooms is lecture and explanation; the teacher's voice predominates, and the students' role is to absorb information, follow directions, and learn the content of the curriculum. In cooperative learning classrooms, on the other hand, *students' voices predominate:* Students do most of the talking, students figure out what to do, and students make missteps and errors along the way. The knowledge that students construct in the process of problem solving and working with new ideas, then, *becomes* the curriculum that is guided and nurtured by teacher construction of complex, productive tasks. I once heard someone say, "The more the teacher talks, the more the teacher learns"; cooperative learning is based on the obverse of that statement.

SHARED RESPONSIBILITY FOR LEARNING

The second key characteristic of cooperative learning is that *no one can complete an assigned task without the participation of other members of the group* (Cohen, 1986); consequently, students teach, assist, and guide one another, give directions, listen, criticize, and complement each others' efforts. Here again, the classroom dynamic changes from one that traditionally has been competitive to one in which individual success depends on group success. This new dynamic does not occur magically, nor can its occurrence be left to chance. Teachers can and must guide students toward cooperative learning behaviors, and we will discuss at length ways to do this later in this chapter. Once students become adept at group participation, however, such creative group problem solving yields important gains for students in the form of opportunity to: (1) learn from one another, (2) engage in higher-order thinking, and (3) experience authentic intellectual pride in their accomplishments (Cohen, 1986, p. 13).

MIXED-ABILITY GROUPING

A third characteristic of cooperative learning activities is that *groups are mixed-ability and mixed regarding other status characteristics* (gender, race, ethnicity, etc.) so that they represent the classroom and school population as a whole. This is particularly significant for students whose cultural and family backgrounds include core values in which individuals with different strengths and abilities share and help one another as specific abilities are needed (LittleSoldier, 1989).

In middle and junior/senior high schools, traditionally entrenched ability-tracking plans have given way, or are in the process of giving way, to nontracked schools and classes; cooperative learning approaches are one way schools can, and do, effect the change from tracked to untracked class placement (Braddock, 1990). In fact, these activities are the most reasonable alternative to the traditional read-lecture-explain-test format that is so difficult to accomplish successfully with mixed-ability classes.

COMPLEX ACADEMIC TASKS

Finally, critical to the success of cooperative learning activities are the *tasks* themselves. Cohen (1986) recommends that groupwork tasks should have more than one answer or more than one way to solve problems; be intrinsically interesting and rewarding; allow different students to make different contributions; use multimedia; involve sight, sound and touch; require a variety of skills and behaviors; require reading and writing; and challenge students (pp. 57–58).

Clearly, all of these characteristics point to cooperative learning tasks that are complex, rich, and full. Many, but not all, cooperative learning activities require more than one class period to complete; these generally involve rather extended, polished final products. Complex group tasks can be completed in the space of a class period, however; it becomes a matter of adjusting the scope of activities to fit the time and activity constraints of the course.

COOPERATIVE/COLLABORATIVE LEARNING, LANGUAGE, AND LITERACY

What, then, do cooperative and collaborative learning have to do with developing students' reading and writing abilities? The answer is, "a lot." In fact, you already know, or sense, the extent and magnitude of this relationship because of the emphasis placed on it in other chapters of this text and the number of instructional activities developed there that require cooperative group or partnership work to complete.

Ann Shea Bayer (1990) uses Vygotsky's (1978) notions about the social origins of learning to make a case for what she calls "collaborative-apprenticeship learning" (CAL) in which student language and thinking are central to the learning process (Bayer, 1990, p. 18) and are enhanced through social interactions. She, Vygotsky, and others (McCaslin, 1990; Ruddell, 1991) contend that learning is deepened and enhanced through language and social interactions that occur as learning progresses. Bayer makes the following assertions about these interrelationships (the assertions in italics are Bayer's; the explanations in plain text are mine):

1. *Language is the mechanism through which the negotiation of meaning occurs.* Until we can give voice to our thinking, it remains inchoate, confused, and unformed. Language allows us to sort through confusion, name ideas, and mark our own progress toward insight; students cannot effectively learn subject area content without using language to negotiate and construct meaning.

2. *Students need regular opportunities to talk, read, and write as they attempt to construct explanations that make sense to them.* Without these, students are engaged in what I call "lonely learning," which systematically limits their potential for learning and increasing literacy abilities by denying them access to the thinking of those around them. Listening to the teacher's explanation is not nearly as effective in "getting it" as working through an idea or process with the help of other learners.

3. *Expressive language allows the learner to express freely thoughts, feelings, and opinions about a subject, and is the beginning point for coming to terms with new ideas.* Expressive language doesn't sound academic, and may, in fact, be mistaken for informal conversation; nevertheless, it is the language we all use to "noodle" with ideas, explore and experiment, and become accustomed to new concepts and thinking. Expressive language is the language we use before and while we gain mastery over the subject area itself and is often the language we use for rehearsal, or "trying out," new ideas.

4. *As students work out meanings for new concepts, their talk becomes less expressive and more formal, and includes appropriate use of specialized vocabulary.* Students begin to talk, write, and think like scientists, poets, historians, welders, and mathematicians only after they've had many opportunities to try out the language, experiment with new ideas, and explore new ways of thinking. They cannot do this solely within their own heads; they need the audience, the reactions, the other points of view that group interaction permits to extend their own thinking.

INTERRELATIONSHIPS BETWEEN COOPERATIVE/COLLABORATIVE LEARNING, LANGUAGE, AND LITERACY

If we now add to Bayer's assertions the principles of thinking, reading, and writing set forth by this text, we begin to see the full extent of the interrelationships between cooperative/collaborative learning, language, and literacy. Essentially, the logic goes like this:

1. Thinking, reading, and writing are cognitive processes that have as their intended outcome the construction of meaning.

2. Language, whether oral or written, is the medium through which we explore, extend, and grapple with ideas while thinking, reading, and writing to arrive at new insights and construct new knowledge.

3. Opportunity to use spoken and written language and to share insights, explorations, extensions, and questions with others increases everyone's fund of knowledge, reveals alternative logic systems, influences viewpoints, and enriches the total experience base we have available to bring to the reading/writing act.

4. This enriched experience, including increased knowledge and alternative logic systems and viewpoints, in turn, increases our ability to construct rich meanings as we transact with text.

Thus the relationship between cooperative and collaborative learning and students' abilities to read and write in subject areas is a direct and important one, and the relationship between language (including literacy abilities) and subject area learning is just as direct.

And so, the extraordinary, and singularly important, linkages between thinking, language, social interaction, literacy abilities and subject area learning are sufficiently compelling, I think, for us to conclude that instruction in subject area classrooms must, indeed, account for all these variables and their interactions. Bayer (1990) proposes a two-stage Collaborative-Apprenticeship Learning model (CAL I and II) to operationalize the relationships between collaboration, language, literacy and subject area learning. The model is shown in Figures 9.1 and 9.2. Notice the CAL emphasis on language interaction, reading, and writing in learning. Notice also that the final

FIGURE 9.1   *CAL Teaching Model, Part I*

SAMPLE TEACHING–LEARNING CYCLE	STUDENTS USING LANGUAGE TO LEARN
Select major concept. Expand/modify to include student interests.	
Elicit student interest.	Students write/talk about discipline related interests.
Start with what individual students know about concept. How? Use focused freewriting; use brainstorming.	Students write what they know. Students talk about what they know.
Make public what students know. How? Use small groups so students can pool their knowledge; small groups share knowledge with whole class. Collective prior knowledge becomes accessible to instructor and to each other.	Students collaborate with each other using expressive talk. Students look for confirmation of their current knowledge in scaffolding activities.
Build on what students know. How? Demonstrate the concept; model the concept/procedure. Place student-generated knowledge within conceptual framework.	Students engage in scaffolding activities.
Focus student reading. How? Students use what they already know and the concrete activities to make predictions about text material.	Students read to confirm own predictions.
Discover areas of student confusion. How? Use small groups so student can discuss what is or isn't clear. Use think/write logs so students can write what is or isn't clear.	Students collaborate with each other using expressive talk. Students collaborate with instructor using expressive writing.
Encourage application of ideas. How? Students independently (or in collaboration with others) engage in long-term projects of interest to them. Use writing response groups and peer research groups.	Students use writing, talking, listening, and reading as they engage in long-term projects.

application stage of each cycle assumes that students will become increasingly independent from teacher guidance and interdependent with one another through the use of "scaffolding" activities; that is, activities that support students during periods of

FIGURE 9.2   *CAL Teaching Model, Part II*

SAMPLE TEACHING–LEARNING CYCLE	STUDENTS USING LANGUAGE TO LEARN
Focus reading.	Students write what they know.
How? Use focused freewrite; students read text looking for confirmation of current beliefs.	Students read to confirm own predictions.
Students expand on what each knows.	Students collaborate with each other using expressive talk.
How? Use small groups so students can clarify and expand on each other's thinking about ideas in text.	
Share small group interpretations with whole class.	
Teacher fills in gaps.	Teacher uses scaffolding activities for whole class instruction (if necessary).
How? Provide missing connections, if any, in students' interpretations via concrete examples.	
Discover areas of student confusion.	Students collaborate with instructor by using expressive writing.
How? Use think/write logs so students can write what is or isn't clear.	
Encourage application of ideas.	Students use writing, talking, listening, and reading as they engage in long-term projects.
How? Students independently (or in collaboration with others) engage in long-term projects of interest to them.	

uncertainty and as they assimilate new ideas. By the time students move into Part II of CAL, they are working increasingly independently from the teacher who, at the same time, remains an important resource. The predominant theme of CAL II is *students guiding themselves* through long-term project study rather than simply responding to teacher guidance. If you look carefully at Bayer's model for collaborative-apprenticeship learning (see Figure 9.2), you will see that it incorporates activities and learning approaches strikingly similar to many we've discussed in this text. Bayer states clearly that she does not consider her learning model to be prescriptive (p. 22); rather, it will require modifications to meet specific subject area needs, requirements, and conventions.

Many learning activities focus both on (1) learning content through cooperative and collaborative action and (2) promoting language and literacy abilities. Such activities would appear to be one of the most productive ways for implementing the kind of instruction Bayer's CAL model represents. The cooperative/collaborative learning activities presented in the next section of this chapter are all compatible with Bayer's model even though each activity addresses the model in its own way. These activities all highlight the linkages between thinking, social and language interaction, literacy, and subject area learning.

COOPERATIVE AND COLLABORATIVE LEARNING ACTIVITIES TO PROMOTE LITERACY AND CONTENT LEARNING

At this point, it should be clear that we have been discussing instructional activities that combine literacy and content learning with cooperative and collaborative learning throughout this text. Virtually every instructional strategy I've presented, from the DR–TA in Chapter 3 to the Reading Response Groups in Chapter 5 to the Double Entry Journals (DEJs) in Chapter 6, is at least one of the following:

1. Explicitly focused on literacy/content learning combined with cooperative/collaborative learning.
2. Partially focused on literacy/content learning combined with cooperative/collaborative learning.
3. Readily adaptable to various small group and partnership formats.

With minor adjustments—letting students direct reading discussions, or allowing students to work together to do part or all of the activity tasks, for example—these activities acquire all of the characteristics requisite for cooperative and collaborative learning. Essentially, such activities use mixed-ability groups to explore specific aspects or topics of a lesson, respond to teacher prompts or questions, and arrive at consensus regarding an intended outcome of the lesson (Eeds & Wells, 1989; Johnson & Johnson, 1979; O'Flahavan, 1989). Johnson and Johnson (1986) even provide directions for "guided controversy," in which group members first argue one side of an issue, then switch roles and argue the other side, and, finally, arrive at a consensus.

The wide variety of activities compatible with cooperative/collaborative learning illustrates clearly that once teachers understand and accept the basic structure of group planning and problem solving, the possible formats and specific activities are limited only by teachers' imaginations. Cooperative and collaborative learning activities, therefore, can take many different forms; the one constant among them, however, is that most do require group construction of a final learning product such as a report, a videotape, an experiment, a presentation, a model, a panel discussion, and so forth.

Cooperative and collaborative learning activities lend themselves to many different kinds of language and literacy uses. Further, they promote content learning by providing extended opportunity for students to explore and discuss topics, ideas, events, issues, and procedures, which are the heart of the content itself. The instructional activities detailed next share these characteristics and are useful cooperative/collaborative learning activities. Each activity is adaptable in various ways.

JIGSAW GROUPING
By now, *Jigsaw Grouping* is well-known and frequently used in one form or another. Jigsaw Grouping was introduced by Elliott Aaronson for the purpose of encouraging active participation in group settings by students from different ethnic, cultural, and racial backgrounds (Aaronson et al., 1975; Aaronson et al., 1978). Jigsaw Grouping is

based on the characteristics of a jigsaw puzzle: Students are given interlocking parts of a whole picture; each student learns and communicates her/his part, but no one can see the whole picture until all of the parts are in place.

To do Jigsaw Grouping, the teacher establishes mixed-ability groups of four to five students and assigns one-fourth or one-fifth of the unit of study to each student. Students read their own part and meet with members from other groups who were assigned the same part; this new group meets to discuss and clarify their understanding of the material read, and, in the course of that discussion, becomes the Expert group on that section of the unit. Members then return to their original groups to teach the group the important information from their part. The group then works to incorporate these interlocking parts into a construction of the whole unit. Following this initial shared teaching, the group may go back to any or all parts of the material to gather additional information or clarify areas of confusion.

Slavin (1986) expresses concern over the use of Jigsaw Grouping with typical classroom texts. His point is that most texts are not written so that unit sections can be easily separated out; the only way teachers can make the sections independently comprehensible is to rewrite and/or add considerable amounts of text (p. 339). I agree, in part, with Slavin; I've used Jigsaw Grouping with adults and have encountered this problem. On the other hand, many texts are readily subdivided into sections that stand alone.

Even when text does not lend itself to subdivision, however, the following are ways around the problem that do not involve extensive rewriting:

1. Using library and other resource materials to supplement the classroom text so that comprehensible, free-standing text units are put together from various sources.

2. Combining Jigsaw with an adapted Content DR-TA or K–W–L in which groups list and record everything they know about the lesson topic before reading, share these with the class, and then read their assigned sections of the unit and do their Expert grouping. The Content DR-TA/K–W–L brainstorming thus provides a common core of background knowledge that assists students in constructing meaning as they read separate sections of the unit.

3. Helping students to become accustomed to a situation in which *some of the information they need is missing*; in this case, part of the purpose of the Expert group discussion would be to identify information gaps, propose alternative ideas for filling those gaps, and predict how some of the pieces of the Jigsaw will ultimately fit together. This approach also encourages students to work cooperatively to elicit important (perhaps missing) information from one another during discussions, a central point of the exercise itself.

JIGSAW II

Slavin proposes a useful alternative to Jigsaw Grouping (1986). His idea is to have all group members read the complete text, but then each member is assigned a topic within that unit of text about which he or she is to become the Expert. Every group has at least one member assigned to each topic. Teacher-generated questions on an Expert Sheet direct students' attention to the area for which they are to develop expertise. An important standard for development of these topics is that none of the topics represents subsections of the text; to address each topic fully, students should need to read and make connections within the entire text and connect this information with prior knowledge. In a family-living class unit on consumer knowledge, for example, the Expert topics (which adhere to the standard just mentioned) might be as follows:

1. What are some ways consumers use money wisely?
2. What are some unwise consumer habits?
3. What regulations control consumer spending, borrowing, and repaying of money?
4. What protections are available to consumers?
5. What actions are available to you if you find you have gotten too deeply in debt and need to get out of debt?

Each student in the group is assigned one of these topics on which to become The Expert. After the reading, Expert Groups meet (same-topic students) to discuss and extend individual responses to the topic questions, and students then return to their original groups to teach their topics. Following small group knowledge exchanges, final products are developed.

How to do . . . .

JIGSAW AND JIGSAW II

Jigsaw Grouping can be such an addition to your teaching repertoire that you would do well to consider using either form or both in your classroom. It is easily combined with other instructional strategies, especially mapping and VSS. Below are steps for implementing Jigsaw and Jigsaw II.

JIGSAW

1. Determine the material to be studied and the lesson or unit objectives.

2. Divide the reading material into four or five roughly equal sections.

3. Establish cross-ability and cross-status groups of four or five students each; the number of students in each group should correspond to the number of sections of reading material.

4. Assign one section of the chapter (or other reading material) to a student in each group so that the total reading assignment is covered within each group.

5. Allow reading time.

6. Ask all students assigned to each section (e.g., section 1, section 2, etc.) to meet in Expert groups to: (a) consider, discuss and clarify the

information in their assigned reading, and (b) prepare for returning to their original groups and teaching the material to that group.

7. Convene original groups for students to teach their part of the reading to other group members.

8. Conduct full-class discussion of the chapter or other reading material for further clarification and/or research.

JIGSAW II

1. Determine the material to be studied and the lesson or unit objectives.

2. Write four or five topic questions for the Expert Sheet; answers to these questions should require integration of information within the entire text.

3. Establish cross-ability and cross-status groups of four or five students each; the number of students in each group should correspond to the number of topic questions on the Expert Sheet.

4. Assign one question on the Expert Sheet to a student in each group so that all of the topic questions are covered within each group.

5. Allow reading time.

6. Ask all students assigned to each question (e.g., question 1, question 2, etc.) to meet in expert groups to: (a) consider, discuss and clarify ideas and responses to their assigned question, and (b) prepare for returning to their original groups and leading discussion of the topic question.

7. Convene original groups for students to teach their topics and guide additional discussion of the topic questions.

8. Conduct full-class discussion of the chapter or other reading material for further clarification and/or research.

GROUP INVESTIGATION

Sharan and Sharan (1980, 1986, 1989–1990) have developed the Group Investigation approach, which uses interest-centered cooperative groups as the means for students to plan and carry out extended project investigations and productions. They propose a six-stage progression of cooperative events:

Stage 1—Identify the topic and organize research groups

Stage 2—Plan the investigation

Stage 3—Investigate

Stage 4—Prepare a report

Stage 5—Make final presentations

Stage 6—Test and evaluate

Huhtala and Coughlin (1991) decided to use Group Investigation for a Middle East unit in an interdisciplinary, team-taught, sophomore English and government class beginning in the fall of 1990. This was a timely decision and a daring one, given the subsequent need for them to teach world events as these events were happening during the buildup to the 1991 Persian Gulf War. Huhtala and Coughlin describe the successes and the problems they encountered in using Group Investigation for the first time. Of real import is that, problems and all, in comparison with other, nonteamed classes, in the Group Investigation class, "Absenteeism was reduced by a third. Grades of D and F were reduced from twenty to thirteen percent" (p. 50).

THE GROUP READING ACTIVITY (GRA)

The Group Reading Activity (GRA) (Manzo, 1974; Manzo & Manzo, 1990) divides responsibility for initial learning and presentation of topic information among five or six collaborative learning groups within the classroom. The teacher determines topic divisions and assigns a topic and corresponding reading to each group. For example, for a unit on the Middle Ages, the following topics and assignments might be made:

Topic	Assignment
Byzantium	pp. 115–119
Peoples, Cultures, and Leaders	pp. 119–126
Feudalism	pp. 126–131
Crusades, Religions, and Religious Leaders	pp. 135–142
Town, Guilds, and Merchants	pp. 142–147
Education, Science and Art	pp. 147–151

Additional resources are available in the room and in other areas in the school.

Each group must determine: (1) what is the most important information in the assigned textbook reading, (2) what, if any, other information is needed to understand the topic, and (3) how the group can best present the topic information to the rest of the class. Presentation options include written summaries and outlines, annotations, oral reports, panel discussions, dramatizations, audiovisual presentations, and any other type of product useful for informing the class and preparing everyone for unit evaluation.

Following group deliberations, the teacher appoints a student critic from each group to move to another group to listen to the proposed ideas for class presentation. The student critic is expected to provide constructive criticism. Groups use this information to revise and rearrange their proposals, which they then present to the teacher. The teacher consults with the group and assists further in adapting the presentation plans, if needed. Groups complete all preparations and do the presentations.

The class then works as a whole to determine what areas of the unit need further reading and study as well as how that study could be carried out; students are encouraged to "rapid read" those sections presented by other groups. Final arrangements for follow-up activities are made. At the end of the unit, student knowledge is evaluated using assessment strategies that are appropriate to the students, the unit, and the type of information learned.

How to do . . . .

THE GRA

The GRA is similar to Jigsaw Grouping by its provision for Expert groups about limited topics within the unit of study. It differs from Jigsaw by giving the Expert groups more working time together, and by making the Experts responsible as a group for teaching their part of the unit to the rest of the class. I like the GRA because it requires precisely the kind of social and verbal interaction Bayer (1990) described as being so critical to learning and because the task of producing something for use in teaching the topic further assists groups in moving from expressive to formal language. The focus is evenly divided among collaboration, reading, language interaction, learning, teaching, and production of a teaching aid. Writing is used spontaneously and naturally throughout and is often the chosen medium (or a major aspect of the chosen medium) for transmitting information to the rest of the class. The GRA is readily adaptable to units of various size and length and fits reasonably into most subject areas. The following steps should assist you in using the GRA:

1. Determine the material to be studied and the lesson or unit objectives.

2. Divide the reading material into four, five, or six topic sections.

3. Establish four, five, or six cross-ability and cross-status groups. The number of groups should correspond to the number of topic sections established.

4. Assign one topic of the reading material to each group. Each group is to determine: (a) what is the most important information in the section, (b) what other information is need to understand the topic, and (c) how the group can best present the topic to the rest of the class.

5. Appoint one student critic from each group to go to listen to that group's plan for presenting its material to the class.

6. Allow time for the student critic to make constructive recommendations.

7. Consult with each group regarding its plans for presentation.

8. Allow time for presentations to be finalized.

9. Have groups present.

10. Conduct full-class discussion for further clarification and research of project ideas.

THE CREATIVE THINKING-READING ACTIVITIES (CT–RAs)

The Creative Thinking-Reading Activities (CT–RAs) (Haggard, 1978, 1979, 1980) are short, warm-up activities for developing students' creative problem-solving abilities. CT–RAs require cooperative learning groups to generate: (1) as many possible solutions as they can think of for a problem or incongruity; and then (2) combine possible solutions, or generate from them, a final solution that the group determines to be the "best" according to a given criterion.

CT–RAs use standard creativity tasks such as *Unusual Uses* ("Think of all the unusual ways you can to use a brick"); *Circumstances and Consequences* ("What would happen if we all had eyes in the backs of our heads?"); *Product Improvement* ("Think of all the ways you can to improve school desks"); and *New Inventions* ("With your group, think of as many ideas as you can for a new toy. Invent a toy, name it, and write out directions or explanations for it."). These may be used in their "pure" form (e.g., "Think of as many unusual uses as you can" for any common object) or adapted to a specific content area (e.g., "Think of as many unusual games as you can using a volleyball," or "Invent a tool to be used around the house in the year 2020"). Consider that only a short time ago, a subject-specific CT–RA could have been, "What would happen if the Berlin Wall fell?"

In completing the CT–RA, groups are required to follow the original ground rules Osborn developed (1963) for brainstorming:

1. No criticizing anyone's ideas, not even your own.
2. List as many ideas as possible.
3. Freewheeling is encouraged—the wilder the idea, the better.
4. New ideas may be formed by combining and adding to ideas already listed.

After the brainstorming, the groups use their list of possible solutions to arrive at a final answer; they may be asked to decide their final most useful answer, their funniest answer or combination of answers, or the solution they think is most likely to occur in the future. These final answers are then shared with the whole class.

Using CT–RAs   CT–RAs are easy. They can be done in 10 to 15 minutes at the beginning or end of the class period (5 minutes of brainstorming; 5 minutes of polishing final solution; and 5 minutes of sharing with whole class) and can then be recalled for application to subject content. They're also good for days when interruptions or an altered school schedule destroys the continuity of the class routine (i.e., days with assemblies, early dismissal, pep rallies, field trips, etc.).

I used CT–RAs for one full semester in a high school remedial reading class and discovered at least four things. First, my "low academic" kids were marvelously creative. Anyone who didn't know this was a remedial reading class and who observed the students' CT–RA discussions would have labeled my students "bright" (my students *were* bright, by the way). The students certainly looked and acted bright doing CT–RA; in fact, this is the group that wanted to improve school desks by putting hydraulic lifts on the legs so the students in the back of the room could see as well as the ones in the front (Haggard, 1986)!

Second, my students *loved* doing CT–RAs. For many of them, it was the first time they'd ever *felt* bright, in control, and powerful in the classroom. If I tried to cancel

CT–RAs, the students let me know about it in no uncertain terms. Never have I had such a population of students complain so much if I cancelled a school task.

Third, I learned that the interest inherent in the task overrode all problems associated with cooperative group work. I had no difficulty with students staying on task and with students participating cooperatively. Keep in mind that these were the students whom most people would predict would be the *least* likely to work well together; many of them were considered by other teachers and students to be the most difficult in the school.

Finally, I learned to capitalize on the thinking students did during CT–RA and transfer it to academic tasks. So, when a freshman student asked me how to write the paragraph on skiing he needed to take to his English class, I could begin by saying, "Remember the thinking we did this morning in our CT–RA (unusual uses)? Sit down, and *using that same kind of thinking*, list everything you know about skiing." He did this without hesitation and without needing clarification. Following that, we clustered his ideas, narrowed them down, and he wrote his paragraph.

The importance and value of the small and large group discussions in CT–RA cannot be overemphasized. Although initially, high achievers and/or highly verbal students may dominate the small cooperative group discussions, this lasts only until the hesitantly offered suggestion of a quieter member knocks everyone's socks off for its wit, its wackiness, or its sheer beauty. As groups share their efforts in full-class discussion, "oohs" and "ahs" echo spontaneously around the room when particularly ingenious responses are read; students quickly learn that these comments frequently were contributed by class members who rarely contribute anything to class.

A CT–RA Activity: Biology   Bob Tierney (1985) describes a CT–RA-like activity he uses in his tenth-grade biology class in which each student draws an animal, real or imaginary, with a felt-tipped pen. Students then cut their animals out, cut off the head, and pass the head to the student sitting next to them. Students paste the new head on the animal body they've retained. Tierney then provides the class with a list of Latin and Greek word roots and asks each student to give his or her animal a scientific name and write a description of the animal's habitat and behavior. Students read their descriptions to one another and group the animals according to similarities. Following this, Tierney launches his lesson on binomial nomenclature and classification.

This lesson needs only the addition of cooperative groups to make it a cooperative learning activity. After the new animals are pasted together, groups or partners (rather than individuals) brainstorm possible names, habitats, and behaviors for each person's animal; using these ideas, students then work individually to write descriptions of their animal's habitat and behavior. Small groups reconvene to share names and descriptions and determine tentative criteria for classification of the animals in that group. Oral summaries of the small group discussions are then shared with the whole class.

How to do . . . .

CT–RA

Creative problem solving is *fun* and becomes increasingly so as it is shared with others. Creativity is based on incongruity and free-wheeling mental play; it therefore invites spontaneity and risk-taking, wild speculation, and humorous response. (Be prepared for noise and laughter.) CT–RAs lead to wonderfully generative thinking that produces innovative, unpredictable problem solutions. That does *not* mean the solutions or answers are frivolous. They are the models and prototypes of solutions that come from brainstorming and creative problem solving *in subject areas*. The fact that they are fun does not make them less academic. The fact that they are done in small group cooperative settings means that they stimulate precisely the kind of social and language interaction that content learning requires. The following steps should be useful in developing CT–RAs for your classroom:

1. Decide how CT–RAs fit into the curriculum, unit, and/or lesson plans (daily, periodic; general, specific).

2. Write CT–RA prompts and final answer criteria: for example, "What would happen if everybody all over the world recycled paper, plastic and glass?" The final answer criterion is to choose the answer you think most likely to happen.

3. Divide students into cross-ability and cross-status groups.

4. Allow 5 minutes for brainstorming, 5 minutes for considering final answer, and 5 minutes for group sharing of answers with the whole class.

5. Conduct full-class discussion to determine possible follow-up of ideas generated.

ASK SOMETHING

Paul Crowley's Ask Something approach (1988) is based on the notion that students can improve writing drafts by learning from peer reactions. Students bring to class a piece of their writing; this may be from learning log entries, a piece of writing following reading, or the result of a direct teacher assignment. Students work in small groups where each student passes his or her paper to the person on the left (or right). Students read the new papers and write at least one question in the margin or at the bottom of the paper that they believe needs to be addressed. The papers are then passed to the next person for the same purpose. When all members of the group have asked one or more questions, papers are returned to the author. Authors then choose which questions they wish to address and make revisions. Following the initial activity, groups may reconvene to share their revised work, discuss particularly useful questions, make plans for final revision, or do any combination of the three.

The value of Ask Something is its demonstration of how writing can be a collaborative process in which, once again, students assume most of the responsibility for the learning event. Clearly, any content can be addressed in the writing itself, whether it is analysis of a mathematical procedure, elaboration of a current event, literary response, or recordings taken during a science project. The teacher's role here is to monitor individual and group progress.

VALUING COOPERATIVE/COLLABORATIVE LEARNING

By now, I've become so convinced of the value of cooperative and collaborative learning that the advantages seem self-evident. Certainly, I've incorporated more and more group work into my own classes over the years. Twenty years ago, when I began my college teaching career, I taught almost totally from a lecture-demonstration model that was more lecture than demonstration. I was a good lecturer; I knew my stuff, had an upbeat and dynamic speaking presence, and threw in stories and dramatic humor to keep things interesting. My students left the room each class period shaking their aching hands and telling me *how much* they'd learned. They not only performed admirably on my rather rigorous tests, but also gave me very high teaching evaluations and wrote personal notes to me about how they liked the class. There was no reason to change—until I began to think about the incongruity of my standing in front of a class lecturing about the importance of language interaction for content learning (I was the only one "interacting"!) and until I perceived that having students work through new ideas in small group discussion and written products might be more important than giving tests to see how much course content they could remember. And so I changed. Beginning in my second or third year of college teaching, I began adding more and more small group discussion and participation so that now, even in so-called lecture classes, not a class period goes by without one or more extended periods of small group cooperative or collaborative learning.

AMBIGUITY, RISK, AND COOPERATIVE/COLLABORATIVE LEARNING

My decisions about cooperative and collaborative learning grew from a combination of classroom experience, what I know and am still learning about language interaction and content learning, and my own research and study. I've spent some time examining issues related to ambiguity and risk in the classroom, specifically with regard to how students construct meaning when faced with ambiguous classroom tasks (Haggard, 1989; Ruddell, 1991a) and have hypothesized about a certain type of advantage cooperative/collaborative learning activities provide.

Ambiguity refers to the extent to which a precise and predictable formula for student action in generating a task product is defined (Doyle & Carter, 1984); that is, a task is considered ambiguous when students are not told everything they need to know or do to fulfill task requirements. Recent research suggests that students disambiguate classroom tasks in one of two ways: (1) reducing the task to a low-level, formulaic assignment (Doyle & Carter, 1984; Haggard, 1989; Ruddell, 1991a), or (2) redefining or reconstructing the task itself (Haggard, 1989; Murphy, 1988). Interacting with ambiguity in classrooms is the element of *risk*, or the degree to which students face heavy consequences for failure to meet task demands (Doyle & Carter, 1984). When both ambiguity and risk are high, students are persistent in their efforts to reduce one or both (Doyle & Carter, 1984).

Cooperative and collaborative learning activities reduce individual student risk in the face of complex, ambiguous classroom tasks (Hoffman, 1990; Ruddell, 1991b); this is important because complex, ambiguous classroom tasks very often are precisely the kinds of higher-order thinking tasks required for real learning in content areas. Reduction of risk comes in cooperative/collaborative groups not only from the psychology of "strength in numbers," but from many other sources as well.

By reducing risks, cooperative/collaborative learning activities offer the following advantages:

Cooperative/collaborative learning activities focus on student construction of knowledge rather than reproduction of answers from text. Students, do indeed, engage in higher-order learning tasks that are nonformulaic, and for which there are no pat, easy answers. Learning is active, assertive, and student-directed.

Cooperative/collaborative learning activities allow student thinking to determine much of the content of lesson discussion and the lesson itself. Recall my earlier statement that students' constructions of knowledge *become* the curriculum; this occurs when complex, ambiguous tasks allow multiple viewpoints in problem solution. This is not "out of control," directionless curriculum; rather, it is true connectedness between what students know and what they are learning.

Cooperative/collaborative learning activities place the teacher in the role of facilitator of learning and friendly monitor of classroom events. The teacher serves as an important resource person as students work through cooperative/collaborative tasks; the term *friendly monitor* is intended here to convey a mentoring teacher role. The teacher as facilitator is always aware of curricular and student needs but steps back sufficiently to allow student self-determination.

Cooperative/collaborative learning activities contain guidelines, guideposts, and directions for focusing response. Students are not expected simply to sink or swim. Scaffolding activities and resources, including teacher modeling, guidance, and assistance, are available as students need them to support learning.

Cooperative/collaborative learning activities encourage independent thought and action. Cooperative/collaborative learning activities leave plenty of room for individuality and independent thinking. Because of the high ambiguity and low risk, students are free to make choices and pursue uncharted waters without fear of being "wrong"; teacher guidance and support encourage this process.

Cooperative/collaborative learning activities provide "practice time" for rehearsing new ideas, thoughts, and theories. Progression from expressive to formal language occurs during this practice time. As students manipulate ideas in language, they begin to see nuance and make important connections between prior knowledge and new learning. Their efforts are informed by insights and ideas expressed by others.

Cooperative/collaborative learning activities require much oral and written interaction between classroom participants. This includes all participants, students and teachers, and serves as a means for students to sort through the ambiguities and make sense of the task and the new learning. Further exploration of ideas occurs in the course of carrying out language interactions.

Cooperative/collaborative learning activities promote interdependence with peers and other resources. While this may sound contradictory to developing independent thought and action, it is not. Independence and interdependence would seem to be very important cohabiting qualities. It is through this combination that students come to trust their own voice and viewpoints while simultaneously listening to and understanding many voices and other viewpoints. This is particularly important in classrooms and schools in which students with homogeneous experiential backgrounds and values are being joined by students with diverse cultures, attitudes, values, and ideas (LittleSoldier, 1989).

INTEGRATED STUDIES AS A MEANS FOR COLLABORATIVE LEARNING IN SUBJECT AREAS

Recent attention on interdisciplinary and integrated instruction has led to many interesting interpretations and applications of team learning and teaching (MacIver, 1990; Pace, 1995a). Almost all of these include—and some in fact highlight—collaborative learning activities. I think this is because many of the assumptions underpinning one apply equally as well to the other; central to both integrated instruction and collaborative learning, for example, are notions of *connectedness* between subject areas and between individuals as learners.

MAKING CONNECTIONS

Connectedness makes it seem reasonable to reduce artificial barriers between subject areas and find ways for learning in each to complement and enhance learning in all others. This, in turn, makes reasonable a view of learning that demands that the learning process itself be de-mechanized and increasingly holistic. In other words, if we believe that one doesn't learn optimally when *individuals* are isolated and separated from one another, it is much easier to accept the notion that one doesn't learn subject areas optimally when discipline knowledge is isolated and separate from other subject areas, either.

This view of learning is well in line with what George, Stevenson, Thomason, and Beane (1992) characterize as the new vision of middle level education. This vision, they assert, is "learner-centered" and consonant with good general curriculum theory. Such curriculum should include:

1. *A learner-centered environment.* This means:

   curriculum is derived from students' questions and concerns and negotiated by the teacher and students, not tightly controlled by specifications and mandates from outside the classroom;

curriculum is constructivist, "enabling young people to construct their own meanings rather than simply accept those of others"; and

teachers and other adults in the school are also viewed as learners.

2. *An integrative curriculum.* This means:

doing away with traditional separate subject boundaries;

viewing cognitive and affective activities as interrelated, not separate; and

developing knowledge and skill through purposeful use in the process of pursuing meaningful, worthwhile questions and issues.

3. *Appropriate evaluation processes.* This means abandoning narrowly defined performance objectives for learning goals that:

address "self and social questions";

identify significant themes, activities, knowledge, and the finding of resources; and

respect the fact that while students "engage common questions and concerns," they do not all "learn the same particular information" (George, et al., 1992, from Pace, 1995b).

Perceiving interconnections between subject areas and agreeing with the vision of curriculum suggested by Paul George and his associates is somewhat easier than designing instruction to create interconnectedness in educational settings in which philosophical and physical plant traditions are based on separation of subject areas. Even so, redesigned instruction is happening today in middle and junior/senior high schools, and the vehicle that appears most promising for its implementation is project-based learning.

PROJECT-BASED LEARNING

Project-based learning, as its title suggests, centers around major projects that students, as a class or in small groups, decide to undertake. In an integrated studies environment, projects may address community needs ("Cleaning Up the Neighborhood"); explore personal, family, and community histories ("The Families, Lives, and Times of Odessa, Missouri"); engage students in exploration of global issues ("Money Makes the World Go 'Round"); or develop any of a myriad other big ideas. Effective development of these project topics requires two conditions: (1) topics must grow from students' felt needs, and (2) project development involves resources from and exploration of multiple subject areas.

Jerry Harste (1994) emphasizes the importance of inquiry as the foundation for project-based learning. He is not talking about inquiry as a methodology here, but rather inquiry as a deeply felt, inner need to know. He states, "Viewing curriculum as inquiry means that I envision classrooms as sites of inquiry, or as communities of learners. Inquiry is not a technical skill be to applied at will, but rather a philosophical stance that permeates the kinds of lives we choose to live" (1994, pp. 1230–31). Inquiry becomes the starting point and sustaining element that propels a classroom project itself and thus emerges as the driving force of project-based learning.

I find the notion of inquiry, as Harste envisions it, to be powerful. Essentially, he is saying that students and teachers should examine what they know, look around their world, and decide what it is they want to know. *Then learning should grow from class ex-*

ploration of questions generated in determining what the group wants to know. The idea that deeply felt needs should guide curriculum choices in classrooms, that questions students and teachers ask and then energetically seek to answer are more important than state- or district-mandated curriculum guides, and that intensely focused reading and writing stemming from the inquiry topic may be more legitimate than assigned textbook reading and learning how to write formal lab reports and expository essays is *revolutionary.* And it is worth our attention.

In addition, I like the idea of projects as a focal point and center for learning. We have all seen pre-adolescents and adolescents go after an idea or hone a skill with absolute concentration and determination (think about their pursuit of athletic, musical, or thespian abilities; their amazing ability to surf the World Wide Web; their absorption with 'toons and comic books and popular music). *That's* the energy and motivation that projects based on true inquiry capture. Consider for a moment how, as part of an "Our Bodies, Ourselves" project, student-conducted experiments during a visit to an amusement park (e.g., wind resistance during roller coaster rides; heart rate and pulse studies on various rides; the speed of the roller coaster in contrast to the speed of the ferris wheel, the carousel, and the bumper cars; etc.) lead naturally both to insight and learning and to new questions and additional study. Along the way, students read and write as it serves their project needs.

To institute project-based learning in your class, begin by leading a class discussion about "Things We Know" (about a particular topic). Let students work in pairs or groups to list what they know; give them plenty of time and expect ideas to range considerably. Share these in whole class discussion. Then let them go back to their partner or group and first list "Things We Don't Know" and later "Things We Want to Know." Perry Marker (1993) suggests the following progression of questions to guide a similar process. He views this as a means for students' development of ideas and issues into thoughtful, transformative projects: (1) What do we know [about this topic]? (2) What don't we know? (3) What do we want to find out about what we don't know? (4) How can we find information? (5) What resources do we have to find the information? (6) How can we present and share our findings? and (7) What specific proposals can we make to implement our findings? (pp. 82–83). Either of these approaches for launching inquiry projects may cover several days and may require that

you "prime the pump" a bit; students are wholly unused to being asked what they'd like to learn in school and given the freedom to develop their own projects. Your role is to assist student groups in shaping project ideas and guiding them as they work in collaborative groups to completion of the projects. Develop procedures and record-keeping systems *before you begin the projects* so they are ready to go from the start (more about this in the next section).

PROCEDURES FOR IMPLEMENTING, GUIDING, AND EVALUATING COOPERATIVE/COLLABORATIVE GROUP WORK

If I had to identify the single greatest barrier to group learning in classrooms, it would undoubtedly be concern teachers have about "turning the class loose" or "losing control" in the classroom. This is a well-founded concern: We've all seen or experienced classrooms that were out of control. If you consider this for a moment, however, you'll probably conclude that, most of the time, students working in groups did not cause the loss or lack of control. Other things did, and those other things would have been present whether the class was in small groups or not.

It would be foolish to claim that there are no problems associated with cooperative/collaborative group instruction. Of course, there are; but careful planning can do much to reduce the probability that such problems will occur.

PREREQUISITES TO GROUPING FOR COOPERATIVE LEARNING

Preparation for cooperative/collaborative learning is essential to success. In schools or districts in which students are experienced group workers and learners, preparation and prior planning for cooperative or collaborative work need only be minimal. If students are not used to working with one another, then preliminary planning must be detailed and carefully thought out. At the very least, you should arrange the following conditions before using cooperative/collaborative learning groups in your classroom:

1. *Before you even consider moving students into learning groups, you must establish an orderly learning environment.* This does not necessarily mean "pin-drop quiet" or even quiet most of the time. It does mean that, whatever the class rules and expectations are, everyone knows them and generally abides by them.

2. *Your classroom should demonstrate to any and all who enter a clear focus and intent on learning.* There can be no mistaking that this is a classroom in which everyone works and everyone gets things done. Expectations are high, and teacher behavior consistently reflects this.

3. *Whatever your class is, it is consistently that.* Students can trust that teacher behavior, expectations, and responses will be much the same day in and day out. Decide, and let students know, what you will tolerate and what you will not. Maintain a generally even disposition, and don't play favorites. Expect adolescents to test the boundaries, and respond to each test the same way you responded to the one before and the same way you will to the one after.

INTRODUCING COOPERATIVE/COLLABORATIVE LEARNING GROUPS

One attitude that will serve you well in introducing cooperative/collaborative learning activities is that it is worthwhile to spend a little time introducing and clarifying cooperative/collaborative learning concepts before attempting to have students work in learning groups. Time spent here is small in comparison to time spent reducing chaos or confusion and removing problems. Consider doing the following:

1. *Physically arrange the room to be as conducive as possible to accommodate interactions and resource needs of cooperative/collaborative learning groups.* Try to plan the room arrangement to reduce noise, movement, and confusion; you will also need to consider specific needs and equipment for your subject area. If you do not have your own room, plan ways to rearrange and arrange back quickly and quietly each class period.

2. *Establish working rules for operation of learning groups.* These may be developed cooperatively with your class, or you may announce and explain them. Rules need to account for:
   a) Procedures for getting into and out of groups each day.
   b) Amount of movement permissible in room during group work (e.g., you may want to specify that only two people may be up and moving around the room at a time).
   c) Movement to other resource areas in the school (the library, film room, storage area, computer lab, etc.).
   d) Signals for starting and stopping work each day.
   e) Instructions/procedures for using computers and other classroom resources.
   f) The signal you will use to get students' attention when the room is noisy with working conversations.

IDENTIFYING SOCIAL SKILLS FOR EFFECTIVE COOPERATIVE/COLLABORATIVE GROUP PARTICIPATION

MaryEllen Vogt (1996) suggests that a useful beginning activity for introducing cooperative/collaborative activities is to engage students in a conversation about what constitutes an effective working group. This may be initiated by asking, "What do participants do to make a group work?" As students brainstorm ideas ("listen to one another," "do the work you say you're going to do," "be prepared," "don't fool around," "encourage others' participation," etc.), the teacher records ideas on the board. After the brainstorming, students select one social skill (e.g., "listen to one another") and as a group develop a Looks Like/Sounds Like/Feels Like chart that summarizes what a learning group will look and sound like when it is operating well (Figure 9.3). Other social skills are explored in the same manner: charts are recorded on large easel paper and then posted in the room as friendly reminders.

ESTABLISHING ROLES FOR INDIVIDUALS IN COOPERATIVE/COLLABORATIVE LEARNING GROUPS

Most teachers using groups for the first time like the idea of role assignment because it adds structure that helps students understand specifically what it is they are to be

FIGURE 9.3   *Looks Like/Sounds Like/Feels Like chart*

Social Skill: **Listening**

Looks Like	Sounds Like	Feels Like
heads nodding	one person speaking	I am important
people are interested	a "busy buzz"	what I have to say is important
people are leaning forward	questions and answers	what I think matters
there is eye contact	appropriate disagreement	I can help others figure things out
people are taking turns	people are reading and learning	good

doing. Just as importantly, role assignment gives a clear message to students that this is business; it has certain *goals*, certain *expectations* for student performance, and certain *structures* to guide student behaviors. Such messages go a long way in developing students' abilities to work independently. Over time, specific roles are rotated among group members so that everyone has an opportunity to assume each role. The following roles are useful for learning groups (each role may not be necessary every time groups function, depending on the group task):

The *Facilitator* is responsible for moving the group process along, making sure everyone has a chance to participate, encouraging reticent members, helping talkative members curb their input, and making sure the task is completed.

The *Recorder* is responsible for keeping notes and informal minutes of the discussion, ideas generated by the group, alternative solutions, explanations, and any other important information; the Recorder does the final write-up, as needed.

The *Timer* allocates and monitors time so that all parts of the task are completed as required; the Timer notifies the group throughout of time considerations.

The *Worrier* is responsible for worrying about content and procedural issues; for example, whether the group is "bird walking" (off the subject), whether the ideas being generated are on track with the task goal, or whether the operational "grand plan" of action can be accomplished in the time available, and so forth. The Worrier begins most sentences with, "I'm worried that . . ."

The *Reporter* is responsible for reporting progress and/or final solutions to the class during wrap-up time; the Reporter may also be responsible for taking periodic reports of the group's progress to the teacher.

For some cooperative/collaborative learning activities, you may want to add the following roles:

The *Messenger* serves as liaison between the group and other groups, the resource center(s), and/or the teacher; the Messenger may be the only group member designated to be out of the group working area without special permission.

Set-up/Clean-up Persons are responsible for collecting and returning materials and equipment, checking to see that personal belongings and trash are removed from the working area, and requesting any additional materials and equipment the group needs for continued work.

The *Author* is responsible for final write-up of written report or project using material and drafts developed by the entire group. There may be two or more Authors per working group.

The *Editor* is responsible for reviewing and revising drafts developed by the Authors and/or other members of the group. The Editor works closely with the Authors in production of the final product. There may be two or more Editors per working group.

The *Checker* makes sure that individuals have completed their work and submitted it to become part of the group product and helps Authors and Editors meet final deadlines.

There is clearly overlap across roles, places where two roles could be combined, and perhaps a gap or two from the perspective of your subject area, and that's fine. These are not etched in stone; many adaptations and additions may be used to tailor the roles to a given subject area or class. Similarly, the responsibilities I've attached to each have been gleaned over time using group learning activities in my classes and from what others have described. They, too, are recommendations only, and can and should be adapted to fit the needs of a given task, class, and teacher.

One cautionary note about group roles is warranted: Bonnie Raines, in a master's thesis study of collaborative literature group discussions in middle grades, found that assigning roles and requiring students to facilitate or lead discussions did not always produce positive results (Raines, 1991). Because of inexperience, Facilitators sometimes asked questions that interrupted the flow of discussion and limited student thinking or speculation. Raines found that groups in which students were given clear discussion tasks and worked as a group toward that task, rather than in specific roles, produced higher-level discussions than did structured, role-assigned groups.

In your subject area and for the cooperative and collaborative group tasks you develop, group roles may not be an issue; it may be that the choice of whether or not to assign them is clear and compelling. You may find it helpful, however, to monitor the effectiveness of assigning group roles, to try various arrangements, and then make adjustments as they are needed.

GUIDING COOPERATIVE/COLLABORATIVE LEARNING GROUPS

The teacher's role as students work in groups is a critical one. Whatever you do, don't be misled into thinking that once the groups are operational, your work is over. Far from it. You have many important functions to perform, even though they differ significantly from traditional teacher roles. As groups work, you should do several things.

STAY WITH THE ACTION

One of the most valuable "teacher rules" for effective cooperative/collaborative group learning is that the teacher's time when groups are working should *not* be used to grade papers, plan other instruction, leave the room, or do any of the myriad paperwork or other tasks that you have to do. You need to be alert, "with it," and on top of things at all times.

STAY AWAY WHEN YOU SHOULD

Probably the hardest thing for you to do is to stay back and let students work. If you don't already know how to do it, learn to tune in and out of group discussions from a distance; you'll be surprised how easy it is. You'll see groups having problems and be tempted to settle the issues. Resist the urge. Give them some time to make mistakes or work through solutions themselves.

GET CLOSE WHEN YOU SHOULD

When you see a group that appears to be off task, go stand near it; you may or may not want to have any verbal interaction whatever with the group. Simply stand there, and see whether your presence gets the group back on task. You may see a group caught in a problem too large or too complex for students to work out; go ask if there is any way you can help. Periodically stop by each group and ask how students are doing, if they need anything, and what you might do to facilitate their progress. Be particularly watchful, alert, and close when group work has any implications for student safety.

PROJECT MANAGEMENT

When students are working in cooperative or collaborative groups, and especially when the work they are doing is project-based, one of the most important things you can do to make the experience successful is to maintain an organizing system that assists students in focusing their attention and energy each day on the work at hand. A very simple way to do this is to provide time at the beginning of class each day for stating the work to be done today and at the end of class reflecting on the day's accomplishments and planning for the next day's work. I recommend a "status-of-the-group" roll call at the beginning of class (Ruddell & Ruddell, 1995) that asks each group in turn, "What are you doing today?" and "What do you plan to accomplish?" At the end of class, guide students similarly in reflecting on the work done; this gives groups and individuals opportunity to monitor their own progress ("What did we accomplish today?" "What will you be doing tomorrow?") and share with other students and the teacher what they've found in their research and/or problems they're encountering.

Analytical discussion of this kind increases students' ability to self-monitor their working progress and develops their planning and strategic inquiry skills. It also keeps you informed of the progress they're making and provides information for your record keeping and evaluation procedures.

Figure 9-4 illustrates one way to maintain records of group planning and progress. Make a copy of the Project Work Management Sheet for each working group. Put the group's name or project topic at the top and list all group members in the space allotted. Each day at status-of-the-group roll call, record (in abbreviated form) each group's outline of its plan for the day. Later, during reflection time ("What did you accomplish today? What do you need for continued progress?"), record group accomplishments. Make note of any other pertinent information.

FIGURE 9.4   *Project Work Management Sheet*

Group: _____

Members: _____

_____

_____

_____

_____

Date	Work Planned	Work Accomplished

EVALUATING AND GRADING COOPERATIVE/COLLABORATIVE GROUP WORK

Evaluation and grading are critical components to successful cooperative/collaborative group functioning and are made all the more so by the fact that we don't have a group work evaluation/grading tradition to guide what we do. Ultimately, you'll have to decide how and what you want to evaluate from the group work, and each decision will be based on the complexity and extent of the group task and the product from the group interaction. It's difficult to give hard and fast rules here; however, I recommend that you seriously consider using some form of portfolio assessment (see Chapter 7) incorporating individual and group self-evaluation. Specific recommendations follow.

GRADING CRITERIA

Before launching cooperative or collaborative learning groups, decide upon your grading criteria and procedures and do not deviate from them. Unless what you devised is patently unfair, capricious, or prejudicial, continuing with flawed procedures generally causes fewer problems than changing grading criteria and procedures in midstream. If you do see a need to change, find a way to remove or reduce the effect of the flaws. Be sure your grading criteria and procedures are clearly outlined for students.

GROUP AND INDIVIDUAL GRADES

Consider awarding a group grade for the final product with provision for some type of individual evaluation. This may require that students keep individual journals chronicling their own participation and contributions to the group effort. You may want to include some sort of individual assessment—an individually written or developed product (test, essay, etc.) based on the group work.

STUDENT PERCEPTIONS OF GROUP PROGRESS

Consider also administering a questionnaire periodically to see how students perceive the progress of the group project. Cohen's questionnaire (1986) is based on students' perceptions of how interesting and difficult the work was, how actively the individual participated, and how effective the group was in allowing equal participation by all students. You can write a short, 5-minute questionnaire for use to maintain periodic connection with student perceptions.

SOME FINAL WORDS ON COOPERATIVE/COLLABORATIVE LEARNING

In most of the other chapters, I've developed my own "final words." In this one, I want to use the words of one of my students. Below is an excerpt from an end-of-semester report written by David Hathorne (1991) about his field experience in secondary reading. This excerpt just about says it all to summarize our discussion of cooperative/collaborative learning, literacy instruction, and subject area learning. (I might add that it does so with delightful humor and eloquence.)

One of the more significant events which occurred while I was observing the class, and certainly the event most relevant to the teaching of reading and writing in a math class, was a cooperative unit on geometrical measurements. The lesson to be learned was ostensibly how to use geometry to make indirect measurements—that is, measurements that would be otherwise difficult or even impossible to make. And, in fact, methods for making such measurements were learned, but so were other things, such as how to interpret, how to think, and how to write clearly.

The easy and most obvious way to teach such a lesson would be to give the kids a set of instructions and then let them make the measurements. That would have worked, and something of value would have been learned, but Janie (not her real name) was more clever than that. What she did was to divide the class into teams of four students and give each group a very sketchy set of instructions. The tasks to be performed were described, and the instruments to be used for each task were enumerated. Some hints as to how to go about making the measurements were given, but students had to use pre-existing knowledge and a bit of intelligence in order to come up with complete schemes to make accurate measurements. Each group was required to pool their geometrical resources and write out a complete description as to how the measurements were to be made. This report was handed in and graded before the actual field work was performed.

Now this in itself constitutes, in my opinion, one excellent lesson. It has math, it has groups, it has thinking, it has writing. What more could one ask for? Well, this is where Janie put the most interesting spin on the project. When the groups got the reports handed back, they each got a report written up by another group. So to do the actual measurements, the groups had to pretend that they didn't know how to proceed, and follow explicitly the set of instructions written by another group. Keep in mind that the groups knew that this was going to happen, so, in addition to the grade they received on the initial report, there was an element of competition between groups to produce the best report. . . .

Even though I took no part in writing the initial report, I did get to join one of the groups in the actual performance of the measurements. Our tasks were to measure the height of the school library clock tower, the height of the flag pole, the distance across the street in front of the school, and the height of a tree on campus. Each of these measurements was done using a different method. The first one required the use of a large sighting protractor, which the students were required to construct. The day before the measurements were to occur, I took it upon myself to construct the protractor for our group. It turned out to be a super-deluxe whizbang unit with custom sighting arm, tripod mount, and bubble leveling device for precision accuracy. This did not hurt getting me in good with my group, and besides it was fun to make. So we gathered our data, did our calculations, and got our answers. Pretty damn good ones too!

But the real capper to the whole exercise occurred when we all gathered back in the classroom. Each group, it seemed, was absolutely convinced that the set of instructions they wrote up was a masterwork of mathematical prose—elegant in its conciseness and sheer genius in its clarity. The piece of trash that they had to work with, however, they were convinced had been dashed off by a group of crazed opium-eaters coming down from eight days on bad stuff. There's a lesson there somewhere. The most difficult part for me was letting the students do most of the work. It was, after all, their exercise and not mine.

D O U B L E   E N T R Y   J O U R N A L

_____
_____
_____
_____
_____
_____
_____
_____
_____
_____
_____

Go back and look at your prereading DEJ notes about your own experiences with cooperative/collaborative learning. Given those experiences and what you've learned reading this chapter, how do you think you might effectively use cooperative/collaborative learning groups in your classroom? What steps will you take to make such learning a positive experience for students? What do you see as the "pros" and "cons" of using cooperative/collaborative learning activities in your subject area? How willing would you be to try your hand at integrated studies? Share your ideas with a friend.

REFERENCES

Aaronson, E., Blaney, N., Sikes, J., Stephan, C., Snapp, N. (February 1975). The Jigsaw route to learning and liking. *Psychology Today*, 43–50.

Aaronson, E., Stephan, C., Sikes, J., Blaney, N., & Snapp, M. (1978). *The jigsaw classroom.* Beverly Hills, CA: Sage.

Alexander, W. M. (1987). Toward schools in the middle: Progress and problems. *Journal of Curriculum and Supervision, 2,* 314–329.

Allington, R. L. (1990). What have we done with the middle? In G. G. Duffy (Ed.), *Reading in the middle school* (2nd ed.), (pp. 32–40). Newark, DE: International Reading Association.

Atwell, N. (1987). *In the middle: Writing, reading and learning with adolescents.* Portsmouth, NH: Heinemann.

Bayer, A. S. (1990). *Collaborative-apprenticeship learning: Language and thinking across the curriculum, K–12.* Mountain View, CA: Mayfield.

Braddock II, J. H. (1990). Tracking the middle grades: National patterns of grouping for instruction. *Phi Delta Kappan, 71,* 445–449.

Caught in the Middle. (1987). Report of the Superintendent's Middle Grade Task Force, California State Department of Education. Sacramento, CA: Department of Education.

Cohen, E. G. (1986). *Designing groupwork.* New York: Teachers College Press.

Condon, M. W. F., & Hoffman, J. V. (1990). The influence of classroom management. In G. G. Duffy (Ed.), *Reading in the middle school* (2nd ed.), (pp. 41–59). Newark, DE: International Reading Association.

Crowley, P. (1988). Ask something. In C. Gilles, M. Bixby, P. Crowley, S. R. Crenshaw, M. Henrichs, F. E. Reynolds & D. Pyle (Eds.), *Whole language strategies for secondary students* (p. 47). New York: Richard C. Owen.

Doyle, W., & Carter, K. (1984). Academic tasks in classrooms. *Curriculum Inquiry, 14,* 129–149.

Eeds, M., & Wells, D. (1989). Grand conversations: An exploration of meaning construction in literature study groups. *Research in the Teaching of English, 23,* 4–29.

George, P. S., Stevenson, C., Thomason, J., & Beane, J. (1992). *The middle school—And beyond.* Alexandria, VA: Association for Supervision and Curriculum Development.

Goodlad, J. I. (1984). *A place called school.* New York: McGraw-Hill.

Haggard, M. R. (1978). The effect of creative thinking-reading activities (CT–RA) on reading comprehension. In P. D. Pearson & J. Hansen (Eds.), *Reading: Disciplined inquiry in process and practice.* 27th Yearbook of the National Reading Conference (pp. 233–236). Clemson, SC: National Reading Conference.

Haggard, M. R. (1979). Creative thinking-reading activities (CT–RA): Catalysts for creative reading. *Illinois Reading Council Journal, 7,* 5–8.

Haggard, M. R. (1980). Creative thinking-reading activities (CT–RA): Bridging the gap between creative thinking and creative reading. *Reading Newsletter, No. 10.* Boston: Allyn & Bacon.

Haggard, M. R. (1986). Instructional strategies for developing student interest in content area subjects. In D. Lapp, J. Flood, & N. Farnan (Eds.), *Content area reading and learning: Instructional strategies* (pp. 70–80). Englewood Cliffs, NJ: Prentice-Hall.

Haggard, M. R. (1989). Reducing ambiguity: How students and teachers make sense of school. In

S. McCormick & J. Zutell (Eds.), *Cognitive and social perspectives for literacy research and instruction,* 38th Yearbook of the National Reading Conference (pp. 445–451). Chicago: National Reading Conference.

Harste, J. C. (1994). Literacy as curricular conversations about knowledge, inquiry, and morality. In R. B. Ruddell, M. R. Ruddell, & H. Singer (Eds.), *Theoretical models and processes of reading* (4th ed.), (pp. 1220–1242). Newark, DE: International Reading Association.

Hathorne, D. (1991). Reading curriculum field experience. Unpublished manuscript.

Hoffman, J. V. (1990). The myth of teaching. In J. Zutell & S. McCormick (Eds.), *Literacy theory and research: Analyses from multiple paradigms,* 39th Yearbook of the National Reading Conference (pp. 1–12). Chicago: National Reading Conference.

Huhtala, J., & Coughlin, E. B. (1991). Group Investigation, democracy, and the Middle East. *English Journal, 80,* 47–52.

Johnson, D. W., & Johnson, R. T. (1979). Conflict in the classroom: Controversy and learning. *Review of Educational Research, 49,* 51–70.

Johnson, D. W., & Johnson, R. T. (1986). *Learning together and alone* (2nd ed.). Englewood Cliffs, NJ: Prentice-Hall.

Lewin, K., Lippett, R., & White, R. (1939). Patterns of aggressive behavior in experimentally created 'social climates.' *Journal of Social Psychology, 10,* 271–299.

LittleSoldier, L. (1989). Cooperative learning and the Native American student. *Phi Delta Kappan, 71,* 161–163.

Manzo, A. V. (1974). The group reading activity. *The Forum.* College Reading Special Interest Group. Newark, DE: International Reading Association.

Manzo, A. V., & Manzo, U. (1990). *Content area reading: A heuristic approach.* Columbus, OH: Merrill.

MacIver, D. J. (1990). Meeting the needs of young adolescents: Advisory groups, interdisciplinary teams, and school transition programs. *Phi Delta Kappan, 71,* 458–464.

Marker, P. (1993). Not only by our words: Connecting the pedagogy of Paulo Freire with the social studies classroom. *Social Science Record, 30*(1), 77–90.

McCaslin, M. M. (1990). Motivated literacy. In J. Zutell & S. McCormick (Eds.), *Literacy theory and research: Analyses from multiple paradigms*. 39th Yearbook of the National Reading Conference (pp. 35–50). Chicago: National Reading Conference.

Moore, D. W., & Stefanich, G. P. (1990). Middle school reading: A historical perspective. In G. G. Duffy (Ed.), *Reading in the middle school* (2nd ed.), (pp. 3–15). Newark, DE: International Reading Association.

Murphy, S. B. (1988, February). *The problem with reading tasks: Watching children learn*. Paper presented at the Eastern Educational Research Association, Miami Beach, FL.

O'Flahavan, J. (1989). *An exploration of the effects of participant structure upon literacy development in reading group discussion*. Doctoral dissertation, University of Illinois-Champaign.

Osborn, A. F. (1963). *Applied imagination* (3rd ed.). New York: Scribner's.

Pace, G. (1995a). *Whole learning in the middle school: Evolution and transition*. Norwood, MA: Christopher-Gordon.

Pace, G. (1995b). Whole learning and a holistic vision of the middle school: Principles that guide practice. In G. Pace (Ed.), *Whole learning in the middle school: Evolution and transition* (pp. 11–26). Norwood, MA: Christopher-Gordon.

Phi Delta Kappan (1990, February). Special feature edition on middle school education (pp. 436–469).

Raines, B. (1991). Response and collaboration in literature discussion groups: A two-year study of an intermediate grade classroom. Master's thesis, Sonoma State University, Rohnert Park, CA.

Ruddell, M. R.-H. (1991a). Students' metacognitive response to ambiguous literacy tasks. *Reading Research and Instruction, 31*, 1–11.

Ruddell, M. R.-H. (1991b, May). *Use of ambiguous literacy tasks: Guiding students toward complex comprehension*. Paper presented at the International Reading Association, Las Vegas, NV.

Ruddell, R. B., & Ruddell, M. R. (1995). *Teaching children to read and write: Becoming an influential teacher*. Boston: Allyn & Bacon.

Sharan, S. (1980). Cooperative learning in small groups: Recent methods and effects on achievement, attitude, and ethnic relations. *Review of Educational Research, 50*, 241–271.

Sharan, S., & Sharan, Y. (1986). *Small-group teaching*. Englewood Cliffs, NJ: Prentice-Hall.

Sharan, Y., & Sharan, S. (1989–1990). Group investigation expands cooperative learning. *Educational Leadership, 47*, 17–21.

Sherif, M., Harvey, O. J., White, B. J., Hood, W. E., & Sherif, C. W. (1961). *Intergroup conflict and cooperation: The Robber's Cave experiment*. Norman, OK: University of Oklahoma Book Exchange.

Siu-Runyan, Y., & Faircloth. *Beyond separate subjects: Integrative learning at the middle level*. Norwood, MA: Christopher-Gordon.

Slavin, R. E. (1980). Cooperative learning. *Review of Educational Research, 50*, 315–342.

Slavin, R. E. (1986). A cooperative learning approach to content areas: Jigsaw teaching. In D. Lapp, J. Flood, & N. Farnan (Eds.), *Content area reading and learning: Instructional strategies* (pp. 330–345). Englewood Cliffs, NJ: Prentice-Hall.

Stephenson, C., & Carr, J. F. (1993). *Integrated studies in the middle grades: Dancing through walls*. New York: Teachers College Press.

Tierney, B. (1985). In the fifth grade, they all raise their hands. *Learning, 85*, 34.

Vogt, M. E. (1996). Creating a response-centered curriculum with discussion groups. In L. B. Gambrell & J. F. Almasi (Eds.), *Lively discussions: Creating elementary classrooms that foster engaged reading* (pp. 181–193). Newark, DE: International Reading Association.

Vygotsky, L. (1978). *Mind in society: The development of higher psychological processes*. Cambridge, MA: MIT Press.

BUILDING TABLE

CHAPTER 9	JIGSAW I AND II	GROUP INVESTIGATION	GRA	CT–RA	PROJECT BASED LEARNING
FOCUS ON	Content reading & discussion; information organization and articulation	Content reading & discussion; information organization & articulation	Content reading & discussion; information organization & articulation	Content problem solving; reading & writing articulation	Integrated content learning
GUIDES STUDENTS	Before, during, and after reading and writing	Before, during and after reading and writing	Before, during and after reading and writing	During reading and writing	Before, during, and after reading and writing
USE TO PLAN	Lessons, units	Units, semesters	Lessons, units	Lesson, units, semesters	Units, semesters
MAY BE USED	Cooperative groups	Cooperative groups, Collaborative groups	Cooperative groups	Cooperative groups	Collaborative groups
MAY BE COMBINED WITH (known strategies)	VSS, GMA, REAP, Writing Workshop, Journals. Learning Logs	DR–TA, DRA, Writing Workshops, Journals, Learning Logs	VSS, GMA, Writing Workshop	Content DR–TA, GMA, Semantic Mapping, Writing Workshop, Journals, Learning Logs, DEJ, Group Investigation	VSS, Writing Workshops, Journals, Logs
MATERIALS PREPARATION	Moderate to extensive	Light	Moderate	Light	Light
OTHER PREPARATION	Moderate	Moderate	Moderate	Moderate	Moderate
OUTSIDE RESOURCES	Necessary	Necessary	Necessary	Not needed	Necessary
HOW TO DO	Pages 280–281		Page 283	Page 286	

10

DIVERSITY IN THE CLASSROOM: MEETING THE NEEDS OF ALL STUDENTS

Write the word diversity *in the center of your jour-*

nal page. Around it, write all the ideas and associa-

tions you have with regard to the notion of

"diversity." Classify and categorize your associations.

Make a semantic map of your ideas.

Diversity is becoming the norm in U.S. classrooms. Where once our schools housed populations of relatively similar students, we now find more and more schools with students representing diverse cultures, language backgrounds, family structures, socioeconomic classes, ethnicities, sexual orientations, learning styles, and physical and learning abilities. This new diversity results, in part, from legislation reflecting social changes in the United States, beginning perhaps as early as mandatory attendance laws, but more significantly with *Brown vs. Board of Education* (1954), which initiated the end of legal segregation of students into racially homogeneous schools. Legislatively mandated changes further increased classroom diversity in the federal law, P. L. 94-142, stipulating the "least restrictive environment" for students with various physical and learning disabilities by mainstreaming them out of special schools and classrooms into regular public schools and classes to the fullest extent possible.

Other social and school conditions add further to the diversity of our classrooms. One such condition is the recent large wave of immigration to this country that began in the 1970s and is continuing to increase today (McLeod 1992); such numbers of immigrant entry into the United States are, by far, the largest since the turn of the century (Kellogg, 1988; McLeod, 1992). Portes and Rumbaut (1990) state, "Each year during the 1980s an average of six hundred thousand immigrants and refugees have been legally admitted into the country, and a sizable if uncertain number of others enter and remain without legal status, clandestinely crossing the border or overstaying their visas" (p. ivii). Nearly one-third of these immigrants currently settle in California. The others live in large cities (New York, Miami, and Chicago—often in ethnic enclaves of former immigrants) or disperse in areas surrounding these cities. Undocumented immigrants appear more likely to settle in rural areas than do legal immigrants (Portes & Rumbaut, 1990).

Adding to the cultural mix created by immigrant students in schools are special programs directed toward retention of immigrant and indigenous students with traditionally high drop-out rates; these populations include teenage mothers, low socioeconomic students, gifted minority students, and students with special interests and talents. The net effect is that our schools look different today than they did even a few years ago. It is not unusual today to hear several languages in the halls of middle and secondary schools, and in large urban schools serving immigrant populations, the number of different languages and dialects spoken in one school can be 20, 30, or more. Because of PL94-142 and the mainstreaming practices it mandated, students who were once sequestered in special classes and schools now are sitting in regular classes—sometimes in wheelchairs or accompanied by guide dogs, notetakers, and American Sign Language (ASL) interpreters, and sometimes physically indistinguishable from their peers. Girls and young women appear in advanced mathematics, science, and government courses in growing numbers, and students of all races, abilities, and talents are given support and encouragement to stay in school and continue on to college or other postsecondary education.

This variation and diversity is further reflected in a perceptible move from the "melting pot" tradition characteristic of previous immigrant movements into the United States in which cultural, ethnic, and linguistic groups adopted mainstream values and behavior to become absorbed into the majority culture; now, attitudes lean more toward a "salad bowl" mixture in which groups retain and celebrate their differences and contribute their unique qualities to the larger society (Banks, 1994). Thus, students from diverse cultures, both immigrant and indigenous, are less likely today to seek absorption by adopting majority traits; rather, they are maintaining ties and identification with their primary culture by holding to the behaviors, language, attitudes, and values of the group or groups with which they identify, whether these groups are culturally, linguistically, academically, ethnically, or socially defined.

Diversity, variation, and difference are very much a part of today's schools, and these qualities contribute greatly to providing a rich, multicultural, multiperspective education for all students. The presence of such diversity and difference has caused schools to change from practices that assume homogeneity and from practices that deny or denigrate student characteristics, languages, or qualities. This change is by no means completely accomplished; schools and districts are currently increasing their efforts to bring about changes appropriate to the new diversity and will continue to do so in the future. Teachers and administrators in school districts are participating in workshops, in-service programs, and graduate study to increase their understanding of the diverse populations entering schools, whether these populations are learning disabled students, various immigrant groups, gifted students, low-income indigenous and immigrant students, students with physical and health disabilities, students with special talents, bilingual students, or any combination of these.

Along with knowledge gained in study about various populations, it is helpful to have a framework for understanding diversity in all its forms. Such a framework allows us to gain perspective regarding the broad spectrum of student diversity and guides how we think about and respond to diverse student abilities and needs. The Difference Model framework (Weiner & Cromer, 1967) gives us such perspective and a positive means for conceptualizing diversity. It is presented in the next section of this chapter as one of several available models and along with instructional implications. Specific instructional activities for teaching in a diverse, multicultural environment follow.

THE DIFFERENCE MODEL AS A MEANS FOR VIEWING DIVERSITY

Weiner and Cromer (1967) identified four models to explain and describe instructional implications for students experiencing reading difficulties. These models grew from research on students with reading problems and were developed to explain characteristics of that population. However, they represent assumptions commonly applied to other types of diversity as well, particularly those involving physical and learning disabilities, cultural and language differences, and socioeconomic status.

The models, each with its own assumptions, diagnostic requirements, and instructional implications, serve as alternate means for understanding diverse student abilities—specifically, language and literacy abilities—in subject area classrooms. In presenting these models as representative ways to view many aspects of diversity, I am extending them beyond Weiner and Cromer's original intent (1967). My thesis here, however, is that one of them, the Difference Model, is useful for responding to all types of diversity and is particularly helpful to subject area teachers for analyzing student needs and developing literacy instruction and support to accompany subject area instruction.

Weiner and Cromer's four models for characterizing problem readers are summarized in Figure 10.1 (1967). As you look at these four models, at least two attributes are readily apparent. One is that the first three models have names and assumptions that involve pathology: that is, defect = something *wrong*, deficit = something *missing*, and disruption = something *interfering*. In contrast, the Difference Model carries no pathology: Nothing is wrong, missing, or interfering academically, socially, economically, linguistically, or culturally. Something is *different*. The student responds in a way that is simply different from the expected response, and this difference may range from responses that indicate problems or inability to construct meaning to those that go well beyond the expected response.

THE DEFECT AND DISRUPTION MODELS

A second attribute is apparent in the instructional implications of each model. Two of them, *defect* and *disruption*, are well outside the purview of the subject area teacher (see Figure 10.1); the one requires "correction of the defect," whereas the other recommends removing the source of trauma and/or repairing its effects. Certainly, teachers are responsible for referring students to specialists when they believe students need vision, hearing or some other physical screening or emotional or psychological counseling. Nevertheless, there is often a limit to the amount of correction that can be done for any given problem as well as a limit to the number of physical and emotional problems that are correctable.

FIGURE 10.1   *Four Models for Understanding Literacy Abilities*

MODEL	ASSUMPTIONS	DIAGNOSIS	INSTRUCTION
DEFECT	Something is *wrong* that causes a problem (e.g., vision or hearing loss).	Find the problem.	Correct the defect.
DEFICIT	Something is *missing* that causes a problem (e.g., word-recognition or comprehension skills).	Find the missing element(s).	Teach student skills that are missing.
DISRUPTION	Some sort of physical or emotional trauma has occurred that *interferes* with reading and causes a problem (e.g., emotional difficulties).	Locate the cause of the trauma.	Remove the source of trauma and/or repair effects.
DIFFERENCE	Some *difference* exists between the student's usual mode of response and the expected mode that causes the problem; (e.g., word-by-word reading or noncomprehension).	Identify the area of difference.	Adjust instructional approach or materials, or adjust response mode to minimize difficulties.

The fact is, students will be sitting in your classroom with any number of temporary and permanent physical and psychological problems ranging from very mild to major, and you are powerless to change the fact that these problems exist or to make the causal circumstances go away. Sometimes these problems will impinge on language and literacy functioning, and sometimes they will not; regardless, you can't change them. You *are* responsible for the academic and emotional well-being of these students in your classroom; however, you will need to do something other than look for the "defect" and correct it or identify the event that "disrupted" a student's progress. The defect and disruption models simply do not offer productive avenues for subject area teacher action in the face of various kinds of diversity in their classrooms.

THE DEFICIT MODEL

The *deficit model* is equally, if differently, problematic. The deficit model assumes that the best way to handle literacy problems is to look for whatever is missing and then teach it. It is, in fact, the most universally accepted model of instruction in Title I reading programs and many learning disability programs (Johnstone & Allington, 1991). I have some serious reservations about the value of this model in any form, as do Johnstone and Allington (1991), because of its emphasis on "teaching to the weakness." Essentially, the deficit model suggests that appropriate instruction for students with reading or learning problems involves finding out what students can't do (or don't have), teaching them how to do it, and then having them practice doing it. From just about any perspective, this seems like a questionable practice; it certainly is from the students' vantage point.

Consider for a moment one of the things you do least well (perhaps, for example, batting a softball); now consider having to go to a place and learn about and practice doing that thing for 1 hour every day, 5 days a week. *That's* deficit-model teaching; that's "teaching to the weakness." I don't want to be on the receiving end of it, and I suspect you don't either. Furthermore, I suspect that at one time or another you've been exposed to plenty of instruction in how to do whatever it is you don't do well: *It didn't "take."* No matter how many hours you go to a place and learn about it and practice doing it, instruction probably wouldn't take now. The greatest fallacy, in my mind, about deficit-model teaching is that the model itself fails to account for the fact that whatever it is we're trying to teach now has probably already been taught and was not learned. Continuing to focus on that weakness and not on the individual's strengths is self-defeating.

Aside from these issues surrounding deficit-model teaching in reading classes is the incontrovertible fact that subject area teachers do not have time to teach students "missing" skills unless the skills are directly related to learning in subject areas. This entire book concerns your responsibilities for increasing students' literacy abilities *in your subject area*, and they are considerable. But to expect you as science or social studies teachers, mathematics teachers, and home economics teachers to interrupt subject area instruction to teach the so-called basic literacy skills is unrealistic and unfair.

The fact that you have five students in your class "missing" English fluency does not mean that you are expected to stop class and teach English; instead, you are responsible for seeing to it that these students learn as much as they possibly can in your subject area in English. The same holds true for other literacy abilities. The fact that some students in your class are "missing" some aspect of their ability to construct meaning from text does not mean you are to suspend content instruction to teach "basic" comprehension skills; instead, you are responsible for finding ways to increase the probability that these students can construct meaning using available subject area texts. There are ways you can do both of these, which we'll discuss later; however, the kind of instruction suggested by the deficit model is not helpful here and is as much outside the purview of secondary teachers as is the instruction implied from the defect and disruption models.

THE DIFFERENCE MODEL

The *difference model* offers an alternative to the defect, disruption, and deficit models as a means for viewing and responding to diversity, whether this diversity resides in language and literacy abilities or elsewhere. The difference model, as we suggested earlier, assumes no pathology; nothing is "wrong" with the student or missing or interfering with anything. The difference model is neutral in that regard. The teacher does not seek to find problems; rather, she or he identifies the student's response, compares it with the expected response, and evaluates the difference. This is a significant and important change from the other models in the way we look at students. We quit asking, "What's wrong here?" and begin asking, "What is the magnitude and nature of the difference?" We quit blaming students for not being everything we think they should be in our classroom, spending hours finding labels and symptoms for so-called problems that seem to grow even larger as we toil and generally operating from a mind-set of pathology and fault finding.

Of major significance here are the instructional implications the difference model suggests. Recall in our models chart, the "Instruction" section for the difference model reads, "Adjust instructional approach, instructional materials or response mode to minimize difference." *Here* is where subject area teachers respond positively to diversity in their classrooms, and here is where your responsibility is most important. Notice that the model is still neutral. You are not going to change the instructional approach or materials because something is wrong with the materials or with students; rather, you are doing it because you notice a difference between what your students are doing and what you want them to do. In every sense, this entire book and others like it are about the many ways you can adjust instruction or instructional materials to minimize the difference between what your students are doing and what you want them to do.

AT-RISK STUDENTS, THE DIFFERENCE MODEL, AND DIVERSITY

In her elegant analysis of the parallels between quantum physics and reading theory, Constance Weaver (1994) describes the "quantum leap" as the collapsing of possibilities of what one might observe in the transaction he or she is observing. Weaver explains, ". . . when a human observer intervenes to measure some aspect or quality of a particle, such as its position or momentum, the person *actualizes* one possibility (makes it happen) and collapses all other possibilities (negates the possibility of their happening)" (p. 1188). In other words, the transaction between the observer and the observed creates in a very real way the observer's construction of meaning about the behavior of the observed. I think this is an extraordinarily powerful notion. Applied to the difference model, it suggests that *how we view students* affects substantially our interpretations of students' behaviors and abilities. If we choose to assume pathology, we will, indeed, find things "wrong" or "missing" or "defective" in our students; if, on the other hand, we approach students from the difference model, we will identify how and in what ways students' responses differ from our expected responses and adjust instruction and materials accordingly.

The difference model also leads us away from the fallacy of associating all diversity (or difference) with the general category of students "at risk." *At risk* is a term that has gained great popularity and widespread use growing from the widely disseminated and widely quoted study, *A Nation at Risk: The Imperative for Educational Reform* (National Commission on Excellence in Education, 1983), which led the educational reform movement of the 1980s. My concern, and the concern of others (Pearson, 1990), is that we may begin to label too many students "at risk," bringing into our definition students who exhibit any difference from the mainstream, including, for example, bicultural/bilingual students and students with talents other than traditional academic skills.

There are, indeed, students in our schools who are truly at risk for failure, and their numbers are greater than any of us wish; but they cannot be defined by diversity or difference alone. I will discuss the specific characteristics of at-risk learners in the next section of the chapter. For now, the difference model is a useful reminder that not all diversity is associated with problems or difficulties; difference is not always to be equated with "at risk."

It is, of course, impossible to list and discuss every kind of difference or diversity found in today's schools. Nevertheless, there are broad categories of diversity useful for guiding our discussion here; within each of these categories there are variations and individual differences. Let's now look at specific types of diversity and ways that classroom teachers can reduce differences between how students respond and how teachers want them to respond.

READERS AND WRITERS IN TROUBLE

Ken Goodman uses the term "readers [and writers] in trouble" to refer to the students most commonly referred to as "disabled" or "problem readers" or other such names (1996). He and others (Crowley, 1995) use this terminology because they want to remove stigma and fault assumption from students, teachers, school, or homes. (Interestingly, Peter Johnston and Dick Allington [1991] refer to young readers in trouble as "children who did not learn to read on schedule"—another neutral term.) Readers and writers in trouble are students whom we most frequently consider to be at risk. Vacca and Padak (1990) offer a specific definition of "at risk":

In times of war or crisis, men and women serving on the front line are often described as being "in harm's way." They're vulnerable to attack by the enemy and open to physical danger. In times of schooling—our times—some children and youth experience a different type of vulnerability and danger. For a variety of reasons, . . . these students are in danger of school failure. They are also in harm's way, but not in the sense of physical danger or attack. Their danger, and society's potential loss, is more social, economic, and psychological in nature. From a school perspective, the students to whom we refer are said to be "at risk" (p. 486).

Central to our discussion in this section are those students truly at risk and, specifically, those at risk of failing to acquire literacy levels necessary for academic success. Origin of birth, ethnicity, and/or language background do not, alone, define the risk. Rather, Vacca and Padak describe such students as fitting into one or more of the following categories (pp. 487–488):

1. *Students who are alienated from a system that has failed them.* These are students who never learned to read effectively and rarely make any attempts to read at all.

2. *Students who learned to read but whose participation in school is marginal.* These students can read but do so only under duress and only to fulfill minimal requirements.

3. *Students who demonstrate characteristics of "learned helplessness."* These students feel that they do not have the resources for overcoming failure and are further limited by various other attributes and characteristics. Included in these attributes are: (a) narrow understanding of reading processes, (b) lack of metacognitive skills, (c) low self-image, (d) negative attitude and interest in reading, and (e) limited set of strategies for approaching reading tasks.

Mike Rose, in *Lives on the Boundary* (1989), depicts poignantly the feelings and trajectory of adolescent students at risk from the students' own perspective:

You'll see a handful of students far excel you in courses that sound exotic and that are only in the curriculum of the elite: French, physics, trigonometry. And all this is happening while you're trying to shape an identity; your body is changing, and your emotions are running wild. If you're a working-class kid in the vocational track, the options you'll have to deal with this will be constrained in certain ways: You're defined by your school as "slow"; you're placed in a curriculum that isn't designed to liberate you but to occupy you, or, if you're lucky, train you, though the training is for work the society does not esteem; other students are picking up the cues from your school and your curriculum and interacting with you in particular ways. . . . you turn your back on all this and let your mind roam where it may. What . . . so many [students] do is protect themselves from such suffocating madness by taking on with a vengeance the identity implied in the vocational track. Reject the confusion and frustration by openly defining yourself as the Common Joe. Champion the average. Rely on your own good sense. F[ ] this b—s—. B—s—, of course, is everything you—and the others—fear is is beyond

you: books, essays, tests, academic scrambling, complexity, scientific reasoning, philosophical inquiry.

The tragedy is that you have to twist the knife in your own gray matter
to make this defense work. You'll have to shut down, have to reject intellectual stimuli or diffuse them with sarcasm, have to cultivate stupidity, have to
convert boredom from a malady into a way of confronting the world. Keep
your vocabulary simple, act stoned when you're not or act more stoned than
you are, flaunt ignorance, materialize your dreams. It is a powerful and effective defense—it neutralizes the insult and the frustration of being a vocational kid and, when perfected, it drives teachers up the wall, a delightful
secondary effect. But like all strong magic, it exacts a price (pp. 28–29).

The picture Rose paints here is all too accurate and all too familiar to those of us who
have spent time with adolescent readers and writers in trouble, and, when accompanied by poverty and segregation, the loss, in terms of potential achievement, is extraordinary. Jonathon Kozel, in *Amazing Grace* (1995) documents the drop-out and
"discharge" rate of poor, at-risk students: only 200 graduating seniors in a school of
3,200 students—a statistic of what he calls "human ruin" (p. 150).

Gentile and McMillan (1987) explain that readers and writers in trouble have to
deal simultaneously with their lack of academic prowess and the stress that accompanies failure to succeed in school. This produces a "fight or flight" reaction in which
students either act confrontationally when faced with literacy tasks or retreat altogether (pp. 19–22). Johnstone and Allington (1991) attribute these behaviors to the
"ego-involving situations" so commonly found in classrooms. Ego-involving situations are those in which the public nature of the situation causes one's ego to be exposed (p. 1004); readers and writers in trouble are unable to tolerate such vulnerability.

INSTRUCTION FOR READERS AND WRITERS IN TROUBLE

Certainly, we see readers and writers in trouble in secondary classrooms, and by the
time they get there, they have established their own personal responses to school and
literacy tasks. Some students may be brash, "difficult," and rejecting of traditional academic values (Ogbu, 1988); others may retreat into quiet passivity; and still others
camouflage their academic problems with acting out behavior, clowning, or obse-
quiousness. Whatever the overt behavior, it is important that these students not be
thrust into ego-involving situations; specifically, Gentile and McMillan (1987) recommend that teachers not do any of the following with students who have difficulty
reading (pp. 3–4):

1. Require students to read aloud in front of other students.
2. Require students to read from books or materials that are long and hard.
3. Ask students to stop reading because they have made too many errors or
   appear lost or flustered.
4. Require students to do the same kind of reading day after day.
5. Require students to read materials that parallel specific traumatic events in
   their lives.

This list eliminates three of the most frequent activities associated with textbook reading in subject area classrooms: (1) Round Robin Oral Reading, (2) reading from textbooks that are too difficult for the readers, and (3) unending, unvarying, routine reading assignments and tasks. Earlier, I emphasized in this text that unrehearsed oral reading has no place in the classroom, and I reiterate it here. Unrehearsed oral reading is the source of real fear and embarrassment for readers in trouble, and *it does little, if anything, to ensure that they are constructing meaning from text*. In fact, these students are so consumed by the discomfort of anticipating their turn and living through and remembering their embarrassment while reading that very little of their energy can be directed toward cognitive processing of content information. These students are just as poorly served by inappropriate materials and assignments that do not vary from one day to the next. We've discussed at length in other chapters the importance of friendly, accessible text as well as availability of many useful instructional strategies for teaching subject area content and literary skills.

Clearly, we must engage readers and writers in trouble in *task-involving situations* in which students get caught up in the activity, and, in so doing, define themselves as successful (Johnstone & Allington, 1991). In addition, we must give these students the support of working with others to achieve academic and literacy success; in this way, they are not overwhelmed by being solely responsible for everything they do in the classroom. We also must provide learning environments that look and feel like the classrooms described by various "whole language," "meaning-based," and "process-writing" educators (Cambourne & Turbill, 1988; Holdaway, 1988). These are classrooms in which the following conditions exist:

> *Students are immersed in literacy.* Students cannot avoid or escape print. It is everywhere—on the walls, chalkboards and bulletin boards; in books, magazines, folders and papers; in their journals, logs, and texts.
>
> *There are ample demonstrations of how print works.* Students have many opportunities to see literate people being literate (especially in subject areas), including their peers, the teacher, other school faculty and staff, and themselves.
>
> *The teacher has high expectations that everyone will achieve.* The clear message to students is that they will "of course" learn; the teacher, in turn, is tolerant of students' risk taking, experimentation with ideas and language, and different constructions of meaning.
>
> *Students accept responsibility for their own learning.* Students, rather than teachers, choose texts to be read, writing topics and group projects; students explore and actively seek answers; and students engage in questioning and exploration.
>
> *Approximation is valued.* Approximate attempts—things students do that are partially but not quite right—whether they involve reading, spelling, writing, or using a protractor, are not viewed as "wrong"; rather, they are seen as one step toward being right. *Students have lots of opportunity to use and practice what is learned.* This involves authentic reading and writing—that is, reading and writing with a purpose and reading and writing that contribute to content learning.

Students have frequent opportunity for approval. Approval comes both from the teacher and from peers. Students work collaboratively in various group and partnership configurations sharing the work of learning content and coming to admire others' efforts and contributions.

And finally, if we are going to change the lives of readers and writers in trouble in any real sense, if we are going to remove the need for them ". . . to protect themselves from such suffocating madness by taking on with a vengeance the identity implied in the vocational track" (Rose, 1989), then we must change the way we view them (remember the quantum leap) and the way they view themselves. Paul Crowley (1995) urges us to help readers in trouble revalue the reading process and themselves as readers. He states:

> Middle school is not too late to help readers in trouble. Students come to us with a wealth of language experiences, and curiosity that form a solid basis for a meaning-centered reading program. The challenge for us is to strip away the sense of failure, to overcome the defensive attitude, and to involve them as members of a community of readers. This is not an easy task, but helping readers revalue themselves and what they know about reading is the starting point (p. 11).

We help readers and writers in trouble revalue themselves as literate beings by arranging instruction so that students are supported and successful, both in becoming increasingly strategic readers and writers, and in learning subject matter content. To do this we must provide "scaffolds"—structures that support students as they grapple with new ideas and new literacy needs (Cambourne & Turbill, 1988). The instructional approaches developed below, and those discussed previously in this text, all have built into them various kinds of scaffolds to support all readers and writers, including readers and writers in trouble.

INSTRUCTIONAL ACTIVITIES FOR READERS AND WRITERS IN TROUBLE

It is important at this point to state explicitly that instruction in subject area classes for readers and writers in trouble *must be instruction that occurs as a natural part of the classroom and that has content learning as its primary goal.* That means you are in no way expected to "take students aside" and teach them separately from the rest of the class; nor are you to water down materials, slow down instruction, or otherwise impede progress of other students in order to teach "remedial" reading and writing.

Rather, judicious choice of well-designed instructional activities that combine literacy and content instruction allows you to teach in such a way that supports the needs of readers and writers in trouble *while providing appropriate, rigorous content instruction for all.* All of the instructional strategies presented in this section are useful for teaching in virtually any classroom. Only one of them, ReQuest, was specifically designed for teaching readers in trouble, and it has already been discussed as an appropriate content-focused instructional strategy. Any of the others could just as reasonably appear in other chapters in this text (e.g., comprehension, reading across the curriculum, or cooperative/collaborative learning). My choice to include them here is based on the direct and explicit means these activities provide for developing students' metacognitive abilities and knowledge regarding their own literacy and learning. That is, these activities assist students in becoming strategic readers—figuring out how subject area texts work, monitoring their progress through text, and developing effective response strategies for text reading and other learning events.

The first three, ReQuest, Question/Answer Relationships (QAR), and ReQAR, all fit into a category of instruction generally labeled "reciprocal teaching" (Palincsar & Brown, 1984) that has been used successfully to teach readers in trouble (Manzo, 1969a, 1969b; Palincsar & Brown, 1984; Raphael, 1982). New efforts are currently being launched at the Center for the Study of Reading to study further the usefulness of such teaching with adolescent students (Anderson, personal communication, 1992).

ReQuest

Although we've already discussed ReQuest as a means for developing comprehension in subject area texts (see Chapter 3), it deserves mention here because it was originally designed specifically for students with reading problems (Manzo, 1969b; Manzo & Manzo, 1990). ReQuest is particularly effective in one-to-one situations with individual students, which is how I used it in my Title I reading classes. As a regular classroom teacher, however, you will rarely have the opportunity to work one-to-one with your students. If you do, ReQuest is a good instructional choice, especially if students have already experienced it in whole-class settings. In that case, I recommend that you proceed one sentence at a time, following all the criteria listed in Chapter 3, when you work with readers in trouble and that your questions focus both on content information and on useful literacy behaviors for constructing meaning while engaged with text.

You'll probably use ReQuest most often with the whole class and have the combined objectives of increasing content comprehension and providing assistance specifically for readers in trouble. Here again, you may also want to use sentence units for the initial experience (as opposed to paragraphs, which I suggested in our Chapter 3 discussion). In all probability, your targeted students will not be the ones to volunteer a question or a response. While some people recommend calling on students to get the quieter ones to participate (Helfelt & Lalik, 1976), I'm hesitant to do this, even when conversation is initially dominated by the better students. As long as everyone is attentive, I'm content to assume that the more vocal students are serving as yet another model of questioning behavior that others can emulate at a later time. If more hesitant students aren't forthcoming relatively soon, then put everyone into multi-ability groups and let them do ReQuest under the guidance of a peer leader. The smaller groups are less public and therefore less ego-involving and threatening to students who are unsure of themselves as readers and learners.

Helfeldt and Henk (1990) recommend combining ReQuest with another questioning strategy called QAR (Question/Answer Relationships) (Raphael, 1982, 1984, 1986). We will look first at QAR and then consider the combination of ReQuest and QAR.

QUESTION/ANSWER RELATIONSHIPS (QAR)

QAR (Raphael, 1982, 1984, 1986) is an activity in which students categorize comprehension questions according to how and from what sources the questions are answered. Raphael (1986, p. 517) uses the schematic shown in Figure 10.2 to describe relationships between questions and answers.

In the Book relationships are those in which: (1) answers are "Right There," explicitly stated in one sentence, or two contiguous and pronominally related sentences; or (2) answers require the student to "Think and Search" (that is, answers are available in one or more forms in text, but must be put together from information throughout the reading).

In My Head relationships involve: (1) answers that require "The Author and You" by combining readers' background knowledge with elements from text in such a way as to integrate prior knowledge and text information; or (2) answers achieved "On Your Own" that come primarily from readers' background knowledge unrelated to text information. The point of QAR is to develop students' understanding that both the text and their own knowledge base are important sources for constructing meaning while reading. Readers are then asked to consider specifically how text and background knowledge interact in the meaning-construction process.

The teacher may initiate instruction in QAR by modeling an introspective process (Helfeldt & Henk, 1990) or by probing students' responses during question-answer episodes with such follow-up questions as, "How did you know that?" and, "Where did you get that answer?" After identifying the QAR taxonomy, the teacher begins

FIGURE 10.2   *QAR Relationships*

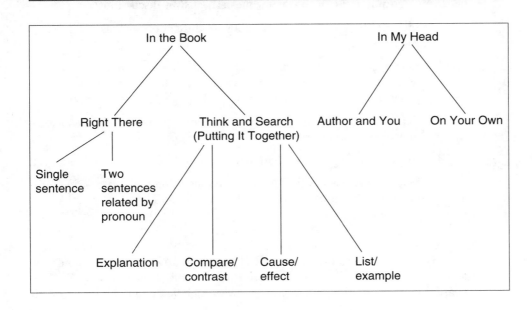

making response relationships explicit; for example, "Oh. You had to look in several places *In the Book* to find that answer; that's a Think and Search, isn't it?" or, "Good. You used information from the book and stuff *In Your Head* to arrive at your answer. You were using Author and You there."

Raphael (1986) suggests that teachers may want to begin by distinguishing only between the two main categories—*In the Book* and *In My Head*—and spending some time allowing students to analyze responses on those two dimensions only. After students become comfortable with that analysis, then begin extending to the subcategories (Right There, Think and Search, The Author and You, On Your Own), concentrating first on one type (e.g., *In the Book* category) and then including the other.

How to do . . . .

QAR

QAR has any number of advantages for all students, and its use need not (and should not) be limited to classes with a significant number of readers in trouble. It is intended for use in all classes. Nevertheless, for readers in trouble, it is particularly useful because it highlights the value and importance of connecting prior knowledge and text information. (One way these students' response to text is different from the expected response is that they frequently do *not* make that connection.) It also serves as a basis for developing students' abilities to locate information in text, understand different text structures (e.g., explanation versus comparison-contrast), and recognize whether information is explicitly stated in the text or implied (Raphael, 1986). The following steps will help you incorporate QAR into your question-answer discussions:

1. Identify the QAR taxonomy using an illustration such as the one in Figure 10.2.

2. During a question and answer discussion, connect students' answers with the QAR taxonomy; for example, "You had to look in several places *In the Book* to find the answer. That's a "Think and Search."

3. Begin asking students to connect their answers with the QAR taxonomy at the *main category* level (*In the Book*, *In My Head*).

4. Continue doing this until students become skilled and confident at it.

5. Have students identify QAR connections using main categories and *subcategories* (Right There, Think and Search, The Author and You, On Your Own).

ReQAR

Helfeldt's and Henk's (1990) combination of ReQuest and QAR is intended to be used after students are thoroughly familiar with both ReQuest and QAR separately. ReQAR uses the basic ReQuest questioning structure; however, Helfeldt and Henk suggest alternating between student-questioning and teacher-questioning after each question-answer sequence. In its original form (Manzo, 1969a, 1969b; Manzo & Manzo, 1990), the ReQuest procedure allows students to ask as many questions as they wish to ask before turning the floor over to the teacher; this is followed by the teacher asking as many questions as she/he wishes to ask. I prefer the original form because it allows the teacher to follow up, as needed, in any areas not covered by students' questions and to provide as extended a model of questioning and answering as he or she deems necessary.

Using the ReQuest structure, ReQAR begins by focusing on the two main QAR categories: *In the Book* and *In My Head*. A student asks a question that the teacher answers in the following sequence:

1. The teacher answers the question.
2. The teacher identifies the QAR category (*In the Book* or *In My Head*).
3. The teacher gives reasons why he/she chose that QAR category.

This same procedure is used when students answer the teacher's questions.

After students demonstrate consistent proficiency in identifying main QAR categories, the second phase of ReQAR is initiated in which the questioner specifies a QAR category for the answer-giver to use, and the answer-giver identifies the source, or subcategory (Right There, Think and Search, Author and You, On Your Own) used in developing an answer. The sequence looks as follows:

1. The student asks question(s) and specifies QAR category (*In the Book* or *In My Head*).
2. The teacher answers question(s) and identifies QAR source (Right There, Think and Search, The Author and You, and On My Own).

In the final phase of ReQAR, all identification of QAR categories and sources is done by students. The teacher's role at this point is simply to field answers and questions; students determine which categories and sources describe their own and the teacher's questions and responses.

ReQAR has much to offer readers in trouble. First is the amount of analytical thinking going on in any question-answer episode. My experience with this population of students is that, usually, they are very good thinkers who haven't had many opportunities or much encouragement to use their intellectual capacities in school; at the very least, they *perceive* this to be the case. While they may hesitate at first, when given the opportunity to think and talk and problem solve, they do so with amazing energy and skill. ReQuest and QAR each encourage analytical thinking, even when used singly; combined, the effect is enhanced. My recommendation is that you not push quiet or hesitant students into participating during ReQAR; give them time to see how it works and let them feel comfortable with it. Once the activity is well known, use small groups to make participation easier for them.

Another advantage of ReQAR is that by focusing on answers, the teacher and students will learn just as much about questions. Students who generally lack strategies for getting information and learning school subjects will therefore have access to kinds of questions to ask, kinds of information and combinations of information useful in school learning, and ways to find out what they want to know.

How to do . . . .

REQAR

Helfeldt and Henk (1990) recommend using ReQAR over time, and I concur. Like ReQuest, ReQAR will take a little time for its full power to be felt. Make it a short-and-sweet daily routine, gradually progressing from one stage to another. Don't feel pressed to do everything all at once. Teach ReQuest first; play with it and let students get comfortable in their new role as question-askers. Give them experience in small groups playing the "teacher" role as well. Then move on to QAR. Spend lots of time thinking out loud analyzing the question-answer relationships and then draw students' analyses from them with easy, nonthreatening probe questions. When everyone is thoroughly successful with ReQuest and QAR, *then* try the combination ReQAR and use it over time as well. The following steps are useful with ReQAR:

1. After students are familiar with ReQuest and QAR, in a ReQuest discussion, after answering a student's question, identify the QAR category (*In the Book, In My Head*) and give a reason for the category you chose.

2. Continue doing this for a while.

3. After a student answers your question, ask the student to identify the QAR category and give a reason for her or his choice.

4. Continue this until students are skilled and confident doing it.

5. Have a student ask you a question and identify the QAR category.

6. Answer the question and identify the QAR subcategory (Right There, Think and Search, Author and You, On Your Own).

7. Ask students to make all identifications.

THE CONE OF EXPERIENCE

Richard Sinatra (1991) uses Dale's (1969) "Cone of Experience" as the basis for integrating language and literacy activities into content learning (see Figure 10.3). The Cone of Experience approach is a useful way to develop lessons and units that give needed assistance to readers and writers in trouble.

The key to the Cone of Experience is designing instruction on a continuum from Activities of Action (including direct, purposeful experience, contrived experiences, and dramatic participation), to Activities of Observation (demonstrations, field trips, exhibits, motion pictures, and audio/videotapes, still pictures), and, finally, to Abstract Representations (visual symbols and verbal symbols). Important to the Cone of Experience is that the Action and Observation activities precede and provide the environment and context for Abstract Representation activities, so that by the time students read and write on a topic, they are well prepared and ready to do so.

FIGURE 10.3   *Dale's Cone of Experience (adapted)*

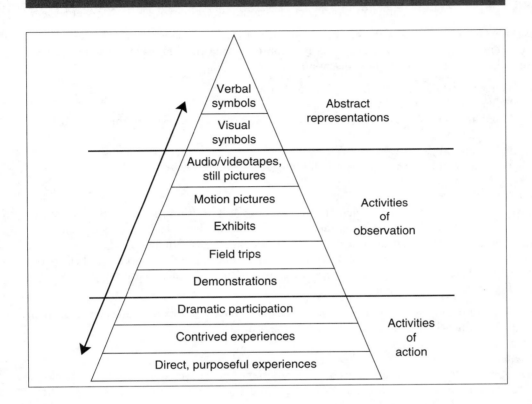

The lesson or unit should begin with a "hands-on cooperative endeavor," in which students become immersed in the experience and the language of the topic (Sinatra, 1991, p. 427). Following the direct experience or simulation, the lesson progresses to one or more observational activities that contain elements from the action experience and add to that experience. Finally, students, perhaps back in their groups, launch into full-scale reading and writing about the topic in whatever form and medium that best fit the topic itself. Below is a short outline of a unit using the Cone of Experience:

UNIT   *Westward Expansion*

CONE OF EXPERIENCE OUTLINE

ACTIVITIES OF ACTION

Setting: Students will be divided into five groups. Each group will represent *one* of the following groups: Farmers/settlers ready to leave Independence, Missouri on the Santa Fe Trail;

Wives, daughters, and other female family members of the farmers and settlers; Mexican families living in the New Mexico Territory; Native Americans living in Kansas, Oklahoma, Texas, and New Mexico; and cattle ranchers of various cultures in target areas for settlement.

Task: From the perspective of the groups they represent, each student group is to develop a statement of their group's attitudes and position regarding the westward movement using the following questions to guide discussion:

1. What is at stake for you in the westward movement?
2. What benefits can/will you get?
3. What are the demands, dangers, and problems for you as a result of the westward movement?
4. What will be your response? Why?
5. What do you believe is your probability of succeeding? Why?

ACTIVITIES OF OBSERVATION

Following whole-class sharing of each group's attitudes and position regarding the westward movement, the class will watch and then discuss a multimedia slide show or video such as Ken Burns's *The West* that incorporates all five vantage points. Student groups will analyze how the presentation did or did not represent the viewpoints and perspectives of the people they represent (farmer/settlers, female family members, Mexican families, Native Americans, and cattle ranchers).

Possible additions: movies such as *So Big, Dances with Wolves,* and others; museum field trip; computer simulations and/or reference information.

ABSTRACT REPRESENTATIONS

Each group chooses one or more aspects of its experience in the westward movement to research and produce a written account of its research along with a performance or graphic visual product. Groups must consult at least one source in each of the following categories:

Museum products or visits

Realia

Primary documents

Historical fiction

Biography/autobiography

Various kinds of maps

How to do . . . .

CONE OF EXPERIENCE

One of the main values of the Cone of Experience progression for lessons and units is that it leads you, the teacher, toward careful consideration of how to establish an environment and context for reading and writing in your subject area. That's a bonus for all students, but critical for readers and writers in trouble. The focus on cooperative group activities of action is also helpful, giving students opportunity to contribute a variety of knowledge and skills to the group and then add to their own repertoire of literacy abilities in the visual representation stage. Use the following steps to develop lessons and unit using the Cone of Experience:

1. Identify unit or lesson content and objectives.

2. Determine Activities of Action and the introductory "hands-on" experience.

3. Identify, collect, and/or prepare resources for Activities of Observation.

4. Determine how the Activities of Observation connect to unit/lesson objectives and Activities of Action.

5. Determine alternatives for Abstract Representations and the prompt(s) you will use to guide students in completing Abstract Representations requirements.

6. Establish criteria and guidelines for students to use in meeting the Abstract Representations requirements.

7. Determine how the Abstract Representations requirements connect to the unit objects and the Activities of Action and Observation.

STRATEGY REVIEW

Before leaving our discussion about readers and writers in trouble, I think it's important to remember that many of the instructional strategies and activities discussed in other chapters are very helpful for addressing the needs of this group. We needn't discuss them further here, but do review and consider using the following: DR–TA and mapping (Chapter 3); VSS (Chapter 4); Content DR–TA, PReP, K–W–L, and DIA (Chapter 5); Learning Logs and Double Entry Journals (Chapter 6); Jigsaw, GRA, and CT–RA (Chapter 9).

GIFTEDNESS, GENDER, AND OTHER DIFFERENCES

We've discussed at some length the diverse populations in today's middle and secondary schools. Even if you teach in somewhat homogeneous schools, it's safe to predict that you will have many kinds of students come through your classroom daily; over the years, you will undoubtedly see a wide spectrum of human abilities, intelligences, attitudes, behaviors, appearances, and actions. It's impossible to address the needs of each and every one of those students in a text such as this; nevertheless, there are three additional populations I'd like to mention and discuss briefly.

GIFTED STUDENTS

Gifted students may be the most neglected group of students in schools. This is because, in so many cases, gifted students are able to achieve, and in fact soar, without very

much institutional or classroom attention. Many, many students gifted with extraordinary academic talents delight teachers daily with their wit, insight, and sterling-quality
work. For gifted students whose talents lie outside academic areas, challenge or go beyond teachers' understanding and beliefs, or are masked by inability to perform well
on standardized academic achievement tests, this is not necessarily the case (Sternberg, 1986). In fact, some gifted students can, and do, have problems in school. Tuttle (1991, p. 373) identifies the characteristics and sample potential difficulties that
gifted students have (see Figure 10.4).

When you have gifted students in your classes, you will find that multiple-ability
grouping activities, project-based learning, and many different writing activities lend
themselves to individual investigation and enrichment assignments that are appropriate
and challenging for gifted students (Davis & Hunter, 1990; Tuttle, 1991). Such assignments require students to choose areas of personal interest, read and conduct other research about the chosen topic, and produce written and other projects that reflect their
research and learning. Essentially, assignments such as these provide opportunity and
encouragement for gifted students to use their individual talents to go well beyond what
others in the class are doing on any given topic and allow classroom teachers to make
personalized, individual adjustments for students with special talents and intellect.

Parents of gifted students are often critical of mixed-ability grouping practices
because they believe their children will be "slowed down" or held back by other
students in the group. *Their concern is misplaced as long as the instruction used with these*

FIGURE 10.4 *Characteristics Associated with Giftedness*

CHARACTERISTIC	SAMPLE POTENTIAL
Curiosity	Continually raises questions that sometime interfere with the teacher's lesson; needs access to a variety of materials
Persistence	Focuses on areas of personal interest, sometimes at the expense of work in other areas often required by the teacher; is viewed as stubborn
Critical Thinking	Is reluctant to submit work that is not perfect: may not even begin a project because of feeling that it may not reach own excessively high standards; criticizes peers and teachers, causing negative reactions and feelings
Abstract Thinking	Neglects details once generalizations are mastered; jumps to conclusions about specifics; impatient with teacher's focus on specific steps or details in a procedure; becomes frustrated by others' inability to understand general concepts quickly; designs own procedures that may be in conflict with those taught by the teacher
High Verbal Ability	Dominates class and informal discussions; is sarcastic of others; argues for the sake of argument, detracting from the progress of the lesson; uses humor not always understood or accepted by others

mixed-ability groups involves complex problem-solving tasks—in other words, the kind of instruction we discussed at length in Chapter 9. Subotnik (1988) emphasizes the value of interdisciplinary, thematic instruction for gifted students because of their ability to "see relationships and make generalizations" (p. 279). Throughout the literature on giftedness (Maker, 1982; Van Tassel-Baska et al., 1988; Wheatley, 1988), there is a clear focus on the need for gifted students to be engaged in high-level problem-solving tasks involving intuitive expression, analogies, discrepancies, organized random search, tolerance for ambiguity, creative reading and writing, creative thinking, and visualization (Williams, 1972). Such instruction is very much in line with what should be going on in every classroom and is particularly appropriate for gifted students because it allows full use of their abilities and interests.

GENDER DIFFERENCES

In the past two decades, pioneering work has been done on the cognitive, moral, academic, and language development of girls and young women by, among others, Carol Gilligan and her associates (1990) at the Harvard Center for the Study of Gender, Education and Human Development, by the work of the Education for Women's Development Project (Belenky, McVicker-Clency, Rule-Goldenberg, & Tarule, 1986), by Deborah Tannen (1990) in her study of language differences between males and females, by Myra and David Sadker in their longitudinal studies of girls' academic achievement, and by the American Association of University Women in its national study, *The AAUW Report: How Schools Shortchange Girls* (1992). This work is significant because so much of our understanding of human development—and preadolescent/adolescent behavior especially—is rooted in theory and research from primarily male populations (Belenky et al., 1986; Gilligan, 1990). It was not until the 1980s that assumptions from male-based theory and research were examined in light of controlled research using female subjects.

What we know from the recent research on female development is that cognitive, moral, academic, and language development of girls and young women are different from that of boys and young men, and current studies are beginning to identify specifics regarding these differences. For example, Gilligan (1990) found 11- and 12-year-old girls to be confident, resistant to interlopers or things outside what they know, willing to stand up for their ideas and willing to disagree—even reluctant to back down. By the age of 15 or 16, however, adolescent girls are likely to have gone "underground" with their resistance and appear much more tractable; they become less confident in their own abilities (or willing to subordinate them) and focus primarily on making and maintaining connections with others. These connections have been found to be central to women's lives (Miller, 1976), and adolescent girls encountering conflict face the additional dilemma of deciding how (or whether) to protect themselves while simultaneously maintaining connections with others (Lyons, 1991). Further, we have documented evidence of the alarming progression of girls in school (Sadker & Sadker, 1994; Barbieri, 1996):

- In the early grades, girls are ahead of or equal to boys on almost every standardized measure of achievement and psychological well-being. By the time they graduate from high school or college, they have fallen back. Girls enter school ahead but leave behind.

- In high school, girls score lower on the SAT and ACT tests, which are critical for college admission. The greatest gap is in the critical areas of science and math.
- Girls score far lower on College Board Achievement tests, which are required by most of the highly selective colleges.
- Boys are much more likely to be awarded state and national college scholarships.
- From elementary school through higher education, female students receive less active instruction, both in the quantity and in the quality of teacher time and attention.
- Eating disorders among girls in middle and secondary schools and college are rampant and increasing (Barbieri, pp. 35–36).

The point of this discussion is that the decline in assertiveness and in achievement documented for middle-level and high school young women is deeply rooted in the culture of schools and classrooms as well as in the general social environment. Teachers and researchers report that girls "recede" in classrooms (Barbieri, 1995; Sadker & Sadker, 1994) where boys' voices and participation dominate. Gender stereotypes continue to pervade classrooms and teacher and student behavior, even when teachers are attempting to be sensitive and responsive to all students' needs. Nancy McCracken (1996) highlights the effects of such gender bias in schools:

> Girls are not the only ones harmed by gender role effects in language arts. While middle school girls have been the focus of much of the recent research on gender bias in the schools, it is important to recognize that all middle school kids, male and female, are harmed by pervasive, unaddressed gender stereotypes in schools, in language arts as well as in science and math. . . . Boys and girls who *don't* fit the stereotypical gender-role expectations are also profoundly disadvantaged in classrooms and schools where gender stereotypes go unchallenged (p. 9).

OTHER DIFFERENCES

On occasion, you will have students with special differences who require the services and/or expertise of special teachers and staff. These include severe emotional, psychological, or learning disorders; homelessness and/or migrant family life patterns; severe home and family problems; and physical problems that require in-school treatment, medications, or major accommodations. For students with such differences, you will need to work very closely with special teachers and staff in order to provide what is best for individuals while simultaneously caring for the needs of the other 30 or 35 students in the class. Your allies in this effort will be counselors, nurses, resource room teachers, vice principals, school psychologists, reading teachers, and various representatives of outside agencies, including social workers, police, psychologists and psychiatrists, physicians and nurses, and university clinical faculty.

Programs for pregnant teens, teen parents, HIV-positive students or students suffering from AIDS, and teen 12-step drug and alcohol recovery programs may also be operating within the school, or available outside it, and may be a significant part of your students' personal and academic lives. In order for you to address your students' cognitive needs, to teach them content and develop their ability to read and write in your subject area, you will have to maintain contact with school and community agency representatives who are working to support students psychologically, emotionally, physically, socially, and economically. Working with these professionals also supports you and your efforts in the classroom. As a rule, everyone benefits from close and frequent communication and collaboration.

OTHER APPROACHES FOR MEETING THE NEEDS OF STUDENTS IN SCHOOLS WITH DIVERSE POPULATIONS

Teacher teams are a promising means for meeting the needs of diverse school populations. Formed for a variety of reasons, including interdisciplinary teaching, school and teaching reform (Erickson, 1990), and curriculum improvement, teacher teams provide opportunity for several teachers to work concurrently with one group of students. Frequently, such teaming involves released time for planning or whatever the teamwork involves, some degree of training to prepare teachers for teamwork, coordination by a principal or other designated site individual, and resources for bringing about the team task (Erickson, 1990). However, teacher teams, while often productive, can be expensive; released planning time alone requires the commitment of substantial resources from the school district. So it is that actual use of teacher teams tends to flourish in the good times and wane in the bad; or, teacher teams continue to flourish in bad times, but no resources are allocated for support.

When such teams are institutionalized in schools, new concepts about valued teacher characteristics, roles, and abilities emerge. Cynthia Pilar (1991) describes the teacher team configurations, called "Houses," used in the 1600-student high school where she is principal. One House may consist of four teachers with teaching specialties in English, driver education, physical education, and computer keyboarding. This House team is responsible for specific sophomore curriculum and students and decides itself how to allocate that responsibility, how each teacher's workday is divided, and how instruction and students will be evaluated. In order to function, such structures require teachers with the following characteristics (Pilar, 1991):

- Ability to collaborate.
- Ability to cross curriculum areas.
- Willingness to coach rather than criticize.
- Ability to use a variety of instructional strategies and materials.
- Ability to structure lessons effectively.

- Tendency to contribute less teacher talk and stimulate more student talk.
- Recognition that "covering content" or "covering ground" is less important than developing students' knowledge base and engaging them actively in learning.

Such structure and team approaches offer many advantages to students and teachers; however, actual implementation and institutional support for interdisciplinary teams may lag considerably behind acceptance of the idea. Consequently, in many schools, teacher teams are established and maintained informally and personally by teachers themselves. Models for doing this vary widely and can take many different forms. For example, Roehler and her associates (1990) report that to accommodate for the amount of time it took to develop integrated units of study and the isolation teachers felt in their separate classrooms, teachers created "units banks" (p. 191) in which units of study developed for one class were exchanged and used by different teachers. There are many other ways, ranging from simple to elaborate, for teachers to engage in teamwork and provide mutual support.

CREATING A COMMUNITY OF READERS

Susan Clark (1991) describes a team effort used by community college faculty for making connections not only across subject areas, but between different physical plants and three campus sites as well. The point of the project was to increase interdisciplinary involvement with literature for the express purposes of: (1) fostering literacy, (2) encouraging faculty and students to read beyond textbook assignments, (3) demonstrating the value of lifelong reading habits, (4) enjoying the social benefits of a community of readers, and (5) incorporating literature-based activities into subject area instruction (p. 381).

The project began with the selection of Kurt Vonnegut's *Galápagos* as a centerpiece literary work for school-wide class and campus activities. *Galápagos* met the selection committee's criteria for choice: It had application to various disciplines, affordability, suitable length, substantive content, literary merit, broad appeal, and a living author. Each campus then used elements and aspects of *Galápagos* for various special events (e.g., a themed beach party), course assignments, contests, and activities. After he was notified of the project, Vonnegut wrote a letter to students and later joined a telecommunications interview by a panel of local celebrities.

This same idea can be applied to middle, junior high, and senior high schools as well, and it can be done with relatively little additional resources or time. It is helpful to have a steering committee to guide the effort, but, in essence, this project requires only that a book with elements and implications from a number of academic disciplines be chosen (Clark recommends a high degree of student participation in the selection) and made available and encouragement given to all teachers to find ways to connect that book with their subject area. The book in Clark's project was a novel; there is no reason, however, why well-written high-interest nonfiction books could not be used just as easily.

Assistance and suggestions from reading and writing specialists may be helpful in this project; certainly, those teachers who see the value of connecting literature with content are important resources for other teachers. The point here is for an entire school and separate subject areas to do variations on a theme provided by the central book. How they choose to do so and the form these variations take are highly individualistic.

I'm charmed by this idea for several reasons. It's a relatively simple approach for getting teachers from different subject areas to talk to one another by giving them a central content-related focus. Such conversations are bound to be interesting and lively. Further, it allows many layers of interdisciplinary connections without stepping on toes or making teachers feel they're being asked to teach something other than their subject area. There's a lot of freedom here for faculty to do what they are comfortable doing, and yet, this community of readers (an entire school reading the same book) is bound to get conversations going, and to have teachers talking not only about the content of the book itself but also about how that content was used in various classes. From this, other interesting connections will result. I think it's worth a try, even if you limit the project to one book during one grading period. After a successful in-school project, consider extending another project to include a similar school in a neighboring district or develop a joint middle school/senior high project within the same district.

GETTING TO KNOW, AND LIKE, PREADOLESCENT AND ADOLESCENT STUDENTS

Beyond designing and using effective instructional approaches, teachers also need to get to know their students well. Teachers don't have to "love" kids to be able to teach well, but they do need to like them and understand what lies beneath the surface of the carefully constructed personas that adolescents present to the world. Elizabeth Kean (1991), a high school teacher, writes movingly about what she learned about teaching as she watched her own son progress through adolescence:

> High school students are simply high school students, not underage college kids. Like many inexperienced high school teachers, I'd been teaching literature by trying to reproduce my favorite college classes. Having a child in high school brought me and my embarrassingly unrealistic expectations back to earth. My son also helped me discover a side of my students I would have otherwise missed. Preparing for a 9th grade oral report on Greek mythology, Rob took a Tupperware bowl from the kitchen, covered it with aluminum foil, and wore it as a helmet. I was astonished. He was a jock. He worked at being "cool." Yet he was willing to put a foil-covered bowl on his head in public (p. 7).

One of the ways we learn about what lies behind students' public faces is in the daily contact and interaction we have with them. Critical to this are the classroom routines, events, and rituals that define the learning environment and that come to define the teacher herself or himself. Much of what I'm talking about here falls under the heading of "classroom management" and has to do with everything from how class is called to order, to what the operational classroom rules are and how they are monitored and enforced, to teacher mannerisms and habits, to the consistency of the teacher's demeanor and personality from day to day and week to week. My point is that how the teacher establishes classroom routines, events, and rituals has a major effect on the classroom environment, and, therefore, on the human interactions that occur within that environment. This, in turn, affects the substance of what students and teachers say to one another and what they come to know about each other.

Any number of good books are available to guide you in making decisions about how you establish and maintain the environment in your classroom. My favorite, and the one I think all student teachers and new teachers should read (even though it is old), is Jenny Gray's *The Teacher's Survival Guide* (1969); it gives specific, useful, step-by-step advice for establishing an orderly classroom and for developing the classroom management skills that make teaching an art. My own advice for maintaining a classroom environment conducive for getting to know and like students has three central rules:

1. Establish clear, explicit expectations and make sure everyone knows them.
2. Be consistent.
3. Have a short memory.

EXPECTATIONS

It matters not how you determine *expectations* for student behavior in the classroom or precisely what those expectations are. You may wish to determine the rules of the road and simply tell them to students; conversely, you may want each class to work cooperatively at setting its own standards. You may find also that your idea of what constitutes appropriate and useful classroom behavior may not match other teachers'. That's okay too, although I encourage you to check the *Survival Guide* for ideas about appropriateness and inappropriateness. The important thing once these rules or standards have been developed is to make sure they are explicitly communicated to students and, I might add, written and displayed prominently in your substitute teacher file for the days when you will not be in the class. You may even wish to display them in the room. The reason for explicit rules and clear communication is so that everyone in the room knows precisely what these expectations are and has no reason to be unclear or unsure about how he or she is to act.

CONSISTENCY

Consistency means that you respond to students and student behaviors pretty much the same way every day. Consistency also means that, whatever the classroom rules and regulations are, they are enforced the same way every day and with every student. Whether you choose to run a highly structured classroom or one that allows considerable leeway for student actions is not the central issue; students generally adapt easily to different classroom styles *as long as each style is clearly defined and constant*. What is at issue is consistency. Whatever classroom style choice you make is your choice, *but make it and stay with it*.

Inconsistency is the kiss of death in a middle school, junior high, or senior high classroom; students want and need to know what the limits are and how far you are willing to be pushed. If you laugh one day at behavior you censured the day before, or if you allow chaos and out-of-control behavior one day and demand pin-drop silence the next, students will not be able to find the boundary limits or the point at which your flexibility ends. They will keep testing the limits and trying your patience. A true measure of your consistency is the number of times you have to *yell* to quiet the room, the amount of unproductive noise that swells when you turn your back or leave the room, and the degree to which student behavior careens from held-in-check to uncontrolled. If there's a lot, you're not.

Consistency also applies to how you treat students, and the rule here is, don't play favorites. Be thoroughly consistent in your treatment of students. You're bound to like some students better than others: some students will charm you silly while others will put you off, and you will find it difficult to see any redeeming features about some of the students you teach. These feelings and responses are normal, natural aspects of human interaction. *But when it comes to how you treat students in your classroom, you must set these feelings aside.* Be assiduously fair, objective, and emotionally reasonable in your responses to student behavior, and, I might add, in your grading practices; the consequences for any act and the reward for any work must be absolutely the same for all students.

SHORT MEMORY

Having a *short memory* for what students do wrong is one of the greatest assets you can bring to the classroom. When problems occur, when student behavior is difficult, rebellious, or unacceptable, handle the problem immediately and completely. Get all issues attended to, and apply appropriate sanctions or disciplinary measures objectively and firmly. Then forget it. Be prepared to be stern and unyielding with a student one moment and capable *in the next moment* of addressing that same student in your normal, cheerful voice and accepting manner. That's not a particularly easy attribute to develop, but it's an important one for conveying to students that what is at issue here is their behavior and not themselves. Further, it demonstrates that you are not keeping a mental scoreboard of student "transgressions" that will accumulate throughout the school year. (Interestingly, the very act of moving rapidly from sternness to normal demeanor in such situations actually does help you avoid starting and maintaining scoreboards.) The ultimate message to students is, "I may not always accept your behavior, but I always accept you." It's an important message, and it goes a long way in developing liking and trust between students and teachers.

The reason I've taken time to address classroom management issues is my strong belief that chaotic classrooms, or classrooms in which students feel frightened, or angry, or unsure of themselves produce very little in the way of productive learning. Many different kinds of classrooms, on the other hand, provide positive environments. Characteristic of such classrooms, and notwithstanding a variety of classroom styles, is that students and teachers alike perceive the classroom to be a safe, orderly place where honest mistakes are allowed, risk-taking is encouraged, and hard work is rewarded. Further, the class environment must be conducive to such feelings if schooling is going to accomplish its primary goal of educating young people. Students learn very little content, and very little that is positive, in classes where they feel disconnected, angry, or out of control.

THE DIFFERENCE MODEL REVISITED

By this time, it should be clear why I believe the difference model to be so powerful for explaining student diversity and developing appropriate instruction to meet various student needs. I like the difference model because:

1. It allows us to take a healthy, rather than pathological, look at diversity in all its manifestations.

2. It contains implications for instruction that are reasonable and workable within the context of subject area classrooms.

3. It reinforces the notion that sound, well-developed instructional approaches, with minor adjustments and adaptations, are just as appropriate for "diverse" learners as they are for mainstream learners. That's the whole point of this chapter.

You simply *cannot* attend to and correct every academic, language, social-emotional "problem" students exhibit as they file through your classroom to the tune of 150 to 180 per day; such defect and deficit model goals are self-defeating, if only due to sheer numbers alone. You can, however, make needed adjustments in instruction and activities to adapt for differences that are present in student responses and in the students themselves. Your decision to use instructional activities that support students' language and literacy abilities increases the likelihood that students with diverse abilities, language backgrounds, talents, and skills will succeed in your class.

REFERENCES

American Association of University Women (1992). *The AAUW Report: How Schools Shortchange Girls*. Washington, DC: AAUW.

Banks, J. A. (1994). *Multiethnic education: Theory and practice* (3rd ed.). Boston: Allyn & Bacon.

Barbieri, M. (1995). *Sounds from the heart: Learning to listen to girls*. Portsmouth, NH: Heinemann.

Barbieri, M. (1996). Words under the words: Learning to listen to girls. *Voices from the Middle, 3*(1), 33–40.

Belenky, M. F., McVicker-Clency, B., Rule-Goldberger, N., & Tarule, J. M. (1986). *Women's ways of knowing*. New York: Basic Books.

Cambourne, B., & Turbill, J. (1988). *Coping with chaos*. Portsmouth, NH: Heinemann.

Clark, S. R. (1991). Turtles, blue-footed boobies, and a community of readers. *Journal of Reading, 34,* 380–383.

Crowley, P. (1995). Listening to what readers tell us. *Voices from the Middle, 2*(2), 3–12.

Dale, E. (1969). *Audio-visual methods in teaching* (3rd ed.). New York: Holt, Rinehart & Winston.

Davis, S. J., & Hunter, J. (1990). Historical novels: A context for gifted student research. *Journal of Reading, 33,* 602–606.

Erickson, L. G. (1990). How improvement teams facilitate school-wide reading reform. *Journal of Reading, 33,* 580–585.

Far West Laboratory (Fall, 1989). The new classroom diversity: Crisis or opportunity? *Research*

D O U B L E   E N T R Y   J O U R N A L

Go back to your "diversity" semantic map. Re-arrange, revise, and add to it in any way you choose.

Add a place for the category "Teaching I Can Do to Provide for Student Diversity" and fill it in with ideas from this chapter appropriate for your subject area. Share your map with your partner or group.

Explain the reasoning behind your map structure and content, and tell why you chose to map as you did.

& Practice (pp. 1–6). San Francisco: Far West Laboratory.

Gentile, L. M., & McMillan, M. M. (1987). _Stress and reading difficulties: Research, assessment and intervention._ Newark, DE: IRA.

Gilligan, C. (1990). Teaching Shakespeare's sister: Notes from the underground of female adolescence. In C. Gilligan, N. P. Lyons, & T. J. Hanmer (Eds.), _Making connections: The relational worlds of adolescent girls at Emma Willard School_ (pp. 6–27). Cambridge, MA: Harvard University Press.

Gillotte, H. (1991, January). _Multicultural content in subject matter programs._ Paper presented at the Celebrating Diversity: Preparing the Educators of Today for the Schools of Tomorrow Conference. Oakland, California.

Goodman, K. S. (1996). Principles of revaluing. In Y. M. Goodman & A. M. Marek (Eds.), _Revaluing readers and reading: Retrospective miscue analysis._ Katonah, NY: Richard C. Owen.

Gray, J. (1969). _The teacher's survival guide_ (2nd ed.). Belmont, CA: Fearon.

Helfeldt, J. P., & Henk, W. A. (1990). Reciprocal question-answer relationships: An instructional technique for at-risk readers. _Journal of Reading, 33,_ 509–514.

Helfeldt, J. P., & Lalik, R. (1976). Reciprocal student-teaching questioning. _The Reading Teacher, 30,_ 283–287.

Holdaway, D. (1988, July). _Towards joyful language teaching through homely models._ Address delivered at the Twelfth World Congress on Reading of the International Reading Association. The Gold Coast, Australia.

Johnstone, P., & Allington, R. (1991). Remediation. In R. Barr, M. L. Kamil, P. B. Mosenthal, & P. D. Pearson (Eds.), _Handbook of reading research: Volume II_ (pp. 984–1012). New York: Longman.

Kean, E. (1991). Other people's kids. _Teacher Magazine,_ August, 6–7.

Kellogg, J. B. (1988). Forces of change. _Phi Delta Kappan, 70,_ 199–204.

Kozol, J. (1995). _Amazing grace._ New York: Crown Publishers.

Lyons, N. P. (1990). Listening to voices we have not heard: Emma Willard girls' ideas about self, relationships and morality. In C. Gilligan, N. P. Lyons, & T. J. Hanmer (Eds.), _Making connections: The relational worlds of adolescent girls at Emma Willard School_ (pp. 30–72). Cambridge, MA: Harvard University Press.

Maker, C. J. (1982). *Curriculum development for the gifted*. Rockville, MD: Aspen.

Manzo, A. V. (1969a). *Improving reading comprehension through reciprocal questioning*. Doctoral dissertation, Syracuse University. (University Microfilms No. 70–10, 364).

Manzo, A. V. (1969b). The ReQuest procedure. *Journal of Reading, 13*, 123–126.

Manzo, A. V., & Manzo, U. C. (1990). *Content area reading: A heuristic approach*. Columbus, OH: Merrill.

McCracken, N. M. (1996). Resisting gender-binding in the middle school. *Voices from the middle, 3*(1), 4–10.

McLeod, R. G. (1992, February 3). Immigration at a 48-year high. *San Francisco Chronicle*, p. A2.

Miller, J. B. (1976). *Toward a new psychology of women*. Boston: Beacon Press.

National Commission on Excellence in Education (1983). *A nation at risk: The imperative for educational reform*. Washington, DC: U.S. Government Printing Office.

Ogbu, J. U. (1988, May). *Minority youth and school success*. Paper presented at the Teaching At-Risk Youth conference. Baltimore, Maryland.

Palincsar, A. S., & Brown, A. L. (1984). Reciprocal teaching of comprehension-fostering and comprehension-monitoring activities. *Cognition and Instruction, 1*, 117–175.

Pearson, P. D. (1990, May). *Who's at risk? Our students, our schools, our society? A research and policy perspective*. Paper presented at the annual meeting of the International Reading Association. Atlanta, Georgia.

Pilar, C. (October, 1991). *Issues in teacher education*. Phi Delta Kappa conference, Rohnert Park, California.

Portes, A., & Rumbaut, R. G. (1990). *Immigrant America: A portrait*. Berkeley: University of California Press.

Preparation to teach crossculturally: A guidebook for teacher candidates. (1988). Irvine, CA: Office of Teacher Education, University of California, Irvine.

Raphael, T. E. (1982). Teaching children question-answering strategies. *The Reading Teacher, 36*, 186–191.

Raphael, T. E. (1984). Teaching learners about sources of information for answering comprehension questions. *Journal of Reading, 28*, 303–311.

Raphael, T. E. (1986). Teaching question answer relationships revisited. *The Reading Teacher, 39*, 516–522.

Roehler, L. R., Foley, K. U., Lud, M. T., & Power, C. A. (1991). Developing integrated programs. In G. G. Duffy (Ed.), *Reading in the middle school* (pp. 184–199). Newark, DE: International Reading Association.

Rose, M. (1989). *Lives on the boundary*. New York: Penguin Books.

Sadker, M., & Sadker, D. (1994). *Failing at fairness: How America's schools cheat girls*. New York: Scribner's.

Sinatra, R. (1991). Integrating whole language with the learning of text. *Journal of Reading, 34*, 424–433.

Sternberg, R. J. (1986). Identifying the gifted through IQ: Why a little bit of knowledge is a dangerous thing. *Roeper Review, 8*, 143–147.

Subotnik, R. F. (1988). Teaching gifted students. In J. A. Banks & C. A. McGee Banks (Eds.), *Multicultural education: Issues and perspectives* (pp. 269–285). Boston: Allyn & Bacon.

Tannen, D. (1990). *You just don't understand: Women and men in conversation*. New York: Ballantine.

Tuttle, F. B., Jr. (1991). Teaching the gifted. In J. Flood, J. M. Jenson, D. Lapp, & J. R. Squire (Eds.), *Handbook of research on teaching English and the language arts* (pp. 372–379). New York: Macmillan.

Vacca, R. T., & Padak, N. D. (1990). Who's at risk in reading? *Journal of Reading, 33*, 486–488.

Van Tassel-Baska, J., Feldhusen, J., Seeley, K., Wheatley, G., Silverman, L., & Foster, W. (1988). *Comprehensive curriculum for gifted learners*. Boston: Allyn & Bacon.

Weiner, M., & Cromer, W. (1967). Reading and reading difficulty: A conceptual analysis. *Harvard Educational Review, 37*, 620–643.

Wheatley, G. H. (1988). Matching instructional strategies to gifted learners. In J. Van Tassel-Baska, J. Feldhusen, K. Seeley, G. Wheatley, L. Silverman, & W. Foster (Eds.), *Comprehensive curriculum for gifted learners* (pp. 383–394). Boston: Allyn & Bacon.

Williams, F. (1972). *A total creativity program kit*. Englewood Cliffs, NJ: Educational Technology Publications.

BUILDING TABLE

CHAPTER 10	QAR & ReQAR	CONE OF EXPERIENCE	COMMUNITY OF READERS
GUIDES STUDENTS	After reading	Before, during, and after writing	Interdisciplinary content learning, reading and writing
USE TO PLAN	Lessons	Lessons, units	Before, during and after reading and writing
MAY BE USED	Whole class, small groups	Whole class, cooperative groups	Units, Whole class, cooperative groups
MAY BE COMBINED WITH (known strategies)	DRA, GMA, ReQuest, VSS, REAP, Learning Logs, DEJ	GMA, VSS, List-Group-Label, Semantic Mapping, REAP, Journals, Learning Logs, DEJ	DR-TA, DRA, GMA, VSS, Writing Work-shop, Journals, Learning Logs, DEJ, Jigsaw I & II, Group Investigation, GRA, Cone of Experience
MATERIALS PREPARATION	Light	Moderate	Light
OTHER PREPARATION	Moderate	Moderate to extensive	Moderate to Extensive
OUTSIDE RESOURCES	Not needed	Necessary	Useful
HOW TO DO	Pages 318–320	Pages 322–323	

CHAPTER 11

TEACHING BILINGUAL/ BICULTURAL STUDENTS IN MULTILINGUAL/ MULTICULTURAL SETTINGS

DOUBLE ENTRY JOURNAL

Picture yourself, a successfully literate adult and competent learner, newly arrived in a country whose language and culture is different from your own. Jot down some of the problems and feelings you might experience in such a situation. Now imagine yourself a preadolescent or adolescent in school in this new

country, language, and culture; spend a little time listing the likely problems and feelings you might have had as an adolescent. What strategies might you have used to function successfully in that environment and learn the content of school subjects? Share your perceptions with a friend.

BILINGUAL/BICULTURAL AND NON-ENGLISH-SPEAKING STUDENTS

Bilingualism is a relatively recent issue in U.S. education. This is probably because prior to the late 1960s, immigrant and other non-English-speaking populations moved rapidly away from their primary languages toward assimilation into the mainstream culture by shifting to the mainstream language (Portes & Rumbaut, 1990). Political and social conditions today are such that more bilingual/bicultural people are choosing to retain their primary language while gaining fluency in English and to encourage their children's competence in both languages as well. Thus, U.S. classrooms are increasingly multilingual and multicultural with various combinations of bilingual/bicultural students in them. It should be noted that individuals' intent to develop bilingual fluency and literacy (or, in some cases, multilingual fluency and literacy), while relatively new to most monolingual U.S. Americans, is not considered unusual in many parts of the world (Glazer, 1993; Portes & Rumbaut, 1990, pp. 182–183). Unfortunately, the issue of bilingualism is all too often viewed as a *problem* in this country (you need only to read the popular press to perceive the magnitude of this belief), when in fact just the opposite should be true. Nathan Glazer (1993) describes an alternative high school in New York City in which one of the admissions requirements is fluency in Spanish. He then situates the advantages of bilingualism in the United States:

> When we treat the knowledge of Spanish as an ability to be nurtured and developed, we do not, by that token, say that the knowledge of English in an English-speaking country is unnecessary. It is essential. We are saying that knowing two languages means that one is provided with two competencies rather than one. We are also saying that to effectively learn one language and develop it to the highest level of fluency does not require the eradication of another (p. 320).

As we discuss issues associated with non-English-speaking students and bilingualism, keep in mind that, for many students, English is not a second language, but a third or fourth. Our discussion will focus on bilingualism and bilingual learning because that is the most common pattern; however, concerns I raise and suggestions I make for bilingual students apply to multilingual students as well.

Keep in mind also the very close connection between language, culture, and community (Banks, 1988; Moll, 1994; Moll & Gonzalez, 1994; Ovando, 1988). Regardless of whether students are learning English as a second, third (or even fourth) language, much of what they bring to school from their primary language represents the beliefs, attitudes, behaviors and values of their home, their primary culture, and community as well. Kiana Davenport, in her novel *Shark Dialogues* (1994), speaks of both the close relationship between language and culture and the pain associated with eradicating one's primary language:

> And entering university in Manoa Valley, frightened every day. What am I doing there, who do I think I am? . . . Silently swearing I will wear my fingers down, my eyes, I will die becoming something better. Smoothing out my

English. Swallowing Pidgin, denying it, saving it for home, for "slang." This tongue I was born with, raised on, this part of my mouth demeaned, thrown out like garbage. Mama trying to keep up with me, ironing out her Pidgin, ironing other people's clothes (p. 193).

To teach bi- and multilingual students effectively, we need knowledge and understanding of their language, culture, and community; we need to honor and respect the funds of knowledge represented by students' homes and communities (Moll, 1994; Moll & Gonzalez, 1994); and we need to understand the relationships between these important influences on students' lives. We need also to recognize that many monolingual English-speaking students are at the same time bicultural. Some of the issues regarding bilingualism are just as appropriately applied to monolingual/bicultural students as they are to bilingual/bicultural students.

For the most part, non-English-speaking students in United States schools are immigrant rather than indigenous. Bilingual students, on the other hand, may have been born in the United States to immigrant parents or reared in a family where a language or dialect other than English predominates in the home; these students may or may not be literate in their first language. In addition, there are geographically isolated groups of indigenous populations whose primary language has been slow to yield to English; in these families, as well, the primary language is the first language in which children gain spoken fluency. The Navaho, Eskimo-Aleut, and other Native Americans and the Louisiana French are examples of such populations (Ovando, 1988; Portes & Rumbaut, 1990). Various other populations speak Creole and/or dialect English (e.g., native Hawaiians, Sea Islanders from the Carolinas to Northern Florida, and African Americans) as a first language, either exclusively or in addition to mainstream English (Ovando, 1989). Tiedt and Tiedt (1990) suggest that due to regional and other differences, we all speak dialects of one kind or another (pp. 137–138).

All of these variations—from immigrant non-English-speaking students, to indigenous students with primary language fluency preceding English language fluency, to students whose primary language and/or dialect develop concurrently with English—are present in our schools. Furthermore, all of these variations of language learning in some way affect students' language and literacy development in English. The remainder of this chapter addresses issues related to second language acquisition, bilingual students and programs, and appropriate subject matter instruction for bilingual/bicultural students in multilingual/multicultural settings.

SECOND-LANGUAGE ACQUISITION

How we acquire and become literate in a second language has been the topic of much research and theory building over the years. Numerous theories exist to explain this process (Freeman & Freeman, 1994), each addressing second language acquisition from a specific perspective. I'll not attempt to summarize all of them here; rather, I'll present two of the predominant theories and their implications for instruction. You should know that, while language acquisition theories differ, they are not necessarily conflicting. Nearly all of them acknowledge the central role of first language fluency and literacy in the acquisition of second language fluency and literacy. Further, all but the nativist theories (those attributing language acquisition to innate abilities) account for, and in fact highlight, the importance of social interactions and transactions in second language development. Finally, all theories focus on the learner (or "acquirer," as Stephen Krashen would say) and his or her home culture as central to the process; that is, that second language acquisition is a process of "personal invention shaped by social convention" (Goodman & Goodman, 1990; in Freeman & Freeman, 1994, p. 106).

KRASHEN'S SECOND LANGUAGE ACQUISITION THEORY

Stephen Krashen (1981, 1995) posits a model of second language acquisition based on five hypotheses.

THE ACQUISITION-LEARNING HYPOTHESIS
The first hypothesis is the Acquisition-Learning Hypothesis, in which *acquisition* of a language occurs as a subconscious process as we encounter and use a second language for some communicative purpose. Conscious *learning* of a language, on the other hand, occurs as we study formally the grammar, structure, and lexicon of a language. Krashen considers acquisition, rather than learning, to be the primary means for second language development.

THE NATURAL ORDER HYPOTHESIS
The Natural Order Hypothesis refers to the general order in which elements of a second language are acquired. Simply put, it means that we acquire the grammatical structures of a second language in a predictable order, even though linguists do not have complete understanding of what that order is for every structure in every language.

THE MONITOR HYPOTHESIS
The Monitor Hypothesis explains the relationship between acquisition and learning. While acquisition—encountering and using language for specific communicative purposes—is responsible for fluency in a second language, conscious learning—what we know and can articulate about that language—serves as a monitor or editor in language use. Recall our discussion of cognitive monitoring in Chapter 2, that facility of the mind that lets us know when things are going well and also when things are not (e.g., when it signals "Whoa. Go back. This is not making sense"). The second language monitor serves the same purpose; it alerts the second language speaker/reader/writer that the language construction she or he just used is not appropriate and allows for self-correction. Krashen emphasizes that for the monitor to be effective, the second language user must *have time* to consult or reflect on language rules (such time is rarely available in normal conversation), *focus on form* or be thinking about correctness, and *know the rule*—a difficult task given the number and complexity of the rules and the time it takes to learn them.

THE INPUT HYPOTHESIS

The Input Hypothesis is, I think, the heart of Krashen's model. The input hypothesis states that we learn a second language by understanding language containing linguistic structures that are just beyond the structures we already know. Krashen calls this *comprehensible input* and symbolizes it as i (input) + 1. The notion of i + 1 is not at all unlike Vygotsky's Zone of Proximal Development (again, discussed in Chapter 2); it is that place just a little bit beyond our current level of competence within which we are able to construct new meaning. We construct this new meaning (in this instance, understand the content of the communication and acquire more of the second language) using what we already know about the language, world knowledge, contextual information, and extralingual information. Krashen emphasizes that we acquire new structures in a second language (new words, new grammar rules, etc.) not by focusing on the structures themselves, but by understanding the meaning of a communication containing those new structures.

Two interesting phenomena are explained by the input hypothesis. One is the *silent period*, the time during which the second language acquirer does not speak. This is a time for collecting information, for getting a "feel" for the language, and for learning words and language structures by listening (although not all of the input is comprehensible). The silent period is an important stage in second language acquisition, and one in which the acquirer is particularly vulnerable, possibly even fearful, if he or she is required to produce language too early. I know, for example, that I am in a silent stage in acquiring Spanish: Given plenty of supporting context, I can read and construct reasonable meaning for sentences and even paragraphs in Spanish and can get the gist of *some* conversations—not all I hear—about common, ordinary topics and/or events in the immediate environment (but not technical or abstract topics). I do not participate in these conversations, however, beyond the word level ("bueno," "gracias"), even when I know that the other participants would willingly tolerate errors. Since occasion to receive comprehensible input is relatively rare for me, my silent period continues; with additional input and time to acquire more language, I could progress.

The second phenomenon associated with the input hypothesis is the *Din in the Head* experience first described by Barber (1980). A linguist on a trip to Russia and struggling to bring her Russian to fluency, Barber noticed by the third day "a rising Din of Russian in my head; words, sounds, intonations, phrases, all swimming about in the voices of the people I talked with." This Din has been studied by other linguists (Bedford, 1985; Krashen, 1983; McQuillan, 1995; McQuillan & Rodrigo, 1995) and is often noted to be melodic. Bedford (1985) describes it as a "noticeable din or jumble of words, phrases, or even characteristic melody patterns" (p. 286). The Din is thought to be an involuntary mental rehearsal of bits and pieces of the new language that happens as we have i + 1 input; messages in the Din contain linguistic information not yet learned and allow the learner to practice the language mentally before having to produce and/or comprehend it. Once fluency is achieved or input is removed, the Din goes away.

THE AFFECTIVE FILTER HYPOTHESIS

Krashen identifies three affective variables that serve as "filters" or mental blocks that may inhibit second language acquisition. *Anxiety, motivation,* and *self-confidence* are the influencing filters: In situations where we feel comfortable, where motivation is high for acquiring the language, and where we see ourselves as capable learners, acquisition of the second language is enhanced; the opposite effect occurs when anxiety is high and motivation and self-confidence are low. In the case of my Spanish language acquisition, the affective filter is working full-tilt. Even when I'm with friends and friendly acquaintances who will slow their speech and wait for me and ignore my mistakes, my concern about correctness (self-imposed high anxiety), ability to get along very nicely in the English-language world I'm in at that moment and insecurity about my current level of fluency all serve to slow my progress. Immersed in a Spanish-language environment, my need to get and give information (motivation) would at some point override the anxiety and insecurity. (A friend once told me that when visiting a country where the language is not one you know, the first words you learn are, "Where's the bathroom?".) To the extent that the environment is friendly, inviting, and tolerant of my imprecise language attempts, my progress toward fluency would be heightened.

Krashen summarizes his theory this way: "People acquire second languages when they obtain comprehensible input and when their affective filters are low enough to allow the input in" (1995, p. 101). He suggests further that second language acquisition will occur in classes taught in the second language if the student can understand what is going on in the class; that is, when input is comprehensible.

CUMMINS' COGNITIVE AND LANGUAGE CONTEXT THEORY

Jim Cummins (1984) introduced the terms *basic interpersonal communication skills* (BICS) and *cognitive academic language proficiency* (CALP) to distinguish between students' second language fluency and proficiency in social settings and their fluency and proficiency in classrooms. Essentially, this distinction is between the informal, ordinary language of daily life and the more structured, technical, and abstract language of academic discourse. Cummins estimates that ESL students acquire age-appropriate conversational proficiency (BIC) in about 2 years, while academic proficiency (CALP) requires 5 to 7 years. He cautions us, therefore, to refrain from assuming that second language students' proficiency in conversational English is a true measure of their proficiency in science, or social studies, or mathematics. This is particularly true in the situation in which we are using English language tests to measure intelligence or academic skills. Cummins rightfully asserts that schools have all too often given ESL students "one-way tickets to special education classes" (1994, p. 39) through inappropriate testing practices based on faulty assumptions about students' English language proficiency.

Cummins explains the discrepancy between the acquisition of social and academic language proficiency ideas by examining communicative interactions associated with social and academic discourse. Figure 11.1 identifies two intersecting continua of cognitive and linguistic elements of language transactions (please note that this explanation is applicable to *all* language transactions, not just to those encountered by second language learners). The horizontal continuum describes the linguistic elements of context-embedded versus context-reduced language events. Context-

FIGURE 11.1 *Range of Contextual Support and Degree of Cognitive Involvement in Communicative Activities*

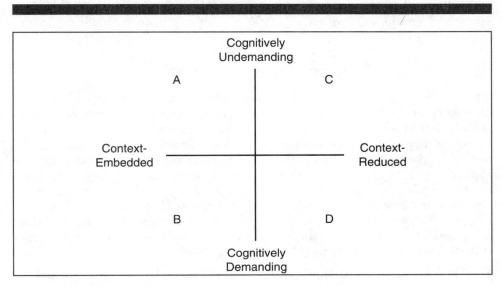

embedded events are those in which "participants can actively negotiate meaning (by indicating when a message has not been understood, for example) and the language use is supported by a range of meaningful interpersonal and situational cues" (1994, p. 40). Social conversations, banter among friends, rereading well-known books or reading books by an author you've read frequently are all examples of context-embedded language transactions. Context-reduced language events, on the other hand, are those in which participants must rely heavily on their knowledge of the language, rather than on interpersonal or situational cues, to construct meaning. Many classroom events are context-reduced: reading from informational texts, writing reports and essays, and learning new vocabulary, to name a few.

The vertical continuum describes extremes of the cognitive demand placed on participants in communicative events. Cognitively undemanding situations are ones in which we already have lots of background and/or other information to support our participation in the language event and are thus easily able to enter into the event (recall our discussion of redundancy in Chapter 2). Cognitively demanding activities are those in which we are learning new concepts and content or are articulating what we know about relatively new information—tasks that are commonplace in classrooms.

As you view the quadrants (A,B,C,D) created by these intersecting continua, you can see that social language proficiency (BIC) clusters in quadrant A, which is context-embedded and cognitively undemanding; academic language proficiency (CALP), however, is primarily within quadrant D and is context-reduced and cognitively demanding. Thus we can see the reason for the 3-to-5-year lag between students' acquisition of social language proficiency and the acquisition of academic language proficiency. Cummins makes the further point that even as ESL students are acquiring skill in academic discourse, so too are native English speakers; thus, ESL learners must "catch up with a moving target" (1994, p. 43) if they are to match the proficiency of native English speakers.

IMPLICATIONS FOR INSTRUCTION

The clear implication of the Krashen's and Cummins' models is that ESL students need to be in classrooms in which they receive sufficient comprehensible input to allow both the learning of content information and the further acquisition and development of English language proficiency. Further, instruction for ESL students must include support and scaffolding activities represented particularly by quadrant B of Cummins' intersecting continua; that is, when cognitive demand is high, instruction must be highly context-embedded to give students many extralingual and situational cues for constructing meaning. This has the effect of reducing negative affective filters (e.g., high anxiety, low self-confidence, low motivation), boosting positive affect, and increasing students' willingness to participate in learning events. Jim Cummins (1994) summarizes school responsibilities for ESL students:

1. The educational and personal experiences that ESL students bring to schools constitute the foundation for all their future learning; schools should therefore attempt to amplify rather than replace these experiences (p. 53).

2. Although English conversational skills may be acquired quite rapidly by ESL students, upward of 5 years may be required for ESL students to reach a level of academic proficiency in English comparable to their native-English-speaking peers; schools must therefore be prepared to make a long-term commitment to supporting the academic development of ESL students (p. 54).

3. Access to interaction with English speakers is a major causal variable underlying both the acquisition of English and ESL students' sense of belonging to the English-speaking society; the entire school is therefore responsible for supporting the learning and need for interaction of ESL students, and ESL provision should integrate students into the social and academic mainstream to whatever extent possible (p. 54).

4. If ESL students are to catch up academically with their native-English-speaking peers, their cognitive growth and mastery of academic content must continue while English is being learned. Thus, the teaching of English as a second language should be integrated with the teaching of other academic content that is appropriate to students' cognitive level. By the same token, all content teachers must recognize themselves also as teachers of language (p. 56).

5. The academic and linguistic growth of ESL students is significantly increased when their parents see themselves and are seen by school staff as coeducators of their children. Schools should therefore actively seek to establish a collaborative relationship with parents of ESL students that encourages them to participate in furthering their children's academic progress (p. 57).

BILINGUAL STUDENTS AND PROGRAMS

In the literature of bilingualism, you will find a number of generally standard terms and abbreviations used to describe or refer to non-English-speaking and bilingual students. It is helpful to learn these terms, and, in so doing, begin to get a sense of the students themselves.

LEP refers to Limited English Proficient students, those who demonstrate some level of oral-language fluency in English but who have not attained minimal levels of academic and oral-language English proficiency (Watson, Northcutt, & Rydell, 1989).

FEP refers to Fluent English Proficient students who communicate rather easily in English in general conversation, in the classroom, or both. FEP students have acquired minimal proficiency in English oral language and academics (Watson et al., 1989).

SAE refers to Students Acquiring English (Lapp & Flood with Tinajero, 1994); SAE is a relatively new term that is beginning to replace LEP as the preferred means for referring to ESL students. Students Acquiring English has a more positive cast than does Limited English Proficient.

L1 stands for "first language"; *L2* is "second language." Various authors use the terms *primary language*, *native language*, or *mother tongue* to refer to L1.

ESL, or "English as a Second Language," is used to designate classes that are immersion English classes. In these classes, students generally have various primary languages and varying levels of English literacy and oral fluency. As suggested earlier, students in the classes may be learning English as a third or fourth language. Often, ESL classes are taught by teachers who are monolingual English speakers; instruction is in English and focused on acquisition of English language skills. Most L1 interaction in ESL classes is between students with common primary languages. ESL is also commonly used synonymously with SAE and LEP to refer to students who speak English as a second language, whether or not those students are actually in ESL classes.

Bilingual education programs provide instruction in students' primary language, focusing on content area learning, while providing instruction in English during part of the school day. Most bilingual classes are in elementary schools, and most of those are at the primary grade level. Some do exist at intermediate grades and in middle schools, and a few can be found in junior high or high schools. Bilingual classes require that everyone in the class have the same L1 and so generally are found in schools with large concentrations of immigrant students from the same country or who speak common languages; they also require teachers who are fluently bilingual and bilingually literate.

Transition programs are intended to bridge ESL and bilingual classes and regular classrooms. Students who have been in ESL and bilingual classes who need a bit more assistance before being completely immersed in regular classes are often put into transition classes. Many transition classes focus on sheltered

English as the primary means for instruction; some are even called "sheltered" classes. We will discuss sheltered English at some length later in the chapter. Transition classes are often found in middle school, junior high, and senior high schools.

Maintenance Bilingual Programs are available in some very few middle and secondary schools for the purpose of maintaining and developing students' language and literacy proficiency in their first language (Loeza, 1995). Such programs are grounded in two key beliefs: (1) that unless SAE students have opportunity for continuing instruction in their primary language, they are at risk of becoming "partial bilinguals and semi-literates [in their first language]" (Loeza, 1995, p. 6); and (2) that eradication of students' first language may very well undermine cultural identity and cause loss of communication between parents who maintain the first language and English-only children, a generational rift that Lily Fillmore (1990) describes as "tragic." She states, "What is lost is the ability for parents and children to communicate about the deep and critical experiences of growing up. What the parent has to teach the child and what the child is able to share with the parent are irretrievably lost when their means of communication are lost to them" (p. 46). Maintenance bilingual programs validate students' primary language and culture, develop their L1 language and literacy abilities, and assume bilingualism to be an advantage.

APPROPRIATE PLACEMENT IN PROGRAMS FOR BILINGUAL STUDENTS

Lee Gunderson (1991) emphasizes the importance of appropriate instruction for ESL students and appropriate placement of these students into available bilingual, ESL, reading, and regular classrooms. He uses a graduated scale to define degrees of English (L2) oral-language proficiency that is helpful in understanding stages of second language development. Please note that Gunderson's "0-Level English" and "Very Limited English" may, in fact, describe a student in the silent period. The levels he uses are described below (adapted from Gunderson, 1991, p. 26):

0-Level English

　Cannot answer yes/no questions

　Unable to identify and name any objects

　Understands no English

　Often appears withdrawn and afraid

Very Limited English

　Responds to simple questions with mostly yes/no or one-word responses

　Speaks in 1- to 2-word phrases

　Attempts no extended conversation

　Seldom, if ever, initiates conversation

Limited English

Responds easily to simple questions

Produces simple sentences

Has difficulty elaborating when asked

Uses syntax/vocabulary adequate for personal, simple situations

Occasionally initiates conversation

Limited Fluency

Speaks with ease

Initiates conversations

May make phonological or grammatical errors

Makes errors in more syntactically complex utterances

Freely and easily switches codes

Gunderson uses a "decision heuristic" that combines students' L1 literacy (the number of years they have experienced literacy instruction and/or literacy in their primary language) and L2 oral-language proficiency (English) to guide decision-making about ESL student placement (p. 27). The secondary decision heuristic—English Ability— is shown in Figure 11.2.

This heuristic may be used to decide what kind of instruction would be most beneficial for students: Students with 0-Level or Very Limited L2 proficiency and none or very few years of L1 literacy instruction (upper-left box in Figure 11.2) would be very unlikely to benefit from placement in regular subject area classrooms; students with limited oral fluency and 7 or more years of L1 literacy would probably function very effectively in regular classes. Between these extremes, students would probably function better or less well in regular classrooms, depending on where their abilities fall on the heuristic.

I present Gunderson's oral-language proficiency description and the decision heuristic here because my experience suggests, and reports from middle school and secondary teachers confirm, that bilingual and non-English-speaking students are often misplaced in schools, particularly at the senior high level. This occurs with greater frequency as resources dwindle and teachers and staff with expertise and experience in bilingual and ESL programs are removed from schools. As a rule, elimination of positions begins at the senior high school and works its way downward.

In the event that you find yourself in a school that has minimal staff and facilities for evaluating and placing bilingual students in programs and classrooms, you need to have some basis for making this evaluation yourself. Similarly, even with staff and facilities, you may find bilingual students in your class whom you believe to be misplaced. To check the placement and appropriate instruction for students in your classes, use the authentic assessment instruments discussed in Chapter 7, as appropriate, and check records to determine everything you can about students' prior schooling and L1 literacy; then apply that information to Gunderson's heuristic. You may or may not be able to change students' placement if this analysis suggests they are

FIGURE 11.2   *The Secondary Decision Heuristic—English Ability*

L1 Literacy	L2 Oral Proficiency		
	0-Level Very Limited	Limited	Limited Fluency
None			
2 to 6 Years			
7+ Years			

misplaced; however, at the very least, knowledge gained from the analysis should guide your decision making about classroom instruction and activities for these students.

ACADEMIC SUCCESS AND BILINGUAL/BICULTURAL STUDENTS

It is important to emphasize at this point that *many* bilingual/bicultural students succeed splendidly in school. Their success stories are not only well known, but the students (and their stories) are in front of our eyes daily. Research in the thinking and literacy processes of successful bilingual readers and writers, although relatively sparse, is beginning to yield interesting insights. Robert Jiménez, Georgia García, and David Pearson (1996) examined what strategies successful middle school Latina/o readers use as they read. They found that successful Latina/o readers (1) understand the unitary nature of reading, whether the process is in Spanish or English (e.g., "When I learned to read in English I just needed to know the pronunciation and spelling of the words." "[E]verything's the same that you have to know [to read in English and Spanish]." [p. 99]); (2) use a variety of techniques to identify unknown vocabulary, including context, prior knowledge, inferencing, searching for cognates

(English/Spanish words with similar pronunciation), and translating; (3) monitor their comprehension by checking to make sure their constructions of meaning make sense; (4) make large numbers of inferences during reading that serve as temporary meaning units to be confirmed or disconfirmed by further reading and/or additional information; and (5) occasionally ask questions to assist in meaning construction. You can see from this list that successful Latina/o readers reading in English use strategies that are strikingly similar to strategies used by successful monolingual English readers (recall the discussion of "expert" or "thoughtful" readers in Chapter 3).

Other students do not succeed, and we must recognize that fact. Their experience may reflect attitudes they hold about English language acquisition and usage that they acquired through cultural experiences. John Ogbu (1988) distinguishes between immigrants—people who moved "more or less voluntarily" to the United States for economic, political, or personal reasons—and involuntary minorities—people who were brought into U.S. society through slavery, conquest, or colonization (p. 41). Involuntary minorities in the United States include African Americans, Native Americans, and Mexican Americans of the Southwest. Ogbu makes the point that differential success rates of various cultural groups in acquiring fluent English, independent literacy, and academic success may be explained, in part, by differences in how different cultures were originally brought into the mainstream culture. He suggests further that among involuntary minority youth, behaviors that reject mainstream culture, language, and academic values may reflect students' ". . . disillusionment about their ability to succeed in adult life through the mainstream strategy of schooling" (p. 54), rather than reflect differential abilities and intelligence for school learning across racial and ethnic groups.

INSTRUCTION FOR BILINGUAL/BICULTURAL STUDENTS

One of the most important concerns in the education of non-English-speaking and bilingual students is the degree and quality of communication between all parties involved. All too often, there is too little, it is too late, or the lines of communication break down (Diaz, Moll, & Mehan, 1986). If you have bilingual students in your classes or students who speak very little English, you need to initiate contact with whomever is responsible for counseling, making assignments and watching over these students' progress if that person does not contact you. Do whatever is needed to maintain close communication.

A second concern relates to characteristics and contents of classrooms for bilingual students. Fillmore and Valadez (1986) note that the classroom environment is best when there is a balance between ESL students and native-English-speaking students and when interactions in the class facilitate language learning as well as communication of content knowledge. Since the teacher may have little control over the ESL/native-English-speaking balance, it is therefore doubly important to plan instruction to accommodate for needed language interactions. Such classrooms also should have, or there should be within the school, an ample supply of fiction and non-fiction literature by, for and about people of many cultures and languages, and particularly those represented by the students in that school.

As you work with bilingual/bicultural students, you may want to use this as an opportunity to become familiar with old standards and new books by, for, and about people of cultures different from your own. The titles in Figure 11.3 below are books read by my students that they recommend for middle school and adolescent readers. Undoubtedly, you will discover many others. Pugh and Garcia (1990) and Isabel Schon (1990), in every September issue of the *Journal of Adolescent & Adult Literacy* (previously called the *Journal of Reading*), provide evaluation checklists and reviews of trade books appropriate for multicultural classrooms and schools.

Once again, the point must be made that instruction for bilingual/bicultural students need not, and indeed *should not*, be "remedial" in nature. Rather, it should be the kind of *good instruction* emphasized throughout this text, involving

- rich language interaction
- focus on students' prior knowledge base
- careful lesson planning
- integrated/collaborative learning
- cultural breadth
- emphasis on student strengths
- authentic assessment
- multiple sources of information

Bilingual students are best served by solid, well-designed instruction suitable for all students that focuses on content learning and that provides needed support for students who are in the process of developing English language and literacy skills. Further, such instruction should provide for cultural attributes other than language,

FIGURE 11.3   *Good Books By, For, and About People of Various Cultures and Life Experiences*

Achebe, Chinua (1959). *Things Fall Apart.* New York: Fawcett.
Anaya, Rudolpho (1972). *Bless Me Ultima.* Berkeley, CA: Tonatiuh-Quinto Sol, Intl.
Bambara, Toni Cade (1972). *Gorilla My Love.* New York: Random House.
Boyd, Candy Dawson (1987). *Charlie Pippin.* New York: Macmillan.
Carter, Forest. *The Education of Little Tree.* Albuquerque, NM: University of New Mexico Press.
Crew, Linda (1989). *Children of the River.* New York: Delacorte.
Davidson, Robyn (1980). *Tracks.* New York: Pantheon.
Ellison, Ralph (1972). *The Invisible Man.* New York: Vintage Books.
Hamilton, Virginia (1987). *A White Romance.* New York: Philomel.
Highwater, Jamake (1986). *I Wear the Morning Sun.* New York: Harper & Row.
Hobbs, Will (1989). *Bearstone.* New York: Antheneum.
Houston, Jeanne Wakatsuki, & Houston, James D. (1973). *Farewell to Manzanar.* Boston: Houghton Mifflin.
Hurston, Zora Neale (1990). *Their Eyes Were Watching God.* New York: Harper.
Irwin, Hadley (1988). *I Be Somebody.* New York: Atheneum.

including nonverbal communication, perspectives and world views, behavioral styles, values, methods of reasoning and validating knowledge, and cultural identification (Anderson, 1988, *Preparation for Teaching Crossculturally: A Guidebook for Teacher Candidates*).

Hee-Won Kang, Phyllis Kuehn, and Adrienne Herrell (1994), in an ethnographic study of Hmong adult literacy classes, found numerous areas of cultural misunderstanding between the Hmong students and their native U.S. teachers. For example, much laughter was heard in the room as students worked, enough so that one observer concluded that the Hmong students were not serious about their study. Closer observation showed, however, that students laughed or giggled when they made a mistake, or were having problems, or were unsure about what they were doing or saying in English. Thus, instead of being a sign of lightheartedness or play, the laughter was a signal to the teacher that the student needed help.

SHELTERED ENGLISH

Sheltered English is the instruction viewed today as most effective and appropriate for students in ESL transition classes and in subject area classes that house students who are not fully fluent in English and have not achieved English literacy (SAE).

Sheltered English instruction includes all of the elements of good instruction listed above (rich language interaction, focus on students' prior knowledge, etc.), with the addition of the following:

- attention to language
- more time for everything
- repetition of ideas and concepts
- allowance for students to choose which language to use at any given moment
- low-risk environment for second language use
- deemphasis of on-the-spot correction of language miscues

Watson and colleagues (1989) and Hernández (1989) suggest that teachers use sheltered English techniques to bridge the gap between students' English language and literacy abilities, the teacher's language, and the content to be learned. Sheltering involves the following:

1. Adjusting language demands of a lesson by modifying speech and vocabulary, providing rich context, using models and visuals to illustrate concepts, and relating instructions to students' experiences.

2. Teaching both the content vocabulary and the words used to explain the lesson.

3. Using and repeating the same general lesson format (not activity) initially so that students do not have to figure out how the teacher is presenting information from day to day.

4. Minimizing lecture time, making lectures short and direct, and emphasizing small-group cooperative learning activities.

5. Providing charts, schematics, pictures, organizers, and other visual items to illustrate and support information and concepts developed through oral or written language.

6. Using pictorial schematics to illustrate directions for completing tasks and activities.

7. Incorporating tasks into lessons, as appropriate, that do not depend heavily on language and literacy abilities. The following sample lesson demonstrates one way to create a sheltered English lesson. This lesson is an adaptation of the DIA lesson in Chapter 5.

SAMPLE LESSON   *Directed Inquiry Lesson with Sheltered English—Science Adaption of DIA Lesson*

BRINGING THE LESSON TO LIFE
Bring to class items and objects for illustrating energy; for example, hammer, nail, and board; light socket and light bulb; hotplate and teakettle; magnets, and so on. Begin the lesson by using the items and objects to illustrate forms of energy; invite students to offer explanations and other illustrations.

SETTING THE STAGE
Divide the class into five groups. Have the groups work together to make predictions for each of the Inquiry Questions.

1. What are the different forms of energy?
2. How do we use energy, and what are the implications of energy use?
3. Why is it important to consider issues related to energy resources?
4. How do we distinguish between kinetic and potential energy resources?
5. What are some important questions we need to explore? Share some of the predictions.

PRETEACHING VOCABULARY
Prep: "Tell me anything that comes to your mind when I say 'energy' (write students' free associations on the board). What made you think of _____ when I said 'energy' (point to specific response). Based on our discussion, have you any new ideas about energy? Add these to your group predictions." Spot check for student understanding of items used to illustrate energy ("Everybody understand 'magnet'?), "kinetic," and "potential"; remind class of group responsibility for making sure others in group understand.

GUIDING INITIAL LEARNING
Before reading commences, assign each group one of the Inquiry Questions that it is to become expert on. After reading, each group is to respond to all questions and prepare to be the Resident Expert on its assigned question and to have a plan for further exploration of that question.

GUIDING PRACTICE
While groups are discussing and working, be the friendly monitor ready to offer suggestions and/or resource availability.

GUIDING INDEPENDENT PRACTICE

During whole class discussion, assist each group in refining its plan for further explanation of their question. Establish timelines for project completion and grading standards. Have each group prepare a written contract for the project it is to complete.

How to do . . . .

SHELTERED ENGLISH LESSONS

The principles of sheltered English instruction are not at all unlike the kind of content and literacy instruction we've discussed throughout this text. These principles outline instruction that makes learning easier for all students. Following these principles is critical, however, if content instruction for students with limited English proficiency is to be effective. Watson et al. (1989) recommend a Seven-Step Plan for sheltered English instruction. The following steps are adapted from their Seven-Step Plan:

Step 1   *Preplan the year by developing themes.*
   - Decide what the students need to master.
   - Organize content around themes.

Step 2   *Think of ways to bring lessons to life.*
   - Develop objectives for content and language.
   - Identify visuals and manipulatives.
   - Identify concrete and pictorial materials to illustrate ideas, concepts and task directions.

Step 3   *Set the stage.*
   - Present a broad overview of the unit/lesson content.
   - Begin each lesson with a short review of what was learned yesterday and/or predictions of what will happen today.

Step 4   *Preteach two vocabulary sets.*
   - Teach words necessary for understanding content.
   - Teach words that will be used to explain content.

Step 5   *Guide initial learning.*
   - Use consistent lesson formats, at least initially.
   - Find ways to animate instruction with role-playing, realia, experiments, and activities.

continued

How to do   *continued*

Step 6   *Guide practice.*

- Provide examples and tryouts.

- Demonstrate explicitly how practice activities relate to initial learning.

Step 7   *Guide independent practice.*

- Maximize student interactions (dyads, groups, cooperative learning).

- Evaluate students using student-developed products and tests.

SHELTERED ENGLISH COLLABORATIVE PROJECTS

Sinatra, Beaudry, Stahl-Gemake, & Guastello (1990) recommend a "visual literacy" activity for culturally and linguistically diverse students that has students working in pairs to construct photo and written essays. In the sixth and seventh grade classrooms Sinatra and his associates describe, the teacher used 20 cameras donated by a camera manufacturer as the basis for the collaborative project (disposable cameras are available if you haven't got access to donated cameras, and they're recyclable).

Students are given the task of creating photo storyboards, using a semantic map framework, around a central theme. Themes at this level are general. For example, students in the Sinatra and colleagues project were exploring various aspects of their own neighborhood community; hence, the theme, "Wonderful Williamsburg" [New York] (Sinatra et al., 1990). With this activity, each student pair is responsible for deciding what aspect or subtheme it wishes to photograph, planning specific shots, and taking the pictures. As soon as the pictures are developed, pairs determine the organization of their storyboards, prepare and mount the photos, and follow that with a written essay based on the photo essay. The beauty of visual literacy activities is their application to widely various themes. Themes and storyboard and written essays may include scientific as well as social observations, analysis of physical movement as well as art or literature, and commentary on plant or animal as well as human attributes.

The value of this activity is the extended, independent collaborative planning and decision making it requires, along with the language-rich environment such planning and decision making create. The activity begins with a class-determined project. Then student pairs must discuss the topic theme and subthemes at some length to arrive at their own plan for developing an idea. Next they must sort, classify, and organize their photos to communicate whatever they wish to say. Sinatra and his associates (1990, p. 614) found three patterns of storyboard organization developed by the students (see Figure 11.4). These organizational patterns provide support for students engaged in the final collaborative activity of constructing a written essay to accompany their photo essay.

FIGURE 11.4   *Three Patterns of Storyboard Organization for Photo Essay and Written Composition*

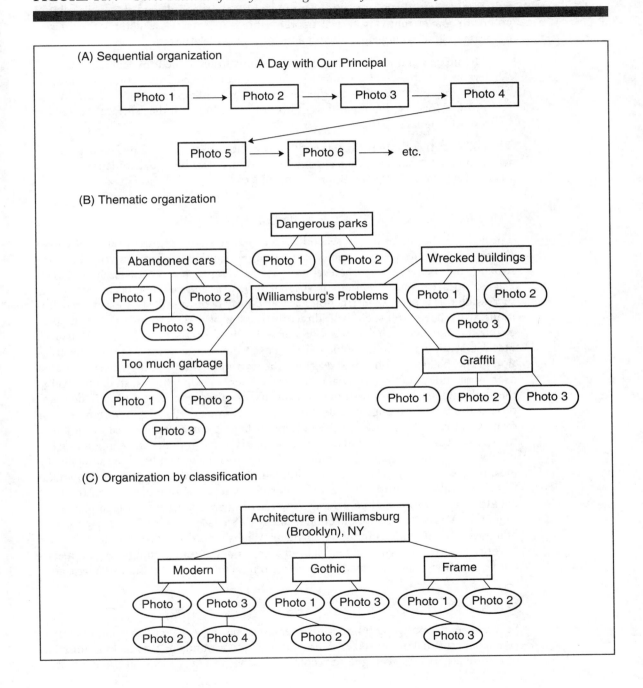

For students learning English as a second language, the amount of language interaction during planning and preparation of the storyboards and the availability of photos to convey mutually agreed-upon meanings increases considerably their access to meaning and to language. Sinatra and colleagues (1990) state

> The images and ideas captured by the photos transcended the language differences of this diverse student population while providing a common base for communication. Indeed, the "deep" structure of a picture is processed by a viewer for meaning regardless of his or her facility with the "surface" structure of language (p. 613).

The collaborative strategy Sinatra and his associates propose, with its language interaction and photo support, thus encourages and increases bilingual students' oral and written English language development in subject areas.

VOCABULARY KNOWLEDGE AND ESL LEARNERS

Throughout the literature on second language acquisition, a great deal of attention focuses on vocabulary learning and instruction (notice the emphasis on vocabulary instruction in sheltered English teaching). With bilingual learners, as well as native-English speakers, our tradition of vocabulary instruction has not been particularly successful; this is because instruction has relied heavily on word lists, look-it-up definitions, worksheets, and such, with direct instruction of predetermined words the preferred method of teaching (see Chapter 4 for further discussion of these issues). Hee-Won Kang and Anne Golden (1994) make the critical point that direct instruction of vocabulary must be viewed as only the starting point for bilingual learners, that a far more important instructional task is for teachers to help bilingual students develop the skills and abilities to learn new vocabulary on their own. Kang and Golden emphasize the need for bilingual students to learn words that they see as important to their own situation and interests and to become skilled at constructing meaning for new words from contextual cues and information (this is how comprehensible input—$i + 1$—increases language fluency). According to Kang and Golden, simply telling students the meaning of English words is of very limited usefulness in vocabulary development: "The least valuable information about a word is a word in another language" (p. 66). I could not agree more, and I encourage you to consider very seriously the implementation of the Vocabulary Self-Collection Strategy (VSS) (see Chapter 4) as a way to assist bilingual students in becoming independent English word learners, to increase their sensitivity to the language of your subject area, to develop their ability to gain meaning from context, and to provide rich, active transactions with the English language.

OTHER ISSUES

Several issues concerning bilingual learners must be addressed at this point. The first issue concerns making mistakes. Hernández (1989) reminds us that making mistakes is a normal part of learning. She recommends that teachers focus on the content of what bilingual students are saying or doing rather than such surface features of language as pronunciation, syntax, and grammar. She suggests further that correction of surface features should be covert (that is, rephrasing or repeating with correct pronunciation) rather than explicit. I support her recommendations: This is what I meant when I discussed "valuing approximation" in Chapter 10. An eighth-grade English teacher I know has a sign in her room. It says,

> We learn from our mistakes. Make lots!

The intent of the sign is to encourage risk-taking, and this teacher reinforces that encouragement often. For ESL students, such an attitude and approach gives them the freedom to concentrate on learning content without worrying about language differences. English language learning will occur, as does L1 learning, rapidly and naturally with continued exposure to a language-rich environment and experimentation with English.

The second issue is one I've touched on earlier in this chapter and in Chapter 10 as well. It concerns our perception about second language learners and the effect that perception has on them. Recall in Chapter 10 my discussion of Constance Weaver's notion of the quantum leap, in which how we choose to view students affects our interpretations of students' behaviors and abilities. I suggest here that it also affects how students view themselves as individuals and as learners. It is therefore essential that ESL students' cultures and primary languages are respected and valued in classrooms, that classroom situations and activities are structured to include ESL students *as mainstream participants in the class*, and that bilingual students are treated as capable, contributing class members. Thus, we must allow ESL students the latitude to respond variously in English, in their primary language, in other visual forms, and in assorted combinations secure in the knowledge that each response system supports their English language and academic development. We must create and construct classroom activities that invite ESL students to contribute information from their cultural and knowledge base that might not have been available without their presence in class, and we must develop requisite understanding of cultures represented in our classes so that behaviors and abilities are not misinterpreted (Kang, Kuehn, & Herrell, 1994). We must ensure that bilingual students have access to academic conventions and strategies that lead to success in school (Delpit, 1995). And finally, we must encourage students' first language and literacy development through maintenance classes and programs, thereby asserting the advantage of bilingualism in this society.

The final issue I want to address concerns families, communities, and bilingual/bicultural learners themselves. Luis Moll and his associates (Moll, 1994; Moll & Gonzalez, 1994) have spent considerable time over the past few years studying households of language-minority communities; what they have found is a complex, rich system of "funds of knowledge" through which individuals, families, and other groups share information and skills for the betterment of each. Moll makes the point that not only are these community resources often unperceived by teachers and schools, but, more importantly, that teachers, classrooms, and schools would benefit greatly by having access to them. This requires reaching out to the community rather than waiting for parents and community leaders to come to school. Such reaching out is particularly important when you consider the reality of bilingual/bicultural students' lives. Voon-Mooi Choo and Taffy Raphael (1995) characterize bicultural students as "walking in two worlds" and characterize the experience as follows:

> 1) learning to walk in different worlds is complex; 2) the journey involves dealing with the unknown; 3) [for adolescent students this] can be a lonely journey; and 4) [students] exist in a confused, confusing, and deeply troubled hybrid world (p. 3).

Given this, it seems powerfully important that teachers and schools not wait for parents and the community to come to them; the only reasonable way to provide support for students walking in two worlds is to develop programs and events that bridge those worlds.

WRITING IN A SECOND LANGUAGE

All of the strategies and activities we discussed about writing across the curriculum in Chapter 6 are useful for teaching ESL students. Perhaps we could even say they are not merely "useful," but imperative. Diaz and colleagues (1986) emphasize the importance of using the students' L1 language skills ". . . in the service of academic goals in their second language" (p. 218) and recommend development of academic activities that connect the home and community with the school. Such activities are particularly effective when students' primary language and culture are incorporated into content learning. Diaz and associates emphasize also that writing activities for ESL students, as for all students, should focus on writing for communication and intellectual advancement.

The use of mixed-ability/mixed L1 collaborative learning groups that engage students in such writing activities provides much support for bilingual students at all levels of English proficiency. It is to be expected that SAE and native-English-speaking students will contribute differentially to the final group product; the important goal is for all students to be engaged in comparable activities that are intellectually demanding (Diaz et al., 1986, p. 213).

STRATEGY REVIEW

I recommend that you review instructional strategies in other parts of the book for use with ESL students. Because of the clear need for continuing and consistent attention to vocabulary, I particularly encourage you to use some form of VSS (Chapter 4) with ESL students. In addition, the comprehension strategies (Chapter 3), reading across the curriculum activities (Chapter 5), writing activities (Chapter 6), and collaborative learning activities (Chapter 9) are likewise appropriate and adaptable to ESL populations.

SOME FINAL WORDS ABOUT TEACHING BILINGUAL/BICULTURAL STUDENTS IN MULTILINGUAL/MULTICULTURAL CLASSROOMS

Recently, I supervised a student teacher in a tenth-grade mainstream social studies class in which about half the students were native-Spanish speakers of varying English language fluency. The teacher, Nancy Case (a former student of mine), is fluently English-Spanish bilingual. When Nancy was in the room, I noticed that she chatted with students in English and Spanish, often mixing the languages in one conversation. Students did the same, with her and each other. The room itself was filled with student-created posters, maps, art work, and written reports; much of the 95-minute class periods were spent in group projects and activities in which students were grouped by the teacher (or by themselves) cross-culturally and in which lots of student talk—both on- and off-task—went on (most of the off-task talk was after work was finished and groups waited for other groups to complete their work). As the semester progressed, I noticed that Eric Wycoff, the monolingual English student teacher, began using some of the conversational Spanish (a word here or a phrase there) frequently heard in the room. Students responded to him in kind. Eric proudly announced to me toward the end of the semester that his Spanish was "really getting better." What became clear to me was that this was a classroom where *everyone* felt comfortable and both first and second languages were honored and respected; where code switching from Spanish to English was valued and encouraged; where students grouped themselves by friendship and interest criteria and across language and cultural boundaries; and where a great deal of learning was going on. In short, it was a classroom in which all of the following questions could be answered with a resounding "yes" (Schifini, 1994, pp. 161–162):

1. Are second-language learners who are new to English given the opportunity to perform many language tasks involving real (or at least realistic) communication?
2. Do they receive understandable language and multisensory input throughout the day?
3. Do they engage in reading and writing for authentic purposes daily?
4. Are the reading selections at the appropriate level of complexity, based on the student's evolving language and literacy skills in English?
5. Are second-language learners encouraged to take risks with language?
6. Are they integrated with native-English speakers in meaningful contexts?
7. Do they have access to challenging subject matter material and expository text delivered with a language-sensitive approach?
8. Is their growth in language assessed in an authentic fashion?

These are questions that must be asked frequently and continually by teachers of bilingual/bicultural students. To the extent that the answers are "yes," then we can be assured that ESL students are acquiring the content knowledge they need, acquiring fluency and literacy in English, and acquiring the skills for academic success.

D O U B L E   E N T R Y   J O U R N A L

Go back to your list of problems and feelings you might experience as a monolingual-English speaker attempting to acquire subject matter knowledge in a new culture and language. Now think about ESL students in your classroom and school. List some of the problems and feelings they might have. What can you do to help them "walk in two worlds" successfully? How can you alleviate some of the problems and assist in their English language and subject matter acquisition?

REFERENCES

Banks, J. A. (1988). _Multicultural education_ (2nd ed.). Boston: Allyn & Bacon.

Barber, E. (1980). Language acquisition and applied linguists. _ADFL Bulletin, 12,_ 26–32.

Bedford, D. (1985). Spontaneous playback of the second language: A descriptive study. _Foreign Language Annals, 18,_ 279–287.

Choo, V-M., & Raphael, T. E. (1995, December). _Literacy use and power: A case study of a teenager negotiating the boundaries between two cultures._ Paper presented at the National Reading Conference, New Orleans, Louisiana.

Cummins, J. (1984). _Bilingualism and special education: Issues in assessment and pedagogy._ Clevedon, UK: Multilingual Matters.

Cummins, J. (1994). The acquisition of English as a second language. In K. Spangenberg-Urbschat & R. Pritchard (Eds.), _Kids come in all languages: Reading instruction for ESL students_ (pp. 36–62). Newark, DE: International Reading Association.

Davenport, K. (1994). _Shark dialogues._ New York: Penguin.

Delpit, L. (1995, December). _Other people's children._ Paper presented at the National Reading Conference, New Orleans, Louisiana.

Diaz, S., Moll, L. C., & Mehan, H. (1986). Sociocultural resources in instruction: A context-specific approach. In _Beyond language: Social and cultural factors in schooling minority students_ (pp. 188–230). Sacramento, CA: Bilingual Education Office, California State Department of Education.

Fillmore, L. W. (1990). Language and cultural issues in the early education of language minority children. In S. L. Kagan (Ed.), _10th Yearbook of the National Society for the Study of Education, Part 1_ (pp. 30–49). Chicago: University of Chicago Press.

Fillmore, L. W., & Valadez, C. (1986). Teaching bilingual learners. In M. C. Wittrock (Ed.), _Handbook of research on teaching_ (3rd ed.), (pp. 648–685). New York: Macmillan.

Freeman, D. E., & Freeman, Y. S. (1994). *Between worlds: Access to second language acquisition.* Portsmouth, NH: Heinemann.

Glazer, N. (1993). Where is multiculturalism leading us? *Phi Delta Kappan, 75*(5), 319–323.

Goodman, Y. M., & Goodman, K. S. (1990). Vygotsky in a whole language perspective. In L. Moll (Ed.), *Vygotsky and education: Instructional implications and applications of sociohistorical psychology.* Cambridge, England: Cambridge University Press.

Gunderson, L. (1991). *ESL literacy instruction: A guidebook to theory and practice.* Englewood Cliffs, NJ: Prentice-Hall Regents.

Hernández, H. (1989). *Multicultural education: A teacher's guide to content and process.* Columbus, OH: Merrill.

Jiménez, R. T., García, G. E., & Pearson, P. D. (1996). The reading strategies of bilingual Latina/o students who are successful English readers: Opportunities and obstacles. *Reading Research Quarterly, 31*(1), 90–112.

Kang, H-W., & Golden, A. (1994). Vocabulary learning and instruction in a second or foreign language. *International Journal of Applied Linguistics, 4*(1), 57–77.

Kang, H-W., Kuehn, P., & Herrell, A. (1994). The Hmong literacy project: A study of Hmong classroom behavior. *Bilingual Research Journal, 18*(3&4), 63–83.

Krashen, S. (1981). *Second language acquisition and second language learning.* London: Pergamon Press.

Krashen, S. (1983). The din in the head, input, and the second language acquisition device. *Foreign Language Annals, 16*, 41–44.

Krashen, S. D. (1995). Bilingual education and second language acquisition theory. In D. B. Durkin (Ed.), *Language issues: Readings for teachers* (pp. 90–115). White Plains, NY: Longman.

Lapp, D., & Flood, J., with Tinajero, J. V. (1994). Are we communicating? Effective instruction for students who are acquiring English as a second language. *Reading Teacher, 48*(3), 260–264.

McQuillan, J. (1995, May). *Reading, acquisition, and the "din in the head": A new way to examine literacy.* Paper presented at the International Reading Association, Anaheim, California.

McQuillan, J., & Rodrigo, V. (1995). A reading "din in the head": Evidence of involuntary mental rehearsal in second language readers. *Foreign Language Annals, 28*(2), 1–7.

Moll, L. C. (1994). Literacy research in communities and classrooms: A sociocultural approach. In R. B. Ruddell, M. R. Ruddell, & H. Singer (Eds.), *Theoretical Models and Processes of Reading* (4th ed.) (pp. 170–207). Newark, DE: International Reading Association.

Moll, L. C., & Gonzalez, N. (1994). Lessons from research with language-minority children. *Journal of Reading Behavior, 26*(4), 439–455.

Ogbu, J. U. (1988, May). *Minority youth and school success.* Paper presented at the Teaching At-Risk Youth conference, Baltimore, Maryland.

Ovando, C. J. (1988). Language diversity and education. In J. A. Banks & C. A. McGee Banks (Eds.), *Multicultural education: Issues and perspectives* (pp. 208–227). Boston: Allyn & Bacon.

Portes, A., & Rumbaut, R. G. (1990). *Immigrant America: A portrait.* Berkeley, CA: University of California Press.

Pugh, S. I., & Garcia, J. (1990). Portraits in Black: Establishing African American identity through nonfiction books. *Journal of Reading, 34*, 20–25.

Schifini, A. (1994). Language, literacy, and content instruction: Strategies for teachers. In K. Spangenberg-Urbschat & R. Pritchard (Eds.), *Kids come in all languages: Reading instruction for ESL students* (pp. 158–179). Newark, DE: International Reading Association.

Schon, I. (1990). Recent good and bad books about Hispanics. *Journal of Reading, 34*, 76–78.

Sinatra, R., Beaudry, J. S., Stahl-Gemake, J., & Guastello, E. F. (1990). Combining visual literacy, text understanding, and writing for culturally diverse students. *Journal of Reading, 33*, 612–617.

Tiedt, P. L., & Tiedt, I. M. (1990). *Multicultural teaching: A handbook of activities, information and resources* (3rd ed.). Boston: Allyn & Bacon.

Watson, D. L., Northcutt, L., & Rydell, L. (1989). Teaching bilingual students successfully. *Educational Leadership, 46*, 59–61.

BUILDING TABLE

CHAPTER 11	SHELTERED ENGLISH	SHELTERED ENGLISH COLLABORATIVE PROJECTS
FOCUS ON		Content reading and discussion; information organization & articulation
GUIDES STUDENTS	Before, during, and after reading and writing	Before, during, and after reading and writing
USE TO PLAN	Lessons, units, semesters	Lessons, units
MAY BE USED	Whole class, cooperative groups, partnerships, individuals	Whole class, cooperative groups, partnerships
MAY BE COMBINED WITH (known strategies)	DRA, DR-TA, Three Level Guides, DIA, Content DR-TA, VSS, Semantic Mapping, Journals, Learning Logs, List-Group-Label, DEJ, Cone of Experience, Group Investigation	Writing Workshop, Cone of Experience, Group Investigation, Community of Readers, Sentence Collecting
MATERIALS PREPARATION	Moderate to extensive	Moderate
OTHER PREPARATION	Moderate to extensive	Moderate to extensive
OUTSIDE RESOURCES	Necessary	Necessary
HOW TO DO	Page 354	

12

DEVELOPING LIFELONG READERS AND WRITERS

List as many books, articles, and other materials as you can that you read more for pleasure than for study. What about such reading makes it pleasurable? On what occasions do you write "just for the fun of it"? What, if anything, does the reading and writing you do "for fun" have to do with you as a learner and as a subject matter specialist?

INVITATION

If you are a dreamer, come in,
If you are a dreamer, a wisher, a liar,
A hope-er, a pray-er, a magic bean buyer . . .
If you're a pretender, come sit by my fire
For we have some flax-golden tales to spin.
Come in!
Come in!

I begin this chapter with Shel Silverstein's "Invitation" (1974) to turn your attention to the teacher's role as an opener-of-doors. Everyone who has read and loved (and reread and loved some more) Silverstein's *Where the Sidewalk Ends* knows that on the pages behind that poem lies a world that is forever interesting, joyful, and touching for readers anywhere from the ages of 4 to 88. Silverstein opens doors by saying things we've never said before, finding unerringly the points of universal experience, and leading us to self-discovery through humor and his own healthy irreverence tinged with a sweetly sane view of the world and the humans in it. If all we had to do was read Shel Silverstein poetry to students all day, discipline problems would go away, kids would rush to get to our classes, and life at school would be fine indeed!

Of course, we can't read wacky and wonderfully insightful Silverstein to students all day, but just the thought of it gives us a yen to do something more than preside over days and months of unending passive routines that John Goodlad (1984) and others (Applebee, Langer, & Mullis, 1988; Flanders, 1970) describe as typical of secondary schools.

Opening Doors

"Opening doors" is about capturing students' natural curiosity, interest, and energy and showing them the possibility of new ideas and new ways to view the world of a particular subject area. It occurs when teachers slip quietly from the role of teacher into the role of mentor, spending much less time telling and much more time suggesting, encouraging, pointing the way, identifying resources, and monitoring students' independent progress.

When I think of mentoring and opening doors, I always think of Auntie Mame (Patrick, 1955), that exuberant, irrepressible, bohemian aunt who, in 1929, took her orphaned nephew to rear in the midst of freethinkers, cocktail parties, an ever-changing apartment decor to match her own changing personal interests (Siamese to Southern Belle to ultra modern), and an incipient stock market crash. Auntie Mame opened doors of delight, wonder and new ideas to Patrick:

> "My dear, a rich vocabulary is the true hallmark of every intellectual person. Here now"—she burrowed into the mess on her bedside table and brought forth another pad and pencil—"every time I say a word, or you hear a word, that you don't understand, you write it down and I'll tell you what it means. Then you memorize it and soon you'll have a decent vocabulary. Oh, the adventure," she cried ecstatically, "of molding a little new life!" She made another sweeping gesture that somehow went wrong because she knocked over the coffee pot and I immediately wrote down six new words which Auntie Mame said to scratch out and forget about (p. 22).
>
> I still have some of the vocabulary sheets of odd information picked up at Auntie Mame's soirees. One, dated July 14, 1929, features such random terms as: Bastille Day, Lesbian, Hotsy-Totsy Club, gang war, Id, daiquiri— although I didn't spell it properly—relativity, free love, Oedipus complex— another one I misspelled—mobile, stinko—and from here on my spelling went wild—narcissistic, Biarritz, psychoneurotic, Shönberg, and nymphomaniac (p. 24).

INFLUENTIAL TEACHERS: TEACHERS WHO OPEN DOORS

Teachers, of course, have for generations opened doors for students. Robert Ruddell's original study of Influential Teachers (1981) supports this claim; Ruddell asked sophomores, juniors, and seniors in high school to identify and describe teachers who had been influential in their (the students') academic or personal lives. The students were able to do this in some detail, averaging about three Influential Teachers apiece and writing descriptions that Ruddell and I later analyzed to derive categories of Influential Teacher attributes (Ruddell & Haggard, 1982). Forty-six percent of students' responses indicated "Quality of Instruction" to be most significant in prior teachers' influence on them; the next highest response was [assists in student's] Life Adjustment (21 percent), followed by Personal Characteristics [of the teacher] and Attitude toward Subject (14 percent each), and Understands Learner Potential (5 percent) (Ruddell & Haggard, 1982).

What was most striking in that study was the degree to which students valued high-quality instruction over personal characteristics and other teacher attributes. In the analysis comparing these students' views of Influential Teachers with the teachers' views of themselves (Ruddell & Haggard, 1982), we were further surprised to discover that Influential Teachers' ratings were quite different from the students': Influential Teachers rated Personal Characteristics most frequently (47 percent) as their most prominent attribute and Quality of Instruction relatively low (16 percent). Clearly, these students differentiated teachers more on the basis of what went on in classrooms than on personality and personal characteristics and had strong, positive memories of teachers who demonstrated effective teaching skills. And it does not seem too great a stretch from the study of Influential Teachers to suggest that from students' connection with such teachers, students begin making decisions to become physicians, athletes, merchants, actors, teachers, scientists, dancers, attorneys, accountants, historians, poets, psychologists, singers, and such.

OPENING DOORS TO LIFELONG LEARNING

One of the attributes of mentors and influential teachers is that they transform students from people who "study math" (or any other subject) to people who *"Do math"* (or any other subject), and Doing math or science or literature or football means one reads and writes in that area for the rest of his or her life, regardless of whether that lifelong involvement is part of a career choice. That is what this chapter is about: turning students into avid learners and lifelong readers and writers in your (and other) subject areas and engaging their interest and energy for independent learning that goes well beyond the confines of classroom and school walls.

Throughout this text, we have discussed instructional strategies and activities for involving students actively in content learning. In this chapter, we will look at other ways for teachers to open doors and to encourage students to become lifelong readers and writers.

FINDING OUT ABOUT READERS AND WRITERS

One of the most important things you can do is find out about your students as readers and writers. I'm talking here not about knowledge of students' basic reading and writing abilities, but students' literacy attitudes, interests, and proclivities as well. And I'm suggesting that every teacher needs to get this information.

"Why," you ask, "do I, the physical education [music, art, science, math, vocational education] teacher, need to know about my students' reading and writing interests, attitudes and habits?" The answer is, because you cannot really understand your students, individually or as a group, until you have a sense of how they view themselves; so much of school is tied to literacy that students' self-esteem at school is often rooted in their literacy, behaviors, and interests. Gaining access to students' literacy attitudes, interests, and habits gives you real insight into their attitude toward your subject area, other subject areas, school in general, and themselves as learners. This understanding is critical to our goal of developing lifelong readers and writers; we need to know what kind of readers and writers students are now, how they view themselves as readers, writers and learners, and what interests they have. Such knowledge, in turn, allows us to connect students with the right book or right idea and encourage their continued interest, involvement, and participation in learning.

QUESTIONNAIRES

Questionnaires are useful instruments for finding out about students; they are generally nonthreatening and may be used at various times throughout the year. Recall (or go back and look at) the reading and writing questionnaires that were introduced in Chapter 7. These questionnaires reveal students' literacy attitudes, interests, and behaviors and are open-ended enough to allow widely diverse responses. Whether you decide to use them early in the year or semester (as "ice breakers," as mentioned in Chapter 7) or later, be sure you emphasize to students that the questionnaire has no bearing on grades. You may want to consider letting students choose whether to sign the questionnaire or respond anonymously; signed responses will give you individualized information, and anonymous ones will give you a sense of group attitudes, interests, and habits.

The questionnaire is intended to give you an overview of how students view their own literacy abilities, how they see school literacy, and the kind of reading and writing they do independently and of their own choice. It may be just as revealing to do this without knowing specifically who thinks what as it is to have identities divulged. On the other hand, you may want detailed information about each student. Use your judgment in deciding which you wish to do.

Feel free also to adapt the questionnaire to your own subject area and the area of student interests and attitudes that are important to you. I may not have included questions that you'd like to have asked, or I may have asked questions that you do not consider useful. Note particularly items 6 and 7 on each questionnaire. These are intended to tap resources and ideas students have that may be incorporated into class content and materials options. Avid readers and writers may contribute especially good suggestions here.

These certainly are not the only questionnaires available for surveying students' reading and writing habits, although I like them because they're short and sweet and they get at important attitudes, interests, and habits. Nancie Atwell (1987) includes similar, but slightly longer, open-ended reading and writing questionnaires in her text. Readence, Bean, and Baldwin (1995) recommend the use of the "BJP Middle/ Secondary Reading Attitude Survey" (Baldwin, Johnson, & Peer, 1980), which students respond to anonymously and teachers use to gain an understanding of how students as a group view reading (see Figure 12.1). Readence and his associates assert that reluctant and/or less proficient readers may react negatively to questionnaires that reveal each individual's identity; such students may respond by writing down what they believe the teacher wants rather than what they really feel (p. 190). That can happen, but here again, you may want to give students a choice of putting their name on the questionnaire or not, as they wish.

TALKING TO AND OBSERVING STUDENTS

It's amazing how much information you can get by simply noticing the books and other things students bring to your class each day. Some of this cargo is regulated by where students' lockers are in the building in relationship to your classroom location, but for the most part students carry with them the things that are personally meaningful to them. Pay attention, and you'll see all manner of things (some of which, perhaps, you'd just as soon not see).

A standing, and cardinal, rule of my classroom always was, "Bring some sort of pleasure reading material to my class every day." Possibilities were broad—comic books, magazines, library books, books from home, paperbacks, fiction, nonfiction; limitations were narrow—no nudity and no smut. Students were told that they needed free reading material available in the event that they finished all their work and had class time to fill; a penalty was assessed if students were observed with time on their hands and no book or magazine to read.

The refrain I used was, "You never have nothin' to do" as long as you've got your free reading book in my class. Students who did find themselves without a free reading book were allowed to choose something to read from materials available in the room (after the penalty); they were *not* allowed to go back to their lockers to get their own. Quiet reading time was frequently enjoyed by the entire class for the 5 or 10 minutes before dismissal; on days on which schedule disruption was so intrusive as to destroy any semblance of normalcy—when the whole school's collective attention was on picture day, prom, or the championship game, and sometimes in that week before winter holidays—I used quiet reading time for part or all of a period as a means for calming the crowd, restoring everyone's jangled nerves, and/or as relief from a day of unabated excitement and anticipation.

Granted, I was an English teacher, but it should not be just in English classes that students read something interesting to fill time or as a reward for getting work done. Nor is it only English teachers who occasionally want to let students cool out a bit in

FIGURE 12.1   *The BJP Middle/Secondary Reading Attitude Survey*

Directions: This survey tells you how you feel about reading and books. The survey is not a test, and it is anonymous. It will not affect your grades or progress in school, but it will help your school to create better programs. Answer as honestly as you can by circling the letters which tell how you feel about each statement.

SA = Strongly agree   A = Agree   D = Disagree   SD = Strongly disagree

1.	Library books are dull.	SA A D SD
2.	Reading is a waste of time.	SA A D SD
3.	Reading is one of my hobbies.	SA A D SD
4.	I believe that I am a better reader than most other students in my grade.	SA A D SD
5.	Reading is almost always boring.	SA A D SD
6.	Sometimes I think kids younger than I am read better than I do.	SA A D SD
7.	I enjoy going to the library for books.	SA A D SD
8.	I can read as well as most students who are a year older than I am.	SA A D SD
9.	1 don't have enough time to read books.	SA A D SD
10.	I believe that I am a poor reader.	SA A D SD
11.	I would like to belong to a book club.	SA A D SD
12.	I like to take library books home.	SA A D SD
13.	Teachers want me to read too much.	SA A D SD
14.	You can't learn much from reading.	SA A D SD
15.	Books can help us understand other people.	SA A D SD
16.	I almost always get As and Bs in reading and English.	SA A D SD
17.	I like to have time to read in class.	SA A D SD
18.	Reading gets boring after about ten minutes.	SA A D SD
19.	Sometimes I get bad grades in reading and English.	SA A D SD
20.	I like to read before I go to bed.	SA A D SD

60–80 = Good
40–59 = Fair
20–39 = Poor

Scoring: The positive items are 3, 4, 7, 8, 11, 12, 15, 16, 17, 20. Give four points for an SA, three points for an A, two points for a D, and one point for an SD. For the negative items, 1, 2, 5, 6, 9, 10, 13, 14, 18, 19, score four points for an SD, three for a D, two for an A, and one for an SA. Scores can range from 20 to 80.

times of high excitement. I think it would be a good idea for a "bring a free reading book to class every day" standard to be adopted by an entire school to promote independent and pleasure reading.

John Shefelbine (1991) makes the point that good readers are students who read a lot outside of school and outside school assignments. This *practice reading*—just like practice playing the piano or playing basketball—is the key to high-level accomplishment (p. 6). Anderson, Wilson, and Fielding (1988) found that as little as 10 minutes a day of reading outside of school contributed positively to students' reading proficiency and growth and that teachers' attention to and provision for reading that goes beyond class assignments contributed significantly to students' overall reading abilities. It seems very reasonable that the Anderson and associates (1988) findings hold true for writing. If I were teaching now, I'd give students an option; to fill free time in my class, students could: (1) read their free reading book or (2) write in their journal housed in my class.

You may be uncomfortable with the idea of letting students read just any free reading book in your class or write on topics outside your subject area. If you are, fine. Stock up on books and magazines that you *do* approve, or prepare a list of books and other reading material students may read when they have extra time in your class. Prepare a file box of general writing prompts that are appropriate to events and content in your classroom: for example, "What I found hardest about today's class." Use content-based free reading and writing activities to demonstrate to students that reading and writing are pleasurable and esteemed free time activities; if you can impress on them additionally that reading and writing *in your subject area* are pleasurable, so much the better.

When students routinely engage in independent reading and writing in your classroom, your role is to pay attention to what they read and write. Look to see what books and magazines are on their desks; chat with them about their reading and writing. Share books you are reading or have read, and make suggestions and recommendations. You will learn an enormous amount about students as you talk about reading and writing with them and observe them as they read and write independently. You will learn what interests them and what doesn't and see them from a new perspective. In the meantime, your attention, willingness to share your own pleasure reading and writing with them, and knowledge of books, magazines, articles, and ideas that coincide with their interests will validate their reading and writing behaviors. As students see that you value literacy and that you promote and engage in avid reading and writing, they, too, will begin to adopt such attitudes and behaviors.

FINDING OUT ABOUT YOURSELF

We have all faced the old "Do as I say, not as I do" dilemma. We encountered it as youngsters on the receiving end of the admonition (or its equivalent), and have probably handed it out on occasion as adults. As is most generally the case, "Do as I say, not as I do" doesn't get it when we're attempting to encourage our students to become lifelong readers and writers. On the up side, its opposite, "Do as I say *and* as I do," *does* get it. Without a doubt, one of the most powerful things you can do to increase your students' willingness and desire to be independently literate is to be so yourself and to share parts of your literacy with them.

You might want to begin by filling out the reading and writing questionnaires we discussed in the last section; or, you may want simply to spend some time thinking about your reading and writing habits. Would you characterize yourself as a Reader (capital R) or Writer (capital W)? Do you find that you "never have enough time" for reading and writing? Are you a little ashamed to admit you'd rather read Joan Collins or Louis L'Amour than Jane Austen or William Faulkner? Do you have a file of poems and other writing stuck way back in a drawer that you pull out and read occasionally (or haven't read in a long, long time)? When you saw the poem "Invitation" at the beginning of this chapter, did you recognize it immediately as Shel Silverstein whom-you-love-and-have-read-over-and-over-and-over, and you've read *Light in the Attic* (1981), *The Giving Tree* (1964), and *Uncle Shelby's ABZ Book* (1961)? These, and many other questions, may be asked as you explore your own literacy. The answers you get should give you new insights about yourself and some ideas about how you can influence your students' literacy.

Donald Graves talks about this in his book, *Discover Your Own Literacy* (1990). He believes that before we, as teachers, can begin to influence and affect students' literacy, our own literacy must be addressed. He states, "Professionals are people who make decisions. Literate professionals make decisions about their own literacy and of the [students] they teach" (p. 15). He then sets forth a plan that teachers may follow to become readers and writers from any starting point.

BECOMING A WRITER

Graves recommends that to become a writer, one should commit a daily 10-minute period, situated to coincide with his or her own individual schedule and biorhythms, to writing. The purpose here is to write about familiar things—thoughts you've had, events and scenes you've observed, ideas you want to consider. He recommends the following guidelines (p. 24):

1. Write about what you know.
2. Write with details; sketch rapidly.
3. Don't revise in early drafts.
4. Experiment, but be yourself.

To which I add:

5. Write with whatever medium you like—pencil, pen, typewriter, computer—rather than whatever medium you believe you "should" use.
6. Find a writing place or places you like and write there.

Graves continues to advise: (1) write daily (recall Joe Bob Briggs's "Write every day. Write every day. Write every day. That is all there is." from the end of Chapter 6); (2) keep lists of ideas, details, and feelings that you may want to use in your writing; (3) be playful and unabashed by beliefs that "writing is serious business;" and (4) find some readers. Graves concludes that two of these 10-minute periods a day for two weeks will launch anyone into becoming a writer.

I believe him. I find that the more I write, the more productive I become; further, I find that a frequent, consistent writing schedule helps me "find the groove" in which I write with ease, fluency, and a feeling that comes close to exhilaration (Ruddell, 1991). Also, I have learned to follow my own writing needs and instincts. Winston Churchill dictated to his secretaries late at night (between 11:00 P.M. and 4:00 A.M.) prodigious volumes of books and speeches, pacing back and forth in his study at Chartwell, and working from texts and notes on a stand-up Disraeli desk (Manchester, 1988). All of this supposedly occurred with Churchill stark naked and the study room heated to body temperature by furnace and fireplace, while his secretaries sweltered (Curator, Chartwell museum, 1990, personal communication). Charmed though I am by the eccentricity of this arrangement, I couldn't do it—not any of it.

However, I have my own idiosyncrasies. I arrange my desk in a certain way, begin each writing session with a specific routine and plan, and have my own system for maintaining and locating my working informational sources. (The "system" consists of piling each source on my desk as I use it and then locating it later.) Since I work with others who write professionally, I've had opportunity to note that they, too, have highly individualistic writing routines, preferences, quirks, styles, and approaches. We all, in fact, maintain very different writing routines and organizational styles—it's a "You say 'tomato' and I say 'tomahto' " kind of thing. Graves's point is (and I concur), to become a writer, find your own pace, style, routines, and preferences, and follow those.

BECOMING A READER

The process of becoming a reader is parallel to that for becoming a writer. All you need to do is read. You need to commit to reading time and then find the things you wish to fill that time. Graves (1990) recommends that you *not* feel constrained by any of the "myths" about reading, including those suggesting that you should be reading the classics, or professional journals, or "really difficult" text, or that you should not read popular fiction and nonfiction, children's books, or enjoyable literature (p. 41).

I've been a consumer of books since before I learned to read, so this part has always been easy for me. When I began teaching, I decided that a standing, and cardinal, rule for myself would be, "Always read from the library your students read from" (not good grammar, but good advice). And my first year of teaching (sixth grade) offered me the opportunity to go back and read some of the books I'd read as a youngster. My very first book that very first year was *Caddie Woodlawn* (Brink, 1935); I went on to read *My Side of the Mountain* (George, 1959), *Big Red* (Kjelgaard, 1945), *Up a Road Slowly* (Hunt, 1966), and many, many others. When I began teaching high school, I rediscovered *A Tree Grows in Brooklyn* (Smith, 1943), and Mazo de la Roche's Jalna series (1944); I discovered *The Outsiders* (Hinton, 1967), *Mrs. Mike* (Freedman & Freedman, 1965), LeCarré's *The Spy Who Came in from the Cold* (1963), and, of course, Paul Zindel. Sadly, our most recent research indicates that teachers—even English teachers—are often unfamiliar with the books that preadolescents and adolescents like to read (Applebee, 1992; Krickeberg, 1996; Samuels, 1982). In a national survey of English teachers, Sandra Krickeberg found that "teachers have personally read very few notable young adult novels" (1996, p. 2); further, she found that teachers believe such novels are appropriate only for 9th and 10th grade average and below average students. Krickeberg concludes, "Young adult literature presents realistic portrayals of adolescents and topics relevant to their lives. Teachers' lack of knowledge about young adult literature appears to limit its inclusion in literature classes" (p. 2). I would add that this lack of knowledge about what kids are reading not only limits the possibilities for literature study but also limits severely teachers' knowledge about the kids themselves, and renders impossible the goal of developing lifelong readers and writers. I recommend you consider rediscovering some old favorites or discovering other books from the library your students use. It's an easy, interesting way to become a reader, and it's great fun.

MY PARTIAL LIST OF GOOD AUTHORS

You may want to look for books by some of the authors I've read over the years (see Figure 12.2). Undoubtedly, you will have to find some of these authors' books in the library rather than the bookstore because many of them are "golden oldies."

If reading from one of these lists or a school or public library doesn't appeal to you, find whatever does—bestsellers, books around the house, newspapers, magazines, how-to books, and so on—and read, even if it is for 10 minutes a day.

CLASSROOM CLIMATES FOR LITERACY

As you go about the business of finding out about yourself, look around classrooms and begin thinking about how classroom environments encourage or discourage literacy. It doesn't take much to create a literate environment. You need books; to get them, you can join paperback book clubs, subscribe to magazines relevant to your subject area, eke out as much as you can from your yearly budget to buy books, accept offers of giveaways from the librarian, or bring books and magazines from home. You need bookshelves, bookstands, writing folders, journal storage space, and shelves; for these, you may need to beg, borrow, and build whatever you can, scavenge from storage rooms, or consider joining a cut-rate office supply outlet. You need time; all this requires is that you allocate reading and writing time each day, use a variation of mandated free reading and writing options in your class ("You never have nothin' to do"), and talk about books and literacy between classes when students cluster around and want to talk.

Consider also how you can make pleasurable reading and writing central to your classroom curriculum. As you read and become acquainted with interesting trade books, find ways to incorporate parts or whole books, fiction and nonfiction alike, into the major materials and resources you use with a given unit. *Look* for opportunities for students to write about how their lives and experiences intersect with classroom content. Interesting, vital materials and ideas for teaching content in all subject areas abound. Use them. Learning does not have to be drudgery; find and use the materials that make learning exciting.

FIGURE 12.2   *Selected List of Interesting Authors*

Bess Streeter Aldrich	Kay Gibbons	Chaim Potok
Harriet Arnow	Janice Holt Giles	Conrad Richtor
Margaret Atwood	Gael Green	Harold Robbins
Jean Auel	Allan Gurganus	Tom Robbins
James Baldwin	Victoria Holt	Kenneth Roberts
Maeve Binchy	John Irving	Rafael Sabatini
Barbara Taylor Bradford	Susan Isaacs	Helen Hoover Santmyer
Gwen Bristow	Erica Jong	Dorothy Sayers
Rita Mae Brown	Ken Kesey	Anya Seton
Taylor Caldwell	Francis Parkinson Keyes	Sidney Sheldon
Bebe Moore Campbell	Judith Krantz	Anne Rivers Siddons
Truman Capote	Anne LaMott	Betty Smith
James Carroll	John LeCarré	John Steinbeck
Tom Clancy	Harper Lee	Mary Stewart
Arthur C. Clarke	Robert Ludlum	William Styron
James Clavell	Alistair MacLean	Jacqueline Susann
Pat Conroy	William Manchester	Amy Tan
Annie Dillard	Gabriel García Márquez	Trevanian
Ivan Doig	Armistead Maupin	Ann Tyler
Daphne DuMaurier	Colleen McCollough	Leon Uris
Ann Fairbairn	Helen McInnes	Alice Walker
Howard Fast	Larry McMurtry	Morris West
Edna Ferber	James Michener	Phyllis Whitney
Ken Follett	Farley Mowat	Robert Wilder
Fredrick Forsythe	Gordon Parks	Herman Wouk
Marilyn French	Rosamunde Pilcher	

READING AND WRITING WITH STUDENTS

READING WITH STUDENTS

Sustained Silent Reading (SSR) (McCracken, 1971) is probably the most widespread approach for encouraging reading in classrooms. SSR is a time when everyone in the classroom reads (teacher included), and everyone reads a book or magazine of his or her own choice (a *Newsweek* "Buzzwords" column once reported that students have dubbed SSR "Sit down, Shut up and Read"! [Zeman, 1991]). SSR periods can be anywhere from 5 to 15 minutes long, although most people use 10 or 15 minutes. Central to SSR is that the time is spent reading for pleasure; textbook reading, homework from or for other classes, and book report requirements for SSR books are all not allowed.

Getting started with SSR requires some planning and thinking. You will need first to explain the activity to students (many of them will be experienced SSR-ers from elementary school) and identify policies and procedures. Decide how many minutes make sense for your students; to begin, it's usually a good idea to underestimate, rather than overestimate, time. (You can always add minutes gradually to work up to an ideal time.) Decide what will signal start and stop time and other "rules of the road"—what reading matter is permissible and what is not, what bonus will be given for good performance and what penalty for poor performance (pluses and minuses, points, etc.), and other details.

In my classroom, I allowed students to use their free reading material for SSR (applying the same possibilities and limitations mentioned earlier in the chapter) and used the tardy bell as signal for reading to begin; I used 15-minute SSR periods and gave the signal when to stop. I awarded grades for SSR: *A* if you did it, *F* if you didn't. It only took about 3 days for kids who'd rarely seen an A on anything to begin collecting them routinely. My directions were, "During SSR, you must read; if you are not reading, you must at least be turning pages and passing your eyes over print. Neither talking nor sleeping counts as SSR." I spent a minute or two observing as students settled into reading and then began reading my book. I was able to monitor student participation quite nicely by looking up occasionally and sweeping the room with my eyes. (Pin-drop quiet rooms, however, require very little monitoring.)

In some districts, whole schools take time out for SSR every school day; during school-wide SSR, everyone reads (students, teachers, the principal, the janitor, the secretaries, etc.), and special accommodations are made for visitors arriving at the school during that time. Jim Trelease (1989) describes the turnaround brought about in a middle school of 400 students in Boston by a principal who instituted SSR, among other new activities, as part of a campaign to improve students' academic performance. In this school, SSR was done the last 10 minutes of every school day, and every teacher in the building was assigned to participate with a group of students. Initially viewed with skepticism and some resentment by some teachers, whole-school SSR became quite successful. Trelease describes the effect:

> Within a year, [the principal's] critics had become supporters and the school was relishing the quiet time that ended the day. The books that had been started during SSR were often still being read by students filing out to buses—in stark contrast to former dismissal scenes that bordered on chaos (p. 15).

I *really* like the idea of teachers reading with classes. In your classroom, you may not want to do it every day as I did. Try two or three times a week, always on the same schedule; or alternate SSR with journal writing or some other activity. You may wish to encourage school-wide adoption of SSR. The main thing is to do it—to read. You'll be surprised at how interested students are in what you're reading; you may also be surprised to find that students begin listening to your recommendations for books more attentively or even begin asking you to suggest good books to read. If you have an avocation or hobby, bring something to read that reflects it; let kids see a side of you they don't know about. All of this has real impact on students. Through such activities, you become a model of literate behavior, and you develop bonds with students that otherwise could not be.

READING TO STUDENTS

Reading to students is just as important as reading with them. Jim Trelease, in his *The New Read-Aloud Handbook* (1989), makes a strong case for both. According to Trelease, reading aloud to students does ". . . what the great art schools have always done: [provide] 'life' models from which to draw" (p. 15).

I read to my university students every class period, and you should see the faces of my "Reading and Writing across the Curriculum" class students the very first time I do. They're shocked, and a little embarrassed, by a grown woman standing there in front of other grown men and women reading Dave Barry's hilarious "How to Make a Board" (1982). I read everything to them—excerpts from favorite books, columns from newspapers and magazines, Shel Silverstein, children's books, adolescent literature, cookbooks, new discoveries and golden oldies, my very favorite childhood book (*Flibberty Gibbet and the Key Keeper*), and on and on.

I want to prove the point that no one ever gets too old to enjoy being read to, and make the point that my students should read to their middle school, junior high, and high school students, too. The first point always gets proven (and I hope the other point gets made). By the third or fourth week, students see me reach for my reading material and I see them begin to put things away and *arrange* themselves for the reading. I'm always surprised by the number of full-grown adults who close their eyes to listen to me read.

Read to your students. Read what *you* like, and they'll like it too. I once charmed a very difficult freshman English class (right after lunch, 24 boys and 2 girls, de facto low-ability/difficult student group) into cooperative, productive behavior by reading *They Call Me Mr. 500* by Andy Granatelli (1970) to them for the first 15 minutes of class every day. The class came to me straight from after-lunch playground activity and exuberance and could not seem to make the transition to academic tasks successfully; we needed something to calm the exuberance and turn their attention to school work. The book did it. Thus it was not "wasted time." I found we accomplished more in the remaining 40 minutes after the reading than we could in the 55 minutes without the transition activity.

Very shortly after I began reading to the students, an interesting thing happened. I had the only copy of the book owned by our library, but I looked up one day to see Larry Baldwin (one of the most difficult students in this very difficult class) reading along with me in what was clearly a library-owned copy of the book. Since I was reading out of the one from the school library, I knew that Larry had made the effort to go to the neighborhood public library to find the book. He probably had to *get* a library card in order to get that book. As far as I'm concerned, that's success.

I am always astonished at what reading to students accomplishes. With my adult students over the years, I've seen some amazing things on the last night of class when they read to one another: A man *sang*, a cappella, a song that was part of the novel of Appalachia he was sharing with us; another young man read one of John F. Kennedy's speeches (7 or 10 minutes long) completely in JFK dialect; and yet another student fought back tears repeatedly, *but kept on going*, as she read to us from a novel paralleling the life of her immigrant grandmother.

Younger students, junior high and senior high reluctant readers and kids truly "at risk" have told me many times that mine was the first class during which they'd read a book "all the way through." Maybe that's the only complete book they'll ever read. But maybe not. Maybe from that experience they'll be willing to try another, and then another. If they're read to in every class, if the physical education teacher and the mathematics teacher, and the social studies teacher, and music teacher all periodically and consistently read newspaper stories and articles or book excerpts and poems to them, how much more powerful that would be. How much more likely it would be that we create a nation in which ". . . 90 percent of the children can read and willingly choose to do so" (Trelease, 1989, p. 18), and I might add, a nation where "90 percent of the adults can read and willingly choose to do so."

WRITING WITH STUDENTS

Just as we can implement SSR, so can we have periods of sustained writing. I've known of teachers and schools to refer to Sustained Silent Writing (SSW). With the growth of the process writing movement, the often-found presence of journals and learning logs in middle and junior/senior high classrooms, writing workshop, and the ideals of writing across the curriculum, students are much more commonly today writing in many subject area classes than they were even a few years ago.

Nancie Atwell (1987) emphasizes the importance of teachers writing with students to demonstrate the seriousness of the writing workshop and to provide a model for students to emulate. She describes her way of doing this after she's given students all the rules of the writing workshop:

> Then I sit down at an empty student desk—so kids can clearly see what I'm doing—with my favorite white paper and my favorite Flair pen. I label my manuscript DRAFT #1, put my head down, and start writing one of the stories I'd considered in the mini-lesson. I don't look up. I'm not watching to see who's writing and who isn't. I'm busy, I mean business, and my posture demonstrates that I'm expecting everyone else will become a writer and join me. And they do. After ten minutes or so, when I finally look up from my own writing, everyone is writing. Always (p. 84).

Atwell goes on to describe how she then quietly begins moving among students to confer with them as needed. This model, this teacher writing, is just as powerful as the teacher reading with and to students. It projects a very strong message that says (among other things), "Writing is important. I am a writer, and here is how I begin. You can be a writer, too."

You need not write with your students in exactly the way Atwell does, but you can find many ways to write. As your students are working with their partners to write lab reports, you can be writing your own report to share and compare with students'. While students write end-of-class summaries of how they worked through the day's lesson on probability, you can write a summary of your successes and frustrations as you taught the lesson. Your writing can and should be shared with students.

WRITING TO STUDENTS

One of the most effective vehicles for writing to students is their journals. Many teachers and students like the letter format for corresponding back and forth, commenting on ideas in each other's previous letters, and as a way of conveying important information to one another (Atwell, 1987). Graves (1990) recommends this as a way to share responses to books and other reading students and teachers do. He comments on how dramatically the writing changes when students quit writing neutral accounts and summaries of their books and begin writing about their responses to the books. He marvels further over how dialogue is often sustained for several weeks about a single subject (p. 56).

This kind of writing is substantially different from the notes in the margin and other notes we frequently write to students to alert them to things that are missing or wrong or need fixing in their work. Journal letters are exchanges between individuals writing as equals. They become another powerful tool for making literacy natural, easy, and self-sustaining.

RESOURCES FOR DEVELOPING LIFELONG READERS AND WRITERS

One of the first issues to be addressed as you decide how independent reading and writing will be used in your class is what and where are the resources available to support your decision to do so. Specifically, you will want to know where you can go to locate the kind of books kids really like to read and where you can get ideas for encouraging students' writing. There are many, many resources available to you.

RESOURCES FOR INDEPENDENT READING—FINDING GOOD BOOKS

SCHOOL LIBRARIANS
The very first resource I can think of for finding books is your school librarian. School librarians know and love books; all too often, however, they are viewed as catalogers and library monitors rather than what they really are—veritable storehouses of knowledge about books and what kids like, what's new, what's old and still usable, what books would be perfect to use with your unit on "transitions," and a host of other important areas. Working with the librarian, you can get classroom sets of books on a given topic to be kept in your room during a unit of study, make arrangements for bringing or sending your students to the library during class periods, gain access to computer files and book lists and other resources, and accomplish any number of useful goals.

I always made a point to make friends with my school librarian very early in the academic year and found my success rate over the years to be 100 percent. To a person, they were cooperative, delighted to offer services and have the opportunity to be a resource to students, willing to try various joint ventures and plans for accommodating my and the students' needs, and utterly generous with their time and knowledge.

STUDENTS

Another major resource for books is the students themselves. Students know what books they like and don't like, and they will tell you. Furthermore, they are quite willing to hold onto their own beliefs and opinions, even when those do not coincide with adults' beliefs and opinions. In the early 1970s, when *The Exorcist* (Blatty, 1971) hit the bestseller lists and details from the movie production became common fodder for gossip columns, this lengthy book (about 2" thick in paperback) became the reading rage in high schools. Never mind that teachers didn't consider the book appropriate, never mind that it was anything but "young adult" fare, and never mind that it was not particularly easy reading—kids read it (many of them the very students everyone believed to be "low," "slow," or "below" readers).

Adolescent readers are not at all averse to reading the complete works of any given author. Stephen King books enjoy this status, as do Paul Zindel's, S. E. Hinton's, Judy Blume's, and others. Adolescents also like book series; many of you may be graduates of the *Dune* series (Herbert, 1965), the *Narnia Chronicles*, or even the old perennials Nancy Drew and the Hardy Boys. Lately, the *Babysitter's Club* series has been highly popular with middle school girls.

Following, in Figures 12.3. and 12.4, are lists of favorite books recently voted on by students in middle school and high school; no claim is made here that these lists are nationally representative of students' interests—they are simply lists I was privy to. They probably do, however, resemble lists collected from other students in other schools and other geographical areas. Please note the position of *The Outsiders* on the high school list; for 10 years, this book was my number-one no-fail-book-I-could-give-to-the-most-reluctant-reader-I-had. It has an amazingly timeless appeal for adolescents.

PUBLISHED BOOK LISTS

There are any number of excellent book recommendation lists available for assisting you in selecting titles for your own reading, gathering books for in-class use, or making suggestions to students. Most of these are annotated or provide discussion of some type about the content and quality of the books appearing on the list. They are in addition to standard review sources such as the American Library Association *Booklist* and the *Hornbook* magazine and major newspaper review sections (e.g., *The New York Times*, *The Christian Science Monitor*, and others). The following book lists and reviews are highly useful resources:

Abrahamson, R. F., & Carter, B. (Eds.) (1988). *Books for You: A Booklist for Senior High Students*. Champaign, IL: NCTE.

Carlsen, G. R. (1980). *Books and the Teenage Reader* (2nd ed.). New York: Harper & Row.

Davis, J. E., & Davis, H. K. (Eds.) (1988). *Your Reading: A Booklist for Junior High and Middle School Students* (7th ed.). Champaign, IL: NCTE.

Davis, J. E., & Davis, H. K. (Eds.) (Spring 1989). Books for the Junior High Years. Special edition of *Focus*, 1–115. Champaign, IL: NCTE.

FIGURE 12.3   *Favorite Books—High School*

Favorite Books—High School (voted on by entire school)
1. S. E. Hinton, *The Outsiders*
2. Stephen King, *Pet Sematary*
3. Stephen King, *Christine*
4. V. C. Andrews, *Flowers in the Attic*
5. Stephen King, *Cujo*
6. Judy Blume, *Tiger Eyes*
7. Stephen King, *The Shining*
8. Lois Duncan, *I Know What You Did Last Summer*
9. Stephen King, *Night Shift*
10. Stephen King, *Dead Zone*
11. V. C. Andrews, *Heaven*
12. S. E. Hinton, *Tex*
13. Douglas Adams, *The Hitchhiker's Guide to the Galaxy*
14. Jean Auel, *Clan of the Cave Bear*
15. Stephen King, *Salem's Lot*
16. Stephen King, *Firestarter*
17. V. C. Andrews, *My Sweet Audrina*
18. Paul Zindel, *The Pigman*
19. Jay Bennett, *The Executioner*
20. Norma Fox Mazer, *Summer Girls, Love Boys*
21. S. E. Hinton, *Rumblefish*
22. V. C. Andrews, *If There Be Thorns*
23. Stephen King, *Carrie*
24. Stephen King, *The Stand*
25. Norma Fox Mazer, *Up in Seth's Room*

Donelson, K., & Nilsonk, A. P. (1985). *Literature for Today's Young Adults* (2nd ed.). Glenview, IL: Scott, Foresman.

IRA Committee on Literature for Adolescents (1990). Young Adults' Choices. *Journal of Reading, 34,* 203–209. (New book popularity polled from representative U.S. student samples. Published annually in the *Journal of Adolescent and Adult Literacy* (formerly the *Journal of Reading.*)

Matthews, D. (Ed.) (1988). *High Interest–Easy Reading for Junior and Senior High School Students.* Champaign, IL: NCTE.

Pugh, S., & Garcia, J. (1990). Portraits in Black: Establishing African American Identity Through Nonfiction Books. *Journal of Reading, 34,* 20–25.

Reed, A. J. S. (1988). *Comics to Classics: A Parent's Guide to Books for Teens and Preteens.* Newark, DE: IRA.

Schon, I. (1990). Recent Good and Bad Books about Hispanics. *Journal of Reading, 34,* 76–78.

FIGURE 12.4   *Favorite Books—Middle School*

Favorite Books—Middle School (voted on by selected English classes numbering 319 students)

1.   Theodore Taylor, *The Cay*
2.   Wilson Rawls, *Where the Red Fern Grows*
3.   Natalie Babbitt, *Tuck Everlasting*
4. (Tie) Robert N. Peck, *A Day No Pigs Would Die*
           L. M. Montgomery, *Anne of Green Gables*
6.   Lynne R. Banks, *Indian in the Cupboard*
7. (Tie) Ann M. Martin, *The Babysitter's Club*
           Robert O'Brien, *Mrs. Frisby and the Rats of NIMH*
           Stephen King, *Pet Sematary*
           Frances Hodgson Burnette, *The Secret Garden*
12. (Tie) Katherine Paterson, *Bridge to Terabithia*
           Stephen King, *Misery*
           Stephen King, *It*
15.   Zilpha Keatley Snyder, *The Egypt Game*
16. (Tie) Vincent B. Jackson & Dick Schapp, *Bo Knows–Bo*
           C. S. Lewis, *The Lion, the Witch and the Wardrobe*
           Jack London, *White Fang*
19. (Tie) Gary Paulsen, *Hatchet*
           Ann McGovern, *Robin Hood, Prince of Thieves*
21. (Tie) Scott O'Dell, *Island of the Blue Dolphins*
           Madeleine L'Engle, *A Wrinkle in Time*
           Sid Fleischman, *Whipping Boy*
24.   R. L. Stine, *The Boyfriend*
25. (Tie) Judy Blume, *Are You There, God? It's Me, Margaret*
           Louis Schar, *There's a Boy in the Girls' Bathroom*
           Paula Fox, *Slave Dancer*
           Franklin Dixon, *The Hardy Boys*
           Roald Dahl, *James and the Giant Peach*

Trelease, J. (1989). *The New Read-Aloud Handbook*. New York: Penguin.
Walker, E. (Ed.) (1988). *Book Bait: Detailed Notes on Adult Books Popular with Young People* (4th ed.). Chicago: ALA.

RESOURCES FOR INDEPENDENT WRITING—GETTING GOOD IDEAS

Good ideas for writing generally are ideas growing from our own experiences. Stimulating students' writing (and your own) is simply a matter of triggering remembrances or exploring current occurrences that are interesting and important in our daily lives. So, a major source you can use is your own ideas about linkages between community, national, world, and global events and the lives of your students and/or yourself. Look around you, read the newspaper, watch CNN, and choose one event; then develop a question that allows students to link that event with their own lives, a memory, or something they know. Their writing may explore that issue, draw and explain the parallel, or discuss insights revealed by the analogy.

Students' lives, and your own, are marvelous resources for writing. Donald Graves emphasizes the value of daily events and observations as sources for writing (1990). These may be "little" events—savoring morning solitude or experiencing the buoyancy and exertion of a good swim—or they may be larger—feelings about community or world events, enumerations of lifetime goals, or speculation about how one's knowledge in an academic discipline fits into the Grand Scheme of Things. The stuff of daily living is very much an appropriate topic for writing.

Memory, especially, can be the source for much writing. David Fisher and Patty Brown (1990) provide the title annotation, "Use your recollections of the past to bring pleasure to the present" in *The Book of Memories*. In this book, Fisher and Brown and their colleagues ask questions and recommend the following:

> Read the question or suggestion, then just close your eyes and think about it. The idea is not just to remember something, but to savor that memory, and enjoy the feeling that it provokes—the way something looked, or smelled, or sounded, the way something felt in your hand (p. 8).

From these vivid recollections, interesting and exciting writing can occur. The questions in *The Book of Memories* make perfect writing prompts; a few are listed below:

What was your favorite picture of yourself as a child?

What was the hardest you ever laughed?

What was the biggest or ugliest bug you ever tried to kill?

What was your most memorable birthday party?

Who taught you to read?

Whose house did you and your friends usually go to to play?

What was the best time you had being late?

What was the most embarrassed you've ever been on a date?

What were some of the cafeteria classics in grade school?

You get the idea. There are many more in the book, and reading them makes you think of others. There's no reason why questions such as these, those that tap areas of common experience and nostalgia, cannot be slanted toward subject area experiences. Below are some topics I created for activating students' memories surrounding content learning and subject area classes:

What was your moment of greatest exhilaration in a physical education class?

What was the biggest breakthrough you ever made in math?

What was your greatest project flop in home economics [or wood/metal shop] class?

What piece of art or music took your breath away?

Describe the sights, sounds, and smells of the science lab.

How does clay feel in your hands?

How do you know when you've hit the tennis ball just right?

What unit in social studies touched your life the most?

What literary character would you most like to have as a friend?

What science discovery had (or has) the greatest impact on your life?

Finally, you may find videotaped or World Wide Web material and information to be a useful resource for writing ideas. With the availability of many high-quality full-length movies and television programs today and the written and visual information on the Web, video and other media resources can and should be used to stimulate writing or serve to mediate reading and writing. Many of the books students read independently, and many fiction and nonfiction books highly useful with thematic and other units of study, are also available in movie or documentary form on videotape. By all means, use these liberally. Students who might not be able to read the original text gain access to ideas and experiences from video showings; students who wouldn't be caught reading a book at any cost often spend hours surfing the net, and they are often able to respond to new ideas in writing.

SOME CONCLUDING THOUGHTS ABOUT DEVELOPING LIFELONG READERS AND WRITERS

I am absolutely convinced of the importance of working to create lifelong readers and writers. It does us no good to teach students how to read and write if they choose not to, and it does us no good to promote learning in subject disciplines if students are unable to further that learning independently. We *know* how to make students good readers and writers: Give them lots and lots and *lots* of practice reading and writing. We also know that English teachers cannot be expected to assume sole responsibility for providing this practice. The only powerful message comes when *all* middle school and junior/senior high teachers own part of that responsibility and when all teachers willingly become openers-of-doors.

In the course of counting ballots for the middle school favorite book voting reported earlier in the chapter, I came across this response: "I haven't read any book for the past 12 years. So, I can't list any." Coming from a student who is, himself, 12, or 13, or 14 years old, this is, I think, an eloquent and poignant reminder of the result when students *don't* choose to become lifelong readers and writers. We as teachers have, at the very least, the important responsibility of providing encouragement, time and opportunity—of opening the door—for students to choose otherwise. Wayne Otto states, "Giving students time to be with books sets up a context where it's not just the books that are valued, it's the personal and social interactions with books that count" (p. 214). When students come to value their "time with books" and writing time, then we can rest assured that they will continue to read, write, and learn well after they leave our classrooms and schools. That's the point, after all.

D O U B L E   E N T R Y   J O U R N A L

_____

_____

_____

_____

_____

_____

Go back to the prereading list of reading and writing that you considered enjoyable. List ways you could include that type of reading and writing in your curriculum. How and when could "free" reading and writing (SSR/SSW) occur in your classroom? Share your thinking with the group.

REFERENCES

SOURCES CITED

Abrahamson, R. F., & Carter, B. (Eds.) (1988). *Books for you: A booklist for senior high students.* Champaign, IL: NCTE.

Anderson, R. C., Wilson, P. T., & Fielding, L. G. (1988). Growth in reading and how children spend their time out of school. *Reading Research Quality, 23,* 285–303.

Applebee, A. N. (1992). Stability and change in the high school cannon. *English Journal, 81*(5), 27–32.

Applebee, A. N., Langer, J. A., & Mullis, I. V. S. (1988). *Who reads best? Factors related to reading achievement in grades 3, 7, and 11.* Princeton, NJ: ETS.

Atwell, N. (1987). *In the middle: Writing, reading, and learning with adolescents.* Portsmouth, NH: Heinemann.

Baldwin, R. S., Johnson, D. D., & Peer, G. G. (1980). *BJP middle/secondary reading attitude survey.* Bookmatch. Tulsa, OK: Educational Development Corporation.

Carlsen, G. R. (1980). *Books and the teenage reader* (2nd ed.). New York: Harper & Row.

Davis, J. E., & Davis, H. K. (Eds.) (1988). *Your reading: A booklist for junior high and middle school students* (7th ed.). Champaign, IL: NCTE.

Davis, J. E., & Davis, H. K. (Eds.) (Spring 1989). Books for the junior high years. *Focus,* 1–115.

Donelson, K., & Nilsonk, A. P. (1985). *Literature for today's young adults* (2nd ed.). Glenview, IL: Scott, Foresman.

Fisher, D., & Brown, P. (1990). *The book of memories.* New York: Putnam.

Flanders, N. (1970). *Analyzing teacher behavior.* Reading, MA: Addison-Wesley.

Goodlad, J. I. (1984). *A place called school.* New York: McGraw-Hill.

Graves, D. H. (1990). *Discover your own literacy.* Portsmouth, NH: Heinemann.

IRA Committee on Literature for Adolescents (1990). Young adults' choices. *Journal of Reading, 34,* 203–209.

Krickeberg, S. K. (1996, April). *A national teacher survey on young adult literature.* Paper presented at the meeting of the International Reading Association, New Orleans, LA.

Matthews, D. (Ed.) (1988). *High interest—Easy reading for junior and senior high school students.* Champaign, IL: National Council of Teachers of English.

McCracken, R. A. (1971). Initiating sustained silent reading. *Journal of Reading, 14,* 521–524, 582–583.

Otto, W. (1990). Bernie and me. *Journal of Reading, 34,* 212–215.

Pugh, S., & Garcia, J. (1990). Portraits in black: Establishing African American identity through nonfiction books. *Journal of Reading, 34,* 20–25.

Readence, J. E., Bean, T. W., & Baldwin, R. S. (1995). *Content area literacy: An integrated approach* (5th ed.). Dubuque, IA: Kendall/Hunt.

Reed, A. J. S. (1988). *Comics to classics: A parent's guide to books for teens and preteens.* Newark, DE: International Reading Association.

Ruddell, M. R. (1991, December). *Negotiating ambiguity and risk: Scaffolds for proficient readers and writers.* Paper presented at the meeting of the National Reading Conference. Palm Springs, California.

Ruddell, R. B. (1981, May). *Teacher impact on student achievement: Implications for reading instruction.* Paper presented at the International Reading Association meeting, New Orleans.

Ruddell, R. B. (1983). A study of teacher effectiveness variables of influential teachers. In M. P. Douglass (Ed.), *Reading, the process of creating meaning for senses stimuli.* Forty-seventh yearbook of the Claremont Reading Conference (pp. 57–70). Claremont, CA: Claremont Graduate School.

Ruddell, R. B., & Haggard, M. R. (1982). Influential teachers: Characteristics and classroom performance. In J. A. Niles & L. A. Harris (Eds.), *New inquiries in reading research and instruction.* Thirty-first yearbook of the National Reading Conference (pp. 227–231). Rochester, NY: National Reading Conference.

Samuels, B. G. (1982). A national survey to determine the status of the young adult novel in the secondary school English classroom, grades 7–12. *Dissertation Abstracts International, 43,* 2224A. (University Microfilms No. 82-29347.)

Schon, I. (1990). Recent good and bad books about Hispanics. *Journal of Reading, 34,* 76–78.

Shefelbine, J. (1991). *Encouraging your junior high student to read.* Newark, DE: International Reading Association.

Trelease, J. (1989). *The new read-aloud handbook.* New York: Penguin.

Walker, E. (Ed.) (1988). *Book bait: Detailed notes on adult books popular with young people* (4th ed.). Chicago: American Library Association.

Zeman, N. Bureau Reports (1991, September 9). Buzzwords. *Newsweek,* p. 6.

LITERATURE CITED

Adams, D. (1980, 1989). *The hitchhiker's guide to the galaxy.* New York: Crown.

Andrews, V. C. (1989). *Flowers in the attic.* New York: Pocket Books.

Andrews, V. C. (1989). *Heaven.* New York: Pocket Books.

Andrews, V. C. (1989). *If there be thorns.* New York: Pocket Books.

Andrews, V. C. (1982, 1989). *My sweet Audrina.* New York: Pocket Books.

Auel, J. (1980). *Clan of the cave bear.* New York: Crown.

Babbitt, N. (1975, 1985). *Tuck everlasting.* New York: Sunburst.

Banks, L. R. (1985). *Indian in the cupboard.* New York: Doubleday.

Barry, D. (1982). How to make a board. *New Shelter Magazine.*

Bennett, J. (1990). *The executioner.* New York: Avon.

Blatty, W. P. (1971, 1984). *The exorcist.* New York: Bantam.

Blume, J. (1970). *Are you there, God? It's me, Margaret.* New York: Bradbury Press.

Blume, J. (1981, 1984). *Tiger eyes.* New York: Harlequin.

Brink, C. R. (1935, 1990). *Caddie Woodlawn.* New York: Macmillan.

Burnett, F. H. (1911, 1987). *The secret garden.* New York: New American Library.

Dahl, R. (1962, 1988). *James and the giant peach.* New York: Penguin.

de la Roche, M. (1944). *The building of Jalna.* Boston: Little, Brown.

Dennis, P. (1955). *Auntie Mame.* New York: Book-of-the-Month Club.

Dixon, F. W. (1985). *The Hardy boys.* New York: Simon & Schuster.

Duncan, L. (1973, 1986). *I know what you did last summer.* New York: Pocket Books.

Fleischman, S. (1986). *The whipping boy.* New York: Greenwillow.

Fox, P. (1975). *Slave dancer.* New York: Dell.

Freedman, B., & Freedman, N. (1965, 1984). *Mrs. Mike.* New York: Berkley Books.

George, J. C. (1959). *My side of the mountain.* New York: Dutton.

Granatelli, A. (1969). *They call me Mr. 500.* Chicago: H. Regnery Co.

Herbert, F. (1965). *Dune.* New York: Berkley Books.

Hinton, S. E. (1967). *The outsiders.* New York: Viking.

Hinton, S. E. (1975, 1989). *Rumblefish.* New York: Dell.

Hinton, S. E. (1979, 1989). *Tex.* New York: Dell.

Hunt, I. (1966, 1987). *Up a road slowly.* New York: Berkley Books.

Jackson, V. B., & Schapp, D. (1990). *Bo knows–Bo.* New York: Doubleday.

King, S. (1975, 1990). *Carrie.* New York: Doubleday.

King, S. (1976, 1990). *Salem's lot.* New York: New American Library.

King, S. (1978). *The stand.* New York: Doubleday.

King, S. (1978, 1990). *The shining.* New York: New American Library.

King, S. (1979). *Dead zone.* New York: Viking Penguin.

King, S. (1980). *Firestarter.* New York: Viking Penguin.

King, S. (1981). *Cujo.* New York: Viking Penguin.

King, S. (1983). *Christine.* New York: Viking Penguin.

King, S. (1983). *Pet sematary.* New York: New American Library.

King, S. (1986). *It.* New York: Viking Penguin.

King, S. (1986). *Night shift.* New York: New American Library.

King, S. (1987). *Misery.* New York: Viking Penguin.

Kjelgaard, J. (1945, 1964). *Big red.* New York: Bantam.

LeCarré, J. (1963, 1984). *The spy who came in from the cold.* New York: Bantam.

L'Engle, M. (1962, 1976). *A wrinkle in time.* New York: Dell.

Lewis, C. S. (1951, 1988). *The lion, the witch and the wardrobe.* New York: Macmillan.

London, J. (1985). *White fang.* New York: Penguin.

Manchester, W. (1983). *The last lion, Winston Spencer Churchill: Visions of glory 1974–1932.* New York: Dell.

Manchester, W. (1988). *The last lion, Winston Spencer Churchill: Alone, 1932–1940.* Boston: Little, Brown.

Martin, A. M. (1987–1990). *The babysitter's club.* New York: Scholastic.

Mazer, N. F. (1982). *Summer girls, love boys.* New York: Doubleday.

Mazer, N. F. (1989). *Up in Seth's room.* New York: Dell.

McGovern, A. (1987). *Robin Hood of Sherwood Forest.* New York: Scholastic.

Montgomery, L. M. (1908, 1987). *Anne of Green Gables.* New York: New American Library.

O'Brien, R. (1971, 1986). *Mrs. Frisby and the rats of NIMH.* New York: Macmillan.

O'Dell, S. (1960, 1987). *Island of the blue dolphins.* New York: Dell.

Patrick, D. (1955). *Auntie Mame.* New York: Doubleday.

Patterson, K. (1977, 1987). *Bridge to Terabithia.* New York: Harper & Row.

Paulsen, G. (1988). *Hatchet.* New York: Penguin.

Peck, R. N. (1972, 1979). *A day no pigs would die.* New York: Knopf.

Rawls, W. (1974). *Where the red fern grows.* New York: Bantam.

Schar, L. (1987). *There's a boy in the girls' bathroom.* New York: Knopf.

Silverstein, S. (1961). *Uncle Shelby's ABZ book.* New York: Simon & Schuster.

Silverstein, S. (1964). *The giving tree.* New York: Harper & Row.

Silverstein, S. (1974). *Where the sidewalk ends.* New York: Harper & Row.

Silverstein, S. (1981). *A light in the attic.* New York: Harper & Row.

Smith, B. (1943, 1968). *A tree grows in Brooklyn.* New York: Harper & Row.

Snyder, Z. K. (1967). *The Egypt game.* New York: Atheneum.

Stine, R. L. (1990). *The boyfriend.* New York: Scholastic.

Taylor, T. (1976, 1987). *The cay.* New York: Doubleday.

Zindel, P. (1968, 1983). *The pigman.* New York: Bantam.

LESSON PLANS

Many of the instructional activities I've presented in this text do not lend themselves to extensive displays of alternative lesson plans or examples. This is, in part, because successful use of these activities hinges on what the teacher does or says (e.g., "With your partner, go back to the chapter and find two words you'd like to learn or know more about. Be prepared to tell where you found the words, what you think they mean, and why you think we should learn them."), and what the teacher does or says does not change appreciably from one text or setting to another (e.g., "With a title like that, what do you think this chapter will be about?"). That said, there are alternative lesson applications and ways to combine instructional strategies that you may find useful. A few are presented on the following pages. Beginning with "Dinosaur Days," the lesson plans are the work of my students.

LESSON PLAN   *Combined Semantic Mapping and DRA–Science**

(Alternative to the DR-TA lesson, "Motion," shown in chapter 3)

LESSON OBJECTIVES:

On completion of this lesson, students will:

1. Recognize the distinguishing factors among the concepts of speed, velocity, and acceleration.
2. Be able to apply their growing understanding of rate, speed, velocity, and acceleration in practical situations.

DAY ONE

Step 1   Preparation for Reading

A. *Vocabulary Presentation:* Write the words *speed, velocity,* and *acceleration* in the middle of separate sections on the chalkboard or on separate sheets of butcher paper taped to the wall.

1. Ask students to work with a partner to list as many features, aspects, or elements as they can for each word.
2. After partners are finished, share responses in whole class, listing ideas in any order around each word.
3. Ask students to use the class responses and other ideas they have to construct a semantic map for each word. They may work in partnerships or singly, as they wish.
4. Have a few students share their maps, guiding discussion to find out why they mapped as they did.
5. Ask students to keep and revise their maps as the unit progresses.

B. *Focusing Event:* Say something like the following:

"This week we'll be exploring the concept of motion. We'll go through the chapter in your text in sections, allowing you to spend homework time either doing relevant problems from the "Activities" or "Think and Explain" sections at the end of the chapter or creating your own problems to share with us. Here's your first challenge: You hear two friends arguing; one says Carl Lewis runs at 35km/hr, and the other insists he speeds along at 35km/sec. Who is right? Can they both be?" (Write challenge on the board.)

Step 2   Guided Silent Reading

Purpose-Setting Statement: "Read Section 2.1, 'Motion Is Relative,' and write a brief answer to the Challenge questions I've posed. Be sure you can justify your answers.

---

*My thanks to Judith Barnes for this lesson.

When you're ready, share your ideas with your partner and together list two other examples of both rate and relative motion."

Step 3   Comprehension Development Discussion Questions

A. Does Carl Lewis run at 35km/hr or 35km/sec? How do you know?

B. Can both the answers 35km/hr and 35km/sec be right? Why or why not?

C. What additional samples did you list? Why did you choose them?

D. How can we now define "rate" and "relative motion"? Where might we locate "rate" and "relative motion" on our maps?

Step 2 (repeated)   Guided Silent Reading

Purpose-Setting Question: "In a car race last year, the top driver averaged 100 miles an hour over a 200-mile course. The course looked something like this (draw a course on the board containing both straightaways and curves). On the straightaway, he was clocked at 200 miles per hour. Read Section 2.2, 'Speed'; how might you describe the race in terms of instantaneous and average speed?"

Step 3 (repeated)   Comprehension Development Discussion Questions

A. How might you describe the race in terms of instantaneous and average speed? Explain your logic.

B. How do you determine average speed? What was the driver's average speed? How did you figure it?

C. What are some other examples in which instantaneous and average speed are important?

Step 4   Comprehension Development Discussion Questions

A. By any method you choose, determine your average speed of walking. Be prepared to share your findings with the class tomorrow.

DAY TWO

Step 4 (cont'd.)   Skill Development and Application

B. Have students share the results of their average speed of walking experiments. Discuss similarities and differences in measurement units and outcomes.

Step 5   Extension and Follow-up

A. Have students go back to their maps for "rate" and "speed" and make changes, revisions, and additions as they wish. Share maps and elicit explanations for refinements.

B. Three-minute write.

DAYS THREE AND FOUR

Continue guiding reading and discussion of the two remaining sections, "Velocity" and "Acceleration," by posing problems, asking students to read to solve the problems, sharing explanations, and then revising and updating semantic maps. Have students finish the chapter by a sustained journal write in which they identify: (1) what they already knew about motion, rate, speed, velocity, and acceleration, (2) things they learned about motion, rate, speed, velocity, and acceleration, and (3) things they still don't understand or that are giving them problems.

Additional Extension Activity: Have students work in pairs to describe how they might illustrate the relationships between rate, speed, velocity, and acceleration to a fourth-grade class.

THREE LEVEL GUIDE—BIOLOGY (HOMEOSTASIS)

   I. Read the following statements; then read pp. 419–424 in your text. Put a check
       (✓) beside those statements you find in your reading. The statements may or
       may not be worded exactly as found in the book. Discuss the statements in your
       group, making sure everyone understands the reading, and provide evidence for
       your choices.

   _____   The exchange of materials with the environment involves two general
           problems: (1) maintaining homeostasis, and (2) removing wastes.
   _____   Osmosis, diffusion, and contractile vacuoles are mechanisms for materials exchange in protists.
   _____   Dew is a form of waste removal.
   _____   Grasshoppers excrete nitrogenous wastes in the form of uric acid.
   _____   Ammonia is very toxic and requires dilution in large quantities of water.

  II. Read the following statements. Put a check (✓) beside those statements you
       agree with based on the reading assignment. In discussion, give reasons for your
       choices.

   _____   Unproductive transfer occurs when organisms take in unneeded materials or excrete needed ones.
   _____   Contractile vacuoles and flame cells serve related functions.
   _____   Land animals and land plants have the common need to conserve
           body water.
   _____   Land organisms and water organisms have evolved different ways to
           excrete nitrogenous wastes.
   _____   The excretory system of the grasshopper is more complex than the
           excretory system of planariums.

III. Read the following statements. Put a check (✓) by those statements you agree with. Use information from this chapter and any other information you have to support your choices. Discuss your reasoning in your group.

_____ Failure or malfunctioning of the excretory system would cause an organism to die.

_____ An organism's excretory system is a product of both evolution and environment.

_____ In human organisms, the respiratory system serves an important role in the excretory process.

_____ Characteristics of the excretory system of an organism can be determined roughly through knowledge of the organism's environment.

_____ Human organisms have the most complex excretory system of all living things.

THREE LEVEL GUIDE—SOCIAL STUDIES (U.S. HISTORY)

I. Read the statements below. Put a check beside each statement that you believe can be supported by the text. In your group discussion, give evidence for your choices.

_____ Alliances are agreements between countries with common goals to protect each other from common enemies.

_____ Small countries, as well as larger ones, formed alliances and made secret agreements prior to World War I.

_____ Germany's growing economic and military strength upset the European balance of power.

_____ Major disagreements resulted when two large nations both wanted to control the same small nation.

_____ International lawlessness occurred because nations felt there was no objective forum for settling differences.

II. Check the statements below that you believe to be logical inferences that can be drawn from your reading. In your group discussion, support your choices.

_____ Alliances among nations, especially those involving secret agreements, created an atmosphere of international distrust that led directly to World War I.

_____ Alliances formed prior to World War I had both positive and negative effects.

_____ Military buildup in Europe was a natural outgrowth of nationalism and imperialism.

_____ Economic, industrial, and military strength determined each nation's power.

_____ Germany played a key role in all events leading to World War I.

III. Check the statements below that are logical conclusions based on information from the text and other information you have. In your group discussion, explain your choices.

_____   Imperialism can be defined as control of one nation by another.

_____   Patriotism and nationalism are synonymous.

_____   The best interests of one country may not be the best interests of other countries.

_____   Maintaining a balance of power among nations is an important aspect of world peace.

_____   Development of an institution to arbitrate international disagreements is a major factor in averting war.

Below are listed national professional organizations and the journals of likely interest to middle school, junior high, and senior high teachers. Many of these organizations also have affiliated regional, state, and/or local chapters.

LESSON PLAN

THE LAND OF THE LOST

DAILY LESSON PLAN

Unit: "Dinosaur Days"

Week: 1

Day: 1

Topics: Introduction to the semester unit—"Land of the Lost"

Goals: For students to understand semester unit experience; for teachers and students to discuss and develop class rules and regulations; to start the unit via a KWL plus exercise as an introduction to the unit.

Materials: OHP, VCR, TV, Video of "Land of the Lost", pens, file folders, KWL handouts

(0–30)   Hand out syllabus.
Discuss authentic assessment.
Go over project descriptions.
Class Meeting/Students are given their journals.

(30–40)   KWL-Plus lesson (students have returned to their table groups of four once the class meeting is finished); KWL will be done in cooperative groups and the Plus (mapping will be done individually).

Set up scenario: **You have been transported to a prehistoric time period.**

K   What do you already know about dinosaurs, prehistoric times, and survival? Do you think that humans and dinosaurs can coexist? Why or why not?

W   What do you want to learn about prehistoric times, dinosaurs, and survival?

(45–50)   Break

(50–70)   Watch the pilot "Land of the Lost" episode which shows the arrival to the "Land of the Lost" and initial survival strategies.

(70–75)

L   Students will write down everything that they learned from the video. Ask: What did you learn from watching this video? Add as many things as you can to the L list.

(75–85)   Students (individually) will create a "map" of what they saw in the video. In other words, students will demonstrate by words or pictures what took place in the video. Show a sample or two of a fictitious map on the OHP.

(85–100)   Students will share their maps with their table groups and then students may share their maps with the class during the final five minutes of the class.

Homework: Journal Entry #1: Can humans and dinosaurs coexist? Why or why not? Explain your answer.

SAMPLE WORKSHEET   *KWL (English/Spanish)*

K (Know)	W (Want to Know)	L (Learned)

S Sabemos	**Q** Queremos saber	**A** Aprendimos

SAMPLE UNIT *Prejudice*

UNIT OBJECTIVES: PREJUDICE

1. To examine individual rights and the ramifications on individuals of prejudice in an historical context.

2. Students will reflect their learning on how it applies to their lives in their journal writing.

This lesson includes the first three days of a unit that will continue to include some of the following:

1. Students will develop a "Student Bill of Rights" to aid in their understanding of what prejudice and scapegoating and their consequences are.

2. Students will build on what they learn in the previous two objectives and apply that knowledge to Proposition 187 in a debate.

3. Students will develop and carry out a long-term group project on a topic of their choice related to prejudice.

4. Each group of students will select a topical novel to read and share with the class in jigsaw.

Class: 10th Grade English and History
Time: 55 minutes
Unit: Prejudice
Day: One

Lesson Topic: Historical racism

Lesson Objectives:

1. Student will gain an understanding of what it was like for the Japanese-Americans to be moved into internment camps during WW II by participating in a "Cone of Experience" activity.

2. Students will start to develop a working definition of "prejudice" and start to identify with their personal encounters with prejudice through a group brainstorm and journal writing.

Materials Needed: Class set of "Civilian Exclusion Order No. 5"

Activity #1: Cone of Experience (30 minutes)

1. Students will break into "families" (5 groups of 5) and be given orders to evacuate their homes. They will be told only that they are being moved to a temporary camp. They will not know where, for how long, or with whom they will be staying.

2. Each family is given a copy of the "Civilian Exclusion Order No. 5" and told to read through the order and plan, according to the instructions on the order, a list of supplies and belongings to take with them.

FIGURE A.1   *Map*

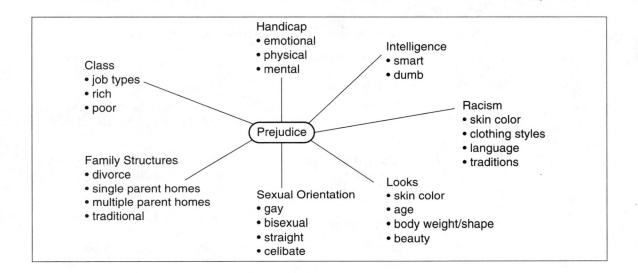

3. After reaching a consensus, one member from each family will share the list with the rest of the class and provide a justification for their choices based upon the needs of the group relative to age, gender, medical needs, and weather.

Activity #2:   Cooperative Brainstorming (15 minutes)

1. Students will participate in a class brainstorming activity in an attempt to create a working definition of the word *prejudice*.

2. Ideas will be written on the board and then grouped into categories based upon student choice.

Activity #3:   Journal Write (10 minutes)
Students will write in their journals on the following topic, "Have you ever been discriminated against? How did it make you feel?"

LESSON PLAN—DAY TWO

Lesson Topic: The Bill of Rights/10th Grade

Lesson Objectives:

1. Students will work in cooperative groups and participate in a Group Reading Activity (GRA). Students will read sections of the Bill of Rights and prepare to present what they learn to the whole class tomorrow.

2. Students will select vocabulary using the Vocabulary Self-Selection Strategy (VSS) to nominate for the class list.

3. Students will reflect and respond to a quote in their journals to demonstrate what they have learned so far in the unit about prejudice.

Materials Needed:

1. "Summary of Constitutional Rights Violated" sheet from WWII.

2. Guidelines for group presentations.

Introduction: (Time: 5 minutes)

Questions: *Today we are going to discuss constitutional rights and how they were violated during World War II. What do you already know about the Bill of Rights?* (Brainstorm on board.)

You have already learned from yesterday's lesson about the removal and incarceration of Japanese-American citizens during WWII. What else do you already know about what happened to them? (Brainstorm on board.)

Step #1: GRA (Time: 30 minutes)

1. Divide students into five cross-ability/cross-status groups. Give each group one page of summary.

2. Direct: *Now you will read the page you are assigned and, as a group, decide how you will present what you learn to the class. You may do this in any way you wish.* Students read and discuss material.

3. Appoint one member of each group as student critic. Teachers also consult with each group regarding its plans for presentation. Presentations will be tomorrow.

Step #2: VSS (Time: 15 minutes)

1. *Nominate one word or term you would like to know more about and that you think should be on our class vocabulary list. Find words/terms that are important to the topic and be prepared to tell*

    a. where you found the word/term in context.
    b. what you think the word means.
    c. why you think the class should learn it.

2. Accept nominations and discuss possible meaning and reasons for learning.

3. Narrow class list.

4. Refine definitions.

5. Direct students to record final list words and definitions.

Step #3: Journal Write (5 minutes)
Respond to the following:

"No one can make you feel inferior without your consent."—Eleanor Roosevelt

LESSON PLAN—DAY THREE

Lesson Topic: Group Presentations

Lesson Objectives:

1.   Students will further their understanding of prejudice and scapegoating.

2.   Students will identify how interpretation of the Bill of Rights changed during World War II as it applied to Japanese-Americans.

3.   Students will self-evaluate the performance of their group.

Materials: Group evaluation forms

Activity 1: 5 group presentations (5–8 minutes each)

Topic—Constitutional guarantees and liberties violated by the internment of Japanese Americans during WWII.

Activity 2: Classroom discussion (teacher-moderated if necessary)

Activity 3: Group evaluations (10 minutes)

Prompt: Evaluate your groups' ability to work together. What strengths and/or weaknesses did you discover about group learning?

GUIDELINES FOR GROUP PRESENTATIONS

However you decide to present your topic to the class, oral presentation or role-playing, be sure that your group presents the information in a well-organized and easily understood manner. Other ideas for presentations are welcome, as long as the teacher okays them.

Presentation Criteria—Be sure that:

_____   your group's presentation clearly demonstrates your understanding of the topic.
_____   each member of the group is actively participating.
_____   your presentation is five minutes in length.
_____   your group shows why your topic is/is not an important part of the Bill of Rights.
_____   your presentation addresses whether this topic is important today.
_____   your presentation is creative.

ALTERNATIVE SAMPLE UNIT   *Prejudice*

CONE OF EXPERIENCE

The following lesson plan would take place as part of a World War II interdisciplinary unit. One of the novels they will have the choice of reading will be *Farewell to*

Manzanar (multicultural text) by Jeanne Wakatsuki-Houston. This text deals with the internment of the Japanese-Americans during wartime hysteria.

ACTION

Setting: Students will be divided into four groups. Each of the groups will represent on of the following groups: Adult Japanese-Americans being interned as the time; children of the families being interned; government officials who were involved with supervising the whole situation; and other American citizens not being interned.

Task: From the perspective of the groups they represent, each student group is to develop a statement of their group's attitudes and position regarding the internment of the Japanese-Americans using the following questions to guide discussion:

1. What was at stake for you in the internment of the Japanese-Americans?
2. What benefits will you get from the situation?
3. What are the possible demands, dangers, and problems for you as a result of the internment of the Japanese-Americans?
4. What will be your response? Why?
5. What do you believe is your probability of succeeding in this situation? Why?

OBSERVATION

Following whole-class sharing of what each group's attitudes and positions would be regarding the internment of the Japanese-Americans, the class will watch and then discuss a multimedia film that incorporates the five vantage points. Student groups will analyze how the presentation did or did not represent the viewpoints and perspectives of the people they represent.

ABSTRACT

Each group will choose one or more aspects of its experience in the internment of the Japanese to research and produce a written account of its research along with a performance, presentation, or graphic visual product. Groups must consult at least one source in each of the following categories:

Museum products or visits

Realia

Primary documents

Historical fiction

Biography/autobiography

Various kinds of maps

Interviews

SELECTED BOOK LIST

Endo, Takado, et al. (1985). *Japanese American Journey.* San Francisco: JACP Inc.
—History, biographies and short stories about Japanese Americans.

Drinnon, Richard (1987). *Keeper of Concentration Camps.* Berkeley: University of California Press.
—A new look at the heretofore respected director of the War Relocation Authority, Dillon S. Myer. the author is explicit in his description of Myer as a racist and U.S. policy towards Japanese Americans during the war severely wanting in point or fairness and justice.

Irons, Peter (1983). *Justice at War, The Story of the Japanese American Internment Cases.* London: Oxford University Press.
—in depth study of the legal cases brought before the Supreme Court.

Ishigo, Estelle (1972). *Lone Heart Mountain.* Los Angeles: Estelle Ishigo.
—Caucasian married to a Japanese American renders the account of her internment at Heart Mountain, Wyoming. Illustrated with the author's art, completed while incarcerated.

Martin, Ralph G. (1946). *Boy from Nebraska.* New York, London: Harper Brothers.
—A biography of Sergeant Ben Kuroki, the Nebraska farm boy, who struggled to be inducted into the Army Air Corps and went on to compile an honorable record as gunner in both the European and Pacific theaters of war.

Myer, Dillon S. *Uprooted Americans.* Tucson, AZ: University of Arizona Press.
—As director of War Relocation Authority, Myer examines the concentration camp history through the eyes of an administrator. Compare with views presented by Richard Drinnon's *Keeper of Concentration Camps.*

Uchida, Yoshiko (1971, 1985). *Journey to Topaz.* New York: Charles Scribner's Sons.
—Story of an eleven year old and her family uprooted from their California home and sent to Topaz, a desert wartime camp.

AUDIO VISUALS

Concentrated American. Michael Yoshida and Jenni Morozumi, producers.
—This film documents the history of wartime removal of Japanese Americans and the efforts to place the issue of redress before the U.S. government.

Days of Waiting. Steven Okazaki, producer/director. Distributor: Transit Media.
—This is an Academy-Award-winning documentary that depicts the story of Estelle Peck Ishigo, a Caucasian married to a Japanese American and incarcerated in the Heart Mountain Camp.

Juxta. Hiroko Yamazaki, producer/director. Distributor: Women Make Movies.
—An emotional journey into the many faces of racism in the U.S. told through the memories of two racially mixed offspring of Japanese war brides and U.S. servicemen.

Through Innocent Eyes. Rennie Mau, producer. Distributor: NJAHS.

—Children reading excerpts from the writings of Poston camp school children who tell about conditions in camp.

Unfinished Business. Steven Okazaki, producer/director.

—This documentary tells the compelling story of three men, Fred Korematsu, Gordon Hirabayashi and Minoru Yasui, who defied Executive Order 9066 and were separately convicted and imprisoned.

Civilian Exclusion Order No. 5

WESTERN DEFENSE COMMAND AND FOURTH ARMY
WARTIME CIVIL CONTROL ADMINISTRATION

Presidio of San Francisco, California
April 1, 1942

INSTRUCTIONS

TO ALL PERSONS OF

JAPANESE

ANCESTRY

LIVING IN THE FOLLOWING AREA:

All that portion of the City and County of San Francisco, State of California, lying generally west of the north-south line established by Junipero Serra Boulevard, Worchester Avenue, and Nineteenth Avenue, and lying generally north of the east-west line established by California Street, to the intersection of Market Street, and thence on Market Street to San Francisco Bay.

All Japanese persons, both alien and non-alien, will be evacuated from the above designated area by 12:00 o'clock noon, Tuesday, April 7, 1942.

No Japanese person will be permitted to enter or leave the above described area after 8:00 a.m., Thursday, April 2, 1942, without obtaining special permission from the Provost Marshal at the Civil Control Station located at:

1701 Van Ness Avenue
San Francisco, California

The Civil Control Station is equipped to assist the Japanese population affected by this evacuation in the following ways:

1. Give advice and instructions on the evacuation.
2. Provide services with respect to the management, leasing, sale, storage or other disposition of most kinds of property including: real estate, business and professional equipment, buildings, household goods, boats, automobiles, livestock, etc.
3. Provide temporary residence elsewhere for all Japanese in family groups.
4. Transport persons and a limited amount of clothing and equipment to their new residence, as specified below.

THE FOLLOWING INSTRUCTIONS MUST BE OBSERVED:

1. A responsible member of each family, preferably the head of the family, or the person in whose name most of the property is held, and each individual living alone, will report to the Civil Control Station to receive further instructions. This must be done between 8:00 a.m. and 5:00 p.m., Thursday, April 2, 1942, or between 8:00 a.m. and 5:00 p.m., Friday, April 3, 1942.

2. Evacuees must carry with them on departure for the Reception Center, the following property:
   (a) Bedding and linens (no mattress) for each member of the family;
   (b) Toilet articles for each member of the family;
   (c) Extra clothing for each member of the family;
   (d) Sufficient knives, forks, spoons, plates, bowls and cups for each member of the family;
   (e) Essential personal effects for each member of the family.

All items carried will be securely packaged, tied and plainly marked with the name of the owner and numbered in accordance with instructions received at the Civil Control Station.

The size and number of packages is limited to that which can be carried by the individual or family group.

No contraband items as described in paragraph 6, Public Proclamation No. 3, Headquarters Western Defense Command and Fourth Army, dated March 24, 1942, will be carried.

3. The United States Government through its agencies will provide for the storage at the sole risk of the owner of the more substantial household items, such as iceboxes, washing machines, pianos and other heavy furniture. Cooking utensils and other small items will be accepted if crated, packed and plainly marked with the name and address of the owner. Only one name and address will be used by a given family.

4. Each family, and individual living alone, will be furnished transportation to the Reception Center. Private means of transportation will not be utilized. All instructions pertaining to the movement will be obtained at the Civil Control Station.

Go to the Civil Control Station at 1701 Van Ness Avenue, San Francisco, California, between 8:00 a.m. and 5:00 p.m., Thursday, April 2, 1942, or between 8:00 a.m. and 5:00 p.m., Friday, April 3, 1942, to receive further instructions.

J. L. DeWitt
Lieutenant General, U.S. Army
Commanding

INDEX

Photo Credits

Chapter 1: Robert Harbison; Chapter 2: Brian Smith; Chapter 3: Brian Smith; Chapter 4: Will Hart; Chapter 5: Will Faller; Chapter 6: Will Faller; Chapter 7: Will Faller; Chapter 8: Will Faller; Chapter 9: Will Hart; Chapter 10: Brian Smith; Chapter 11, Will Faller; Chapter 12: Will Faller.

Text Credits and Acknowledgments

Chapter 2. Page 33: Figure 2.1. Courtesy of Jenny Burcham.

Chapter 3. Page 41: From Maton, A., LaHart, D., Hopkins, J., Warner, M. Q., Johnson, S., & Wright, J. D. *Prentice-Hall Science: Motion, Forces, and Energy.* Copyright © Prentice-Hall, Englewood Cliffs, NJ: 1994. Page 44: Used with permission from Markham, B., *The Splendid Outcast.* Copyright 1987 by North Point Press. Used with permission. Page 57: From Boorstin, D. J., & Kelley, B. M. *A History of the United States.* Copyright © Prentice-Hall, Englewood Cliffs, NJ: 1996. Used with permission. Page 76: Used with permission from Fraenkel, J. R., Kane, F. R., & Wolfe, A. *Civics: Government and Citizenship.* Copyright © Prentice-Hall, Englewood Cliffs, NJ: 1990. Used with permission. Page 83: Used with permission from Davidson, D. M., Landau, M. S., McCracken, L., & Thompson, L. *Prentice-Hall Mathematics: Explorations & Applications.* Copyright © Prentice-Hall, Englewood Cliffs, NJ: 1995.

Chapter 4. Page 98, Figure 4.2: Reprinted with permission of Joan Nelson Herber and the International Reading Association. Page 102, Figure 4.4: Courtesy of Peter M. Santucci. Page 104 and 126: From Miller, K. R., & Levine, J. *Biology,* 3rd edition. Copyright © Prentice-Hall, Englewood Cliffs, NJ: 1995. Used with permission.

Chapter 5. Page 139, Figure 5.3 and page 149, Figure 5.4: Courtesy of Heidi L. Hayman-Ahders and Janet M. Rasmussen. Page 141, Figure 5.5: Reprinted from Ruddell, M. R.-H. "Integrated content and long-term vocabulary learning with the vocabulary self-collection strategy," from Dishner, Beane, Readence, & Moore (Eds.), *Reading in the Content Areas,* 3rd edition. Copyright © Kendall/Hunt Publishing Company, Dubuque, Iowa, 1992. Used with permission. Page 146, Figure 5.7: From Fair, J., & Bragg, S. C. *Prentice-Hall Algebra I.* Copyright © Prentice-Hall, Englewood Cliffs, NJ: 1993. Used with permission. Page 153, Figure 5.8: Excerpted from *Getting Stronger* copyright © by Bill Pearl. $14.95 Shelter Publications, Inc., P.O. Box 279, Bolinas, CA 94924. Distributed in bookstores by Random House. Reprinted by permission. Page 157, Figure 5.9; page 158, Figure 5.10: Reprinted with permission of Eileen Carr and the International Reading Association.

Chapter 6. Pages 171 *ff*: Quotations from Lucy Calkins are used with permission from Calkins, L. Mc. *The Art of Teaching Writing.* Portsmouth, NH: Heinemann Boynton/Cook, 1986. Page 182, Figure 6.1: Used with permission from Daniloff, T. (1991, June). How Czar Nicholas was outfoxed by the guardian angels. *Smithsonian 22* (3), pp. 102–108, 110, 112–113. Page 186, Figure 6.2: From Fraenkel, J. R., Kane, F. T., and Wolf, A. *Civics: Government and Citizenship.* Copyright © Prentice-Hall, Englewood Cliffs, NJ: 1990. Used with permission. Page 189, Figure 6.3: From *The Life and Times of Porgy and Bess* by Hollis Alpert. Copyright © 1990 by Hollis Alpert. Reprinted by permission of Alfred Knopf, Inc. Page 194: Quotation used by permission of Joe Bob Briggs and Creators Syndicate.